SOCIAL INDICATORS AND SOCIETAL MONITORING

AN ANNOTATED BIBLIOGRAPHY

The Jossey-Bass/Elsevier
International Series

Elsevier Scientific Publishing Company
Amsterdam

SOCIAL INDICATORS
AND
SOCIETAL MONITORING

AN ANNOTATED BIBLIOGRAPHY

BY

LESLIE D. WILCOX, RALPH M. BROOKS

GEORGE M. BEAL, GERALD E. KLONGLAN

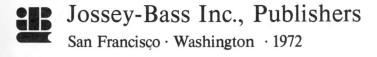 Jossey-Bass Inc., Publishers

San Francisco · Washington · 1972

SOCIAL INDICATORS AND SOCIETAL MONITORING
An Annotated Bibliography
by Leslie D. Wilcox, Ralph M. Brooks,
George M. Beal, and Gerald E. Klonglan

For the United States of America and Canada:
Jossey-Bass, Inc., Publishers
615 Montgomery Street
San Francisco, California 94111

For all other areas:
Elsevier Scientific Publishing Company
335 Jan van Galenstraat
Amsterdam, The Netherlands

Library of Congress Catalogue Card Number LC 72-88862

International Standard Book Number ISBN 0-87589-151-9

Manufactured in The Netherlands

FIRST EDITION

Code 7236

PREFACE

This volume is the result of an extensive literature search and correspondence with individuals working in numerous disciplines, a search which was stimulated by the need to provide greater accessibility to the growing body of literature pertaining both directly and indirectly to current social indicator research. Thus, it is intended both as a tool for those interested in acquiring initial knowledge about social indicators and as a reference work for those with more specialized interests in social indicator research.

The proliferation of literature devoted to the recent topics of societal monitoring systems as well as social indicator research has produced a rapidly expanding body of available printed material. New papers are appearing so rapidly that it is difficult for even those most actively engaged in social indicator research to keep abreast of the tide of literature devoted to these topics. The interdisciplinary nature of this proliferation compounds the difficulty not only in "keeping up" with one's own discipline, but also that of maintaining some level of knowledge of activities in other disciplines. Likewise, the flood of new papers, most of which have appeared during the past five years, has been too great to be readily absorbed in the normal publication channels, resulting in a considerable time lag between preparation and publication of new works. The present bibliography represents an effort to bring together both published and nonpublished sources related to the general topics often found in discussions of social indicators and societal monitoring.

While this bibliography is not a complete listing of sources pertaining to social indicators, it is, we believe, the most comprehensive volume to date, including most of the documents of which we are aware. However, since social indicator research is an international research effort, it is recognized that many documents may be available outside the United States that did not come to our attention during the preparation of this volume.

It is often said that a bibliography is out of date the moment it is published. However, through use of the computer, we were able to update the bibliography, almost daily, right up to the moment of submission of the manuscript to the publisher. Thus, the reader should be afforded greater opportunity to more quickly become aware of current materials of potential utility in his or her work pertaining to social indicators.

A document of this scope would not be possible without the assistance of many individuals. Our correspondence, attendance at professional meetings, and personal interviews placed us in contact with numerous individuals serving in diverse capacities: in various academic disciplines; in business; in universities and research institutes, both public and private, domestic and international; in government--local, state, federal, and international, including the United Nations. Their support and contributions to this volume have provided the extensive listing of sources. We could not begin to express our appreciation to them singularly and, therefore, at the risk of excluding an individual contribution, ask them collectively to accept our gratitude. Their names appear in the Author Index at the end of the bibliography. We hope this addition to the volume will provide a basis for all interested parties to correspond with each other, thus stimulating additional interaction and facilitating the exchange of pertinent ideas to the end that the work in social indicators will be enhanced.

The volume contains over 1,000 separate listings. Of these, we have annotated over 600 articles, books and papers we feel represent a cross section of relevant and related work in social indicators. Our deepest appreciation is extended to K. William Wasson, Harold O'Connell, J. P. Golinvaux, Mary Lees, Michael Price and Kerry J. Byrnes for their intensive efforts in helping with the annotations. Cathy Hendrick and Marlane Diemer provided the clerical support.

Finally, we could not have undertaken this bibliography without the aid of the Cooperative State Research Service of the United States Department of Agriculture through the Iowa Experiment Station. To them we express our deepest appreciation for financial support in this work.

TABLE OF CONTENTS

Page

USE OF THE BIBLIOGRAPHY

To aid the reader in locating articles of interest,
we have provided this brief discussion of the use of the
bibliography. It is divided into four separate indexes:
the Annotated Index, the Author Index, the Key-Word
Subject Index, and the Address Index.

Annotated Index

The first index contains over six hundred individual-
ly annotated articles selected from the larger total
listing of articles, which is found in the Author Index of
this bibliography. These sources were selected to give a
representation of the diffuseness of the social indicator
literature and to provide the reader with a group of relevant readings in each of the annotated bibliographical
categories. We have categorized these annotated articles
into nine major areas: definition, conceptual, general
theory, methodology, policy and planning, application,
criticism and state of the art, bibliography and related.
These various categories were selected to reflect the
type of ongoing work in the initial development of the
social indicator "movement" and, at the same time, to
present the reader with the opportunity of making a
judgment as to the adequacy of current work in each of
these categories. This type of categorization will,
hopefully, stimulate further examination and development
of concepts that need to be operationalized, clarification
of terminology used by those seeking some consensus on
definitions, revision and creation of new methodologies
for analyzing social phenomena, additional examples of
actual application of indicators in society and the possible implications for policy planning.

Author Index

The second index of the bibliography is an alphabetical listing by author of the materials encountered in our
literature review. The response to our written requests
over the past year and a half has exceeded our expectations. Using the computer has allowed us to update the
listing daily. This resulted in a more complete compilation of current sources. With such a wide range of

interest in social indicators and societal monitoring, it
is impossible to be in contact with all relevant sources
of interest. Our intent has been to help interested
people become more aware of work in progress, as well as
provide a means for future interdisciplinary interaction
concerning social indicators, social reporting and social
measurement.

How to Use the Author Index

In scanning the Author Index, the reader will notice
an asterisk (*) in the left margin, i.e. to the left of
the date column, for example, * 1972. The asterisk (*)
indicates that the particular article cited to the right
of the asterisk is annotated in the Annotated Index of the
bibliography. Additionally, the reader will notice that
following each asterisked article are parentheses containing one or more code letters. Each code letter, following
a particular asterisked article, corresponds to one of the
nine categories in the Annotated Index of the bibliography. The following code letters are used to designate the
nine categories:

D=Definition

C=Conceptual

GT=General Theory

M=Methodology

P=Policy and Planning

A=Application

CS=Criticism and State of the Art

B=Bibliography

R=Related

An asterisked article in the Author Index can be
easily located in the Annotated Index of the bibliography.
The first code letter, alphabetic character, inside the
parentheses following an asterisked article indicates the
categorized section in the Annotated Index wherein that
article will be found, listed in alphabetical order of the

author's last name. The second and subsequent alphabetic code letters, if any, refer to other categories to which the particular article might have additional relevance.

For example, if an asterisked article in the Author Index was followed by the code letters (A, P), the reader would locate that article's annotation under the author's last name in the Annotated Index's subsection on Application. The second code letter "P" suggests only that the article might also have relevance to a reader interested in the topical category of Policy and Planning, another subsection of the Annotated Index.

An illustration of this system of code letters is taken from the first page of the Author Index.

Abel-Smith, Brian
 * 1970   "Public expenditure on the social services."
           Pp. 12-20 in Muriel Nissel (ed.), Social Trends.
           London: Her Majesty's Central Statistical
           Office. (M, A)

Thus, the annotation will be found only, in the Methodology section of the Annotated Index. Other aspects, but not major aspects, were categorized as applicable to persons with an interest in the topical area of "Application", the sixth subsection of the Annotated Index.

Key-Word Subject Index

This third section was included to provide a cross-referencing system for persons interested in particular substantive areas. Classification of all articles contained in the Annotated Index was made from the key-word within their title or from the article's annotation itself, when the article's title was not directly indicative of its substantive content.

Over fifty substantive areas have been identified in this index. The following is an illustration of the Key-Word Subject Index.

Planning, financing

        Abel-Smith, Brian   1970   (M)

Thus, the reader will find the subject, or substantive classification, in the capital letters at the left margin of the page. Any modifying or qualifying adjective follows the key-word. In the above example, Planning is the key-word, and subject or substantive clas-

sification. The word "financing" in small letters following is the qualifier, i.e. it is to financing of planning
that the reference following is related.

The indented line contains the name of the particular
author of the article on planning financing. The following four digits refer to the year of the article's publication, 1970. The parentheses at the end of the first
sentence contain the alphabetic code letters indicating
which topical categories those preparing the annotation
classified this article. The codes which indicate subsec-
tions within the Annotated Index are as follows:

     D=Definition

     C=Conceptual

     GT=General Theory

     M=Methodology

     P=Policy and Planning

     A=Application

     CS=Criticism and State of the Art

     B=Bibliography

     R=Related

Thus, a person interested in the subject area of
planning financing would find the annotation for the Abel-
Smith article in the Methodology subsection of the
Annotated Index.

The annotation will be found only in the Methodology
section, alphabetically listed by the author's last name.

Address Index

The fourth and final index in the bibliography contains a detailed address index. It includes the names and
last known addresses of institutes, agencies and individuals currently involved in social indicator research. This
section was included for two reasons. First, many of the
papers have only recently been presented at professional
meetings, or represent initial drafts attempting to describe current activities. These papers or drafts may not

have appeared in sources that can be easily documented or
widely circulated. For this reason, we have included the
names and addresses, as far as possible, of authors of
"fugitive" materials to help the reader locate sources not
presently available in print. Second, and finally, we
hope that this index will facilitate interaction among interested parties to learn more about each other's efforts
in the social indicator "movement".

SOCIAL PLANNING AND SOCIETAL MONITORING

By

RALPH M. BROOKS

Over the past decade, social scientists in various
disciplines, public decision makers involved in social
policy formulation at various levels of government, and
business leaders in the private sector have increasingly
directed their attention to the problems involved in
developing a system of social indicators by means of which
societal change could be monitored and, thereby,
objectively measured. Although most societies have developed some type of information system to aid decision
makers in public policy formulation, specific interest in
the topic of generating social indicators as the component
parts of such an information system is relatively new.
The term "social indicators" (as presently used) was ap-
parently coined by a team of scientists headed by Raymond
Bauer through analogy to the term "economic indicator".
Once introduced, the notion of generating social
indicators to serve as tools to monitor social change
stimulated considerable interest and scholarly discussion,
especially in the United States. Several of the social
science disciplines have devoted major portions of their
annual meetings to the topic of social indicators and its
various ramifications. Similarly, many of the business
societies interested in improved social responsibility and
the problems of quantifying social phenomena have also
focused on social indicators in their professional
meetings. The United States government's interest in the
human dimension of national planning has been evidenced in
initial explorations of the feasibility of future Annual
Social Reports (cf. U.S. Department of Health, Education
and Welfare, 1969) to the nation, as well as proposals for
new statistical publications (cf. Tunstall, 1970).
Additionally, several other national governments, particularly the French and the Canadian, among several others,
have actively undertaken similar efforts.

Most recently, an increasing amount of systematic research has been devoted to the development of a societal
monitoring system based on social indicators. A rapid
scan of several recent bibliographies on social indicators
by Beal, et.al. (1971), Harland (1971a), Agocs (1971),
Tugac (1971), and the Institut National de la Statistique
et Des Etudes Economiques (1971a) indicates that writers
from various academic disciplines, government officials,
and concerned private citizens are contributing to the
vast growing body of literature which focuses on societal

monitoring, social accounting, and the development of
social indicators. Because the initial impact of this research theme had its greatest impact in the United States,
the discussion which follows will largely reflect the
growth and development of the social indicator research
effort in the United States. However, as indicated above,
there have been parallel efforts in other parts of the
world; some of these are discussed in a later section of
this paper.

The widespread interest which has emerged in social
indicators has become, what might loosely be referred to
as, a "social movement". The _first_ section which follows,
titled "Toward the Development of Social Indicators", discusses the early efforts in the United States to measure
social change, considers several of the issues involved in
evaluating the social indicator "movement", and outlines
recent trends toward alternative conceptual perspectives.
The _second_ section, titled "Current Issues in Social
Indicators", discusses the classification scheme utilized
in the Annotated Index of the bibliography; thes categories are reflective of many of the current needs in
advancing social indicator research. The _third_ section,
titled "Social Indicators Research: Current Activities",
reviews some of the current social indicator activities,
both nationally and internationally.

Where appropriate, in each of the following three
sections, reference will be made to some of the
influential documents that have contributed to the evolution of the social indicator "movement".

Toward The Development Of Social Indicators

The initial input for the eventual development of
social indicators within the U.S. came from activities
conducted at the federal level. In 1929, President Hoover
commissioned a group of scientists to consider the
feasibility of pursuing a national survey of social trends
within the United States. The commission wanted to identify specific societal trends, yet cover a broad range of
interests. The results were printed in the Report of the
President's Research Committee on Social Trends (1933) and
contained twenty-nine chapters in the two volume set.
Some of the topics investigated were changing social attitudes and interests, rural life, the family, recreation
and leisure time activities, crime and punishment, population, government and society, health and medical practice
and other related topics. The following quote from this
source demonstrates what the commission hoped to accomplish. "It may indeed be said that the primary value of
this report is to be found in the effort to interrelate
the disjointed factors and elements in the social life of

2

America, in the attempt to view the situation as a whole rather than as a cluster of parts" (Report of the President's Commission, 1933:xii-xiii). The commission recognized the complexity of society and felt that social trend analysis might offer one solution to understanding social phenomena.

Major suggestions coming from the report of that commission indicated that an assessment of the total conditions of society obviously requires more than what one scientific discipline alone can provide. Thus, they called for an interdisciplinary involvement in assessing societal change. Furthermore, a National Advisory Council was proposed which later became the forerunner of the National Council of Economic Advisers. The establishment of that council has contributed greatly to the development of economics and the ability to monitor the economic system in the United States.

After the publication of Recent Social Trends, the interest in assessing social trends gave way to a more immediate concern, stabilizing economic conditions during the depression years of the 1930's. However, even during these years of primary economic concern there was a persistent interest in assessing qualitative social trends. For instance, Bennett (1937) attempted to measure the national "standard of living" of fourteen countries over a ten year period. Recognizing the difficulty of operationalizing the concept of standard of living, he focused primarily on five principle categories of food, clothing, shelter, transport and communication, and professional services. Each of these in turn were further explicated prior to measurement. In his analysis of these five categories, Bennett developed statistical series which reflect the time trends in each category.

Another early research effort reflective of the continuation of interest in the monitoring of qualitative social trends is the work of Goldhammer and Marshall (1953). During this period, it was popularly assumed that mental illness in the United States was on the increase. Goldhammer and Marshall argued that the data frequently used in assessing this assumption was inadequate to properly measure trends in mental health. In their study, they reviewed first admission rates at mental hospitals, and through data analysis, concluded "there has been no long-term increase during the last century in the incidence of the psychoses of early and middle life" (Goldhammer and Marshall, 1953:92). Their work is suggestive of the need for improved social information systems if rational decisions are to be made concerning social development. They also contributed to the gradual return to trend analysis in assessing the qualitative conditions of society.

A continuation of these issues relating to improved social information is expressed in the work of Cabello (1959). He was concerned with the possibility of

assessing social programs through the use of statistics
and, thereby, not be forced to rely on personal judgment
or the political wishes of policy makers. He noted that
social programs are more difficult to evaluate because
"mathematical models describing the effect of social measures on the levels of living, the cost of such measures
and the physical inputs involved have not been established" (Cabello, 1959:207). In spite of such obstacles,
according to Cabello, if one is to raise the level of
living one does so by developing social programs. He then
argues that before these programs can be evaluated, they
need to be translated into statistical terms. Cabello was
also concerned with applying staistics to evaluating
social programs.

From the previous discussion, we see a continuing
interest in quantifying social phenomena. The 1933
President's Commission represented the first joint attempt
of government and social scientists to systematically
assess societal conditions. Bennett continued this effort
by seeking to obtain indicators of "standard of living."
Goldhammer and Marshall were not willing to accept the
general consensus on rising mental illness. Their approach required them to consider the incidence of mental
illness over a number of years and thus proposed that
trend analysis would dispel the traditional beliefs of
rising mental illness.

The challenge for more adequate measurement and the
possibility that accurate information may be useful for
future planning is well taken. The events described from
the early 1930's to the late 1950's contributed to the
preparation of the foundation for a greater research involvement in chartering social trends through social
indicator research.

Increased visibility and societal concern

The increased support for the development of a social
indicator movement began as governmental officials,
leading scientists and professional societies demonstrated
an increased involvement in trying to understand the
social dimension for future planning. In 1960 another
President's Commission was established by order of
President Eisenhower. The purpose of the commission was
to specify some general guidelines to be used for coordination of national policies and programs, and, further, to
establish goals in various areas of national activity.
The general goals suggested by the commission (Report of
the President's Commission on National Goals, 1960) are
first dichotomized between "Goals at Home" and "Goals
Abroad." Among the conceptual areas of concern in the
former goal area are the individual, equality, the
democratic process, education, arts and sciences, economic

growth, democratic economy, technological change, agriculture, living conditions, and health and welfare.

It is interesting to note that six years later, Biderman (1966) delineated eighty-one specific subgoals from the eleven more general goal areas presented by the 1960 President's Commission and attempted to identify indicators of those goals. Using loose criteria, Biderman was able to locate somewhat relevant indicators for only forty-eight of the goals. There were thirty-three goals for which he found no relevant indicator. Goals were being established at the national level, but neither the government nor the private sector had developed indicators of those goals to assess societal progress.

Additional support at the national level for government action in the development of social indicators was demonstrated in the final report of the National Commission on Technology, Automation and Economic Progress (1966). This commission recognized that we are well on our way to perfecting an economic reporting system to measure national economic performance, "but we do not have, as yet, a continuous charting of social changes, and we have been ill-prepared (in such matters as housing, education, or the status of the Negro) to determine our needs, establish goals, and measure our performance. Lacking any systematic assessment, we have few criteria which allow us to test the effectiveness of present policies or weigh alternatives regarding future programs" (Report of the National Commission on Technology, Automation and Economic Progress, 1966a:95). Therefore, the commission recommended that a system of social accounts be established to assess costs and benefits of economic and social change in the areas of social costs and net returns of innovation, social ills (crime and family disruption), defined social needs (for example, education, welfare and housing), and economic opportunity and social mobility.

About this time, one of the most significant events that contributed to the recent concern with societal monitoring took place as a result of the United States space program. The space committee of the National Aeronautics and Space Administration (NASA) became concerned with assessing the possible latent social effect of the space exploration program. Raymond Bauer, a member of that committee, was concerned about possible speculation without the proper data. As a result, he suggested the need for a comprehensive system of social indicators capable of assessing the social impacts of phenomena such as space exploration to aid in the development of social policy, and later brought together some well known social scientists to consider the ramifications of social indicators. The resulting outcome was the now often quoted book, Social Indicators (Bauer, 1966). Due to his work in early years of the last decade, Bauer is sometimes referred to as the "father" of the current social indicator movement.

Since 1967 the growing interest in monitoring the
qualitative social conditions of society has continued to
increase in the United States. A number of activities of
significant importance took place the first year of this
period.

Three professional societies devoted entire issues of
their journals to topics which gave the social indicator
movement greater exposure. The American Academy of
Political and Social Science prepared a special volume
devoted to social indicators from solicited articles. The
response was overwhelming and ultimately led to the
publishing of two separate volumes during 1967 entitled
"Social Goals and Indicators for American Society, Volumes
I and II" (American Academy of Political and Social Science, 1967a; 1967b). The American Academy of Arts and
Sciences invited Daniel Bell to be guest editor for a special edition of Daedalus with the title "Toward the Year
2000." This commission attempted to be imaginative concerning the problems that society would face by the year
2000 and the structural changes that may be necessary.

There were many other events taking place during this
period which gave the notion of social monitoring and reporting greater visibility. Perhaps the most significant
input by the government came in 1966. President Johnson
commissioned the Department of Health, Education and
Welfare to work toward the development of sets of statistics and indicators of general areas of societal concern
that would supplement economic indicators. These were to
be designed for measuring progress toward societal goals
and begin to assess the social well-being of Americans.
The publication Toward A Social Report (U.S. Department of
Health, Education and Welfare, 1969) was released on the
last day of the Johnson Administration and was actually
one of the first attempts to define such abstract terms as
"social accounts," "social indicator," and "social
reports."

Shortly thereafter, Senator Mondale introduced to the
United States Senate the "Full Opportunity and Social Accounting Act" of 1967 and later, the "Social Accounting
Act" of 1969. Commonly referred to as the Mondale Bills,
they were to provide for: (1) an Annual Social Report of
the President, (2) a Council of Social Advisers to aid in
preparing the report and (3) a Joint Committee on the
Social Report to review and transmit the findings to
Congress.

Thus far, the 1969 report has not been followed with
subsequent national social reports, the Council of Social
Advisers has yet to be established and, in fact, this
issue is still heavily debated in Congress.

By this time, however, the level of activity and
interest in the possibility of developing sets of
indicators to monitor social conditions were relatively
high and, indeed, the diversity of the interest is

6

manifested through the extensive bibliography accumulated
in this volume on Social Indicators and Societal
Monitoring. More recent activities related to the generation of a social monitoring system clearly indicates a
maturing of interest in social indicator research. This
in turn has propelled the focus of interest beyond simply
an attempt to sell an idea, toward systematic efforts to
generate social indicators and societal monitoring systems
through an interdisciplinary research effort. One factor
that has aided in this maturing process has been the criticism leveled at early programmatic discussions of this
topic.

Evaluating the social indicator movement

The criticisms levelled at the social indicator
movement stem, in large part, from a reaction to the early
claims made for social indicators. These claims frequently were oriented toward such positive statements as
improving descriptive reporting, developing a balance
sheet, ability to analyze social trends and social change,
assessing the performance of society, anticipating alternative social futures, setting goals and priorities,
acquiring social knowledge for societal control and in
general, the eventual continuous monitoring of quality of
life. Before a discussion of the criticisms of social
indicators, it seems reasonable to first present the often
made claims which should make the criticisms appear more
meaningful. Many of these claims are interrelated and
will be discussed in the following general categories: descriptive reporting, program evaluation, and planned development and societal control.

Descriptive reporting   In order for effective social
planning to become a reality, reliable information concerning the current state of affairs in society with particular emphasis on present societal conditions and social
needs must be readily available. Persons involved in programs of development and social planning have recognized
this need for many years. For example, Wilbur Cohen,
formerly with HEW, strongly argued for the development of
statistics to aid in policy decisions which assess the
present conditions of society and the magnitude of problems that accompany rates of change (Cohen, 1968).
One of the basic functions of social indicators as
perceived by the authors of Toward A Social Report would
be to provide descriptive reports on conditions of
society. Indeed, social indicators could "give social
problems more visibility and thus make possible more
informal judgments about national priorities" (U.S. Department of HEW, 1969:xii). One might wonder if descrip-

tive reporting will be sufficient to accurately portray
societal conditions. One of the many claims for social
indicators, however, is that of providing information
about current needs in relation to national objectives,
thus aiding policy makers in establishing future national
priorities.

Program evaluation   Another claim often made regarding
the function of social indicators is that of program evaluation. Social indicators, it is claimed, will aid in
assessing the effectiveness of policies and programs by
providing insights into national well-being and may
"ultimately make possible a better evaluation of what
public programs are accomplishing" (U.S. Department of
Health, Education and Welfare, 1969:xiii).
     Perhaps nowhere in the discussions of social
indicators does the economic analogy become more apparent
than in the discussions of the potential role of social
indicators in program evaluation. It is assumed that a
reliable system of social indicators will provide the data
base necessary for the establishment of a social accounting system capable of measuring social costs in much the
same way as economic accounts assess the nations economic
well-being. A system of social accounts would allow
society to record not only the gains which result from
social programs, but the social costs as well, and to see
how these costs are distributed.

Planned development and societal control   The third
claim is that of providing requisite knowledge for
societal control and planned social change. It is assumed
by many of the advocates of social indicators that by
making social problems more visible the requisite knowledge would be available to allow society to really become
responsible to its membership, and thereby, be able to
more effectively guide future development.
     It is probably unrealistic, at the present stage of
development, to expect a system of social indicators,
analogous to economic indicators to alert us to social
areas needing possible attention. However, some suggest
that if we had a system it would be useful. "If we now
had a reliable set of social indicators many of the ills
scholars or isolated members of society know about would
be remedied or would not come to pass. Warning signals
would be recognized and action would be taken" (Young,
1970:77). There is a feeling, however, that if it were
possible to establish sets of social indicators, the possibility of averting future social tension and less desirable conditions would be greater than what is now possible. Comments such as those of Young are not uncommon as
more individuals begin to explore the possibility of
establishing some system of social indicators.

8

The possibilities of developing some type of information system capable of achieving the claims discussed thus far ought not tc be discounted. However, as the social indicator movement has matured, several of the more scientifically criented social scientists involved in the movement and writing more recently have addressed themselves to the aims, purposes and goals of the movement. Indeed, their purpose has not been to discredit the movement, rather to suggest caution and the many problems that must be overcome prior to developing usable social indicators. A discussion of the general criticisms of the movement may provide a better understanding of the reasons why some of those involved in the indicator movement are suggesting caution.

<u>Criticisms of sccial indicators</u>   Criticizing the claims made for social indicators is a difficult task because, as yet, a system of social indicators has not been developed. In addition, the criticisms are interrelated in much the same manner as the claims and are difficult to separate.

It is generally accepted that the successes and achievements enjoyed by economics during the past thirty years are due to that discipline's ability to develop a functional economic theory which not only defined but, in addition, specified economic systems. Furthermore, economic theory postulates, either hypothetically or through empirical demonstration, the linkages and interrelations between variables in the system. Input and output factors plus the operation of the system can be assessed in terms of costs and benefits.

If one were to apply this same analogy to sociology, one soon would come to realize that presently no such theory exists. For this reason social scientists such as Gross (1966) and Tiryakian (1967) attempted to generate macromodels of society which would demonstrate interrelationships between variables in the hopes of developing the needed theory. The problem with grand scale attempts at modeling is that it is often difficult to operationalize the concepts or disaggregate the data to meaningful subunits for decision-making purposes. For this reason, some are led to believe that social planners presently are nct provided with the necessary theory and needed conceptualization for a system of social accounts. Perle supports this ccncern and extends it to include the need to empirically verify our conceptual models. Otherwise, they will probably be destined for "idle conversation and intellectual purposes alone" (Perle, 1970:139).

Sheldon and Freeman (1970) are, perhaps, two of the most ardent critics of the social indicator movement. They suggest that the movement can contribute to the three major claims discussed previously, but raise similar concerns as expressed by Perle. According to Sheldon and Freeman, there is presently no social theory that ade-

9

quately defines social system variables nor at the same
time hypothesizes interrelationships. And, one cannot
depend on middle range theories because at this level we
still lack theories having explanatory potential for isolated variables that might be part of some larger system.
It is, therefore, futile to expect social variables to be
capable of providing direction for society in much the
same manner as economic variables have provided guidance
for monitoring the economy because of the current state of
social theory.

The lack of theoretical orientation is perhaps the
most basic criticism and also the most obvious need of the
social indicator movement. Concepts need to be identified
in some taxonomical format with further explication of
subconcepts and their operationalization. Thus far, the
accomplishments in these areas have been less than
adequate.

Implicit in the claims for social indicators is the
assumption that if it were possible to develop a system or
systems of social accounting, the specifications of goals
and priorities about society might be more readily established. Program evaluation would then be possible with
the intent of planning the development of future programs
and activities. Sheldon and Freeman, however, suggest
that goals and priorities are matters of national values
and do not "depend on assembled data" (Sheldon and
Freeman, 1970:99).

The criticism regarding the use of social indicators
for possible societal control stems largely from the definition of social indicators as presented in Toward A
Social Report. The suggestion that social indicators are
statistics of "direct normative interest" (Department of
Health, Education and Welfare, 1969:97) has generated much
discussion. If "normative type" data are to be collected
and, in turn, used for future decision-making, one may
immediately wonder whose normative interests will be used
to determine the selected social indicators from the range
of possible ones. Furthermore, who will use these data in
developing additional goals and exactly who or what
aspects of society will be controlled? These are only a
few of the many concerns which must be considered before
any system of social indicators can be used.

Henriot (1970), in seeking to answer some of these
questions, suggests that conflict of interest rather than
a lack of information has hindered the development of
policies to deal with many social problems. Social problems and processes are often selected which represent current values and bias. Frequently, however, statistics are
used for the purposes of political gain and persuasion according to Bauer (1966) and Biderman (1966). They both
allude to a dual role of statistics for policy decisions.
One role is factual reporting and the other role is that
of political persuasion. The concern with factual reporting is that some may report only those statistics which

10

will tend to support their vested interests. The danger
expressed in the use of social indicators for political
persuasion is that of maintaining the status quo without
allowing change in needed areas.

Sheldon and Freeman also addressed themselves to
these issues, and in particular, the implications of
"normative" indicators for societal control. They stress
that interests change and "what is salient today may not
be so next year." Likewise, what is considered good in
the eyes of some may appear bad in the minds of others.

The criticisms presented in this section are not
meant to dispel the utility of social indicators. Perle
(1970) and Johnston (1971) have, in fact, considered the
potential use and alternative directions for the development of social indicators. The need to acquire some
systematic procedure to monitor constant changes taking
place will not only be sought for by policy planners, but
may in fact be demanded.

The intent of this brief discussion of the claims and
criticisms of social indicators was to present many of the
current concerns which should probably be considered prior
to the development of usable social indicators. Holleb
(1968) and Terleckyj (1970) are but two of the many concerned with social statistics usage for social policy and
the current inadequacies of existing statistical systems
for policy making and analysis of social change. The task
of developing social indicators of societal conditions is
not impossible; in fact, it would appear highly probable.
The important point is to recognize that much additional
work must be done in the areas of theory,
conceptualization, methodology, understanding and specifying interrelationships and needed measurement of sub-
indicators if the social indicator movement is to have an
impact or play a role in the process of planning for
future societal direction.

Toward alternative conceptual perspectives   Thus far,
we have emphasized the early ground work for the eventual
development of the social indicator movement, the various
claims concerning the potential development of usable
social indicators as well as several of the recent criticisms. Throughout the past few years, considerable
maturing of the movement has occurred resulting in more
systematic attempts to deal with these issues. Several
perspectives or orientations to social indicator research
seem to be emerging, each attempting to give direction and
increased sophistication to the problems of
conceptualization, measurement and the future of social
indicators. Even though nearly every writer who has
addressed these issues has suggested their own unique
perspective, there does seem to be a tendency for these
perspectives to converge around a few integrative themes
which will be briefly outlined.

National goals   A popular approach to the development
of social indicators for providing societal guidance is
the specification of national goals. The President's
Commission on National Goals for the Sixties suggested
several major areas of societal concern; however, Biderman
(1966) as previously discussed, was unable to locate relevant indicators for a major portion of those national
goals.

Recently, the Stanford Research Institute (SRI)
released their "Toward Master Social Indicators" (Stanford
Research Institute, 1971) report. The framework for this
report was provided by the major goal areas in the HEW
document of Toward A Social Report. From these major
areas (health, opportunity, environment, standards of
living, public safety, learning and democratic values)
SRI further delineated subcategories for each area and
suggested possible indicators for assessing current
progress in the attainment of those goals for the individual as well as society. They went beyond merely selecting
currently used indicators and in many areas, proposed
indicators which might be considered in future assessments
of national goals and societal change.

This perspective is also supported by those seeking
to adapt the present logical framework of the Programming
Planning and Budgeting System (PPBS) to account for social
dimensions in national program evaluations. Recently, the
National Planning Association received a two-year grant
from the National Science Foundation to conduct research
into the "methods of setting goals for policy purposes"
(Lear, 1972). Although it is difficult to establish generally agreed upon goals, nevertheless, this perspective
has received much support and is reflected in HEW's document as well as some of the works by Gross (1966, 1968),
Olson (1970) and Vestermark's (1968) efforts to develop
indicators of social vulnerability for the Civil Defense
System.

Quality of life   Recognizing the difficulty in
establishing national goals has led some to consider the
possibility of measuring quality of life as another
perspective. Here, social indicators are defined as
indicators of the quality of life. Generally, the approach seems to begin with delineating subcategories that
appear to be general areas reflecting the current state of
quality of life.

This perspective is reflected in the work by Becker
and de Brigard (1970) wherein they explicate quality of
life, which represents "society's overall objective" into
major areas of social, physical and economic environments.
Each of these three major categories were then explicated
to lower level subareas that were either functions of the
state government agency for which the study was conducted,

or had been included in the recent social report by HEW.
For each of the general level societal environments a number of subelements of quality of life are suggested such
as education, housing, health, recreation, social services, economic development, public utilities, public
safety, transportation and natural resources.
Additional examples of this perspective are
exemplified in the works of Jones and Flax (1970b) and
Harland (1971a). The research by Jones and Flax was
conducted at the Urban Institute in Washington, D.C. Although the current activities of this institute will be
discussed later, it is worthwhile to mention their early
work which is reflective of the quality of life
perspective. Basically, several "quality areas" (e.g.,
poverty, air pollution, community concern, social
disintegration, housing, etc.) were considered to be components of quality of life. Each of the fourteen areas,
measured by one indicator, were used to compare "quality
of life" in Washington with seventeen other large
metropolitan cities. It represents one attempt to quantify abstract components of life with the intention of
making inferences for future change. Harland's work with
the Canadian Department of Regional Economic Expansion
also exemplifies "quality of life" research attempting to
consider various components in terms of level, standard,
and norm-of-living.

Viability_and_social_minimums   The emphasis on national
goals and quality of life with the ensuing difficulties
have led some to consider a narrower framework which de-
emphasizes social maximums. This perspective, as suggested by Corning (1970, 1971), draws from evolutionary
biology and assumes that the basic problem of all species
is survival. Therefore, an alternative approach to the
development of social indicators would be to seek those
basic social minimums which tend to indicate how well
society is meeting the basic survival needs of its population.
One criticism of the previous two perspectives is
they both emphasize social maximums and, therefore, tend
to be heavily value laden. Seeking indicators of basic
human needs focuses attention on the generation of an
index of human viability. This same notion has been extended to embrace the problem of assessing social and organizational viability.

Social_problems_and_perception_research   One manner in
which a society can monitor its progress toward a desired
state is to consider assessing current social conditions.
Usually this is defined as an intense concern with social
ills, symptomatic behavior or social problems (cf.
Guttman, 1971) and many indicators are directed toward

13

providing an information base to more adequately
understand those conditions.

The 1969 social report by HEW emphasized the
symptomatic behavior in society and, therefore, proposed
many negative indicators of societal change. This is consistent with their definition of social indicators as
measures of direct normative interest and many of our
present societal conditions seem to promote this
perspective as we are constantly reminded of the level of
crime in the streets and ensuing problems (Wilkins, 1965;
Jones and Flax, 1970a; Ennis, 1969), poverty (Gross,
1965), racial disorders (Palley and Palley, 1969), the
deteriorating environment (Hickey, et.al., 1970) and other
commonly considered social problems. Furthermore, the
University of California at Berkeley is currently involved
in assessing other dimensions of potential social problems, those of discrimination, alienation and the changing
sex roles in the San Francisco Bay area as well as on a
national level.

The issue of perception research is considered
jointly with the social problem perspective because of the
recent emphasis on victimization studies that attempt to
assess the attitudes, experiences and the impact on personality resulting from this and other types of social experience. Most notable contributions in this perspective
come from the Institute for Social Research at the University of Michigan. Campbell and Converse, of the
Institute, emphasize that much of the past social
indicator research has considered structural changes (cf.
Sheldon and Moore, 1968) but little emphasis was given to
psychological aspects which must be included in any complete assessment of social change. The Russell Sage Foundation provided the initial financial support for this research. The findings have recently been released in the
form of an edited book by Campbell and Converse (1972)
entitled, The Human Meaning of Social Change. This is
considered a companion piece to the Sheldon and Moore
publication Indicators of Social Change, and adds a new
dimension to the current perspectives on social
indicators.

Social systems   Given the complexity of social
phenomena and the need to understand this complexity
through an examination of their interrelationships, a more
recent perspective considers social indicators in a
systems framework. The social systems perspective for
social indicators received initial support from Gross
(1966, 1967), who developed "a general model for an international system of national social accounts" which he
calls his structure-performance model. More recently this
perspective gained additional support from Land (1970) in
an extensive treatise on social indicators. He initially
criticized recent theoretical and methodological issues

14

and proposed three criteria which should be employed in the definition of a social indicator with inferences toward social indicators as components in systems. For Land, social indicators are social statistics that : "(1) are components in a model of a social system, (2) can be collected at various points in time and accumulated into a time-series, and (3) can be aggregated or disaggregated to levels appropriate to the specifications of the model" (Land, 1971:4-5). His emphasis on social indicators being a component or parameter in a model is, in part, based on the success economics has enjoyed through macro-economic models of society. He admits that macrosociological models of the type suggested by Gross are much too general to apply in specific social institutions. For this reason, Land suggests the generation of social system models of poverty, health, leisure, the family, education, religion and other related topics.

The concern with monitoring systems performance, in addition to the cause, effect and interrelationship between the variables within the system, is continuing to gain favor among recent writers in the social indicator movement. Further examples of this support, recommended as additional reading, are exemplified in the writings of Fox (1969), General Electric (1970), Brooks (1971), and Dubin (1971). The previous perspectives have not considered the question of how does one go about developing indicators. Instead, the discussions have remained at a general level. If one accepts the general definition by Land that social indicators are components in a social system that provides information about the functioning of the system, a major question for future concern is the methodology to be employed in developing such a system.

Methodology and model building   As Duncan has so effectively pointed out, the current discussions of social indicators tend to polarize around two basic strategies; the theoretical-deductive, and the empirical-inductive. In brief, Duncan (1969) characterizes these two positions by suggesting that the theorist prefers to ponder his problem at great length, then he will feel confident of what must be accomplished by making observations. The empiricist, on the other hand, is concerned with measuring "something" and then standardizing the measurements for purposes of reliability. It would indeed be unfair to argue the inclusion of one to the exclusion of the other. Both are needed in the development of indicators.

Duncan opts for an approach to social reporting that follows more the inductive approach or seems to suggest that we measure what we can without worrying about the framework. He argues that, from his own assessment, "those who have approached the problem of social reporting with the strongest theoretical presuppositions have possibly made the least impressive contribution thus far (Duncan, 1969:9).

On the basis of the inductive approach, Duncan suggests a next step in social indicator research worthy of considerable attention. His basic thesis is that our attention in the immediate future might best be focused on the problem of how changes in value of measured variables are to be detected, rather than focusing on how a general indicator is measured. This would reorient the concern more toward "trend studies" and the measurement of change. This type of research, he suggests, might be best advanced through replication studies of earlier research which are of high enough quality to serve as base data. In other words, we ought to be focusing our attention on learning how to measure change of those things we presently know how to measure. The problem is not only that we do not know what to measure but also that what we presently do measure, we measure incorrectly. Therefore, we would do well to orient our research toward base studies and replication.

The effectiveness of this approach is clearly evident in the excellent study of stratification in America reported by Blau and Duncan (1967) in the book, The American Occupational Structure. In this study, which was the special census survey in 1962, they attempted to construct and estimate the parameters of various path models of the process of social stratification. In many important areas of future sociological analysis, social systems models capable of analyzing input and outputs of social institutions could be built inductively much in the same way as was this study.

At the present, several federal agencies and international organizations continue to compile and publish descriptive statistics on particular social components of society. The Bureau of Labor contributes to this effort through regular releases of occupation and employment data. Likewise, the Office of Management and Budget is preparing a social statistics publication which will provide base data in several areas of societal concern. The data from OMB , however, will be nonevaluative and nonanalytical. It is intended that the data will be used by researchers in building models to aid in understanding the interrelationships of societal phenomena.

Mathematical modeling in social indicator research to better understand the interrelationship between social variables is rapidly gaining support from social scientists. Several sociologists have demonstrated a recent general interest in model building (cf. Coleman, 1964, 1971; Borgatta, 1969; Borgatta and Bohrnstedt, 1970; Costner, 1971; Sonquist, 1970; Gitter, 1970) with their discussions usually related to alternative techniques. Attempts to develop models of health systems are currently in process by Anderson (1970, 1971a, 1971b) utilizing the structure-performance framework developed by Bertram Gross. Fox (1971), an economist, is attempting to develop

16

mathematical models that bring together "quantity of life", "quality of life" and "social indicators" into a common framework which he has labeled, the "gross social product."

In the summer of 1972, the Russell Sage Foundation will sponsor a Conference on Social Indicator Models to emphasize the development of models of primary social processes. Several leading social scientists are invited to attend and present papers which will stress social indicator models paralleling econometric models currently found in applied economics.

Thus far, the discussion has emphasized several themes in the development of the social indicator "movement", leading to the activities of the late 1960's and the first year and a half of the 1970's. Lately, however, the social indicator "movement" in the United States has come to somewhat of a standstill. As yet, the Mondale Bill has not received continued support, a Council of Social Advisors is still in question, and three years have passed since the HEW document was related without regularized annual social reports by the President. While the various evaluative, critical, and state of the art issues continue to be academically and politically debated, a trend is, nevertheless, emerging toward a systematic scientific research effort to develop a system of social indicators. Indeed there is an increasing recognition of the need for a more rigorous approach to social indicators. Gross has succinctly asked: "Wouldn't it first be necessary to develop an ordered set of concepts on which social indicators could be based?" (Gross, 1965:33). This plea for more rigor in concepts can be expanded to include a consideration of methodological, theoretical and definitional problems of social indicators along with the typical concerns for policy planning and application. The next section will focus on some of these issues suggesting relevant sources from the bibliography that reflect these various perspectives.

Current Issues in Social Indicators

One is likely to find, in picking up one of the many references discussed thus far, several issues concerning the development, use and misuse of social indicators in social planning and decision-making. One issue, as an illustration, deplores the current state of social theory and that at the present there does not exist a fully developed system like the economic models to aid in specifying important dimensions and parameters. Of course, the whole question of whether or not social models similar to economic models are needed is also raised. Furthermore, there are only vague suggestions concerning the conceptual underpinnings of any system of social accounts.

Whether one is concerned with quality of life, whatever that may be, to assessing the performance of society and anticipating the future, we believe that issues such as these can be categorized and represent the rationale behind the classification scheme utilized in the annotated portion of the bibliography. For example, the issue on national goals often found in social indicator literature can be subsumed under in the category of "policy and planning." Likewise, assessing the state of society where models may be needed and issues concerning social systems frameworks for social accounting could be a subpart of the category - general theory. For this reason, the bibliography is organized around several categories reflecting current issues in social indicator research. These categories reflect the trend toward a more rigorous scientific investigation of social indicators and may eventually lead to a variety of approaches in the development of social indicators for societal monitoring. The purpose of this section is to outline the various categories in the Annotated Index of the bibliography, briefly define what they are to represent and suggest here and there references from the bibliography that may be relevant in understanding the various underlying issues subsumed under a particular category. Some of the references cited under any cne of the following categories may not appear in the corresponding category in the Annotated Index of the bibliography because (1) they may discuss other issues and, therefore, appear in other categories, or (2) the particular references in question may not have been annotated.

Definition   A typical problem encountered in discussions of social indicators relates to the definition of the term. During the early stages of the movement each perspective seemed to suggest alternative definitions resulting in definitional ambiguity. One perspective considers social indicators defined in terms of their normative aspects and descriptive purposes. Katzman views social indicators "as measurements of social phenomena whose movements indicate whether a particular problem is getting better or worse relative to some goal" (Katzman, 1968:96). Holleb differentiates social indicators and social accounts by suggesting that social measurement must include an assessment of social change, in terms of explicit social goals, which she labels social indicators and "providing a framework for evaluating social policies and programs in terms of their effectiveness in achieving these goals" (Holleb, 1968:83) which she designates as social accounts.

The HEW document defines a social indicator as a statistic of direct normative interest measuring some state cf welfare and if it changes in the "right" direction, can be interpreted as "things have gotten better, or people are better off" (U.S. Department of Health, Education and Welfare, 1969:97). Others reflecting slight variations in defining social indicators along normative lines are Cohen (1968) and Olson (1969) with Kamrany and Christakis (1970) proposing absolute, relative and autonomous indicators and Vestermark (1968) emphasizing the need to take into account three levels of indicators from descriptive to value-relevant in formulating a definition.

A more recent definition, reflecting still another perspective, considers social indicators to be a component of social system models. This definition is proposed by Kenneth Land. He suggests they be "collected over time and accumulated into a time-series and aggregated or disaggregated to levels appropriate to the specifications of the model" (Land, 1971:323).

Conceptual   A next step after defining social indicators might be to consider what social phenomena would be included in those definitions. The articles classified in the category--conceptual, refer to the adequacy of concepts (Bell, 1968), discussions relating to what concepts might be considered in an index of quality of life (Corning, 1971; Gitter and Franklin, 1971; Pett, 1972) and attempts to define measurements of health (Culyer, 1971), social stratification and mobility (Duncan, 1968), leisure (Ennis, 1968; Burkhead, 1971), welfare (Merriam, 1967) and other related concepts. Bertram Gross proposed the development of ordered sets of concepts for which social indicators could be developed. As yet, there are few taxonomies or classifications that meet his proposal.

General theory   A frequent criticism of the current state of social indicator research is the inadequate level of social theory to provide some overall framework. The present bibliography, however, provides evidence that many individuals are experimenting with alternative theoretical schemes as one yet unresolved issue in social indicators. Anderson (1970) adapted Gross' proposed model of a national social accounting system to develop a set of social indicators measuring the impact of innovative programs on the structure and performance of communities. Interrelating variables to develop a theory of nation states, another perspective, is currently being considered by Finsterbusch (1971), with Kunkel (1971) and Dubin (1971) investigating alternative social system perspectives. A new emphasis emerging in general theory focuses on the notion of model building (Coleman, 1971) with some interesting examples from health (Chiang, 1965; Austin, 1971; Chen and Bush, 1971).

Methodology   This category is designed to represent the
manner in which social indicator research is conducted,
alternative techniques, issues of measurement and general
procedures of scientific investigation. These techniques
range from factor analysis (Gitter, 1970), content analysis (Krendel, 1970) and magnitude estimation (Shinn, 1971)
to inductive approaches (Duncan, 1969; Wilcox and Brooks,
1971) and experimental alternatives (Campbell, 1971).
Questions of measurement center on reliability and
validity (Etzioni and Lehman, 1967), suggestions from
other disciplines (D'Agostino, 1971) and operationalizing
abstract concepts (Drewnowski, 1970). Finally, other
sources to consider in this general category suggest
strategies for measuring the quality of life (Flax, 1970;
Jones and Flax, 1970b), social reporting systems for
communities (Albuquerque Urban Observatory, 1971) and
developing social profiles for social action agencies
(Richard, 1969).

Policy and planning   Perhaps this perspective is best
summarized by the titles of recent articles by Leonard
Duhl (1968), "Planning and predicting: or what do you do
when you don't know the names of the variables" and
Senator Mondale's (1967), "Some thoughts on stumbling into
the future." The former refers to policy, the latter to
planning. Decision-makers find themselves in situations
of uncertainty when anticipating the future, planning for
change, establishing goals and evaluating social programs.
All of these are critical components of policy and
planning.
      The articles in this section reflect many of the
above concerns. Evaluative research is assumed to be a
desirable component for future planning. Chaiklin (1970),
Anderson, and others (1970) and Alberts (1971) address
themselves to this issue as well as considering how to
analyze the performance of social programs. Another critical part to be included in this perspective of planning
is the question of social goals and societal feedback.
The former is discussed at great length by Hauser (1967),
Wilcox and Brooks (1971), Biderman (1963) and the National
Goals Research Staff (1970). The latter is represented by
Bauer's (1967) recent article on societal feedback.
      The Full Opportunity Act (Mondale, 1970) and the pro-
posal for a Council of Social Advisers (Samuelson, 1967)
have implications for the making of future policy. The
article by Henriot (1971) discussing political implications of social indicators and Sheldon's (1971)
suggestions for long-term programs in social indicators
propose useful parameters aiding future societal planning
and the establishment of policy.

Application   One might expect to find detailed empirical examples of the application of social indicators to various societal problems. This type of rigor, however, is not demonstrated in the literature. There are several references to real world problems. Ferriss (1969, 1971) is concerned with education and the status of women, with Jones and Flax (1970a, 1970b) considering a range of applied areas subsumed in quality of life. Finally, the study by Wilson (1969) applies nine of the eleven domestic goals included in the Report of the President's Commission on National Goals using each of the states in the United States as the unit of analysis.

Criticism and state of the art   The categories presented thus far can be considered as positive contributions to developing social indicator research. This category, however, refers to all those previously discussed as it contains articles raising many of the basic concerns and challenging the over zealous claims made for potential systems of social indicators. It is through critically questioning the theoretical frameworks, methodologies and how indicators will be used that greater sophistication will result, maturing the "movement".
     Several articles could be suggested as "must reading" to gain an overview of the unrealistic claims or where caution should be exercised in this entire area of research. However, only a few will be mentioned as representative of the areas of concern. One place to start might be with the discussions and debate in the U.S. Senate (1967; 1968; 1969) where testimonies, pro and con, have been presented concerning the Full Opportunity and Social Accounting Act, the Council of Social Advisors and questions relating to systems of indicators in general. Several have criticized the manner in which current policy is formulated (Horowitz, 1968; Perle, 1971; Palley and Palley, 1971), the current use of statistics (Bowman and others, 1960; Gastil, 1970) and political questions about social indicators (Henriot, 1970). Finally, Sheldon and Freeman present a critical overview delineating three areas where they suggest that our current expertise is technically deficient and conceptually inadequate in setting goals and priorities, evaluating programs and developing balance sheets.

Bibliography   In new areas of research, it is difficult to keep abreast of current activities due to inadequate information systems and publication lag. Therefore, several bibliographies have appeared recently to counter these deficiencies. In a recent issue of the Annals, Carol Agocs (1970) prepared a brief listing of sources to suggest the interdisciplinary nature of the social

indicators movement. Beal and others (1971), Tugac (1971)
and Wilcox and others (1972) have provided detailed
listings of current sources with Knezo (1971) preparing a
brief annotated bibliography on the subject of social science policies.

   The classification of the annotated bibliography into
the above mentioned categories was stimulated through
desire to see the movement mature into a scientific
effort. Much work lies ahead before it will be possible
to monitor current social conditions and evaluate social
change in society. It appears inevitable that this will
come to pass and hopefully, the articles mentioned thus
far will encourage others to propose new theoretical alternatives, suggest innovative methods and refine concepts
in advancing social indicator research.

Social Indicator Research: Current Activities

   The last few years have been characterized by the
rapid development of more systematic research efforts in
social indicators, both nationally and internationally.
The primary concern of this section is to review some of
the initial efforts of foreign countries in social
indicator research as well as to consider the wide range
of activities currently taking place within the United
States.

International social indicator activities

France   Social indicator activities in France are
presently conducted by three major research institutes.
Much of the current work was stimulated by a seminar on
social indicators resulting in the book, Les Indicateurs
Sociaux edited by Delors (1971). The intent of these
institutes is to enrich the statistics of the
infrastructure of France. Specific examples are discussed
in the publications by Marie and Dos Santos (1971) on
immigrant workers and French society, Girardeau (1971) on
indicators of education, the Centre National de la
Recherche Scientifique (1971) indicating the present state
of progress pertaining to indicators of work conditions,
and the attempt by the Institute de Recherche Economique
et de Planification (1971) to integrate social indicators
with models of social change.

Great Britain   Social indicator activities in Great
Britain are relatively new but demonstrate a wide range of

interest.   In 1971 the British Social Science Research
Council and the Russell Sage Foundation co-sponsored the
Ditchley Park Conference wherein social scientists
throughout Europe came together to discuss the role of
social indicators in Western Europe.

Thus far, Great Britain has published two excellent
sources of official statistics. These are the two volumes
obtainable from the Central Statistical Office (1970,
1971) under the editorship of Muriel Nissel. They are
relatively small volumes but contain tables and charts
depicting important aspects of current social conditions
in the United Kingdom. Both volumes indicate a strong
commitment to providing regularized reporting on several
important societal dimensions.

Germany   A recent development in Germany was the
establishment of a committee on social indicators by the
German Sociological Association under the chairmanship of
Wolfgang Zapf (1972b). As part of its role in social
indicators, this committee actively encouraged the German
government to consider publishing a document on social
statistics. A result of their efforts is furnished by the
Ministry of Labor establishing a task force to review
indicators currently in use throughout several
governmental departments. The purpose of this task force
is to prepare a common framework for future social reporting. Each department prepares annual reports of their
work and the various introductions to those separate departmental reports are being summarized and bound together
as an initial German Social Report and perhaps the beginning of a regularized "State of the Union" message. Although Germany is just entering this type of research, it
appears that in the near future we can expect an increased
input to the social indicator literature. For those more
interested in the German work we suggest the sources by
Professor Zapf listed in the extensive bibliography.

Canada   Three government related agencies in Canada
presently are involved in different aspects of social
indicator research. The Westrede Institute, at the
request of the Alberta Human Resources Research Council
and the Commission on Educational Planning conducted a
study designed to examine several social phenomena having
an impact on education. The resulting publication by Dyck
(1970) presents a series of forecasts, using the Delphi
technique, for six topic areas. From these six areas,
eleven sets of forecasts are made involving divisions in
Canadian society, value change and ideology, the family,
religion, education, leisure and recreation, politics,
native peoples, relations with others, law and disorder
and mental illness and other social problems.

23

Another social indicator activity currently in progress is under the direction of Douglas Harland (1971a) of the Social and Human Analysis Branch, Department of Regional Economic Expansion. His work represents the relentless search one goes through in attempting to sort out the various components of quality-of-life. Future plans involve report writing with a major emphasis on tables depicting disparities in Canada, by region, along several social indicatordimensions. The intent is to develop social indicator indexes for social reporting and model building for eventual social policy accounting.

A final source which is related to social indicator work in Canada is the publication by the Economic Council of Canada (1971). The report is geared at more effective decision-making and social indicators are considered as a new approach for setting policy objectives.

The discussion thus far is not intended to be an indepth analysis of social indicator activities of an international basis. Rather, it is designed to suggest a general level of activity in Great Britain, France, Germany and Canada. Additional nations involved in social indicator type research are Spain, Japan and Denmark with preliminary steps underway in several other countries.

Involvement of international organizations
There are several international organizations presently involved in social indicator research with an attempt to develop measures in several areas across different countries. One of these, the Organization for Economic Cooperation and Development (OECD) was commissioned by its Ministerial Council to coordinate the fifteen member states in the development of measurement instruments related to quality of life. The duration of the program is for several years and will seek to develop social indicators from an "agreed-upon" list of primary goal areas and social concerns. Some of the specific areas of concern are personal health and safety, time and leisure, the physical environment, the social environment and the political environment (Organization for Economic Cooperation and Development, 1971).

Another international agency involved in social indicator research is the United Nations Research Institute for Social Development (UNRISD). In general, UNRISD is interested in research problems related to social and economic development during various phases of economic growth. Established by a grant from the government of the Netherlands and an additional grant from the United States, its focus is directed to the study of problems from an international point of view that are generally not covered by national universities or institutes.

Some current UNRISD projects include quantitative analysis of socio-economic development, methods of decision-making, preparation of the child for economic and

technological modernization and the measurement of real
progress at the local level. This latter project relates
directly to the recent social indicator movement and puts
forth the hypothesis that "by systematic examination of
real progress at the local level (i.e., in specific
villages, small towns, city districts, etc.) not only can
certain aspects of change, particularly social aspects, be
better assessed but also the nature of change, including
the interrelations between economic and social factors,
can be better observed" (United Nations Research Institute
for Social Development, 1971:1). This emphasis on the
local level is suggested for situations involving social
variables and the need to become familiar with the level
at which interactions are initiated.

The remainder of this introductory paper will be concerned with research activities and opportunities currently in progress in the United States. These activities are
taking place at several levels of government as well as
industry, private research institutes and universities.
It will not be possible to explore each in depth nor discuss fully the entire range of activities. Therefore, the
discussion will center on the various activities at the
national level to sponsor and stimulate social indicator
type research then move to select examples of private research foundations and finally brief mention of university
programs in social indicators which may be of interest in
gaining an overview of work in the United States.

U.S. government and social indicators

At the national level there are currently two organizations playing key roles in the future development of
societal monitoring, social accounting and social
indicators for the purpose of improving social reporting.
The Statistical Policy Division, of the Office of
Management and Budget (OMB) is undertaking the task of
providing a publication (cf. Tunstall, 1970) covering
major social areas with the intent to provide policy
makers and other interested parties with national data for
program guidance and future decision-making. This publication, to be released toward the end of 1972, will not
undertake to analyze nor justify given concern areas.
Rather, its purpose is to present accurate information
about major social concerns.

Thus far, OMB has tried to identify long term significant social issues that are general, not as yet pressing,
within a specifically national and yet comprehensive
focus. These major social concerns are not uncommon in
the social indicator literature, and indeed reflect the
concerns of documents discussed previously from several
foreign countries.

The National Science Foundation (NSF) is another
national organization currently involved in social
indicator activities. However, the role of NSF is to fund

ongoing social indicator research projects in various
areas of interest. The National Science Foundation supports research on social indicators through grants administered by the Division of Social Sciences. Consideration
will be given to theoretical, methodological, and experimental projects which hold the promise of contributing to
the development of social indicators for use in public administration and in longitudinal studies of social change.

The recent surge in social indicator type proposals
has resulted in NSF awarding twenty-two grants in the
fiscal year 1971. These projects cover a wide range of
social indicator activities from political, social and economic to experimental designs, developing goals accounting systems, trend analysis of political opinions, attitudes toward violence, measurement of social indicators,
social and urban indicators as well as a special project
on kinostatistics. At present, NSF has funded three projects for the fiscal year 1972.

The Research Analysis of National Needs section of
NSF also funds social indicator type projects but these
are in the general area of social development and may be
broader than the projects termed as social indicators.
Details about the suggested content and format of proposals are contained in "Grants for Scientific Research" (NSF
69-23) which is available on request to the Foundation at
the Office of Sponsored Research, or its equivalent, at
colleges and universities.

Research foundations and institutes
The Russell Sage Foundation has had a long interest
in supporting social indicators research as part of its
program on the study of social change. Early efforts were
devoted to the collection and analysis of "objective"
indicators of social trends. This resulted in the volume,
Indicators of Social Change: Concepts and Measurements,
edited by Eleanor B. Sheldon and Wilbert E. Moore (1968)
and in the series of monographs on education, American
family, status of women, and health by Abbott L. Ferriss
(1969; 1970; 1971; 1972). Additional efforts have been
devoted to the study of the "subjective" dimension of
social change, and are reported in The Human Meaning of
Social Change by Campbell and Converse (1972). More
recently, interest has focused on community social
indicators with the support of such studies as the replication of earlier Detroit Area Surveys and a Los Angeles
State-of-the-Region Social Report. Finally, recent projects include methods for social indicator analysis in the
form of a Conference on Social Indicator Models. With the
completion of these projects, the Foundation expects to
phase out its social indicators funding.

The Urban Institute, located in Washington, D.C.,
represents a recently established, non-profit research organization currently involved in one particular aspect of

26

the social indicators movement--urban indicators. Organized in April of 1968, the Institute, with a staff of approximately 250 employees, receives its funding from several governmental and non-governmental agencies. In March, 1970, the Institute released its first report, a comprehensive attempt to compare the "quality of life" in Washington, D.C. with seventeen different metropolitan cities of similar size (Jones and Flax, 1970b). Additional work by the Institute reflects their emphasis on urban conditions and in particular, developing descriptive indicators in areas of major social concern. This emphasis is exemplified in past publications by the Institute comparing cities and suburbs (Jones and Flax, 1970a), blacks and whites (Flax, 1971) and generating some statistical benchmarks for selected education indicators in twenty-one major cities (Flax, 1970).

For the future, the Institute plans to expand on previous completed work through updating and broadening previously developed indicators (Flax, 1972). Also, five additional studies are planned (Garn and Flax, 1971:22) involving inter and intra-city indicators of crime, law enforcement and racial equality utilizing data obtained from government agencies and private sources.

Another institute presently involved in social indicator research is the Stanford Research Institute (SRI). This institute's research activities can be summarized in terms of four areas: (1) values and needs of people, (2) social indicators, (3) evaluations of social programs and (4) social change and the future.

The social indicator projects conducted by SRI number six and begin with an approach to devise master social indicators (Mitchell and Markley, 1969). This report emphasized a heuristic model of society, the interrelationships between goals, indicators and attainment levels and a discussion of a comprehensive national social data system. The master social indicators were developed from the general areas suggested in the HEW document of Toward a Social Report. The other projects included attempts to develop scales and indices to measure changing conditions in social indicator areas (Logothetti, 1970), an evaluation of the Office of Economic Opportunity's "Community Profile" data bank which suggests why social reporting is likely to be a regularized practice, a project reviewing recent developments in social accounting and an assessment of indexes of well-being (Hammond and Harvey, 1970).

A different type of social indicators activity involves ten urban cities. The purpose of the Urban Observatories Program is to identify, define and validate measures of urban social conditions that are relevant for public policy formulation, performance evaluation, and decision-making by local officials concerned with such functional areas as health, welfare, manpower training and unemployment, housing, public safety, refuse collection and disposal, environmental pollution control, recreation

27

and culture, and urban transportation.

Each of the ten cities taking part in this two year project have selected areas from those mentioned to focus upon, in greater depth, and then contribute to a synthesis of constructs having a generalizable application. For example, Kansas City (Mid-America Observatory) is directing its efforts to the conceptual problems of developing an indicator system and concentrating on housing and transportation indicators. Thus far, Albuquerque and Atlanta have prepared preliminary reports on their current state of progress. Albuquerque's report (Albuquerque Urban Observatory, 1971) is very detailed and presents key indicators selected to represent major areas of social concern.

Universities and industry   It would be impossible to discuss the many universities currently involved in social indicator type studies. Likewise, the recent movement has also generated concern in industry and many companies are now in the process of instituting new roles in their organization with major responsibilities in the areas of environment, social responsibility and societal analysis. Therefore, we will mention two universities that are engaged in significant indicator activities and then look briefly at two organizations in industry.

The Institute for Social Research (ISR) at the University of Michigan has and will continue to do research in the general field of social indicators. The National Science Foundation recently awarded ISR a large grant to operate the institute with part of the funds being allocated specifically to social indicator research.

At a very general level, the institute will continue its interests in measuring change through the implementation of thirteen various social indicator studies. These range from studies of attitudes and values regarding violence, racial attitudes and behavior to the use of time, meaning of work, surveys regarding reactions to stress, quality of life in cities, mental health and indicators of changes in people's goals, opportunities and economic well-being.

Another research center representing a significant input to social indicator research is the Survey Research Center (SRC) at the University of California (Berkeley). The SRC, under the direction of J. Merrill Shanks, received a grant from the National Science Foundation to conduct a study entitled "Toward the Development of Model Social Indicators" (Shanks, 1971). Professor Shanks is the principal investigator of the study which has two major objectives. The first is to prepare model social indicators and begin measurement in the areas of racial prejudice, political alienation and the changing role of women in society. The second is to contribute to the clarification of common methodological and theoretical

28

problems encountered in social indicator research.

The study is designed for a five year program with five types of data collection. These range from pilot studies and exploratory interviews to large San Francisco Bay Area sample surveys with follow-up studies of special groups, panel studies and periodic national surveys of the general public. The study represents a very sophisticated approach to assessing some of the structural changes in American society.

The final two organizations to be discussed in relation to ongoing programs in social indicators are represented by an example from the field of banking and one from the automobile industry.

In the early part of 1970, the Bank of America's Committee on Social Performance Priorities selected the general areas of minority upgrading, housing, social unrest and environment. These four were considered to be of a sufficient magnitude for the Bank of America to concentrate its resources for the development of possible future action programs to demonstrate its social responsibility.

The automobile industry provides the final example of a large corporation directing its efforts to the area of societal analysis. General Motors has recently organized a new activity in its Research Laboratories called the Societal Analysis Activity under the direction of Dr. Walter A. Albers, Jr. A major interest is the interface of the corporation with society. This newly formed group represents a concerted attempt to develop concepts and methodologies for quantifying social phenomena and externalities of General Motor's operations through a highly qualified team of inter-scientists from economics, physical sciences, sociology, psychology and operations research. This activity may be relatively new, but does appear to provide a stimulating resource base to assess the impact of a corporation on society and at the same time consider a wide range of possible research topics on societal concerns.

Conclusion

The purpose of this paper was to serve as an introduction to the relatively new area of social indicators. The procedure was to provide background information for individuals as yet unfamiliar with this topic. This task was approached by reviewing the social indicator "movement" as it initially developed within the United States, raising some current issues as a basis for the categorization of the sources found in the Annotated Index of the bibliography and to suggest a high level of in-

volvement in social indicator research, both nationally
and internationally. Throughout the discussion, a
recurring theme stressed the need for more rigorous examination of the assumptions, methods and potential usage of
social indicators in societal monitoring. This rigor is
more recently tending toward a scientific effort on the
part of social scientists in response to the demands of
decision-makers. As a result, we may indeed be witnessing
a major revolution in western society as social planning
takes on a higher priority. It may take several decades,
but the need is evident, the momentum is increasing and
hopefully, it will be possible to develop monitoring
systems capable of assessing social change and social
progress.

REFERENCES

Agocs, Carol
    1970   "Social indicators: Selected readings." The
            Annals of the American Academy of Political and
            Social Science (March):127-132.

Alberts, David S.
    1971   "An operations research approach to measuring
            the performance of social programs." A paper
            presented at Annual Meeting of the Ohio Valley
            Sociological Society (April 22-24) Cleveland,
            Ohio.

Albuquerque Urban Observatory
    1971   Social Reporting for Albuquerque: Development
            of a Social Indices System. Preliminary Report.
            Albuquerque, New Mexico: Albuquerque Urban
            Observatory.

American Academy of Arts and Sciences
    1967   Toward the Year 2000: Work in Progress.
            Daedalus. Journal of the American Academy of
            Arts and Sciences (Summer).

American Academy of Political and Social Science
    1967a   Social Goals and Indicators for American
            Society: Volume I. The Annals of the American
            Academy of Political and Social Science 373
            (September).

    1967b   Social Goals and Indicators for American
            Society: Volume II. The Annals of the American
            Academy of Political and Social Science 373
            (September).

    1970   Political Intelligence for America's Future.
            The Annals of the American Academy of Political
            and Social Science 388 (March).

    1971   Social Science and the Federal Government. The
            Annals of the American Academy of Political and
            Social Science 394 (March).

    1972   The Nation's Health: Some Issues. The Annals
            of the American Academy of Political and Social
            Science 399 (January).

Anderson, Claire M., Edward E. Schwartz and Narayan
Viswanathan
    1970   "Approaches to the analysis of social service
             systems." Pp. 42-51 in Edward E. Schwartz
             (ed.), Planning-Programming-Budgeting Systems
             and Social Welfare. Chicago, Illinois: The
             University of Chicago, The School of Social
             Service Administration.

Anderson, James G.
    1970   "Causal models and the evaluation of health
             service systems." Working paper No. 43.
             Lafayette, Indiana: Institute for the Study of
             Social Change, Department cf Sociology, Purdue
             University.

    1971a   "Path analysis: A new approach to modelling
             health service delivery systems." A paper pre-
             sented at the Joint National Conference on Major
             Systems, National Meeting cf the Operations Re-
             search Society of America (October 27-29)
             Anaheim, California.

    1971b   "Social indicators and second-order conse-
             quences: Measuring the impact of innovative
             health and medical care delivery systems." A
             paper presented at the Second National
             Conference on Systems Research for Improving the
             Delivery of Health Care Services, Conducted by
             the Hospital and Health Services Division, Amer-
             ican Institute of Industrial Engineers (February
             4-5) Denver, Colorado.

Austin, Charles J.
    1971   "Selected social indicators in the health
             field." American Journal of Public Health 61
             (August): 1507-1513.

Bank of America
    1971   "Paper recycling: A report on its economic and
             ecological implications." A report prepared by
             the Committee on Social Performance Priorities.
             San Francisco, California: Bank of America.

Bauer, Raymond A. (ed.)
    1966   Social Indicators. Cambridge, Massachusetts:
             The M.I.T. Press.

    1967   "Societal feedback." The Annals of the American
             Academy of Political and Social Science 373

32

(September):180-192. (Reprinted in Bertram M.
Gross (ed.), 1969 Social Intelligence for
America's Future. Boston: Allyn and Bacon).

Beal, George M., Ralph M. Brooks, Leslie D. Wilcox and
Gerald E. Klonglan
    1971   Social Indicators: Bibliography 1. Sociology
            Report No. 92 (January). Ames, Iowa: Iowa
            State University, Department of Sociology and
            Anthropology.

Becker, Harold S. and Raul de Brigard
    1970   Considerations on a Framework for Community
            Action Planning. (Working Paper WP-9)
            Middletown, Connecticut: The Institute for the
            Future.

Bell, Daniel
    1968   "The adequacy of our concepts." Pp. 127-161 in
            Bertram M. Gross (ed.), A Great Society? New
            York: Basic Books, Inc.

Bennett, M. K.
    1937   "On measurement of relative national standards
            of living." Quarterly Journal of Economics 1937
            (February):317-335.

Biderman, Albert D.
    1963   National Goals and Statistical Indicators.
            Washington, D.C.: Bureau of Social Science Re-
            search, Inc.

    1966   "Social indicators and goals." Pp. 68-153 in
            Raymond A. Bauer (ed.), Social Indicators.
            Cambridge, Massachusetts: The M.I.T. Press.

Blau, Peter and Otis Dudley Duncan
    1967   The American Occupational Structure. New York:
            Wiley.

Borgatta, Edgar F.
    1969   Sociological Methodology. San Francisco,
            California: Jossey-Bass, Inc., Publishers.

Borgatta, Edgar F. and George W. Bohrnstedt
    1970   Sociological Methodology. San Francisco,
            California: Jossey--Bass, Inc., Publishers.

Bowman, R. T., Alexander Gall and Israel Rubin
    1960   "Social statistics: Present conditions, future
            needs and prospects." Pp. 74-81 in Proceedings
            of the Social Statistics Section, American Sta-
            tistical Association, Washington, D.C.

Brooks, Ralph M.
    1971   Social Indicators for Community Development:
            Theoretical and Methodological Considerations.
            Unpublished Ph.D. Dissertation. Ames, Iowa:
            Iowa State University.

Burkhead, Danny L.
    1971   "Leisure: A taxonomic approach." A paper pre-
            sented at a Social Indicators Symposium. Ames,
            Iowa: Iowa State University.

Cabello, Octavio
    1959   "The use of statistics in the formulation and
            evaluation of social programmes." Pp. 206-215
            in Proceedings of the Social Statistics Section.
            Washington, D.C.: American Statistical Associ-
            ation.

Campbell, Angus
    1971   White Attitudes Toward Black People. Ann Arbor,
            Michigan: Institute for Social Research.

Campbell, Angus and Philip Converse
    1972   The Human Meaning of Social Change. New York:
            Basic Books.

Central Statistical Office
    1970   Social Trends. Volume 1. London, England: Her
            Majesty's Stationery Office.

    1971   Social Trends. Volume 2. London, England: Her
            Majesty's Stationery Office.

Centre National de la Recherche Scientifique
    1971   "Etat d'avancement de la recherche sur des

indicateurs sociaux des conditions de travail."
Unpublished manuscript. Paris, France:
Laboratoire d'Economie et Sociologie du Travail.

Chaiklin, Harris
1970   "Evaluation research and the
        planning-programming-budgeting system." Pp.
        27-34 in Edward E. Schwartz (ed.),
        Planning-Programming-Budgeting Systems and
        Social Welfare. Chicago, Illinois: The Univer-
        sity of Chicago, The School of Social Service
        Administration.

Chen, M. M. and J. W. Bush
1971   "A mathematical programming approach for
        selecting an optimum health program case mix."
        A paper presented at the meeting of the Opera-
        tions Research Society of America (October
        27-29) Anaheim, California.

Chiang, C. L.
1965   An Index of Health: Mathematical Models.
        Public Health Service Publication No. 1000,
        Series 2, No. 5. Washington, D.C.: National
        Center for Health Statistics.

Cohen, Wilbur J.
1968   "Social indicators: Statistics for public
        policy." The American Statistician 22
        (October):14-16.

Coleman, James S.
1964   Introduction to Mathematical Sociology. New
        York: The Free Press.

1971   Resources for Social Change: Race in the United
        States. New York: Wiley-Interscience.

Corning, Peter A.
1970   "The problem of applying Darwinian evolution to
        political science." Prepared for delivery at
        the VIIIth World Congress of the International
        Political Science Association (August 31-Septem-
        ber 5) Munich, Germany.

1971   "Can we develop an index for quality of life?"
        A paper presented at the Annual Meeting of the

American Association for the Advancement of Science (December) Philadelphia, Pennsylvania.

Costner, Herbert L.
1971   Sociological Methodology. San Francisco,
        California: Jossey-Bass, Inc., Publishers.

Culyer, A. J., R. J. Lavers and Alan Williams
1971   "Social indicators--health." Social Trends No.
        2:31-42.

D'Agostino, Ralph B.
1971   "Social indicators: A statistician's view." A
        paper presented in the Symposium on Social
        Indicators at the Annual Meeting of the American
        Psychological Association (September). Boston,
        Massachusetts: Boston University, Department of
        Mathematics.

Delors, Jacques
1971   Les Indicateurs Sociaux. Paris, France:
        SEDEIS.

Drewnowski, Jan
1970   Studies in the Measurement of Levels of Living
        and Welfare. Report No. 70.3. Geneva,
        Switzerland: United Nations Research Institute
        for Social Development.

Dubin, Robert
1971   "Causality and social systems analysis." A
        paper presented at the Annual Meeting of the
        American Sociological Association (August
        30-September 2) Denver, Colorado.

Duhl, Leonard J.
1968   "Planning and predicting: Or what do you do
        when you don't know the names of the variables."
        Pp. 147-156 in Daniel Bell (ed.), Toward the
        Year 2000. Boston: Houghton Mifflin Company.
        (Also in Daedalus 96 (Summer):779-788, 1967).

Duncan, Otis Dudley
1968   "Social stratification and mobility: Problems
        in the measurement of trend." Pp. 675-719 in
        Eleanor Bernert Sheldon and Wilbert E. Moore

(eds.), Indicators of Social Change: Concepts
and Measurements. New York: Russell Sage Foundation.

1969   Toward Social Reporting: Next Steps. Paper
        Number 2 in Social Science Frontiers Series.
        New York: Russell Sage Foundation.

Dyck, Harold J. and George J. Emery
1970   Social Futures: Alberta 1970-2005. Edmonton,
        Canada: Human Resources Research Council of
        Alberta.

Economic Council of Canada
1971   Design for Decision-Making: An Application to
        Human Resources Policies. Eighth Annual Review
        (September) Ottawa, Canada: Information Canada.

Ennis, Phillip
1969   "Crime, victims, and the police." Pp. 74-81 in
        M. E. Wolfgang (ed.), The Sociology of Crime and
        Delinquency. Toronto: John Wiley and Sons.

Etzioni, Amitai
1970   "Indicators of the capacities for societal
        guidance." The Annals of the American Academy
        of Political and Social Science 388
        (March):25-34.

Etzioni, Amitai and Edward W. Lehman
1967   "Some dangers in 'valid' social measurement."
        The Annals of the American Academy of Political
        and Social Science 373 (September):1-15.
        (Reprinted in Bertram M. Gross (ed.), 1969
        Social Intelligence for America's Future.
        Boston: Allyn and Bacon).

Ferriss, Abbott L.
1969   Indicators of Trends in American Education. New
        York: Russell Sage Foundation.

1970   Indicators of Change in the American Family.
        New York: Russell Sage Foundation.

1971   Indicators of Trends in the Status of American
        Women. New York: Russell Sage Foundation.

1972   Indicators of Trends in Health Status. New
        York: Russell Sage Foundation.

Finsterbusch, Kurt
  1971   "Dimensions of nations: Inductively and
          deductively developed and propositionally relat-
          ed." A paper prepared for the Conference on
          Methodological Problems in Comparative
          Sociological Research of the Institute for Com-
          parative Sociology (April 8-9) Bloomington,
          Indiana.

Flax, Michael J.
  1970   "Selected education indicators for twenty-one
          major cities: Some statistical benchmarks."
          Draft Working paper 136-4. Washington, D.C.:
          The Urban Institute.

  1971   "Blacks and whites - an experiment in racial
          indicators." Working paper 85-136-5. Washing-
          ton, D.C.: The Urban Institute.

  1972   A Study in Comparative Urban Indicators: Condi-
          tions in 18 Large Metropolitan Areas. Washing-
          ton, D.C.: The Urban Institute.

Fox, Karl A.
  1969   "Operations research and complex social
          systems." Chapter 9, Pp. 452-467 in Jati K.
          Sengupta and Karl A. Fox, Economic Analysis and
          Operations Research: Optimization Techniques in
          Quantitative Economic Models. Amsterdam:
          North-Holland Publishing Company.

  1971   "Combining economic and noneconomic objectives
          in development planning: Problems of concept
          and measurement." Unpublished manuscript.
          Ames, Iowa: Iowa State University, Department
          of Economics.

Garn, Harvey A. and Michael J. Flax
  1971   "Urban institute indicator program." Working
          paper 1206-1. Washington, D.C.: The Urban
          Institute.

Gastil, Raymond D.
  1970   "Social indicators and quality of life." Public
          Administration Review 30 (November-December):
          596-601.

General Electric
    1970   "A case study of a systems analysis approach to
            social responsibility programs: General
            Electric's commitment to progress in equal
            opportunity and minority relations." Corporate
            Industrial Relations ERC-49 (10M)8-70. New
            York, New York.

Girardeau, Catherine
    1971   "Elements for a social statistical system." Un-
            published manuscript. Paris, France: Institut
            National de la Statistique et des Etudes
            Economiques.

Gitter, A. George
    1970   Factor Analytical Approach to Indexing
            Multivariate Data Communication Research Center.
            Report No. 43. Boston: Boston University.

Gitter, A. George and S. Franklin
    1971   Subjective Quality of Life Indicators of Sixteen
            Aspects of Life. Communication Research Center.
            Report No. 58. Boston: Boston University.

Goldhammer, Herbert and A. W. Marshall
    1953   Psychosis and Civilization: Studies in the Fre-
            quency of Mental Disease. Glencoe, Illinois:
            The Free Press.

Gross, Bertram M.
    1965   "The social state of the union." Trans-action
            3:5-11.

    1966   The State of the Nation: Social Systems Ac-
            counting. New York: Tavistock Publications.

    1967   "The coming general systems models of social
            systems." Human Relations 20 (Novem-
            ber):357-374.

    1968   "Some questions for presidents." Pp. 308-350 in
            Bertram M. Gross (ed.), A Great Society? New
            York: Basic Books, Inc.

Guttman, Louis
    1971   "Social problem indicators." The American
            Academy of Political and Social Science 393
            (January):40-46.

Hammond, R. J. and E. C. Harvey
    1970   Some Tentative Observations on Social
            Indicators. Menlo Park, California: Stanford
            Research Institute.

Harland, Douglas G.
    1971a   Social Indicators: A Framework for Measuring
            Regional Social Disparities. (July 1, Second
            Draft) Ottawa, Canada: Department of Regional
            Economic Expansion.

    1971b   The Content, Measurement and Forecasting of
            Quality of Life: Volume I - The Literature.
            (October) Ottawa, Canada: Department of
            Regional Economic Expansion.

    1971c   The Content, Measurement and Forecasting of
            Quality of Life: Volume II - Index to the Lit-
            erature. (November) Ottawa, Canada: Department
            of Regional Economic Expansion.

Hauser, Philip M.
    1967   "Social goals as an aspect of planning." Pp.
            446-454 in Hearings before the Subcommittee on
            Government Research of the Committee on Govern-
            ment Operations, United States Senate, 90th
            Congress, first session on Senate Bill S.843,
            the Full Opportunity and Social Accounting Act.
            Part 3, (July 28).

Henriot, Peter J.
    1970   "Political questions about social indicators."
            The Western Politcal Science Quarterly 23
            (June):235-255.

    1971   "Political implications of social indicators."
            A paper presented at the Annual Meeting of the
            American Political Science Association (Septem-
            ber) Chicago, Illinois.

Hickey, Richard J., et al.
    1970   Ecological Statistical Studies on Environmental
            Pollution and Chronic Disease in Metropolitan

Areas of the United States. Discussion Paper
Series: No. 35. Philadelphia, Pennsylvania:
Regional Science Research Institute.

Holleb, Doris
1968   "Social statistics for social policy." Pp.
80-94 in American Society of Planning Officials,
(eds.), Planning: 1968. Chicago: ASPO.

Horowitz, Irving Louis
1968   "Social indicators and social policy." Pp.
328-339 in Irving L. Horowitz, Professing Sociology: Studies in the Life Cycle of Social Science. Chicago: Aldine Publishing Company.

Institut de Recherche Economique et de Planification
1971   "Recherche sur l'integration des indicateurs
sociaux dans les modeles de changement social."
Unpublished manuscript. (September) Grenoble,
France: University of the Social Sciences of
Grenoble.

Institute National de la Statistique et Des Etudes
Economiques
1971a   Inventaire Bibliographique. Unpublished
manuscript No. 320/1163 prepared by the Social
Statistics Group. Paris, France: Institut
National de la Statistique et Des Etudes
Economiques.

1971b   "Les indicateurs sociaux dans le domaine de
l'education." Unpublished manuscript. (November) Paris, France: Commissariat General du
Plan d'Equipment et de la Productivite.

1971c   "Presentation des travaux francais." Unpublished manuscript. (November) Paris, France:
Commissariat General du Plan d'Equipment et de
la Productivite.

1971d   Social Indicators. Unpublished manuscript.
(June) Paris, France: Social Statistics Group.

Johnston, Denis F.
1971   "Social indicators and social forecasting."
Cahiers du Centre de Recherches Science et Vie,
(Paris) No. 2 (September):41-83.

Jones, Martin V. and Michael J. Flax
   1970a   "Cities vs. suburbs - A comparative analysis of
           six qualities of urban life." Working paper
           136-3. Washington, D.C.: The Urban Institute.

   1970b   "The quality of life in metropolitan Washington
           (D.C.): Some statistical benchmarks." Working
           paper 136-1. Washington, D.C.: The Urban
           Institute.

Kamrany, Nake M. and Alexander N. Christakis
   1970   "Social indicators in perspective." Socio-
           Economic Planning Science 4 (June):207-216.

Katzman, Martin T.
   1968   "Social indicators and urban public policy."
           Pp. 85-94 in American Society of Planning
           Officials (eds.), Planning: 1968. Chicago:
           ASPO.

Knezo, Genevieve J.
   1971   Social Science Policies: An Annotated List of
           Recent Literature. (July 8) (71-167 SP) Wash-
           ington, D.C.: Science Policy Research Division,
           Congressional Research Service, Library of
           Congress.

Krendel, Ezra S.
   1970   "A case study of citizen complaints as social
           indicators." IEEE Transactions on Systems Sci-
           ence and Cybernetics. SSC-6 (October):265-272.

Kunkel, John H.
   1971   "Models of man and social systems analysis." A
           paper presented at the Annual Meeting of the
           American Sociological Association (August
           30-September 2) Denver, Colorado.

Land, Kenneth C.
   1970   "Social indicators." In Robert B. Smith (ed.),
           Social Science Methods. New York: The Free
           Press.

   1971   "On the definition of social indicators." The
           American Sociologist 6 (November):322-325.

Lear, John
1972   "Where is society going? The search for
        landmarks." Saturday Review (April 15):34-39.

Lehman, Edward W.
1971   "Social indicators and social problems." Pp.
        149-176 in Erwin O. Smigel (ed.), Handbook on
        the Study of Social Problems. Chicago: Rand
        McNally and Company.

Logothetti, Thomas J.
1970   Social Measurements Handbook. Menlo Park,
        California: Stanford Research Institute.

Marie, Michel and Jose Rodriquez Dos Santos
1971   "Etat d'avancement de la recherche concernat la
        societe francaise et les travailleurs immigres."
        Unpublished manuscript. (December) Grenoble,
        France: Centre de Sociologie Economique et
        Politique.

Markley, O. W.
1970   Alternative Futures: Contexts in Which Social
        Indicators Must Work. Research Note-EPRC
        6747-11. Menlo Park, California: Stanford Re-
        search Institute.

Merriam, Ida C.
1967   "Concepts and measures of welfare." Pp. 179-183
        in Proceedings of the Social Statistics Section
        of the American Statistical Association, Wash-
        ington, D.C.

Mitchell, Arnold, O. W. Markley, et al.
1969   Toward Master Social Indicators. Research Memo-
        randum 6747-2. Menlo Park, California:
        Stanford Research Institute, Educational Policy
        Research Center.

Mitchell, Arnold, Thomas J. Lagothetti and Robert E.
Kantor
1971   An Approach to Measuring Quality of Life. Menlo
        Park, California: Stanford Research Institute.

Mondale, Walter F.
  1967   "Some thoughts on stumbling into the future."
          American Psychologist 22 (November):972-973.

  1970   "Social advisers, social accounting, and the
          presidency." Law and Contemporary Problems
          (Summer):496-504.

Nat'l. Academy of Engineering - Nat'l. Academy of Science
  1970   Policies for Solid Waste Management. Report
          prepared for the Bureau of Solid Waste
          Management. Public Health Service Publictation
          No. 2018. Washington, D.C.: U.S. Government
          Printing Office.

National Commission on Technology, Automation, and Economic Progress
  1966   Technology and the American Economy. Washing-
          ton, D.C.: U.S. Government Printing Office.

National Goals Research Staff
  1970   Toward Balanced Growth: Quantity with Quality
          (July 4) Washington, D.C.: U.S. Government
          Printing Office.

Ogburn, William F.
  1946   The Social Effects of Aviation. Boston:
          Houghton Mifflin Company.

Olson, Mancur, Jr.
  1970   "An analytic framework for social reporting and
          policy analysis." The Annals of the American
          Academy of Political and Social Science 388
          (March):112-126.

Organization for Economic Cooperation and Development
  1971   "Social indicators development programme." Un-
          published manuscript of the Working Party on
          Social Indicators, SI/9, (December 28) Paris,
          France.

Palley, Marian L. and Howard A. Palley
  1969   "Social welfare indicators as predictors of
          racial disorders in black ghettos." A paper
          presented at the 65th Annual Meeting of the
          American Political Science Association (Septem-
          ber) New York, New York.

Perle, Eugene D.
    1970   "Urban indicators: Editor's introduction."
            Urban Affairs Quarterly 6 (December):135-143.

    1971   "Local societal indicators: A progress report."
            Pp. 114-120 in Proceedings of the Social Sta-
            tistics Section, American Statistical Associa-
            tion, Washington, D.C.

Pett, Saul
    1972   "The quality of life." Pp. 13-22 in Rex R.
            Campbell and Jerry L. Wade (eds.), Society and
            Environment: The Coming Collision. Boston,
            Massachusetts: Allyn and Bacon, Inc.

Report of National Commission on Technology, Automation
and Economic Progress
    1966a   "Improving public decision making." Pp. 95-113
            in Technology and the American Economy. Volume
            1. Washington, D.C.: U.S. Government – Print-
            ing Office.

    1966b   Technology and the American Economy. Washing-
            ton, D.C.: U.S. Government Printing Office.

Report of the President's Commission on National Goals
    1960   Goals for Americans: Programs for Action in the
            Sixties. New Jersey: Prentice-Hall, Inc.

Report of the President's Research Committee on Social
Trends
    1933   Recent Social Trends. New York: McGraw-Hill.

Richard, Robert
    1969   Subjective Social Indicators. Chicago,
            Illinois: National Opinion Research Center,
            University of Chicago.

Rokeach, Milton and Seymour Parker
    1970   "Values as social indicators of poverty and race
            relations in America." The Annals of the Ameri-
            can Academy of Political and Social Science 388
            (March):97-111.

Samuelscn, Robert J.
    1967   "Council of social advisers: New approach to
            welfare priorities?" Science 157 (July-August):
            49-50.

Sewell, William H.
    1967   "Review symposium." American Sociological
            Review 32 (June):475-480.

Shanks, J. Merrill
    1971   "Toward the development of model social
            indicators." A proposal submitted to the
            National Science Foundation. Berkeley,
            California: University of California, Survey
            Research Center.

Sheldon, Eleanor Bernert
    1971   "Social reporting for the 1970's." Pp. 403-435
            in Federal Statistics: Report of the
            President's Commission, Volume II. Washington,
            D.C.: U.S. Government Printing Office.

Sheldon, Eleanor Bernert and Howard E. Freeman
    1970   "Notes on social indicators: Promises and po-
            tential." Policy Sciences 1 (April):97-111.

Sheldon, Eleanor B. and Wilbert E. Moore
    1968   Indicators of Social Change: Concepts and Meas-
            urements. New York: Russell Sage Foundation.

Shinn, Allen M., Jr.
    1971   "Magnitude estimation: Some applications to
            social indicators." A paper presented at the
            Annual Meeting of the American Political Science
            Association (September) Chicago, Illinois.

Sonquist, John A.
    1970   Multivariate Model Building. Ann Arbor,
            Michigan: The University of Michigan, Institute
            for Social Research.

Stanford Research Institute
    1969   "Toward master social indicators." Educational
            Policy Research Center. SRI Project 6747, Re-
            search Memorandum EPRC-6747-2. Supported by
            Bureau of Research, U.S. Office of Education.

(February) Menlo Park, California: Stanford Research Institute.

Terleckyj, Nestor
  1970   "Measuring progress towards social goals: Some
          possibilities at national and local levels."
          Management Science 17 (August):B765-B778.

Tiryakian, Edward A.
  1967   "A model of societal change and its lead
          indicators." Pp. 69-77 in Samuel Z. Klausner
          (ed.), The Study of Total Societies. New York:
          Praeger.

Tugac, Ahmet
  1970   "Social indicators and social prediction in
          planning process: A review of literature and
          bibliography." State Planning Organization Pub.
          No. DPT:1124--SPD:243. Ankara, Turkey: Devlet
          Planlama Taskilati, Bakanliklar.

Tunstall, Daniel B.
  1970   "Developing a social statistics publication."
          U.S. Office of Management and Budget. A paper
          presented at the Annual Meeting of the American
          Statistical Association (December 27-30)
          Detroit, Michigan.

United Nations Research Institute for Social Development
  1971   "Proposal for a research project on the measure-
          ment of real progress at the local level." Un-
          published manuscript, UNRISD/72/C.10,
          GE-72.3494. Geneva, Switzerland: UNRISD.

U.S. Department of Health, Education, and Welfare
  1969   Toward a Social Report. Washington, D.C.: U.S.
          Government Printing Office.

United States Senate
  1967   "S. 843: Full opportunity and social accounting
          act." American Psychologist 22 (Novem-
          ber):974-976.

  1968   Hearings before the 90th Congress - 2nd Session.
          Congressional Record 114 (May 8, June 3).

    1969   "Full opportunity act." House of Representa-
            tives Bill #9483. 91st Congress - 1st Session
            (March).

Vestermark, S. D., Jr.
    1968   Indicators of Social Vulnerability. McLean,
            Virginia: Human Science Research, Inc.

Wilcox, Leslie D. and Ralph M. Brooks
    1971   "Social indicators: An alternative approach for
            future research." A paper presented at the
            Annual Meeting of the Rural Sociological Society
            (august 27-30) Denver, Colorado.

Wilcox, Leslie D., Ralph M. Brooks, George M. Beal and
Gerald E. Klonglan
    1972   Social Indicators and Societal Monitoring: An
            Annotated Bibliography. Amsterdam: Elsevier
            Publishing Company.

Wilkins, Leslie T.
    1965   "New thinking in criminal statistics." Journal
            of Criminal Law, Criminology and Police Science
            56 (September):277-284.

Wilson, John O.
    1968   Inequality of Racial Opportunity--An Excursion
            into the New Frontier of Socioeconomic
            Indicators. New Haven: Yale University Depart-
            ment of Economics.

    1969   Quality of Life in the United States: An
            Excursion into the New Frontier of Socio-
            Economic Indicators. Kansas City: Midwest
            Research Institute.

Young, Whitney M., Jr.
    1970   "Prepared statement of Whitney M. Young, Jr.,
            Executive Director, National Urban League." Pp.
            75-100 in U.S. Congress. Senate. Committee on
            Public Welfare. Full Opportunity Act. Hearings
            before the Special Subcommittee on Evaluation
            and Planning of Social Problems, on S.5, 91st
            Congress, 1st and 2nd Session.

Zapf, Wolfgang
    1971   "Social indicators: Prospects for social ac-

counting systems?" A paper presented to the International Social Science Council Symposium on Comparative Analysis of Highly Industrialized Societies (August) Bellagio, Italy.

1972a "Measuring the quality of life." A paper presented at the Social Science Research Council Committee on Comparative Politics Conference (January) Princeton, New Jersey.

1972b "Work on social indicators in the German Federal Republic." A report on a conference (January) Frankfurt, Germany.

DEFINITION

Bestuzhev-Lada, Igor
    1969   "Forecasting--an approach to the problems of the
            future." International Social Science Journal
            21:526-534.

Precise differentiation in usage and concept among the
terms forecasting, planning, programming, and design and
control seemed unnecessary until recently, as the terms
seemed clear and unambiguous. With the proliferation of
writing in this area, clarity can no longer be assumed.
This paper focuses on forecasting and planning, with differences in meaning and implications. For some,
forecasting precedes planning, or is a step beyond
planning, or is contrasted to planning, or even in combination with planning in some relationship may not be suf-
ficiently comprehensive. Forecasting differs from other
approaches to the future primarily in extent of
objectivity and degree of complexity.

Holleb, Doris
    1968   "Social statistics for social policy." Pp.
            80-85 in American Society of Planning Officials
            (eds.), Planning: 1968. Chicago: ASPO.

A brief overview of social indicators and some of the
difficulties involved in developing adequate and effective
indicators. Identifies two aims of social measurement:
1) to systematically record social change in terms of explicit social goals, and 2) to provide a framework for
evaluation of our programs in terms of effectiveness for
achieving these goals. Suggests the two major problems
are either conceptual, in drawing too close an analogy
with economic indicators and accounts, or else pragmatic
in dealing with the inherent difficulties of evaluation.

Kamrany, Nake M.
    1968   "A note on the development of social
            indicators." Santa Monica, California: Systems
            Development Corporation.

Summarizes the present (April, 1968) state of development of social indicators with recommendations for the
special contributions by Systems Development Corporation.

Includes the preliminary report of the Environment Panel for HEW's Social Report, with a table showing environmental variables and corresponding indicators. Presents a conceptual model for developing social indicators, with listing of 16 unresolved problems in both conceptual and theoretical areas.

Katzman, Martin T.
    1968   "Social indicators and urban public policy."
           Pp. 85-94 in American Society of Planning
           Officials (eds.), Planning: 1968. Chicago:
           ASPO.

Indicates a number of the problems involved in development and use of social indicators. Suggests three desirable properties of indicators should be scalability, reliability and validity. Discusses briefly the interaction of social indicators and public policy; most of the examples refer to schools and the educational system although not a detailed analysis.

Kriesberg, Louis
    1970   "Some observations about social conflict." Un-
           published manuscript. Syracuse, New York: Edu-
           cational Policy Research Center, Syracuse Uni-
           versity Research Corporation.

Discussion of the dimensions of social conflict with emphasis upon awareness by the parties involved, degree of intensity from feelings to actual behavior including coercion, degree to which the conflict is regulated and institutionalized, purity of the conflict between parties (in pure conflict what one side loses, the other wins) and the degree of power inequality of one party relative to the other. Characteristics of conflict units are described as boundary clarity and degree of organization of the opposing parties. Social conflict is defined as "a relationship between two or more parties who (or whose spokesmen) believe they have incompatible objectives."

Lamale, Helen H.
    1959   "Present day concepts of income adequacy." Pp.
           103-113 in The Social Welfare Forum, Official
           Proceedings, 86th Annual Forum, 1959 San
           Francisco, National Conference on Social
           Welfare.

Examined in this 1959 paper are the factors relating to a definition of income adequacy, and the component items needed to provide for the social and psychological needs of the individual or family, generally accepted now to be part of the concept of adequacy. Changing standards of living since World War II and family resources are both related to the change in perspective and definition of the concept. Summary of the research at that time with anticipated studies is given.

> 1965   "Poverty: The word and the reality." Monthly
>   Labor Review 88 (July):822-827.

The varied factors involved in defining economic poverty are discussed, in the framework that a precise definition of "means" and "subsistence" is required before the concept can be meaningful and measurable. It is suggested that a single definition to be operationalized with aggregate data at national and regional levels is unrealistic and inadequate, that it is perhaps a series of equations to be solved within specific situations considering needs and resources of individuals and families in relation to the needs and resources of the economy.

Land, Kenneth C.
>   1971   "On the definition of social indicators."   The
>   American Sociologist 6 (November):322-325.

Argues that appropriate framework for relating public policies to social indicators is closer to macroeconomic theory than optimizing theory; indicators as parameters of variables within those models; subsumes social statistics as essential to developing adequate social indicators but not the whole story. Reviews recent criticisms of the claims for social indicators resulting in the need to specify a defining criterion. Viewing social indicators as a component in a social system model is accepted as one criterion. The major unsolved problem in social indicators is "the construction of macrosociological models of social institutions and processes." Emphasizes the need for model building before an optimizing strategy can be applied.

Olson, Mancur, Jr.
>   1969a   "Social indicators and social accounts."   Socio-
>   Economic Planning Science 2:335-346.

This paper defines social indicators as statistics which 1) are measures of direct normative interest (national welfare), and 2) fit into a linear systematic schema from which data can be disaggregated for study of particular problems. He also speaks of the cost-effectiveness analyses also possible with social indicators.

>   1969b   "The plan and purpose of the social report."
>   The Public Interest 15 (Spring):85-97.

52

The author sets out the idea of social reporting in terms of what determines its shape and what it would or would not contain. He deals with the subject under the following headings: the national income and the national welfare, the growth of public problems, a cause of social conflict, information for policy-making, systems analysis and social reporting, and the uses of a conceptual ideal. He concludes by indicating that a social report framework would increase the orderliness of thought and quality of debate about our urgent social problems.

Ontell, Robert
1971   "What is a social indicator?" Unpublished
         manuscript. San Diego, California: Urban
         Observatory.

Reviews social indicator conceptual definitions from Toward a Social Report, Sheldon and Freeman, Land, Demerath and Harland, and critiques each definition of or approach to what is a social indicator. Concludes that while there is general agreement that a social indicator is a kind of social statistic, there is less agreement as to what social indicator specifically refers to, other than generally to "quality of life" as argued by Harland who has proposed approaches for identifying indicators. Harland's approach does not rule out the possibility for investigating other than output social indicators and does not require that a social statistic be related to a social systems model before it qualifies as a social indicator, a requirement which has been proposed by Land.

Patrick, Donald and J. W. Bush
1971   "Toward an operational definition of health." A
         paper presented before the statistics section of
         the Annual Meeting of The American Public Health
         Association (October 14) Minneapolis, Minnesota.

Most quantitative indicators of health include measures of morbidity or mortality. However, a sensitive measure of health should reflect the qualitative as well as the quantitative aspects. The purpose of this paper then is to develop an operational definition of health to bridge the gap between the theoretical concepts of health and their empirical measurements. An adequate conceptual definition of health should consider a number of criteria such as; clearly differentiated components, ability to classify populations as healthy or sick, related to current definitions of classification systems in use by agencies collecting health data, universal in application and view health as a process rather than a constant state.

of well-being. Health is defined as a function of Function Status and Prognosis.

United Nations
    1961   International Definition and Measurement of
            Levels of Living: An Interim Guide. New York:
            United Nations.

    A joint progress report of the UN, ILO, FAO, UNESCO,
and WHO concerning action taken on suggestions the Committee of Experts made in 1954. Components and indicators
appropriate for the international definition and measurement of levels of living are specified with a proposal for
also gathering national background data on demography,
labor, income, expenditure, communications, and
transportation. The explicated components of level of
living are: health, nutrition, education, employment conditions, housing, social security, clothing, recreation
and human freedoms.

United Nations, Department of Social Affairs
    1966   "European programme of current housing statistics." Pp. 1-5 in Conference of European
            Statisticians: Statistical Standards and Studies - No. 7 St/ECE/HOU/29 St/CES/7. Sales No.
            66 II. Mim. 42. New York: United Nations.

    A recommended list of statistics for countries to
compile to measure housing. A complete guide including
definitions, concepts and suggested methods of collection,
but on a very broad international scope.

Abrams, Mark
    1968   "Britain: The next 15 years." New Society 7
            (November):670-673.

    Acknowledging past errors of forecasting, primarily
through extrapolation of available data, this paper
presents some of the likely changes due in the future with
awareness of the many operant variables. Included is consideration of changes in population make-up, work force,
automation and its effects, housing, public education,
building needs and family expenditures. From the history
of forecasting two major concerns are specified. First
are the errors despite the detailed quantitative estimates
available, and second, that public policy has not respond-
ed quickly enough or adequately to even the best documented forecasts.

Alexander, Robert M.
    1971   "Social aspects of environmental pollution."
            Agriculture Science Review 9 (First Quar-
            ter):9-18.

    Categorizes pollution problems into two social issues:
1) how far society can and should go toward a goal of
quality? How much are we willing to pay? Who will pay?
and 2) how decisions are to be made to consider side-
effects. Discusses several alternatives for dealing with
pollution, such as persuasion, adversary procedures, state
regulation, incentive payments, recognition of external
costs, and development of counter technology. The four
alternatives, excluding the first and last mentioned, are
examined in some detail. Summary reassessment of key
social issues.

Bell, Daniel
    1968   "The adequacy of our concepts." Pp. 127-161 in
            Bertram M. Gross (ed.), A Great Society? New
            York: Basic Books, Inc.

    Concepts, social values, and characteristics of
national policy are discussed. Bell calls for a normative
social theory to help identify new problems. The communication pattern of mass society is illustrated, as is the
conventional, private, profit-seeking model of the economy
and each is related to the government's part in them.
Bell urges that a system of social accounts be created to

broaden our concept 'cf costs and benefits and encompass economic accounting. He suggests measurement of the uti- lization of human resources in 1) the measurement of social costs and net returns of innovations, 2) the meas- urement of social ills, 3) the creation of "performance budgets" in areas of defined social needs, and 4) indicators of economic opportunity and social mobility.

1970   "The commission on the year 2000." Futures 2 (September):263-269.

The basic premises on which the commission worked are presented with three methods of social forecasting. Of these methods, analytical identification of social prob- lems, extrapolation of social trends for which there are time series, and model construction that identifies independent-dependent variables, the commission is consid- ered to operate somewhere between the latter two ap- proaches. The commission also identified three general structural changes; national society, communal society and post-industrial society.

Biderman, Albert D.
  1970   "The municipal social indicator leagues." Wash- ington, D.C.: Bureau of Social Science Re- search, Inc.

A hypothetical situation is explored to advance a pro- posal for bringing together certain institutional methodo- logical considerations which may overcome some major flaws in systems for measuring social change. This proposal in- volves the formation of municipal social indicator leagues where municipalities could be compared and contrasted on certain significant indicators of social change.

Broady, Maurice
  1970   "The sociology of the urban environment." Ekistics 29 (March):187-190.

Concerned with urban quality of life as affected by the planning of towns and cities in attempting to achieve social ideals through physical means. Sees change in cur- rent insights to concern with people as human beings, not only as shoppers, employees, residents. Raises the ques- tion of how does one describe, develop or change the social ethos of a town? Case study references to Harlow, England.

Brzezinski, Zbigniew
  1968   "America in the technetronic age." Encounter (January): 16-26.

56

A metamorphosis in human history is examined, in the context of technetronics and its impact in the world. A technetronic society is defined as one shaped culturally, psychologically, socially and economically by the impact of technology and electronics, particularly computers and communication. Seen as a fragmenting and differentiating force, the change confronts America with special obligations. Described as the first society to experience the future, America is looked to for directions for that future. Can the individual and science coexist? Can man, living in the scientific age, grow in intellectual depth and philosophical meaning and thus, also, in personal liberty? Can the institutions of political democracy adapt quickly enough? Implications for the relationships of the developed/underdeveloped nations are discussed. Calls for a world congress on what it is about man's life we wish to safeguard or to promote, going beyond the tangibles of economic development.

Burkhead, Danny L.
    1971   "Leisure: A taxonomic approach." Unpublished
            paper. Department of Sociology. Ames, Iowa:
            Iowa State University.

    Explores time usage, recreation, environment, and attitudinal disposition as related to concept and perception of leisure; not a taxonomy of leisure activities, but one through which those activities could be analyzed.

Calder, Nigel
    1967   "Future research." New Statesman 74 (Septem-
            ber): 399-400.

    A report on the Oslo conference in 1967, the International Future Research Inaugural Congress, convened by "Mankind 2000" of London. With agreement that reliable prediction is inherently impossible, not only because new discoveries and inventions can hardly be anticipated but also because of the intervention of human choice, which responsible forecasters want to cultivate, still provocative statements could be made and useful notions emerge. A sense of the value and compatability of different approaches is reviewed with a general theme of peace and development. Worth noting is that the conference spoke of futures in the plural, as states that have to be, not so much forecasted as, invented.

Caldwell, Catherine
    1970   "Social science as ammunition." Psychology
            Today (September):38-41, 72-73.

The aftermath of the government sponsored survey on education and race, titled Equality of Educational
Opportunity, 1966, is given. Better known as the Coleman
Report, it is one of the few specific requests ever made
by Congress for social research that might provide a basis
for policy. The concept of equal educational opportunity
was the first hurdle in the study, as the concept is not
fixed but changing, meaning different things to different
people. The report took account of three definitions and
measurements: 1) the extent of segregation in the
schools; 2) resource differentials, physical, financial,
intellectual and human; and 3) differential student
achievement scores. Resources are discussed in terms of
effectiveness, not simply the quantification nor availability. The report has been used supportively for very
divergent views; relatively little implementation has occurred.

Campbell, Angus and Philip Converse
    1970   "Monitoring the quality of American life." A
            proposal to the Russell Sage Foundation. Ann
            Arbor, Michigan: Survey Research Center, Uni-
            versity of Michigan.

A proposal for a descriptive survey, repeated over a
number of years, to provide a baseline for subsequent data
comparisons, and some panel analysis. The study is designed to measure the social-psychological aspects of the
goals of Americans as explicated in their aspirations, expectations, satisfactions and dissatisfactions. Initially
it is proposed to examine the individual as unit of analysis and subsequently intergroup variations.

Cassidy, Michael W. A.
    1970   "Social indicators: Accidents and the home en-
            vironment." Working Paper No. 132. Berkeley,
            California: Institute of Urban and Regional De-
            velopment, University of California.

Disaffected with input measures as criteria for the effectiveness or benefits of policy, an attempt is made to
relate domestic accidents as a negative indicator of the
home environment: quality of housing, SES, sex, age and
race, home ownership. Examines both general and behavior
approaches to a theory of accidents, illustrated by data
from available research studies from both the U.S. and
England and Wales, with the often contradictory or
inclusive findings presented graphically, this study concludes that "we are left, then, with no consistent findings on the effect of housing quality on home accidents."
A preface by Melvin M. Webber, however, evaluates the
hypothesized relationship as "highly suggestive and worthy
of further examination."

58

Centre National de la Recherche Scientifique
　　1971　　"Etat d'avancement de la recherche sur des
　　　　　　　indicateurs sociaux des conditions de travail."
　　　　　　　Unpublished manuscript.　Paris, France:
　　　　　　　Laboratoire d'Economie et Sociologie du Travail.
　　　　　　　(November)

　　A brief article indicating the present state of
progress pertaining to the study of indicators of work
conditions.　This is part of a series of studies of long-
term indicators in various fields of the social domain
under study by the French government.

Cerha, Jarko
　　1969　　"The fourth power."　Futures 1 (Septem-
　　　　　　　ber):427-439.

　　Develops the concept that the way of organizing the application of a political idea is of more ultimate importance for the outcome of the political process than the
actual idea itself, such that a humanitarian ideology
enforced by totalitarian organization results in fascist
type society.　Urges "organizational inventors" completely
independent of industry, government, political institutions, or institutions of any kind, to bring the pressure
of "The Fourth Power" (an enlightened public opinion) to
bear on decision-makers to move in the direction of long-
range planning for the public good rather than to act only
on decisions based on political expediency and/or cost or
other short/range factors.

Cohn, Edwin J.
　　1971　　"Social criteria for project and sector
　　　　　　　lending."　Revised draft, PPC/PDA, CP, June 28.
　　　　　　　Washington, D.C.:　Agency for International De-
　　　　　　　velopment.

　　Discusses social, cultural and political considerations
that should be included in the preparation and assessment
of project and sector loans.　Factors considered are those
within responsibility of donor agencies extending development assistance and those analyzable and, at least,
measurable by developing countries, A.I.D. and other donor
agencies.　These factors include:　1) some of the socio-
cultural preconditions which affect the feasibility of
project and sector loans, and 2) some of the implications
of project and sector loans for the distribution of
wealth, power, and status.　Relevant criteria for
assessing social costs and benefits are:　1) access to re-
costs and benefits are:　1) access to re-

sources and opportunities (e.g., land, capital, credit, education, markets), the ways and extent such access is broadened or narrowed; 2) employment; 3) rural displacement, migration, and urbanization; 4) changes in power and participation as between different socio-economic, regional, ethnic and other groupings, and the complications thereof for public policy.

Coleman, James S.
    1971   A Flow Model for Occupational Structures.
            Report No. 101. Baltimore, Maryland: The Johns
            Hopkins University, Center for Social Organiza-
            tion of Schools.

Develops a model for analysis of occupational history data as a step toward the development of a system of social accounts. The model examines flow of men, throughout their lives, through the occupational structure. With data collected from samples of black and white men, the model treats men at age 13 as inputs into different statuses in education and the labor-force, including military, and examines changes through age 39. Hypothetical experiments are made via the model to find the occupational distribution of blacks if their particular educational and occupational experiences were modified to correspond to those of whites. Experiment results suggest usefulness of model both for policy formulation and scientific study of occupational changes.

Corning, Peter A.
    1971   "Can we develop an index for quality of life?"
            A paper presented at the Annual Meeting of the
            American Association for the Advancement of Sci-
            ence (December) Philadelphia, Pennsylvania.

The assumption, accepted by many, that Americans have sufficient income and amenities to warrant measuring quality of life beyond mere survival is rejected suggesting that in fact an index of survival might serve as a benchmark to assess how society is meeting the basic needs of its population. Furthermore, viability of society is proposed as one aspect which could be monitored with intentions on seeking long range goals for future planning to better understand the total system.

Cowhig, James C. and Calvin L. Beale
    1965   "Levels of living among whites and nonwhites."
            Pp. 11-20 in U.S. Department of Health, Educa-
            tion, and Welfare Indicators. Washington, D.C.:
            U.S. Government Printing Office.

60

This article seeks to interpret recent information obtained from published research reports and census volumes on the socio-economic position of the Negro population in the United States. Level of living is operationalized as differences in availability of facilities such as a dwelling unit in sound condition, hot water piped inside the structure, a telephone, and an automobile. The measures of socio-economic status used are income, educational attainment, and housing conditions.

Culyer, A. J., R. J. Lavers and Alan Williams
　　1971　"Social indicators--health." Social Trends No.
　　　　　2:31-42.

Focuses on the development of indicators in the field of health to form policy. Three kinds of social indicators are needed: measures of the state-of-health, measures of the need-for-health, and measures of the effectiveness of health-affecting activities. This article proposes a health indicator, explores the meaning of need, draws conclusions and, in an Appendix, reviews present state of the art in regard to the above three measures.

David, Henry
　　1970　"Assumptions about man and society and histori-
　　　　　cal constructs in futures research." Futures 2
　　　　　(September):222-230.

In this article the author attempts to analyze two problems or dangers associated with the practice of futures research. One of these dangers is the character of assumptions the futures researcher makes about human behavior. The other problem is that of the historical constructs that futures researchers fashion for themselves or borrow from others. Both of these concepts are the basis for their prediction and forecasting; consequently, they must become more aware of their importance and function.

Day, Virgil B.
　　1971　"Management and society: An insider's view."
　　　　　Address presented at the Conference on
　　　　　Management and Public Policy, SUNY (May 21)
　　　　　Buffalo, New York.

Discusses the role of the Business Environment component of General Electric which is engaged in identifying and analyzing long-term social, political, economic, and technological trends, towards forecasting these trends, through 1980, in nine separate segments--international, defense, social, political, legal, economic, financial, manpower and technological. Analysis of segments helps to identify possible policy implications for the future. The Corporation must be considered with public sector expectations for the qualitative aspects of life, objectives of opportunity, preservation of natural environment, development of human resources, and attainment of just and stable society. To achieve these ends the corporation needs sufficient lead time to accomplish the changes, to develop a clear-cut rationale for institutional change, top management commitment to change, long-range strategic planning and "systems approach" to change, establish specific goals and objectives and to revise the measurement and reward system.

Dluhy, Milan
    1969   "Housing and social indicators." Unpublished
         . manuscript. Ann Arbor, Michigan: School of
            Social Work, University of Michigan.

Present housing research is of three general types: 1) technological or physical, primarily concerned with the structural features of housing; 2) social-psychological, concerned with the type housing and neighborhood in their effects on attitudes, behavior and health; and 3) economic analysis, or consumer needs and demands and housing market behavior. The National Housing Act of 1949 specifies as two goals a decent home and a suitable living environment for every American family. Believing that present research concentrates on the first goal and ignores the second, it is suggested serious consideration be given the standards proposed by the American Public Health Association's Committee on the Hygiene of Housing in 1945. By these standards, housing evaluation is considered under facilities (structure, lighting, plumbing, etc.), maintenance of the facilities, and the unit occupancy (room or area crowding). Indicators of these items could provide data: to help cities enforce maintenance codes as well as building codes by landlords; for an index of satisfaction, measuring a family's needs against its present conditions; on neighborhood of local environmental needs. Such indices could give a clearer idea of how we stand in relation to housing needs and a suitable living environment for every American family.

Drewnowski, Jan, Muthu Subramanian and Claude Richard-Proust
    1970   "A planning model for social development." Part
            I in Studies in the Methodology of Social
            Planning. Report No. 70.5. Geneva,
            Switzerland: United Nations Research Institute
            for Social Development.

Two main premises underlie the planning model. First is that the social and economic elements must be planned in relation to each other in an integrated way; the second is the primacy of social over economic elements, with the economic variables as intermediate factors to be used to maximize the level of social variables. Tables are presented of the interdependence of the variables of both a long term model for the present and for the impact of the present plan on the future.

Dror, Yehezkel
    1969   "The prediction of political feasibility."
            Futures 1 (June):282-288.

Discusses methods for more systematic exploration of alternative government policies. Important variables in the construct political feasibility are: 1) main actors-capacities and intentions, 2) inputs into policy area (resources, pressures, political climate), 3) actor-interaction and 4) critical leverage mass or rules of the field. Suggests use of Delphi technique using politicians, senior executives and political observers to develop political feasibility of various alternatives.

Duncan, Otis Dudley
    1968   "Social stratification and mobility: Problems
            in the measurement of trend." Pp. 675-719 in
            Eleanor Bernert Sheldon and Wilbert E. Moore
            (eds.), Indicators of Social Change: Concepts
            and Measurements. New York: Russell Sage Foun-
            dation.

Duncan's chapter discusses problems in the measurement of trends in stratification and mobility for the U.S. since World War I. The first part of the paper is devoted to the opinions of social scientists on the subject matter over this period. The chapter then turns to a highly compressed conceptual exposition intended to identify what should be the major foci of trend studies. Finally a large subdivision contains a detailed appraisal of our present capability to measure one of the kinds of trends thus identified.

    1969   "Human ecology and population studies." Pp.
            678-716 in Philip M. Hauser and Otis Dudley
            Duncan (eds.), The Study of Population: An
            Inventory and Appraisal. Chicago: University
            of Chicago Press.

This chapter deals with population research and how it is related to what is referred to dichotomously as demographic research and theoretical human ecology. A basic systems model of the ecological complex and its assumptions is presented together with suggested hypotheses for analysis at the local community level. "The...paper demonstrates the relevance of ecological considerations to each of the conventional topics of demography," specifically population distribution, composition, growth, vital processes, and movement, as one means of "ordering demographic data intelligibly."

Eisner, Robert
    1970   "Socioeconomic Accounting: Comment." (Working
            Paper) Northwestern University and National
            Bureau of Economic Research.

    General remarks on concepts and measurement of national income and output. Measurement would include "non-income income", consumer services, accumulation of capital in human form as well as physical, labor services and the services of capital. Basic theoretical definition of income is the sum of consumption and capital accumulation.

Ennis, Philip
    1968   "The definition and measurement of leisure."
            Pp. 525-571 in Eleanor B. Sheldon and Wilbert
            Moore (eds.), Indicators of Social Change: Con-
            cepts and Measurements. New York: Russell Sage
            Foundation.

    The discussion of the formidable definitional problems involved in everyday words relating to leisure comprise the first part of this chapter. The second part examines the problems of measuring leisure, dealing with sources of data and difficulties in matching them to the definitions. The third section discusses the distribution of leisure across the social landscape. The fourth section considers the organization and structure of leisure while the final part explores the problem of quality cf leisure.

Etzioni, Amitai
    1970a   "Consensus and reforms in the 'Great Society'."
            Sociological Inquiry 40:113-122.

    Etzioni explores the reasons why the "Great Society" never got off the ground because no programs were aimed at getting consensus among the various interest groups and publics that make up the American society. He recommends 'participatory planning,' of the kind used by the French government in devising its successive four-year plans, to obtain consensus within the population for certain national programs.

1970b "Indicators of the capacities for societal
       guidance." The Annals of the American Academy
       of Political and Social Science 388
       (March):25-34.

This paper discusses the continuation of an effort to
develop indicators for macrosociological concepts. Measurement of the areas of societal knowledge and societal
mobilization are illustrated. The theoretical justification for focusing on these two concepts is briefly discussed, and the merits and shortcomings of various
indicators are explored.

Featherman, David
    1971 "Achievement orientations and socioeconomic
          career attainments." A paper presented at the
          Annual Meeting of the American Sociological As-
          sociation (August 30-September 2) Denver,
          Colorado.

Examines the impact of achievement orientations on
socio-economic career attainments and on the processes of
social mobility from family of origin statuses to destina-
tion statuses. Constructs several path analytic models,
with achievement-related motivations as intervening variables; table of correlation of coefficients given. Little
support found for the assertion that achievement orientations are "highly relevant" to the processes of status
attainment in industrialized societies.

Fox, Karl A.
    1969 "A new strategy for urban and rural America."
          Appalachia (August):10-13.

Under present systems of organization, metropolitan
areas are too large and rural communities are too small.
The author recommends that metropolitan areas be
restructured to establish civic responsibility within log-
ically delineated subareas with a maximum of 500,000
persons. Furthermore, he proposes that nonmetropolitan
areas in America be gathered into 350 multicounty
functional economic units. This will require special programs and efforts to help each unit achieve effective government, generate creative life and efficient community.

Freeman, David M.
    1971 "Sociological intelligence, social conflict, and
          technology assessment in developmental change."
          A paper presented at the Annual Meeting of the
          Rural Sociological Society (August) Denver,
          Colorado.

Contending that technology is a social and political phenomenon, this paper proposes seven criteria for the assessment of technological impact: 1) externality; 2) multi-purpose assessment; 3) allocating burdens of uncertainty; 4) constituency creation; 5) preserving future options and reversibility of action; 6) predicting cumulative effects of scale and 7) predicting impacts of converging technologies. Suggests that the perspective of social conflict, with structures seen as either overlapping or cross-cutting, should be the determinant in choosing alternatives.

Girardeau, Catherine
    1971   "Elements for a social statistical system." Unpublished manuscript. Paris, France: Institut National de la Statistique et des Etudes Economiques.

Accepting the present social information systems as unsatisfactory in France as in other industrialized countries, in part because of the increasing complexity of problems which confront society, the author takes the position that economic statistics are merely a subset of social phenomena and that failure to include appreciation of other aspects of social reality may result in disappointing public policy and action. Reviews forthcoming work to develop the needed elements of a social statistical system: the organization of existing data in terms of topics; "satellite" accounts relating specifically to economic data; the socio-demographic accounts and social indicators for particular fields such as health, education or mobility. Relationships between the four elements are discussed and data sources for each are suggested.

Gitter, A. George and S. Franklin
    1971   Subjective Quality of Life Indicators of Sixteen Aspects of Life. Report No. 58. Boston: Boston University, Communication Research Center.

This study (N = 102 male and female college undergraduates) investigated subjective evaluations of sixteen aspects of "quality of life." The relationship of these evaluations to selected demographic and attitudinal variables was explored. Factor analysis of the evaluations of the sixteen aspects yielded four factors (physical context, security, aesthetic-intellectual, compatibility) accounting for approximately .66 of the variance.

Gitter, A. George and S. Lewis
    1971   Toward a Social Indicator of Crime--A Pilot

Study. Report No. 51. Boston: Boston University, Communication Research Center.

Methods of constructing factor analytical indicators were shown to apply in aggregating multivariate crime data. State and national indicators of (1) change of crime rate, (2) rural crime, (3) violent crime, (4) nonviolent crime, (5) urban crime, and (6) overall crime index for 1967 were computed. Procedures for computing both state and national indicators for any subsequent year were described. The relationships between the 1967 indicators and (a) geographic region, (b) density of population, (c) degree of urbanization, and (d) percent of white population were investigated.

Hanushek, Eric A.
    1970   "Developing local educational indicators--the priorities." (August) Santa Monica, California: The Rand Corporation.

Priority for improving educational system data should be placed, according to this paper, on discovering ways of indicating more about the relationships between schools and what they produce. Data required for the exploration of these relationships would indicate family and school inputs and educational outputs. Selected aspects of existing records are specified as aggregated measures of these inputs and outputs. Hence, it is suggested that input/output analysis could proceed initially from existing records if the data specified are collected for each system's students. Avenues broadening this research approach are also forwarded.

Hauser, Philip M.
    1969   "The chaotic society: Product of the social morphological revolution." American Sociological Review 34 (February):1-19.

Explores impact on man and society of changes in size, density and heterogeneity of population through consideration of four developments and their interrelationship: population explosion, population implosion (density), population diversification, and accelerated tempo of technological and social changes; concept of cultural lag included; role of the social sciences in social engineering and social accounting.

Henning, John A. and A. Dale Tussing
    1970   "Income elasticity of the demand for public expenditures in the United States." (June)

(Working Draft) Syracuse, New York: Educational
Policy Research Center, Syracuse University Research Corporation.

Using U.S. data for years 1900-1968, an econometric
model is developed relating changes in income to changes
in non-defense public expenditures. Mathematical equations are formulated and tables are presented showing
income elasticities of demand for non-defense government
purchases of goods, services, and expenditures, 1900-1968;
government purchases of goods and services 1900-1968 with
the military expenditure variable split, and government
expenditures 1900-1968 with the military expenditure variable split.

Institut National de la Statistique et des Etudes
Economiques
    1971   "Les indicateurs sociaux dans le domaine de
            l'education." Unpublished manuscript. Paris,
            France: Commissariat General du Plan
            d'Equipment et de la Productivite. (November)

One of several long-term studies on social indicators
being conducted by the French government at the National
Institute of Statistics. This particular paper examines
social indicators in the domain of education.

Jantsch, Erich
    1969   "Planning and designing for the future."
            Futures 1 (September):440-444.

Review of two books, Rene Dubos' So Human an Animal,
and Jay Forrester's Urban Dynamics, with some remarks also
on Aurelio Peccei's The Chasm Ahead. Jantsch sees three
notions common to the three books: 1) future of man and
society has to be dealt with within the context of systems
which link them to the environment; 2) these systems form
complex dynamic systems, high-order, multiple-loop, non-
linear, feedback structures, emphasizing feedback; and 3)
actively shaping and planning for the future imply
changing the structure of the systems, not just the variables. Dubos feels we've developed the "know-how," but
not the "know-why," or "know-what" or "know-where-to;"
explores biological limitations of man in relation to
technology and the future. Forrester develops a model,
built from 153 equations described in an appendix, of the
industrial dynamics concept with feedback processes built
into it and carries out computer simulation to explore how
various changes in policy would change urban conditions.

Johnson, Paul
    1969   "Social change not science will shape the

future." New Statesman (March):438-441.

Through the technique of imagining what Samuel Pepys of
1670 would find most novel in 1770, Lord North of 1770 in
1870, Mr. Gladstone of 1870 and 1970, this author attempts
to project us into the world of 2070. His first prediction is for the solution of the color problem, through
intermarriage; second is the solution to over-population
and to food supplies. Two momentous changes foreseen are:
1) such great changes in human relations, sex mores and
child-birth that the family, per se, will have
disappeared; and 2) the freedom to decide when to die, as
medical science is able to sustain life ever longer. Discusses also future education, decision making, privacy,
the human need always for "wildernesses" for the non-
conformists and adventurers, and suggests the
"wildernesses" of 2070 may be the ocean and recreated
Atlantis.

Kahn, Robert L.
    1971   "The justification of violence: Social problems
            and social solutions." Presidential address
            presented to the Society for the Psychological
            Study of Social Issues at the 79th Annual Con-
            vention of the American Psychological Associa-
            tion (September) Washington, D.C.

On the premise that one measure of the quality of life
in a society is the level of violence that people are prepared to justify, this paper discusses social indicators
and relates the current research on the justification of
violence to the criteria for social indicators. The
linkage from social indicators to social policy involves
four elements: the indicators themselves as description
of what is; explanation of relationships underlying the
social processes of which the indicators are signs;
valuation that defines preferred states on the dimensions
identified as indicators; and utilization, the technology
for bringing about change in the relevant dimensions.
Indices of the level of violence justifiable divide into
two parts, that for social control and that for social
change.

Krieger, Martin H.
    1971a   "Planning for an affect based society: Predic-
            tion, indicators and structure." Working Paper
            144B. Berkeley, California: Institute of Urban
            and Regional Development, University of
            California.

Positive mental health of a population as something to

be planned for is the concern of this paper. Discussed are the pre-industrial, industrial, post-industrial, and beyond-post-industrial time periods with the crucial resources and needs of men for each period. The need is seen for increased and improved affect in human relationships in the beyond-post-industrial time. Affect production and change can be monitored, analyzed and perhaps altered. The framework in which people help and advise each other can be changed if we want to do so. Models are given suggestive of such changes with the programmatic and structural implications of the change.

1971b "Social reporting for a city: A perspective and some problems." Berkeley, California: Institute of Urban and Regional Development, University of California.

Discussing some differing needs and uses of social indicators and reporting for cities from those of larger governmental units, this paper suggests that cities need reports geared in content and detail to the tasks that cities can either control or influence. Considered also are the special audiences and interest groups within a city, the nature of the social report needed, and what it should contain. Distinction is made between state indicators describing the situation of a society and service indicators that describe the ongoing activities of the society which, it is felt, are especially relevant to a city report. A tabular presentation is given of some examples of indicators for municipal services including the policy question, relevant indicators, source of data and problems with the indicators.

Kriesberg, Louis
1970 "Toward a social science paradigm for thinking about futures." (Working Draft) (July) Syracuse, New York: Educational Policy Research Center, Syracuse University Research Corporation.

Society as the major unit of analysis. Discusses the bases and varieties of social units, fundamental social process among and within social units, basic conditions of the units, interrelations of processes and conditions and variations in the outcome of different processes.

Lamale, Helen H.
1958 "Changes in concepts of income adequacy over the last century." The American Economic Review 47 (May):291-299.

Considering the changes in standards of living of the

last century, it was inevitable that concepts of income
adequacy would also change. This review of those changes
divides the time into three periods approximating shifts
in emphasis in the empirical approach. The first period,
of 1860-1900, is noted as the subsistence or break-even
concept, marked by rapid industrialization, growth of
public and private welfare institutions. The second
period, 1900-1935, saw the development of the living wage
concept, with agitation for social reforms emphasizing
that income adequacy must deal with real income and
include long-run as well as short-run needs. The social
concept has included the development of budget standards
for different size families with differing needs. The
ability to express these changing concepts and estimates
of needs in quantitative measures is increasingly complex,
and increasingly necessary.

Lee, Philip R.
      1967   "Health and well being." The Annals of the
              American Academy of Political and Social Science
              373 (September):193-207. (Reprinted in Bertram
              M. Gross (ed.), 1969 Social Intelligence for
              America's Future. Boston: Allyn and Bacon).

    Health is discussed as both a generalized and relative
concept, defined to include not only freedom from physical
disease and pain, but also social well-being. In the
past, death rate and morbidity were considered as adequate
health indicators. These no longer yield information
amenable to establishing goals and policy. New indicators
which reflect the emphasis on disability, costs and socio-
psychological consequences of disease are necessary to
evaluate the proliferation of federal programs for
eliminating the shortage of facilities and personnel, or
guaranteeing social access to existing services.

Lippett, Ronald
      1965   "The use of social research to improve social
              practice." American Journal of Orthopsychiatry
              35 (July):663-669.

    Six different patterns are identified for the use of
scientific resources supported by observations and experiences from the Center for Research on the Utilization of
Scientific Knowledge at the University of Michigan. Three
of the patterns are variant methods of bringing special
knowledge or expertise from outside the system, and there
are different ways of developing the knowledge from within
the system. There are six significant differences in
utilization between social practices and research and
those of applied biological and physical sciences: 1)
adoption of new educational or social practice involves

more changes in values and attitudes, with deeper personal
involvement; 2) most significant changes are adaptations
rather than adoptions of others' innovations; 3) no
adequate procedures for identification, documentary description and validation of new practices; 4) little
available feedback on effectiveness; 5) organization of
mental health educational practice provides little stimulus to practioners to take innovative risks; and 6) inadequate linkage for basic applied research to operating
practices.

Lochhead, A.V.S.
    1969   "The search for measurement in social develop-
            ment." Community Development Journal 4:68-73.

    Summarizes some of the work of the United Nations Re-
search Institute for Social Development concerned with
world-wide indicators. Emphasizes need for evaluation of
programs. Four main approaches of the Institute; 1) construction of a levels of living index, 2) attempts at
cost-benefit analysis, 3) social planning, and 4) the
evaluation of experiences of 400 experts in community development field. Findings from this project include chief
mistakes, reasons for success and general reflections for
the future work.

Long, Norton E.
    1970   "Indicators of change in political institu-
            tions." The Annals of the American Academy of
            Political and Social Science 388 (March):35-45.

    Asserts that political science has been largely
unconcerned with developing theory which explains humanly
significant change. The shortcomings of present predictors or indicators will test political science's capacity
for evaluation of humanly important phenomena. And, its
attempt to give such phenomena theoretical comprehension
will suggest indicators which will be necessary for
enhancing this capacity or developing intervention strategies from this comprehension.

Marie, Michel and Jose Rodriquez Dos Santos
    1971   "Etat d'avancement de la recherche concernat la
            societe francaise et les travailleurs immigres."
            Unpublished manuscript. Grenoble, France:
            Centre de Sociologie Economique et Politique.
            (December)

    This paper indicates the state of the current research
on the French society and in particular the immigrant
workers. It is a part of the series of long-term studies

in the social domain and indicates what research has been
done on social indicators in the area of immigrant workers
and French society.

Martin, Margaret E.
    1971   "The Current Population Survey as a statistical
            information system." Washington, D.C.: U.S.
            Office of Management and Budget.

    This article discusses the Current Population Survey as
a statistical information system consisting of input,
processing of the information, output and feedback. The
input is characterized by samples of households on a
monthly basis covering a broad range of topics. The processing of the data is rapid, contains a variety of classifications and is further characterized by the elaborate
system of controls. The output from this survey is a
series of monthly, quarterly and annual tabulations.
Feedback is important to assure greater accuracy, more
detail and improve the quality of information as an input
to the system.

McHale, John
    1968   "Global ecology: Toward the planetary society."
            The American Behavioral Scientist 11
            (July-August):29-33.

    Supporting the world community concept in which there
are no "local" problems anymore, this paper suggests that
the ecological requirements for sustaining that world
community take precedence over the more transient overall
balance till now seen as favorable; there is an urgency to
increase cognizance of the negatives inherent in the
present lack of conscious integration and planning of our
major technological systems. Mandatory needs appear to
be: 1) to recycle the system's metals and materials for
faster turnover and less lag; 2) the increased use of
"income" energies of solar, wind, water, tidal, and nuclear power; 3) changes in food cycle to meet starvation
needs; 4) eco-monitoring systems to check immediate and
long-range effects with positive and negative implications
for the quality of human environment.

Merriam, Ida C.
    1967   "Concepts and measures of welfare." Pp. 179-183
            in Proceedings of the Social Statistics Section
            of the American Statistical Association, Wash-
            ington, D.C.

    Measurement of changes in welfare indicates need for
renewed emphasis on distributive justice and on income

distribution. Present money income is a better measure
than what contemporary concern with other aspects of control over resources would suggest. Aggregate income distribution measures should be supplemented by a series of
subsystem measures for different income units, age and
sex, place of residence, different time periods and for
different classifications of income, including poverty-
line classification. Need to interpret money-income distribution in terms of detailed understanding of interrelationships provided by economic and social analysis as more
important than "correcting" the money-income distribution.

1968   "Welfare and its measurement." Pp. 721-803 in
        Eleanor B. Sheldon and Wilbert Moore (eds.),
        Indicators of Social Change: Concepts and
        Meeasurements. New York: Russell Sage Founda-
        tion.

This chapter has selected one measure of changes in the
general welfare and summarizes some of the major trends
revealed by existing statistics. Two main axes of measurement of welfare were isolated. One axis measures
abundance and indicates that an increasing quantity and
quality of all the elements that make up the level of
living is a basic aspect of welfare. The second major
axis measures the distribution of welfare among the population. The two axes of abundance and distribution are
discussed at length from the perspective of income and
considerable time-series data for the U.S. is presented in
easy reference form.

Miller, S. M. and H. J. Bryce
    1970   "The promotion of social mobility." Pp. 333-344
            in Transactions of the Sixth World Congress of
            Sociology, September 1966. Volume IV. Interna-
            tional Sociological Association.

From the perspective that upward social mobility is not
only an instrument of economic progress, but also a major
measure of the extent of that progress, and one with which
education is highly correlated, this paper identifies some
elements of education which must be enhanced for the
disadvantaged. Discussed are the elements of knowledge,
educational support, stimulation, motivation, attitudes,
rewards, models, confidence and financial assistance, with
broad suggestions for particularistic emphases which could
be provided.

Mindlin, Albert
    1970   "A social indicator system for city and
            neighborhood--Some issues." A memorandum from
            the Chief, Statistical Systems Group, Office of

Budget and Executive Management, Executive
Office of the Mayor-Commissioner, Government of
the District of Columbia, Washington, D.C.

Difficulties of coordinating and integrating presently
available data for optimum utilization; suggests identification of series into clusters called social indicators
"since the various annual reports and other data series
presently available are not integrated into effective
social indicators." Mindlin further discusses issues related to conceptualizing, statistical methodology and the
availability of data to develop meaningful composites.
The District of Columbia is used as the referent in
developing a social indicator system.

Moles, Abraham
    1970   "The future oriented society: Axioms and
           methodology." Futures 2 (December):312-326.

Discusses concepts of how we think about the future and
orient our actions in relation to our time-understanding
of future goals. Develops a table showing the characteristics of time-ordered systems, with four time ranges;
short, middle, long and very long, the time period, mathematical formula, form of reasoning and who is concerned
for each of the time periods. Distinguishes among prediction, projection, prevision, prospective and plan. Suggests a methodology for the future with analytical methods
and socio-analytical analysis.

Mondale, Walter F.
    1967   "New tools for social progress." The
           Progressive 31 (September):28-31.

Noting that the absence of adequate, publicly-announced
social indicators can veil successes and encourage
mistaken interpretation or exploitation of surface indications of failure, the need is presented for statistical
and analytical methods to improve evaluation of the
present state of the nation, where we are, what we have
done and what we ought to be doing. Delineates five purposes of social accounting: 1) sharpen quantitative
knowledge of social needs; 2) measure more precisely our
progress; 3) evaluate efforts at all governmental levels;
4) help in determining priorities; and 5) help in the development and assessment of alternatives without waiting
for failure.

Motes, W. C.
    1971   "Rural development: Economic criteria for as-
           sessment of outcome, and for research inputs."

A paper presented at the Annual Meeting of the
Rural Sociological Society (August 27) Denver,
Colorado.

Presents an overview of rural development with definitions and characteristics. Discusses criteria, goals,
strategies; develops a table of proxies for a set of characteristics by which to categorize communities on the type
of growth policy needed. Items considered are: value
added (capital investment and comparative advantage), population (labor force and local market) and metro proximity
(interaction with major markets).

Munson, Byron E.
    1971   "Substandard housing and social problems." A
            paper presented at the Annual Meeting of the
            American Sociological Association (August
            30-September 2) Denver, Colorado.

A review of housing literature, the basis for this
paper, suggests that substandard housing, low income,
unemployment and other social problems are unrelated to
racial disturbances. A survey by the author to explore
the relationship between urban social structure and racial
riots was made with data gathered on 88 variables for 176
cities, of which 26 had riots and 25 demonstrations between January, 1953 and August, 1967. The data indicates
that the degree of urbanization being directly related to
racial disturbances. Also indicated for further
exploration are the level of discontent, and the gap between expectation and reality.

Murie, Martin
    1971   "Evaluation of natural environments." A paper
            presented at the Annual Meeting of the American
            Association for the Advancement of Science (De-
            cember 27) Philadelphia, Pennsylvania.

This paper presents the rationale for designating two
broad categories, variety and accessibility as evaluation
criteria for natural environments. Variety is indicated
by the wide category of indices of that which is present
in the biotic system; accessibility implies those factors
affecting peoples' chances of making contact with what is
present. This latter factor suggests that land, just capable of holding animals, is not necessarily prime land
for enjoyment of wildlife; and that, perhaps, some large
tracts of wilderness, irreplaceable in the natural
ecosystem, still would be inferior to suburban and farm
areas in wildlife accessibility.

National Wildlife Federation
    1971   1971 EQ Index. Reprinted from October-November,
            1971 National Wildlife magazine. Washington,
            D.C.:   National Wildlife Federation.

    The Third Annual EQ Index is set out in this vividly
illustrated publication. The EQ, for environmental quality, is a collective measure which for 1971 stands at 55.5,
a 1.5 point loss from 1970 but smaller than the substantial loss from 1969. Components of the EQ are water, air,
soil, living space, wildlife, timber, minerals, recycling
wastes and population. Increased environmental awareness,
action and appropriations are noted as still less than
sufficient to reverse the losing trend on every component
except timber.

Olson, Mancur
    1971   "Social indicators for less developed
            countries." Draft, TA/PM/M, August 5. Washing-
            ton, D.C.: Agency for International Develop-
            ment.

    Discusses the problem of knowing if, and how fast, de-
velopment is being achieved. We need to extend measures
of development beyond per capita income to consideration
of other dimensions such as environmental damage (for example, human and animal waste dumped into rivers which are
sources of drinking water) and "institutional capital" and
its improvement, especially in regard to large scale organizations. The choice of kind and amount of aid which
should be given to a country can intelligently be made
only if there is evaluation of general progress of development in that country and the likely consequences of a
particular aid to the country. Also the donor country of
aid should assist developing countries to develop their
own information systems and analytic skills to use information to choose policies more likely to promote development.

Ostrom, Elinor
    1971   "On the meaning and measurement of output and
            efficiency and the production of urban police
            services." Unpublished manuscript.
            Bloomington, Indiana: Indiana University, De-
            partment of Political Science.

    Basic to determining police efficiency are adequate and
specific definitions of the concepts of "output" and "efficiency." One section of this paper begins with diction-
ary definitions as refined for specific usage in the private sector relationships. These definitions are then re-

lated to the public sector with problems of measurement.
The third section develops applications of these concepts
which delineate four types of police activity with possible measurement indicators. The production process is divided into services produced by one patrolman or team of
patrolmen and that involving a department or division; the
consumption process is divided into that used by an individual or one family unit and into that part used mostly
in joint consumption by a larger number of people. Discussed also is the consumer evaluation of the output of
police agencies.

Perloff, Harvey S.
    1969a "A framework for dealing with the urban environ-
           ment: Introductory statement." Baltimore,
           Maryland: The Johns Hopkins Press.

    Defines a universe of environmental elements and their
trade-offs, both natural and man-made which comprise an
urban-environment system. Perloff suggests that a study
of trade-offs between elements comprising the natural,
spatial, transportation/utilities, community/neighborhood,
or microenvironments would quantify the multiple levels of
high density living and define levels of technological development and socioeconomic patterning formed in urban environments. A comprehensive framework of environmental
envelopes is proposed as a decision-making "model" for
developing indicators which can reflect: 1) item average
situations, 2) improvement of deterioration, and 3)
extreme situations deserving special attention.

    1969b The Quality of the Urban Environment.
           Baltimore, Maryland: The Johns Hopkins Press.

    Papers in this volume are essentially theoretical and
empirical progress reports addressing an array of
quality-of-the-environment questions in terms of "urban
resources." Examples of these are: relatively "pure" air
and water, urban space, radio spectrum, and amenity resources. Man-made features figure so heavily in these resources that they are viewed conceptually as constituting
both macro and micro environments which become trade-offs.
This macro-micro trade-off theme is integral to the urban
measures of environmental condition and change which are
suggested by most of the authors for better policy and
decision making.

Pett, Saul
    1972   "The quality of life." Pp. 13-22 in Rex R.
           Campbell and Jerry L. Wade (eds.), Society and
           Environment: The Coming Collision. Boston,
           Massachusetts: Allyn and Bacon, Inc.

From a broad perspective this article describes quality
of life parameters in terms of our environmental problems.
Voicing the common worries about this overcrowded,
computerized, mechanical world, Pett's purpose is to
expose our gross inventory of problems in hopes of
establishing orientations to the full dimensions of our
dilemma. By doing so it was felt that "we could better
judge what to do and how to do it."

Ray, Paul H.
    1968   "Human ecology, technology, and the need for
            social planning." The American Behavioral Sci-
            entist 11 (July-August):16-19.

    Presented here is the view that man is a species in
disequilibrium with the world ecosystem through development of technology and through organization into cities,
bureaucracies and nation-states. The need is to convert
scientific knowledge and technical expertise into
innovations, a problem of decision-making, of planning and
of management. Present societal failure is in the realm
of control - over the environment and over the mutually
inconsistent behaviors within society. Broad outlines are
given of the shape and dimensions of social planning of
the future.

Redick, Richard
    1971   1970 Census Data Used to Indicate Areas with
            Different Potentials for Mental Health and Re-
            lated Problems. No. 3 of Series C, "Mental
            Health Statistics," National Institute of Mental
            Health Series. Public Health Service Publica-
            tion No. 2171. Stock number 1724-0131, 1971
            0-426-439. Washington, D.C.: U.S. Government
            Printing Office.

    Can it be determined in advance of need the kind and
extent of mental health services likely to be needed for
certain area populations? This report of testing and
devising procedures by the National Institute of Mental
Health affirms this potentiality and demonstrates the use
of certain demographic variables in support of their proposal. Indicators are devised in dimensions for social
rank of economic, social and education status; for life
style, and extent of familism; and for ethnicity. Included in the residential area analysis: residential
instability, feminine careerism, area homogeneity and specific indicators of high risk populations. 1968 Census
pretest data for Dane County, Wisconsin, is analyzed from
this framework as an example, with the dimensions and variables presented in tables.

Reeder, William W. and Nelson L. LeRay
    1971   "Some implications of social theory for public
            policy." A paper presented at the Annual
            Meeting of the Rural Sociological Society
            (August) Denver, Colorado.

    Deals with the apparent dilemmas from the practical
problems presented by general-level and low-level theory
and suggests how social theory can be a tool for policy
planning. Uses three master propositions with
elaborations as general framework for high-level theoretical frame of reference; focus on decision content rather
than on decision-making process.

Rice, Stuart A.
    1967   "Social accounting and statistics for the great
            society." Public Administration Review 27
            (June):169-174.

    Reviews the book, Social Indicators, by Raymond Bauer,
prefacing the remarks with some general comments on the
interrelatedness of technological and social change, and
the alterations in that interaction through the years.
Four basic questions: How can we select the most significant relations; find measurable indicators; plot them
systematically; and employ the trend lines usefully? Rice
doesn't feel Bauer's book answers these questions, but
that it can be helpful in pointing the direction. Notes
lack of continuity and cohesion in the book, not
unexpected in a collection of essays.

Rogers, Carl R.
    1968   "Interpersonal relationships: U.S.A. 2000."
            Journal of Applied and Behavioral Science 4
            (July-September):265-279.

    Presented as part of a symposium entitled "USA 2000,"
this author defines man's greatest problem in this
technological age as the quantity of change man can
assimilate and the rate at which he can do so. Though
cognizant of the results of population growth, increased
urbanization and overcrowding, this is yet generally an
optimistic overview. One force for humanization is in
intensive group experiences, where new types and depths of
human relationships are emerging. Included for discussion
within this framework are man-woman and parent-child relationships, institutionalized religion, education, industry
and the tragic trend toward communication breakdown between the privileged and the ghetto.

Sawchuk, R. and A. George Gitter
    1971   Eight Subjective Indicators of Quality of Life.
            Report No. 51. Boston: Boston University, Com-
            munication Research Center.

    This study (N = 125 white undergraduates) examined
subjective evaluations of the quality of seven aspects of
life, and investigated the relationship between these
evaluations and selected demographic and attitudinal variables. Two factors, which accounted for 57 percent of the
variance, were extracted from factor analysis of the
ratings of the seven aspects of life. A multiple correlation of .66 was obtained using the attitudinal variables
as predictors and Factor I--"Quality of Life" as criterion.

Sheldon, Eleanor B. and Wilbert E. Moore
    1968   Indicators of Social Change: Concepts and Meas-
            urements. New York: Russell Sage Foundation.

    This huge volume, containing more than 700 pages, is a
compendium of articles by 14 well-known authors who have
devoted their attention to several components of a social
system from the perspective of outlining the major areas
of social change, the development of social indicators to
monitor such change, and the presentation of considerable
data within each component. Four major areas of structural change form the major divisions of the text and the
demographic base of society, from the point of view of
population; structural features of society, including economic growth, labor force and employment, knowledge and
technology, politics, religion, and family change;
distributive features including consumption, leisure,
health, and education; and the aggregative features of
stratification and mobility and welfare, are the chapter
concerns of the book.

Sullivan, Daniel F.
    1966   Conceptual Problems in Developing an Index of
            Health. Publication No. 1000-Series 2-No. 17.
            Washington, D.C.: National Center for Health
            Statistics, Public Health Service.

    Changing health problems and programs have impaired the
utility of mortality rates as a measure of health for a
population. Considered essential for a more adequate
index are the two factors of sensitivity to the need for
and adequacy of health activities, and its composition of
measurable components. Defining morbidity in terms of the
total impact of illness, disability from disease or injury
which could be measured in cross-sectional surveys, a com-

bined index of morbidity and mortality seems to meet the
minimum criteria. Sources of data, reliability and
validity are discussed in relation to the proposed index.

Sutton, Willis A., Jr. and Jiri Kolaja
    1960   "The concept of community." Rural Sociology 25
            (June):197-203.

    A definition of community from which can be drawn four
variables: 1) number of actors, 2) awareness of action,
3) goal of action, and 4) recipients of action. By cross-
classifying and weighting, a 16-fold table is developed to
classify all actions within the community as to the degree
of "community-ness".

Tunstall, Daniel B.
    1970   "Developing a social statistics publication." A
            paper presented at the Annual Meeting of the
            American Statistical Association (December 27)
            Detroit, Michigan.

    Concepts involved in the social statistics publication
then being prepared (Dec., 1970) by the Statistical Policy
staff in the Office of Management and Budget; book to
include basic social and economic data; listing of nine
goal areas with specific major goal concerns, performance
indicators and analytical information for each of:
health, public safety, education, employment, income,
housing, travel and transportation, physical environment,
and recreation.

Udall, Stuart
    1968   "Population, parenthood, and the quality of
            life." Pp. 122-137 in Stuart Udall, 1976: An
            Agenda for Tomorrow. New York: Harcourt, Brace
            and World.

    Projections of what things would be possible in the
United States in the near future with slow-growth of population, leveling off near 220 million within next decade
according to Dr. Bogue's estimate. Philosophical alternatives to parenthood; advocates design of cities better
adapted to differing life-style, with a few specific references to the pattern in Reston, Virginia, a planned
town.

United Nations Research Institute for Social Development
    1970   "The concept of development and its measure-
            ment." International Social Development Review
            (No. 2):1-6.

82

Development is a process of (a) achieving higher levels
on commonly accepted value continua (health, education,
income, etc.), (b) building up instrumentalities and means
and (c) undergoing structural changes associated in
practice with (a) and (b). This concept does not include
incidental and trivial concomitants or various negative
concomitants. Argues the use of multiple indicators of
development in addition to per capita national income and
presents correspondence analysis on a set of 24 econom-
ic/social indicators of structural factors and
developmental objectives (goals and means). Such analysis
is useful for projections and planning, providing more
elaborate empirical content to the concept of development
than per capita income alone.

U.S. Department of Agriculture
    1969   Some Notes on Quality of Rural Living. Seminar
            during the meeting of the Northeast Rural Soci-
            ology Committee (April 3) Federal Extension
            Service, United States Department of
            Agriculture, Washington, D.C. ER&E-52 (6/69).

Highlights from a one-day seminar, part of the 1969
meeting of the Northeast Rural Sociology Committee. Brief
remarks on the development of the concept, but primarily
discusses the concept of quality of living itself, its
meaning, components and criteria for measurement. Suggests goals, approaches and research for long-range studies and methodology for more adequate conceptualization.

Van Valey, Thomas L.
    1971   "Industrialization and urbanization: An empiri-
            cal assessment of two models." A paper present-
            ed at the Annual Meeting of the Rural
            Sociological Society (August) Denver, Colorado.

This paper attempts to clarify and specify the relation
between industrialization and urbanization, as they are
occurring in rural areas of the southern United States
now. Two models are developed and evaluated through the
use of thirteen indicators. Both models employ three
basic variables: 1) urbanization, 2) facilities for
transportation and communication, and 3)
industrialization. Findings suggest that urbanization
leads to industrialization, which leads to development and
greater use of facilities for communication and
transportation. Noted are instances of rural
industrialization, which may be affected by a regionally-
oriented diffuse process of urbanization. A summary
comment suggests that even with the use of the three variables here as minimum, rural development theory suffers
from incomplete specification and may result in more

confusion than clarification. Relevant correlations are specified in tables.

Ver Eecke, Wilfried
    1970   "Law, morality, and society: Reflections on
           violence." Ethics 80 (January):140-145.

    Presents a brief analysis of man's fundamental psycho-
logical nature, with data and concepts from
psychoanalysis, then draws an analogy from that to man's
attitudes toward rebellion, violence and war. Concludes
from the analogy that man can condemn certain kinds of
violent rebellion, but that he will only be able to
deplore other kinds of rebellions.

Vestermark, S. D., Jr.
    1968   "Social indicators of social effects and the
           social inventory after attack." Pp. 327-363 in
           Proceedings of the Symposium on Postattack Re-
           covery from Nuclear War, held at Fort Monroe,
           Virginia, November 6-9, 1967, under auspices of
           Advisory Committee on Civil Defense, and Office
           of Emergency Planning. Washington, D.C.:
           National Academy of Sciences.

    Discusses the kinds of specific social effects which
should be of concern to post-attack planners and the deficiencies in knowledge about social effects and what might
be done to remedy this situation. Need to know the social
organizational demands that will be put on people after
nuclear attack and the ways in which damage to the social,
ecological, and cultural systems create particular social
policy problems. Need to develop a method and system for
describing the various levels of society in ways which
would allow a rapid calculation of the effects of various
kinds of countermeasure systems in protecting the elements
of society from different kinds of possible attack. The
desirable general characteristics of this system are
outlined as a proposed system of social indicators which
would be incorporated in a National Social Inventory for
Civil Defense.

Vlachos, Evan and Bert Ellenbogen
    1971   "Organizational aspects of irrigation systems."
           A paper presented at the Annual Meeting of the
           Rural Sociological Society (August) Denver,
           Colorado.

    Problematic situation in water management in five
western states; factors related to water supply and
changing social scene; water resources management system;

primary variables of input, the system and output to determine the level of organizational effectiveness of any
water management system.

Warren, Roland L.
    1965   "Types of purposive social change at the
            community level." No. 11 Brandeis University
            Papers in Social Welfare. Waltham,
            Massachusetts: Brandeis University, The
            Florence Heller Graduate School for Advanced
            Studies in Social Welfare.

    Identifies most purposive change as a secondary
adaptive type, a response to uncontrolled changes from
outside, the aggregate of individual decisions within a
community, or response to behavior of various adaptive organizations. Describes three situations for a change
agent as issue consensus, issue difference or issue
dissensus (points on a continuum rather than discrete
states) with strategies for each situation. Definitions
of terms.

    1970   "The good community--What would it be?" Journal
            of Community Development Society 1
            (Spring):14-24.

    Agreeing that everyone wants to "live in a good
community," this paper suggests nine issues necessary to
consider in formulating a model of the "good" community:
primary group relationships; autonomy; viability; power
distribution; participation; degree of commitment; degree
of heterogeneity; extent of neighborhood control and
extent of conflict. Critical questions asked in discussion of each factor; three overall questions: 1) How much
of what we want is actually possible? 2) How much of what
seems desirable do we actually want? 3) How much of a
price are we willing to pay for it when other values are
jeopardized?

Webber, Melvin M.
    1965   "The roles of intelligence systems in urban-
            systems planning." Journal of the American
            Institute of Planners 31 (November):289-296.

    Present urban planning has not kept pace with changing
understandings of urban problems and urban systems. New
strategies hope to be able to foresee second-order consequences of various alternatives, to estimate optimal
timing, and to predict distributions of costs and benefits. Needed is an urban "intelligence center", combining
effectively urban theory and action, becoming agents of
change not serving a single client but rather the urban

system and subsystems. Accepts as inevitable and desirable that value systems of social scientists will be involved, that they will be required by their position to say what they think ought to be as well as what might be.

Wells, Alan
     1971   "Nation-building models and the Nigerian
             dilemma." A paper presented at the Annual
             Meeting of the American Sociological Association
             (August 30-September 2) Denver, Colorado.

By detailed illustration of Nigeria, from the year of independence, 1960, through the Nigerian-Biafran civil war ending in January, 1970, various interpretations of the concept of nation-building are explored. The processes involved in political unification of peoples, the nurturing of national consciousness, cultural homogenization, and the centralization of authority, have acquired somewhat incongruent meanings and may not be universally applicable to newly independent countries. Differences stem from the degree of stress given each element in the overall configuration; models are present schematically as illustration of the varying patterns possible.

Willhelm, Sidney M.
     1964   "The concept of the 'ecological complex': A
             critique." The American Journal of Economics
             and Sociology 23 (July):241-249.

A discussion of the theoretical and methodological assumptions and deficiencies of the "traditional" schools of writings on human ecology, voluntaristic and materialistic; the latter with its two subdivisions, traditional and neoclassical.

Williams, Anne S. and William R. Lassey
     1971   "Pluralistic leadership and area development."
             A paper presented at the Annual Meeting of the
             Rural Sociological Society (August 27-29)
             Denver, Colorado.

Analysis of leadership structure in 8 county development federation in south-central Montana, and its functioning in development efforts. Data supporting pluralistic leadership structure suggest serious problems for organization cohesion of such area efforts.

Wilson, Albert and Donna Wilson
     1971   "Futures-orientation: Toward the

institutionalization of change." Pp. 85-113 in
Magoroh Maruyama and James A. Dator (eds.),
Human Futuristics. Honolulu, Hawaii: Social
Science Research Institute, University of
Hawaii.

Futurology or futuristics, the science of change, is
predicated on the belief that a spectrum of alternative
probable futures exists, and that through our own efforts
we can control the processes of change to enhance or di-
minish the probability of occurrence of any specific
future. Our mode of change must proceed from static stability to dynamic stability, and include the problems of
the methodologies of futurology and their assimilation
into public practice. Also discussed are the
determinative, normative and random aspects of social
change, with definitions and illustrations. A cybernetic
model is suggested, with programs for futures orientation.

Wilson, Ian H.
    1971   "Futures planning: A new dimension of the
            corporate planner." Remarks made at the Inter-
            national Conference on Corporate Planning (De-
            cember 8) Montreal.

Reviews work at General Electric to establish
priorities for future research, especially in relation to
urban/minority problems. As society changes criteria by
which it judges business, in turn, business must change
the criteria by which it judges its own performance. This
entails changing the measurement system used to evaluate
managerial and corporate performance. Among factors which
must be taken into account are the forces for change in
environment outside the firm: developments in international, defense, social, political, legal, economic,
technological, manpower and financial affairs. Analyses
of these forces provides basis for "view of the future"
which then requires "cross-impact analysis" to assign
probabilities (scenarios) and, thereby, provide guidelines
for specifying the course of action which the firm should
pursue which is beneficial for itself and society.

Young, Ruth C.
    1968   "A structural approach to development." The
            Journal of Developing Areas 2 (April):363-372.

This is an attempt to formulate concepts and develop
indices more accurately expressive of the development
process and status than are the usual measures. The concepts of industrial development, communicative development, and external diversity, all with unique and specific
conceptualizations, were formulated and tested with meas-

ures on 50 non-Western countries. Guttman scaling was
used in the study; tables are presented showing the item
content used in the scales, sample proportions and item
errors, and a rank correlation matrix of development measures using Kendall's Tau.

GENERAL THEORY

Adelman, Irma and Cynthia Taft Morris
1967   Society, Politics and Economic Development: A
        Quantitative Approach.   Baltimore, Maryland:
        The Johns Hopkins Press.

Recognizing the interdependence of economic growth and
sociopolitical change, this book develops semiquantitative
insights into the relationships existing between social,
economic and political change and the level and pace of
economic development, focusing primarily on the dynamics
of the development process.   Seventy-four countries are
classified into three groups depicting the level of economic development, for the period of 1957-1962, on the
basis of forty-one factors.   Indicators were chosen to
categorize social variables, portraying principally the
social aspects of urbanization and industrialization,
political variables to indicate emergent modern states,
and economic indices to summarize changes in economic
structure and institutions typical of industrialization
and economic growth.   Separate chapters treat the choices
of indices, the technique of factor analysis used, long-
run relationships, the short-run relationships in
countries at each of three levels of socio-economic development and the broad picture of the development process
and policy implications.

Anderson, James G.
1970   "Social indicators and second order-
        consequences: Measuring the impact of
        intercultural health programs." Las Cruces, New
        Mexico: New Mexico State University Research
        Center.

This paper outlines a social accounting system that is
being developed to measure the social impact of an
innovative intercultural health and medical care program.
A model by Gross has been adapted and this model leads to
the development of a set of social indicators that can be
used to measure the impact of such innovative programs on
both the structure and performance of the community
affected.

Austin, Charles J.
1971   "Selected social indicators in the health
        field." American Journal of Public Health 61
        (August): 1507-1513.

A new set of national health goals is needed due to the recent interest in comprehensive health planning. The assumption is made that current national goals and action plans are being developed in reference to social indicators which are based upon outdated norms. Four conceptual models of planned social change are discussed with emphasis on cybernetic models. More recent health surveys are obtaining data generally not found in traditional national vital statistics. These include adequacy of health and disability insurance, availability of medical and dental care to different sectors of the population and additional information on health status and health care needs. Future health statistics must tell something about the characteristics of the services provided--their accessibility, availability, effectiveness and efficiency. "Much work needs to be done if we are to develop a set of national social accounts in the health field which are developmental rather than rehabilitative."

Bauer, Raymond A. (ed.)
   1966   Social Indicators. Cambridge, Massachusetts:
          The Massachusetts Institute of Technology Press.

This book is a collection of articles by five prominent social scientists who attempt to evaluate the statistical tools relevant to America's social goals. They have devoted themselves to an examination of the defects and limitations of much of our present social statistics, to proposals for improvement in our information systems, and to a critical examination of how information might be used to evaluate the impact of a federal program, such as space exploration. Bauer, Biderman, Gross, Rosenthal and Weiss make contributions to the book.

Bauer, Raymond A. and Alice H. Bauer
   1960   "America, 'mass society' and mass media." The
          Journal of Social Issues 16:3-66.

Deals with the determinant relationship between a society and its system of communications; discusses the myth of the omnipotence of mass media and dissolution of the myth; sections on the role of informal communication, the mass audience as a "mass," the dangers of equating content and effect of mass media.

Biderman, Albert D.
   1971   "Notes on the value selectivity of environment-
          allocating institutions." (April 29) Washing-
          ton, D.C.: Bureau of Social Science Research,
          Inc.

Frames environmental problems as manifestations of our
allocation and utilization system's failure to operate in
a way which reflects particular values. Proposes that a
coherent strategy for coordinating approaches to these
problems may then reside in the value selective features
of these systems. The selectivity of informational system
capacities and the perception/action thresholds of these
allocation and utilization systems are described as being
a function of each informational systems selectivity.
Other aspects of institutional value selectivity are considered within this context.

Boulding, Kenneth E.
    1967   "An economist looks at the future of sociology."
            et al. 1 (Winter):1-7.

    Relating and differentiating economics, political sci-
ence and sociology, Boulding sees all three disciplines
concerned with the total social system from different
viewpoints: economics from exchange and exchangeables,
political science from legitimized threat, sociology from
the integrative system, that is, that aspect of social
life involving the relationships of love, loyalty,
legitimization, and the structure of status, identity, and
community. Recognizes the need for the sociologist to develop a theory of the total social system, as no other
social science discipline is qualified or likely to
undertake this task.

Brooks, Ralph M., Leslie D. Wilcox, George M. Beal and
Gerald E. Klonglan
    1971   "Toward the measurement of social indicators:
            Conceptual and methodological implications."
            Proceedings of the Social Statistics Section,
            American Statistical Association, Washington,
            D.C.

    In the current social indicator movement at least four
perspectives can be identified. Social indicators can be
viewed as "instruments for detecting changes in the quality of life of individuals, groups or societies, as instruments to monitor progress toward societal goals, as social
statistics and as social statistics that measure changes
in variables that are components in a social systems
model." This last perspective according to the authors
offers most for the advancement of the development of
social indicators. Their model of the social system is
adapted from the ecological models with environment,
social organization, population and the cultural system as
basic components in the model. This model is termed the
"community ecosystem" and is utilized as a perspective to
begin the explication of a taxonomy of lower level

indicators that would allow the assessment of current
social conditions within the community. The remainder of
the paper is devoted to a more detailed explication of the
element of population.

Bush, J. W. and M. M. Chen
    1972   "Markovian analysis of disease history and the
            problem of equilibrium." American Journal of
            Public Health (forthcoming).

Mathematical relationships are used to analyze the
history of disease in patients. The stochastic process of
disease development is represented by a stationary Markov
chain. This can be used to understand the impact of
disease and health programs on large populations, and may
make possible an aggregate measure of health levels for a
region or nation.

Chen, M. M. and J. W. Bush
    1971   "A mathematical programming approach for
            selecting an optimum health program case mix."
            A paper presented at the meeting of the Opera-
            tions Research Society of America (October
            27-29) Anaheim, California.

A mathematical programming model is presented for use
in health programs. Health services from such programs
have an output of healthier individuals, a measurement of
which is the quality adjusted years of life. Target populations of these programs are classified by demographic
characteristics and disease forms into smaller modules so
that optimum programs can be developed. The model presented is shown to be more realistic than a cost benefit
procedure.

Chiang, C. L.
    1965   An Index of Health Mathematical Models. Publi-
            cation No. 1000-Series 2-No. 5. Washington,
            D.C.: National Center for Health Statistics,
            Public Health Service.

Using the components of frequency and duration of
illness, severity of illness and number of deaths, models
are formulated for each component and for an overall index
to denote the state of health for a well-defined population over a specific time period, as one calendar year.
As an example, tabular data from the Canadian Sickness
Survey, 1950-1951, gives the number of illnesses within
the calendar year to each individual of a given age group
and the distribution of the subpopulation with respect to
this variable, to indicate the illness frequency compo-

nent. As the value of the index H is affected by the current population distribution, a weighted model is given
for an age-adjusted index of health.

Coleman, James S.
    1971   Resources for Social Change: Race in the United
            States. New York: Wiley-Interscience.

    This book draws together emerging theories of directed
social change by reformulating the resources which are
considered as prime movers for change. Though Coleman addresses only the Negro sub-group problem of gaining power
parity in American society, the framework could be used to
organize any subset of resources towards a desired end
product of improving the deficit position for a population
sub-group relative to others in a society. Since desired
change is appraised in terms of relative action or conversion assets, indicants of social conditions must reflect
relative resource deficits.

Corning, Peter A.
    1970   "The problem of applying Darwinian evolution to
            political science." A paper presented at the
            VIIIth World Congress of the International
            Political Science Association (August 31-Septem-
            ber 5) Munich, Germany.

    This is an extended focus in an effort to show the use-
fulness of applying the Darwinian model of evolution to
analysis of society. The paper traces the impact of
Darwinian evolution on social theory, some characteristics
of a Darwinian model of society, problems in
operationalizing Darwinian theory, a framework for
Darwinian macro-analysis, and finally the applicability of
evolutionary indicators as measures of adaptiveness.

Dillman, Don A. and James A. Christenson
    1971   "Towards the assessment of public values." Un-
            published manuscript. Pullman, Washington: De-
            partment of Sociology, Washington State Univer-
            sity.

    Conceptualizing preferences as values rather than atti-
tudes on the basis values are more general and may
encompass a variety of specific objects and concerns, and
because values imply a hierarchical order, enabled this
study to identify priorities relating to government activities and expenditures. Data was gathered from a questionnaire of 3101 respondents in the state of Washington.
Factor analysis identified the conceptual dimensions of
peoples' public values, yielding 12 factors accounting for

57% of the total variation among the items. High priority
values concerned law and order and pollution control;
medium priorities encompassed protection of the natural
environment, education, employment opportunities, personal
health and security, and urban problems. Low priority
factors included college youth concerns, national defense,
assistance to agriculture, aid to foreign countries and
space exploration. Footnotes give the question-response
categories and listed activities; tables give the varimax
rotated factor loadings of 51 government expenditure
items, and the heirarchical ranking with factor groupings
and their component items.

Drewnowski, Jan
    1971   "The practical significance of social informa-
            tion." The Annals of The American Academy of
            Political and Social Science 393 (Janu-
            ary):82-91.

    This article contends that two important problems in
development cannot be tackled in a satisfactory way without adequate social information: 1) meaningful assessment
of development results and 2) giving social content to development planning. The confusion resulting from the use
of economic variables for these purposes argues the need
to elaborate and apply social indicators. Of the four
classes of social indicators, the methodology and construction of one, level-of-living indicators, is discussed
in some detail as it is considered to be the most critical
class in the development of a coherent system. A
tentative list of level-of-living indicators is presented
in conclusion.

Dubin, Robert
    1971   "Causality and social systems analysis." A
            paper presented at the Annual Meeting of the
            American Sociological Association (August
            30-September 2) Denver, Colorado.

    A general systems approach to the analysis of social
systems is significant in that the theory can be developed
without dependence on the idea of causality, and is thus
equipped to examine complex multivariable systems without
the need to limit the analysis to two variables (or a few)
in looking for causality, or the assigning of primacy to
certain variables. The author finds support for his approach in writings of W. F. Ogburn, Robert K. Merton, and
Talcott Parsons. Two potential dangers mentioned are: 1)
a sense of universality that almost precludes testing
against empirical facts without the assurance that the
test will prove positive; and 2) possible avoidance of
grounding such systems in the empirical world by first

observing its characteristics and then conceptualizing its system features.

Eisenstadt, Samuel
    1971   "Obstacles and reinforcements of development."
            A paper presented at the Seventh World Congress
            of Sociology (September 14-19) Varna, Bulgaria.

Analyzes the "obstacles to development of the social and cultural conditions which influence the development, within different societies, of different ways of coping with the changes due to the impact of forces of modernization." Internal solidarity and cohesion, rigidity and uniformity of the internal division of labor, degree of autonomy and the openness or closeness of one group toward another are considered as important variables in influencing attitudes to change. Finally, the approach to development should not be made on a unidimensional conception of development or modernity.

Eldridge, Eber
    1970   "Community resource and human development." A
            paper presented at the AAEA Annual Meeting
            (August 16, 1971) Carbondale, Illinois.

An economist looks at nonmetropolitan community and re-source development in terms of its objective function. Advances a method of building the function for development wherein variables are included in the function if it de-scribes a primary focus of a development program of some institution, organization or agency. An example for "quality of life" is given where it is described as a function of: purchasing power per person, income distri-bution, economic base, contributions of institutions, infrastructure, capital inventory, cultural level, leadership effectiveness, and performance of services.

Emery, F. E.
    1967   "The next thirty years: Concepts, methods and
            anticipations." Human Relations
            (August):199-237.

The extent of the challenge to the social sciences in the next 30 years is examined in terms of the unique un-derstandings, methods, and institutionalized arrangements for teaching and research, and for relating the social sciences to society. The human effects for consideration are the change in human affects with distress less dominant; alterations in work-leisure ratios, and changes in human relations; significant within the technology are changes in communication and transportation; within the

social-psychological is man's perception of himself and
his world. Changes of this nature are fundamental in the
evolution of society and science and tend to determine the
ways men develop and use the technologies. Conceptual and
methodological difficulties are assessed. The social sciences are seen with the potential for an active role that
expands the alternatives open to men.

Finsterbusch, Kurt
    1971a "Dimensions of nations: Inductively and
           deductively developed and propositionally relat-
           ed." A paper presented at the Conference on
           Methodological Problems in Comparative
           Sociological Research of the Institute for Com-
           parative Sociology (April 8-9) Bloomington,
           Indiana.

    Develops a conceptual scheme of over 50 relevant vari-
ables, of which 26 are utilized to postulate a theory of
nation states as wholes. Discusses the measurement of the
variables, their interrelationships, and some of the more
obvious covariances. The conception involves the nation
as a social system with inputs into, and outputs from the
system, structural characteristics, and system activities
between two points in time; outlines given of the variables related to each, both positively and negatively.
Suggested indicators for each of the variables.

    1971b "The sociology of nation states: Dimensions,
           indicators and theory." (September) Washington,
           D.C.: American Sociological Association.

    Authors of this paper attempt to identify the key vari-
ables for a theory of nation states wherein a state is
conceived as a social system in an environment with inputs
into the system, outputs from the system, system structural characteristics and system activities occuring between
points in time. They proceed towards this objective
discussing the measurement of the 48 variables identified,
forwarding postulates concerning their interrelationships,
considering the testability of the theory, and suggesting
that their 48 variable scheme be reduced to a subset of 23
for inclusion in the theory's first stage.

Ford, Joseph B.
    1971 "Contextual content analysis: A link between
          micro-social and macro-social research." A
          paper presented at the Annual Meeting of the
          American Sociological Association (August
          30-September 2) Denver, Colorado.

    Ford proposes a synthesis of content-analysis and

socio-historical context-analysis to bridge the gap between microsociological and macrosociological research and
theory. Kroeber's macrosociological contextual content-
analysis model is discussed in which he compares cycles of
creativity as indices to larger features of cultural development. Kroeber used biography and history as
indicators to disclose trends in culture growth. Ford
suggests improvements on Kroeber's model to bring it to
the paradigmatic level.

Form, William H. and Joan Huber
    1971   "Sociological theory and occupational rewards:
            An approach to income inequality." A paper pre-
            sented at the Annual Meeting of the American
            Sociological Association (August 30) Denver,
            Colorado.

    This paper discusses the theory of marginal utility and
the functional theory of social stratification in relation
to income inequality. Deficiencies and similarities of
the two theories are noted, and data presented to verify
the argument. Proposes the concept of social power and
control as the important factors accounting for the variance in occupational income.

Fox, Karl A.
    1969a   "Operations research and complex social
            systems." Chapter 9, pp. 452-467 in Jati K.
            Sengupta and Karl A. Fox, Economic Analysis and
            Operations Research: Optimization Techniques in
            Quantitative Economic Models. Amsterdam:
            North-Holland Publishing Company.

    Develops theory and formulae for quantifying inputs and
outputs in social systems; discusses development of a
Gross Social Produce (GSP) comparable to GNP, and what
variables and factors might need to be considered;
generalization of consumption theory to social systems.

    1969b   "Toward a policy model of world economic devel-
            opment with special attention to the
            agricultural sector." Pp. 95-126 in Erik
            Thorbecke (ed.), The Role of Agriculture in Eco-
            nomic Development. New York: Columbia Univer-
            sity Press.

    Development of some of Roger Barker's observations of
the behavior settings of a small midwest town into a mathematical formula for optimal allocation of a person's time
among behavior settings; expansion of the concepts into a
world model divided into 16 functional economic areas
(FEA) with formulae.

Fromm, Erich
    1970   "Humanistic planning." Pp. 59-78 in The Crisis
            of Psychoanalysis. New York: Holt, Rinehart
            and Winston.

    Elaborates the thesis that the analysis of the system
"man" must become an integral part of the analysis of the
system "enterprise" or the system "society." Presently,
we are dealing with the analysis of a social system without adequately considering one of its most important
subsystems. Something which is economically efficient may
thus be humanly and socially detrimental if our real objective is the maximal unfolding of man rather than production and consumption. Concludes that we have the means
to this goal but perhaps not the motivation to undertake
the radical change in our priorities, social structure,
and methods of managing the human resources it dictates.

Gross, Bertram M.
    1966   The State of the Nation: Social Systems Ac-
            counting. New York: Tavistock Publications.

    The author deals extensively with the two concepts,
structures and performance, while developing a model of
national social accounting. He attempts to bring together
in an integrated fashion the relevant concepts developed
by economists, political scientists, sociologists,
anthropologists, psychologists, and social psychologists
and concludes by discussing the difficulties involved in
developing and using social indicators on the basis of
this or any other model of a social system.

Hahn, Erich
    1970   "Sociological system conception and social
            prognosis." A paper presented at the Seventh
            World Congress of Sociology (September 14-19)
            Varna, Bulgaria.

    The scientific prognosis of man demands a scientific
prognosis of society, which demands substantiated system
conception, which demands scientific theory of society as
a whole and is thinkable only as an aspect of this theory.
Hahn further argues that only the socialist theory of
society can offer goals for the satisfaction of human
social needs, that capitalism's over-riding goal of
profits prevents man and society from ever reaching
fullest development.

Heady, Earl O.
    1972   "Objectives of rural community development and

their attainment: Consistencies and competition
among various social and economic aggregates."
A paper presented at the seminar on Rural
Community Development: Focus on Iowa. Ames,
Iowa: Iowa State University, Center for
Agricultural and Rural Development.

The crux of the rural development issue is the
inequitable distribution of benefits and costs of national
economic development. Typical rural communities are
geographically isolated from the major benefits of economic development in the U.S., and the major demographic,
sectoral and economic groups which gain least or sacrifice
most are located in rural areas. Discussed are the various interest groups and their goals, the consensus and
lack of it among them; communities with resources for
growth must be identified and assisted; persons and
families facing migration for employment must be guided
toward optimum relocation for themselves and the
communities; declining communities, which must remain
geared to changing agricultural situations and which contain a large proportion of the "left behind" people, must
be helped adapt to the future away from the atmosphere of
pessimism. There are available various means for these
needs if we are willing to use imagination in devising the
means, and if we accept the premise of an obligation to
these forgotten people and communities.

Heberlein, Thomas A.
    1971   "Some limitations of social science for policy-
            oriented research." Boulder, Colorado:
            Institute of Behavioral Science and Department
            of Sociology, University of Colorado.

Focusing on unique social phenomena, such as the race
riots of 1967, the relationship of explanation and prediction is examined, concluding that what is considered explanation in the social sciences seldom can predict the
initial event itself or the subsequent consequences. The
importance of both accentable variance variables and
explanatory models is also discussed. The use and limits
of experiments, panel studies and longitudinal studies in
development of an explanatory model in general for riots,
and for the specific ASR article by Spilerman (1970), "The
Causes of Racial Disturbances: Comparison of Alternative
Explanation" illustrates the limitations presented. Suggested as adaptive strategies are: social indicators, experimentation or quasi-experimentation, and a combination
of experimental and field survey techniques, with a discussion of the policy issue and costs of these strategies.

Hogg, Thomas C.
    1966   "Toward including ethnological parameters in

river basin models." In Water Resources and Economic Development of the West. Report No. 15. Conference Proceedings Committee on the Economics of Water Resources Development of the Western Agricultural Economics Research Council.

Difficulties entailed with the construction of river basin models and the conceptual problems of incorporating ethnological parameters in them are examined in this paper. Several basic questions which bear on attempts to simulate socio-ecological phenomena--selection of model referents, levels of analysis, and "system" specification--are addressed. An interdisciplinary restatement of formal symbols in semantical terms and formulation of an integrative semantical model is advocated as necessary for arriving at quantitative parameters and eventually mathematical models.

Horowitz, Irving Louis
    1969   "Engineering and sociological perspectives on development: Interdisciplinary constraints in social forecasting." International Social Science Journal 21:546-557.

Considering the unlikelihood that nations faced with material advantages of technological progress would reject that progress because of the cost of social disorganization suggests the need for social scientists to abandon the Luddite response of resistance to innovation and antagonism toward the applied sciences. The author identifies several inadequacies of the engineering perspective toward development, but recognizes that the social sciences also have offered and produced less than was needed. Discusses specific ways through which the social science perspective would be advantageous to engineers, the applied sciences, and, as a result, to the world at large.

Klausner, Samuel Z.
    1971   "Some formal theoretical components for socio-environmental research." A paper presented at the Annual Meeting of the American Sociological Association (August 30-September 2) Denver, Colorado.

Discusses the difficulties of relating biological, physical and social processes in their effects on the environment. Proposes an approach to man-environment research which manipulates the variables of one system while looking to the other for either parametric inputs or as an object of orientation. This would involve the study of

natural systems in the light of human intervention, and
social systems considering physical and biological constraints with the personal and social orientations toward
those restraints.

Kormondy, Edward J.
    1972   "The nature of ecosystems." Pp. 40-45 in Rex R.
            Campbell and Jerry L. Wade (eds.), Society and
            Environment: The Coming Collision. Boston,
            Massachusetts: Allyn and Bacon, Inc.

    Presents an ecosystem process model of noncyclic energy
and cyclic nutrient movement. Relationships between
abiotic and biotic components, autotrophic and
heterotrophic producers, decomposers and recycling are
treated as aspects of ecosystem process dynamics. The expanding human population demands more knowledge of
producer efficiency, energy-flows, nutrient dependence,
and the effects of introducing radioactive or toxic sub-
stances into the natural cycling process. Such knowledge
might help explicate this model and would implicitly require indicants of the contiguity of ecosystem processes
and articulation of environmental interdependencies.

Krendel, Ezra S.
    1969   "The life cycle as a basis for social policy and
            social indicators." Working Paper No. 106.
            Berkeley, California: Institute of Urban and
            Regional Development, University of California.

    The life cycle as a sequence of eight stages, first
proposed by Erik Erickson in 1968, gives a perspective for
evaluating the impact of public programs on individuals.
Comparisons of benefits among different clients of public
services would follow; the model suggested would be used
as a basis for consequent choices in policy formulation.
Reorganization of much presently available social statistics into life cycle terms from the programmatic form
would encourage cross-program analysis, show the integrated effects of programs on individuals, suggest trade-offs
among programs, and point up the failings in the
collective impact of a set of social programs.

        1971a   "Advice as a socially constructed activity."
                Working Paper No. 144C. Berkeley, California:
                Institute of Urban and Regional Development,
                University of California.

    With advice-giving as the model, presented in this
paper are some of the concepts and problems of the knowledge utilization process in private and public life.
Planning is presented as a mode of action for the advice-

giver, with the crucial question, "How can we make more democratic use of what is knowable for public policy purposes?" Reorientation to this basis in current social studies will involve a reexamination of the sources of what we know and a sense of the importance of perceived action, in contrast to sensed behavior, for social knowing.

1971b   "Social indicators and urban systems dynamics." Socio-Economic Planning Sciences 5 (August): 387-393.

A model is presented where the urban resident's perceptions of discrepancies between desired system performance and actual system performance can be made an integral part of urban system's analysis. In this example social indicators are viewed as negative feedback structures whose proper recognition and incorporation in urban subsystem's operating decisions will serve to impact urban quality of life. The urban subsystems considered are city service organizations, such as the fire department, etc.

Kunkel, John H.
1971   "Models of man and social systems analysis." A paper presented at the Annual Meeting of the American Sociological Association (August 30-September 2) Denver, Colorado.

Develops the concept that though social systems consist of men and their behavior, the analysis of systems is influenced by the models of man and of society which one chooses as the basis for analysis. Examines the criteria for psychodynamic and behavioral models, their implications for social systems analysis, internal constraints they place on the systems structure and operation, and the implications of these and other models for options in the design and modification of systems.

Land, Kenneth C.
1970   "Social indicators." In Robert B. Smith (ed.), Social Science Methods. New York: The Free Press.

This is an extended paper which explores analytically the concern for social indicators by authors and public figures both in the past and at present; the theoretical and methodological issues in social indicators including distinctions between social accounting, social reporting, and social indicators; and the potential use of social indicators for public policy. Social indicators are defined and a macro measurement approach is described similar in methodology to much of macro-economic models.

Liu, William T. and Robert W. Duff
1971   "The structural effect of communication flows in
        a pre-industrial city." A paper presented at
        the Annual Meeting of the Ohio Valley
        Sociological Society (April 22-24) Cleveland,
        Ohio.

A study done in the Province of Cebu, central
Philippines, of channels of information about methods of
contraception and the social and cultural factors
affecting those channels. A model is developed showing
that the flow from the source must first circulate within
a homogeneous circle and be legitimized there before effectively being accepted by members outside the circle,
through weak-tie interaction with others; detailed
sampling procedures.

Marcuse, Peter
1970   "Housing policy and social indicators:
        Strangers or siblings?" Working Paper No. 130.
        Berkeley, California: Institute of Urban and
        Regional Development, University of California.

The author suggests that although the goals of our
housing policy as presently stated, to build more and
better houses, are measurable and operational, and
progress toward them is being made, in fact these goals
unclearly state and conceal the real problems of housing.
The way these goals are formulated help some groups and
hurt others; thus the housing problems of the U.S. will be
met only when and if those goals are reformulated in terms
of the overall national interest. While goals criteria
are examined, data and indicators to enable such goal
formulation are not now available. Suggested is a matrix
for adequate indicators of six parallel categories in
which housing inputs can be grouped. Conceptual and
political problems are examined. Evaluation of present
goals suggests they may tell us whether we are moving
forward or not, but they do not specify whether we are on
the right road.

McHale, John
1967   "Science, technology and change." The Annals of
        the American Academy of Political and Social
        Science 373 (September):120-140. (Reprinted in
        Bertram M. Gross (ed.), 1969 Social Intelligence
        for America's Future. Boston: Allyn and
        Bacon).

A definitive comprehensive statement of the causal
connection between science, technology, change and social

indicators. Calls for innovation and integration of present indicators into new conceptual models for social accounting which can generate indicators of qualitative societal aspects. Such is necessitated by obsolescence of extant forms of expressing and conveying societal goal orientations and failure of present indicators to warn of scientific-technical consequences. This work contains many clues to how indicators can be developed along lines of being both a means of predicting and monitoring scientific-technical consequences and an end in framing societal goals.

    1969   The Future of the Future. New York: George Braziller, Inc.

Develops the main theme of man's potential capacity to determine his own futures, the outcome of which will depend on his ability to conceptualize those futures in humanly desirable terms and his willingness to engage himself with those alternatives. Chapters include "The Sense of the Future, The Future of the Past, The Future of the Present, The Future of the Future, Prophets of the Future, and Toward a Planetary Society."

Moore, Wilbert E. and Eleanor B. Sheldon
    1965   "Monitoring social change: A conceptual and programmatic statement." Pp. 144-152 in Proceedings of the Social Statistics Section, American Statistical Association, Washington, D.C.

An early provocative paper concerning the monitoring of large-scale structural transformations in American society, the trends of these changes and how deliberate policy does and could affect those trends. Five major areas are suggested for monitoring: the demographic base, major structural components, distributive features, aggregative features, and welfare, as a measurement of unplanned change and of deliberate social intervention.

Olson, Mancur, Jr.
    1968   "Economics, sociology, and the best of all possible worlds." The Public Interest 12 (Summer):96-118.

Under Daniel Bell and Alice Rivlin as co-chairmen, Olson had immediate responsibility for the Social Report of HEW; discussion of issues raised in Panel on Social Indicators in preparing the Social Report, primarily interdisciplinary differences between economics and sociology; critique of the "ideal" society of both economics and sociology and what Olson sees as irreconcilable differences between the two; continuing and increasing need for multidisciplinary communication and collaboration.

Ozbekhan, Hasan
1969   "Planning theory."   Ekistics 28 (October):296-299.

Develops the theory that the contextual meaning of an event today is far more important than the event itself - a new way of thinking about planning; inadequacies of the Deterministic Planning System of the scientific approach for problems of today.

Richta, Radovan and Oto Sulc
1969   "Forecasting and the scientific and technological revolution."   International Social Science Journal 21:563-573.

From a philosophical orientation relevant to the development of modern civilizations and their futures, this author attempts to clarify the conditions in which futures research may become an active factor in efforts to master the development of society. Suggests the framework will proceed simultaneously and continously through three phases: 1) the scientific phase, defining possible alternative futures and their consequences; 2) based on data from phase one, development of plans for adoption of scientific and technological innovations with particular concern for optimum living and working conditions, material vs. cultural progress, etc.; and 3) with phase one data and phase two decisions, democratic public opinion to determine preferences, goals and social measures, all to allow for comparison, unification and feedback.

Sanders, Irwin T.
1958   "Theories of community development."   Rural Sociology 23 (March):1-12.

Traces the lineage of the concept from community organization and from economic development, and develops theoretical formulations on two levels: that of the practitioner, primarily administrative and action-oriented, and that of the social scientist, largely conceptual in orientation. Suggests four ways of viewing community development: 1) as a process, with a focus upon sequences of interaction; 2) as a method, means to an end; 3) as a program, consisting of content as well as procedures and 4) as a movement, involving personal commitment and emotional dynamics.

Schnore, Leo F.
    1961   "The myth of human ecology." Sociological
            Inquiry (Spring):128-139.

Four approaches to sociological analysis; individual
psychology, social psychology, psychological sociology and
macrosociology are reviewed in an effort to dispel the
"myth" that human ecology is marginal to sociology.
Ecology is viewed as one attempt to cope with the central
problem of sociological analyses and is considered as a
real potential for making a contribution to macro as
against a microsociology.

Stanford Research Institute
    1969   "Toward master social indicators." Educational
            Policy Research Center. SRI Project 6747, Re-
            search Memorandum EPRC-6747-2. Supported by
            Bureau of Research, U.S. Office of Education.
            (February) Menlo Park, California: Stanford Re-
            search Institute.

Stanford Research Institute; key considerations in development of comprehensive national social data system
beyond Social Report of HEW; aggregation of low level
indicators into master indicators; interrelationships of
goals, indicators and attainment levels; tables of
attainment categories, subcategories, and possible
indicators for each of seven areas related to the individual and to society.

Studer, Raymond G.
    1970   "Human systems design and the management of
            change." A paper presented at the Second Inter-
            national Conference on the Problems of
            Modernization in Asia and the Pacific, EAST-WEST
            Center (August 9-15) Honolulu, Hawaii.

A planning culture, toward which the U.S. is moving, is
one in which collective planning strategies are
participated in and supported by the membership as being
both necessary and desirable. The emphasis is upon directed response to the future with objectives identified
and resources mobilized for this purpose. Human behavior
is identified as the relevant unit of analysis in development of a behavior-contingent paradigm for the design and
maintenance of human systems. This paradigm for human
problem-solving tasks is sequential: 1) model (what ought
to be), 2) simulate (what would happen if . .), 3) implement and 4) test (what happens when . .). It is believed
that a controlled approach with varied alternatives to an
uncertain future is within our reach with adequate

management of change.   Various models and adaptations are
presented graphically, including an adaptation of Studer's
(1969).

Suter, Larry E.
    1971   "A 1966 replication of the 1962 occupational
           change in a generation analysis of older men:
           Path models as indicators of social change." A
           paper presented at the Annual Meetings of the
           Population Association of America (April 24)
           Washington, D.C.

    It is shown that components of socioeconomic changes
among minority groups can be measured with multiple
regression models.   This was done with white and Negro men
45 to 54 years old in 1962 and those same men in 1966 in
an attempt to replicate the Blau-Duncan social
stratification model.   In addition to trying to relate education to occupational status, a five variable model of
the socio-economic life cycle containing background characteristics, educational level, occupational status, and a
measure of income was used to relate the path of Negro men
to that of white men.

Terleckyj, Nestor
    1970   "The role of efficiency in achieving national
           goals." A paper presented at the Annual Meeting
           of the American Association for the Advancement
           of Science (December 29) Chicago, Illinois.

    An analysis aimed at development of methodology for
assessing range of available opportunities for achievement
of goals developed at National Planning Association in
National Priorities Study; suggests substantial progress
can be made by 1980 through adoption of certain efficient
innovative approaches and activities.

Tussing, A. Dale and John A. Henning
    1970   "Long-run growth of non-defense government
           expenditures in the United States." (August,
           Working draft) Syracuse, New York: Educational
           Policy Research Center, Syracuse University Re-
           search Corporation.

    Focusing on determinants related to the time trend of
public spending, this study finds a variety of more or
less independent factors operant, some influencing only
certain types of public expenditures, and certain types of
expenditures affected by more than one force.   Examined in
this context are: social insurance, urbanization, income,
displacement effect (Peacock and Wiseman's pattern in the

United Kingdom), war and cold war, stabilization policy, age composition of population, automobile, public-private productivity differentials, revenue productivity, constraints, critical limit theorem, marginal propensity for government expenditure and ideology. Presented in textual and tabular form are results of testing hypotheses relating to these factors (all except ideology, felt to be incapable of statistical test), using the method of least squares. Also examined are issues of taxes and the Federal share of expenditures.

Van Til, Sally Bould and Jon Van Til
    1971   "The lower class and the future of inequality."
            A paper presented at the Annual Meeting of the
            American Sociological Association (August)
            Denver, Colorado.

Contends that neither the "culture of poverty" or "blocked opportunity" hypotheses of lower class behavior are empirically accurate. A third conceptual perspective, "adaptive drift," is proposed to reflect observations that lower-class behavior is characterized by both situational variability and retention of learned cultural modes. The model's policy implications are clearly related to reducing class inequalities and serving to facilitate objective indication of effectiveness--that is, the return of accountable democratic control to both the private and public sectors of society.

Watt, Kenneth
    1970   "A model of society." Simulation 14
            (April):153- 164.

A general environmental model of human society is proposed to explicate the factors which are interdependent with the ecosystem; for a better analysis of the social costs and consequences of policy decisions.

Zucker, Charles
    1971   "Environmental measurement." New York: City
            College of the City University of New York,
            School of Architecture and Environmental Studies, Urban Research Group.

An article reviewing the theory of measurement as it relates to environmental indicators and proposals for innovative procedures.

Abel-Smith, Brian
    1970   "Public expenditure on the social services."
            Pp. 12-20 in Muriel Nissel (ed.), Social Trends.
            London: Her Majesty's Central Statistical
            Office.

In this article, trends in public expenditures on selected social services are analyzed for the period
1951-1968 with special emphasis on the last few years.
The figures quoted are mainly for the United Kingdom.
Sections include the concept of social services, the classification of services, trends in public expenditure,
demographic trends, education services, health services,
welfare and child care and income support.

Alberts, David S.
    1970   A Plan for Measuring the Performance of Social
            Programs. New York: Praeger Publishers.

Methodology based on operations research is used to
formulate a model to measure social goals and programs
from an individualistic viewpoint and from a societal
viewpoint, and then to develop approximate measures of
societal performance from the individual and collective
viewpoints. Data gathered in Philadelphia provided the
basis for the statistical selection of the variables for
use as logical criteria against which the program effectiveness could be measured. Research design, sampling,
questionnaire, data analysis is presented in text and
tabular form, and detailed further in the appendices.

Albuquerque Urban Observatory
    1971   Social Reporting for Albuquerque: Development
            of a Social Indices System. Albuquerque, New
            Mexico: Albuquerque Urban Observatory.

Albuquerque is one of eight cities participating in a
two year social indicator study, Government Impact
Indices, funded by HUD. This report of phase one concerns
identification of the social indicators, while phase two,
to be completed later, will concentrate on testing the
indicators and assessing their reliability. Albuquerque's
model delineates the following areas: education, health,
community participation, equality of opportunity and level
of living, with several indicators of the extent of quality for each area. The five areas were not intended to be

comprehensive of all social conditions, but rather examples of conditions within which specific quantitative
measures could be developed. Included are the sources of
data available and problems with its use for each
indicator measurement. Projections for phase two are
given. An appendix summarizes the work under way in the
other cities of the program: Atlanta, Cleveland, Denver,
Kansas City (Missouri and Kansas), Milwaukee, Nashville
and San Diego, with selected indicators identified in each
city.

Anderson, James G.
    1970   "Causal models and the evaluation of health
            service systems." Working paper No. 43.
            Lafayette, Indiana: Purdue University,
            Institute for the Study of Social Change, De-
            partment of Sociology.

    Path analysis used to construct a causal model of
health service system in New Mexico; allows prediction as
to how change in variables of the population composition
or in the organization and utilization of the health services affect other variables in the system; mathematical
equations for the predictions of the effects of these
changes, estimates of path coefficients based on U.S.
Census data and vital statistics.

    1971   "Path analysis: A new approach to modeling
            health service delivery systems." A paper pre-
            sented at the Joint National Conference on Major
            Systems, National Meeting of the Operations Re-
            search Society of America (October 27-29)
            Anaheim, California.

    Presents a methodology which permits the empirical
validation of hypotheses concerning the effects of socio-
cultural processes on health service systems. Using a
causal modeling technique - path analysis - a structural
model is developed and analyzed which relates social, economic and demographic characteristics of New Mexico
counties to the infant mortality rate as an index of
health. Path coefficients have been estimated and dynamic
programming has been utilized to predict the
direct/indirect effects of changes in population composition on the New Mexico health index.

Applied Urbanetics, Inc.
    1968   Social Maps, District of Columbia Population and
            Social Problems Characteristics: 1968, Data by
            Census Tract. Washington, D.C.: Applied
            Urbanetics, Inc.

110

A summary of the premises, services and operations of
the organization, specializing in the application of computer technology to urban problem solving. The novel emphasis is through computer mapping that analyzes and
combines the effect of all relevant social elements on a
single sheet. Other services are the AID system, a
computerized index to 1400 Federal assistance programs,
REVIEW News Service and Federalist Aid Specialist services. Sample maps, one of the District of Columbia, are
included showing the kind of presentation and information
available.

Babcock, Lyndon R., Jr. and Niren L. Nagda
    1971   "Indices of air quality." A paper presented at
            the Annual Meeting of the American Association
            for the Advancement of Science (December 27)
            Philadelphia, Pennsylvania.

The need for air quality indices is widely accepted.
Governments, scientists, industry and laymen want to know
"how bad it is," preferably through an easy-to-compute,
understandable, combined index. The U.S. Environmental
Protection Agency recently established ambient air quality
standards for six pollutants: oxidants, sulfur oxides,
nitrogen dioxide, carbon monoxide, particulate matter and
hydrocarbons. Despite admitted deficiencies of these
standards, but because they are currently the best available approximations, the Oak Ridge National Laboratory in
cooperation with the National Science Foundation has used
the EPA standards to formulate the Oak Ridge Air Quality
Index (ORAQI), enabling meaningful air quality comparisons
to be made across the country. ORAQI weights and sums
five of the six pollutants. Hydrocarbons are not included
in the model as they are assumed to be a pollutant
precursor rather than an actual pollutant; thus are not
included in the oxidant factor. A monograph for easy computation of the ORAQI is given. Rankings of ten U.S.
cities are made using the index of data from 1962-1967.
Use and limitations of and need for more sophisticated
measures are discussed. Tables show proportions and standards for pollutants.

Bennett, M. K.
    1937   "On measurement of relative national standards
            of living." Quarterly Journal of Economics
            (February):317-335.

An early attempt to derive a static measurement model
for a cross-national comparison of indices of standards of
(national) living. Indices of scores by rank and arithmetic averages are explored.

Bettman, James R.
    1971   "Measuring individuals' priorities for national
            goals: A methodology and empirical example."
            Policy Sciences 2:373-390.

    This study suggests a methodology for measuring indi-
viduals' priorities for national goals on an interval
scale developed by Bechtel. Multivariate, discriminant,
and cluster analytic procedures are then outlined for
gaining policy insights from the scale value data. The
feasibility of this methodology is tested by application
to an empirical example carried out in 1970 concerning
national priorities for eight possible national goals.
Extensions of the technique and further areas of application are proposed.

Biderman, Albert D.
    1971   Kinostatistics for Social Indicators. Washing-
            ton, D.C.: Bureau of Social Science Research,
            Inc.

    Contends that limitations of the print medium make it a
crucial responsibility for social scientists to develop
capacities for conveying indicators using other than
static information media. Established psycho/physical
properties can be applied to displaying data using (a)
more concrete representations than verbal or numerical,
(b) three visual dimensions rather than two, (c) visu-
al/auditory nonverbal communication, (d) color mixes and
motion to represent variable interaction or feedback functions. Hence, the neologism "kinostatistics" refers to
the substantive integration of social content, analysis
technique and display of communication-symbolic or iconic-
media.

Bixhorn, Herbert
    1971   "Cluster analysis: An application to typology
            of urban neighborhoods." A paper presented at
            the Annual Meeting of the American Statistical
            Association (August) Fort Collins, Colorado.

    Discusses the difficulties in using summed-ranks and
principal components in attempting to classify census
tracts on several variables. Suggests cluster analysis as
a technique to classify geographic sub-areas of a city
into a meaningful typology of objects tending to be similar. The ensuing clusters are used as general socio-
economic indicators.

Boruch, Robert F.
    1971a   "Assuring confidentiality of response in social

research: A note on strategies." American
Sociologist 6 (November):308-311.

Two methods are proposed for assuring confidentiality
without jeopardizing either the respondent or the
researcher. The randomized response technique utilizes
statistical manipulations and probabilities for answers to
the question of principal interest to the researcher and
to an innocuous unrelated question. Limitations and
simplifications are discussed. The second technique
employs an administrative or logistical model based on
consolidated longitudinal data about the respondent. The
author evaluates this technique as being simple to
understand and to implement, with perhaps fewer methodological problems than the first strategy.

    1971b "Maintaining confidentiality of data in educa-
           tional research: A systematic analysis." Amer-
           ican Psychologist 26:413-430.

Presenting an integrated picture of the limitations and
problems that the need for confidentiality imposes on longitudinal research, this paper recognizes the social scientist's role and needs as an investigator, and the
respondent's right to personal privacy. An educational
research information flow chart provides the identifiable
steps in the process at which various methods and strategies may be used to provide the maximum confidentiality
required. Procedure moves through the assumptions and
inquiry development, to survey execution, document processing, creation of the statistical file and the identifi-
er file, the data processing, and the final operational
merger. Danger of data abuse is related to the kind of
information solicited and the structure of the information
system. The legal perspective is touched only lightly but
references are given for this aspect.

Boruch, Robert F., John D. Larkin, Leroy Wolins and Arthur
MacKinney
    1970   "Alternative methods of analysis: Multitrait-
           multimethod data." Educational and Psychologi-
           cal Measurement 30 (Winter):833-853.

Evidence has suggested some inadequacies in the
Campbell-Fiske multitrait-multimethod af analysis, in that
measurement error is not allowed for, the model's inherent
assumptions of additivity of effects and homogeneous variances may not be satisfied by the data, and the differences in means and variances of the observations may be a
function of the particular scale. This paper examines the
usefulness of two types of models for specific sets of
data, the first a three way ANOVA model as suggested by

Stanley (1961), and the second a less restrictive factor
analytic model proposed by Wolins (1964). Some additional
information to that obtained through the Campbell-Fiske
method seems worth considering: the extent to which
error, trait and method variance effects the observations
made with a specific measure, consideration of the measures' reliabilities and the possible heterogeneity of
error variance.

Boruch, Robert F. and Leroy Wolins
    1970   "Procedure for estimation of trait, method, and
            error variance attributable to a measure." Edu-
            cational and Psychological Measurement 30
            (Autumn): 547-574.

Two data sets are analyzed by an expansion of the
Campbell and Fiske (1959) multitrait-multimethod matrices.
Findings indicate that with three or more methods of
measuring three traits, one can determine the extent to
which the observation is influenced by each particular
method for each particular trait; the degree of
discriminant validation; and the extent to which individual differences contribute to the observations, independent
of the particular method-trait combination used in measurement. A linear model is developed; goodness of fit can
be indicated through the use of chi-square or the desirability of attributes of a solution.

Boucher, Wayne I.
    1971   "Futures research and national priorities." New
            Priorities Vol. 1, Number 1.

From mere curiosity or diversion, man has moved to
recognition that interest in the future is useful and necessary. Without responsible anticipation, too many
decisions today may have regrettable or disastrous consequences tomorrow. Futures research is concerned with the
process of social judgment and its results, potential
value changes, and new patterns of interaction of people
and institutions; its essence lies in generating alternative futures. Briefly mentioned are some of the
developing methodologies that have been or may be useful:
systems analysis, Delphi technique, mathematical modeling,
operational gaming, scenario writing, cross-impact analysis technique and social indicators.

Brown, Robert M., Nina I. McClelland, Rolf A. Deininger
and Michael F. O'Connor
    1971   "A water quality index - Crashing the psycholog-
            ical barrier." A paper presented at the Annual
            Meeting of the American Association for the

Advancement of Science (December 28)
Philadelphia, Pennsylvania.

Needing a simple, consistent and uniform method of
measuring water quality and a means to convey clearly that
quality level, the Delphi process was used, with 74
experts, for development of a mathematical expression of a
Water Quality Index (WQI). The WQI reflects nine physical
and chemical parameters; dissolved oxygen, fecal
coliforms, pH, 5 day BOD, nitrate, phosphate, temperature,
turbidity, and total solids. Maximum levels were set for
toxic elements and pesticides beyond which the index would
automatically become zero. General versus specific use
indices were evaluated, with the conclusion that the
single SWI was more effective and meaningful than use
indices such as Fish and Wildlife (FAWL) and public water
supply (PWS). A field sampling and evaluation project
begun in May, 1971, is to extend long enough to cover
season variations.

Bryce, Herrington J.
    1971   "Income and general welfare: An identification
            of the socio-economic gaps between low and high
            income regions." Unpublished manuscript. Wash-
            ington, D.C.: The Urban Institute.

Difficulties in identifying the gaps between high and
low income areas for effective program development perhaps
cannot be met either through indicators with simple percentages or more sophisticated techniques as factor analysis. This paper presents an alternative methodology:
choosing variables on the basis of theory, social policy
interest, and acceptable intercorrelation. A discriminant
function was run which defined a linear combination of
variables to differentiate high and low income
metropolitan areas for demography, housing, education and
employment. A table presents Standard Metropolitan Statistical Areas (SMSA) with the probabilities in each of
the four categories for each of the 222 SMSA identified.

Campbell, Donald T.
    1971   "Methods for the experimenting society." Pre-
            liminary draft of a paper presented in abbrevi-
            ated form to the Eastern Psychological Associa-
            tion (April 17) and to the American Psychologi-
            cal Association (September 5) Washington, D.C.

This paper delineates the characteristics of the
experimenting society as action-oriented, evolutionary,
honest, scientific, open, decentralized, responsive,
nondogmatic, etc.; hopefully, the United States is one of
several nations in which such a society might emerge. Ex-

amining the social science methodologist as the servant of
such a society, his job is not to say what is to be done,
but rather to say what has been done, with the goal of
learning more from whatever innovations may be chosen
through the political process. Varied methodologies and
techniques are discussed and evaluated, some alternative
methods are proposed; problems and difficulties are examined to see which difficulties may be alleviated through
adaptation. Archival indicators and voluntary verbal
measures are specifically examined as quality of life
measures for social experimentation.

Central Statistical Office
    1970   Social Trends. No. 1. A publication of the
            Government Statistical Service, Muriel Nissel
            (ed.). London, England: Her Majesty's
            Stationery Office.

    Social Trends is intended to meet the need for measur-
ing social benefits with general economic progress by
drawing together, initially once a year, some of the more
significant statistical series relating to social policies
and conditions. The underlying theme is information about
people, rather than about governments or institutions. It
opens with a series of articles on general developments in
social statistics, public expenditures on social services,
and the growth of population to the end of this century.
Following these articles there is an extensive list of
tables and charts arranging data on the United Kingdom in
terms of public expenditure, population and environment,
employment, leisure, personal income and expenditure,
social security, welfare services, health, education,
housing, justice and law.

Clark, Terry N.
    1971   "Citizens' values and preference revelation:
            Notes on a proposal for operationalization."
            (August) Working draft. Chicago, Illinois:
            University of Chicago, Department of Sociology.

    This working paper reviews alternatives for assessing
public policy. A procedure, based on a set of assumptions
about citizen's values and collective decisions, for
public policy assessment in terms of citizen demand is
suggested. A questionnaire format is proposed for determining this "demand" which assigns each individual a
fixed-equal or weighted-number of votes or resources to
allocate among decisional categories. Various sources of
bias and means of reduction inherent to such a procedure
are considered in relation to the assumptive format that
establishes its boundaries of reliability.

116

Cornblit, Oscar, Torcuato S. Di Tella and Ezequiel Gallo
    1968   "A model for political change in Latin America."
            Social Science Information 7:13-48.

    Sets forth a series of provisional hypotheses which
constitute a simulation model of political and social
change processes which have generated the historical developments within Latin American nations. Using two sets
of definitive variables--actor and societal--thirty empirical hypotheses, readily expressible as linear, finite-
increment equations, are proposed, not deduced, for
explaining or predicting the evolution in time of a given
nation in terms of the model's endogenous variables. The
data bank on Latin American societies being constructed
using this model should refine and integrate these hypotheses into a more comprehensive theory of social change.

D'Agostino, Ralph B.
    1971   Social Indicators: A Statistician's View. A
            paper presented in the Symposium on Social
            Indicators at the Annual Meeting of The American
            Psychological Association. (September).
            Boston, Massachusetts: Boston University, De-
            partment of Mathematics.

    Several interrelated problem areas are of concern to
the statistician and in which he can prove helpful. Among
these are the purposes of social indicators, and indeed,
what social variables should be considered as conceivable
variables related to quality of life; what data should be
collected in view of the difficulty in not being able to
directly measure variables of interest; how does one
collect these time series data guarding against problems
of multicollinearity; and how should the collected data be
handled and analyzed. Particular attention is given to
possible simulation in situations where one has many variables and the data is sparse. In social indicator research it appears that secular trends, cyclical movements,
irregular fluctuations and seasonal variations must be
taken into account. Various techniques are discussed for
relating lead indicators in one time period to coincident
indicators in another period. Finally, the author
presents a select bibliography in canonical correlation,
forecasting, indicators and index numbers, path analysis,
regression analysis, simulation, time series analysis and
other areas useful in analyzing social indicator data.

Day, Lincoln H. and Alice Taylor Day
    1971   "Indicators of social conditions related to
            natality differentials among developed
            countries." A paper presented at the Annual

Meeting of the Population Association of America
(April 22-24) Washington, D.C.

A progress report on research being done in 20
countries which have substantial control over natality and
mortality. Hypothesizes that in these countries natality
will be lowest under two polar sets of conditions: where
the instrumentalities through which individuals as such
(distinct from their statuses as family members) can sat-
isfy their personal needs and interests are either (1)
abundant, or (2) scarce; a causal continuum, the end
points being most conducive to low natality; list of 23
indicators; explanation and illustration of weighting
(grading) procedure.

de Jouvenel, Bertrand
    1966   "A letter on predicting." American Behavioral
            Scientist 9 (June):51.

It is argued that it would be illuminating if forecasts
by a group of experts in some particular field were to be
aggregated into a predictive value, and then checked
against forecasts made by a random group of citizens with
no special relevant expertise. If the comparison were
made against three or four random groups of citizens,
graded for general knowledge, then findings might indicate
whether that aspect of the future being questioned, as a
function of general opinions, increases or decreases as a
rise in the scale of general and then special competence
occurs.

Drewnowski, Jan
    1970   Studies in the Measurement of Levels of Living
            and Welfare. Report No. 70.3. Geneva,
            Switzerland: United Nations Research Institute
            for Social Development.

Studies presented in this volume extend earlier efforts
of the United Nations concerned with the measurement of
levels of living. "Measuring Social Variables in Real
Terms" discusses concepts and principles, while the other
two papers, "The Level of Living Index, New Version" and
"The Level of Welfare Index", seek to transform the concept and principles into operational tools. "The Level of
Welfare" is conceived as a function of the "level of
living", but is not entirely determined by it since
factors other than the flow of goods and services over a
period of time affect the need states of individuals.

Dyck, Harold J. and George J. Emery
    1970   Social Futures: Alberta 1970-2005. Edmonton,

Canada: Human Resources Research Council of
           Alberta.

This report summarizes the results of six forecasting
exercises. The topics covered in these exercises are as
follows: future changes in values and social goal orientations, future of the family, leisure and recreation in
the future, intercultural relations in the future, the
future of politics, and future needs and problems of the
individual. These types were selected for their relevance
to the future of education. The purpose of the study was
to prepare a series of forecasts on social phenomena which
tend to have an impact on education. A "Delphi" process
was used where a group of informed, knowledgeable, and
expert individuals were given questionnaires and were to
rate forecasts in 11 areas: Canadian society, value
change, family, religion, education, leisure, politics,
native people, relations with others, law and disorder,
and mental illness. The results and descriptions of these
forecasts are presented in profile form.

Edwards, Clark and Robert Coltrane
    1972   "Economic and social indicators of rural devel-
            opment from an economic viewpoint." A paper
            presented at the Annual Meeting of the Southern
            Agricultural Economics Association (February
            14-16) Richmond, Virginia.

Valid indicators to describe and explain rural development problems must have these characteristics: 1) be
based on solid theory, not brute-force empiricism; 2) have
analytical content, not be merely descriptive; 3) indicate
structure of multicounty areas, not just aggregative; 4)
be computed for functional economic areas; and 5) be based
on data capable of giving reliable estimates of structure.
State economic areas, Rand McNally trading areas, Office
of Business Economic regions, Governors' delineation under
A-95, and Basic Economic Research Areas are examined as
units of observation, as well as the appropriateness of
alternative delineations, specific variables aggregated
and not aggregated, descriptive properties and interactions. Tables present the framework used to identify the
variables, specific variables and weights, tests and
indicators of differences for specific variables, for the
alternative delineations, and regression and correlation
coefficients. The variables presented are: 1) percentage
of population urban, 1960; 2) percentage of population
farm, 1960; 3) percentage of employment white collar,
1960; 4) percentage of employment finance, insurance and
real estate, 1960; 5) income per capita, 1960; 6) percentage of families with incomes less than $3,000; 7) percent-
age of sound housing units; 8) percentage of persons age
25 and over with high school or more education, 1960; 9)

percentage of commercial bonus with sales greater than $10,000, 1964; 10) retail sales per capita, 1963; 11) bank deposits per capita, 1960; and 12) local government expenditures per capita, 1962.

Engen, Trygg
　　1971　"Use of the sense of smell in determining envi-
　　　　　ronmental quality." A paper presented at the
　　　　　Annual Meeting of the American Association for
　　　　　the Advancement of Science (December 27-31)
　　　　　Philadelphia, Pennsylvania.

Considers the subjective or mental experience of odor with regard to judging the quality of the environment. Odor classification, identification, pollution detection thresholds, scaling and the effects of adaptation, intensity, unpleasantness and quality are discussed. A description is given of the methods which have been developed for analysis of each of these aspects of odor. Concludes that the psychology of how response biases, preferences, and aversions are learned dictates that man's response to his environment goes beyond the measurements of psycho-physical instruments.

Etzioni, Amitai and Edward W. Lehman
　　1967　"Some dangers in 'valid' social measurement."
　　　　　The Annals of the American Academy of Political
　　　　　and Social Science 373 (September):1-15.
　　　　　(Reprinted in Bertram M. Gross (ed.), 1969
　　　　　Social Intelligence for America's Future.
　　　　　Boston: Allyn and Bacon).

Examines the pitfalls and analytical considerations which inhere to "valid" social measurements and the dysfunctions they may have for societal planning. Focusing on the question of internal validity, the problem areas of fractional measurement, indirect measurement, and problems of formalistic-aggregative measurement of collective attributes are considered in terms of two classes of dysfunction: (1) invalid conclusions and erroneous policy decisions, and (2) ignoring conceptual dimensions. Advocates a nongovernmental body should be formed to use this critical perspective to examine the indicators developed or used by government.

Flax, Michael J.
　　1970　"Selected education indicators for twenty-one
　　　　　major cities: Some statistical benchmarks."
　　　　　(Preliminary draft paper 136-4) Washington,
　　　　　D.C.: The Urban Institute.

The second of a projected series designed to evaluate
aspects of the quality of life in one city or metropolitan
area by comparing in similar terms to that in other cities
or metropolitan areas. This paper is an in-depth study of
education; suggests a conceptual framework for
categorizing educational indicators; discusses twenty-
eight possible indicators and presents data on twelve of
these (for which adequate data was available) for the
twenty-one central cities of the eighteen metropolitan
areas covered in the first report. The twelve indicators
are broadly grouped into: 1) educational effectiveness;
2) direct educational input related factors; 3) indirect
educational input related factors; and 4) educational
interest and support. An appendix includes data calcula-
tions and limitations on their use, selected statistics on
the twenty-one cities and the rationale for releasing
achievement test score data to the general public.

Flora, Cornelia Butler and Jan L. Flora
    1971   "Macro-model variables relevant to social ac-
            counting." Contribution No. 34. Manhattan,
            Kansas: Kansas State University, Population Re-
            search Laboratory, Agricultural Experiment
            Station.

Based on data and studies from the Cauca Valley in
Colombia, this paper presents a variety of macro-level
variables for different units of analysis, based on the
premise that such measures should not be aggregate but
rather indicative of a structural property of the unit
under study. Two types of variables are suggested: one
uses group indicators as elements (differentiation,
solidarity and some centrality measures); the second uses
distribution of aggregated characteristics (inequality
indices and some centrality measures). Variables derived
through Guttman scaling techniques and Gini indices are
presented in table form for general differentiation and
organizational differentiation. Other presentations
include: relative centrality, national diplomatic
contacts, and economic dependency; nonelite and local
elite solidarity; organizational boundary maintenance; and
path analysis of structural variables with peasant organizations.

Fontela, E.
    1969   "Introducing sociological forecasting into eco-
            nomic models of the future." Futures 1
            (September):380-381.

A very brief discussion of the necessity of a dialogue
between sociologists and economists in identifying attitude changes towards the economic process. This dialogue,

and the subsequent merging of sociological forecasting and economic forecasting, will be facilitated by the evolution of sociology towards a quantitative oriented discipline, sociometrics, as in the recent year's economics has progressively evolved towards econometrics.

Forrester, Jay W.
    1971   "The computer and social catastrophe."
            Intellectual Digest 2 (November):57-60.

The human mind cannot interpret complex social systems well enough to construct useful models of social systems, thus further hampering the construction of computer models. The use of dynamic models of social systems, such as an urban model, is best yet must be fed by reliable and valid indicators of change in the social system. What is valid for one social system, though, may not be valid for another; witness the U.S.-modeled industrialization of underdeveloped nations. Present policy based on intuition is leading to insurmountable pressures in the future.

Friedly, Philip H.
    1969   "Welfare indicators for public facility
            investments in urban renewal areas." Socio-
            Economic Planning Science 3:291-314.

This paper defines a role for public facility investment in urban renewal areas in terms of benefits and costs accruing to society impacting from such public investment. The author points out the interactions between program objectives and welfare indicators, a structure for public facility analysis, the output effects and public facility benefits, and some policy observations resulting from such analysis.

General Electric
    1970   "A case study of a systems analysis approach to
            social responsibility programs: General
            Electric's commitment to progress in equal
            opportunity and minority relations." Corporate
            Industrial Relations ERC-49 (10M)8-70. New
            York, New York.

Outlines General Electric's new emphasis on equal opportunity and minority relations, requiring a systems analysis approach which takes into account such aspects as environment, corporate role, management support, employee relations, social problems and business opportunities. The question of measurement entails establishing objectives, goals and criteria by which future progress can be measured. As bench marks are established, progress can be

reviewed annually in overcoming problems encountered by
operating components within the organization which
include: recruiting and retention, upward mobility,
management/union/employee understanding, effective utilization of the new work force, and EO/MR community involvement. Appendix D details the EO/MR measurement format instructions.

Gitter, A. George
     1970   Factor Analytical Approach to Indexing
             Multivariate Data. Communication Research
             Center. Report No. 43. Boston: Boston Univer-
             sity.

     This paper presents an approach for aggregating indi-
vidual measures by factor analyzing a state's x variables
matrix to construct social indicators. Factor scores of
selected factors are used as the state's indicators of
major components of the indicator, while the weighted sum
of these scores becomes the state's indicator. Procedures
for deriving national indicators, as well as for computing
post-base year indicator values are discussed.

Gitter, A. George and E. Knoche
     1971   Importance Ratings of Sixteen Aspects of Life.
             Communication Research Center. Report No. 59.
             Boston: Boston University.

     In order to explore the structure of priorities of var-
ious aspects of "quality of life," this study (N = 104
male and female undergraduates) examined the ratings of
sixteen aspects of life, in terms of importance. The relationship between these ratings and selected demographic
and attitudinal variables were investigated. Three
factors (social acceptability, security, aesthetic-
intellectual) which accounted for 65 percent of the variance, were extracted from factor analysis of importance
ratings of the sixteen aspects of life.

Goldstein, Sidney and Kurt Mayer
     1964   "Population decline and the social and
             demographic structure of an American city."
             American Sociological Review 29 (Febru-
             ary):48-54.

     An analysis of the effects of population decline on the
social and demographic structure of an American city of
over 100,000 population. An interesting use of census
data and secondary sources to study social and demographic
variables.

Gordon, Andrew C., Donald T. Campbell et al.
1970   "Recommended accounting procedures for the eval-
        uation of improvements in the delivery of state
        social services." Preliminary draft. Evanston,
        Illinois: Northwestern University, Center for
        Urban Affairs.

Reviews relevant methodology and proposes possible
means for evaluating whether specific changes made in mode
of delivery of state services have had the desired effects
and have been free from undesirable side effects.
Methodology recommended is that of the "control series"
version of the "interrupted time-series design." On question of measurement, multiple indicators, as different as
possible in method, are recommended. Reviews extensively
many categories of problems and possibilities in representing community judgments; for example, measurement of
community opinion to focus on client's perception of
agency performance and the quality of service available
rather than asking personal questions. Also reviewed extensively the many possible ways of conducting the survey.
Specific data-gathering means recommended include:
certified satisfied customers accounting, customer
interviews in the self-certification office or intake
office and staff member evaluations of agency programs.

Gurr, Ted and Charles Ruttenburg
1968   "A causal model of civil strife: A comparative
        analysis using new indices." American Political
        Science Review 62 (December):1104-1124.

The author describes some results of an attempt to
assess and refine a causal model of the general conditions
of several forms of civil strife, using cross-sectional
analyses of data collected for 114 polities. He reviews
the theoretical considerations,the operational measures,
the results of his analyses, and puts forward a revised
causal model to determine the relative magnitude of civil
strife in 114 politics.

Guttman, Louis
1971   "Social problem indicators." The Annals of The
        American Academy of Political and Social Science
        393 (January):40-46.

This is a progress report on the development of a
"mapping sentence" which defines a universe of observations for social problem indicators to guide policy formation by Israel's ministries. Emphasis of the theoretical
discussion is focused on the concept of "problem" and the
need to distinguish these observations from other behav-

ior. Illustrations are given from the Continuing Study
which have used the "mapping sentence" for designing observations for "social problem indicators."

Hage, Jerald
    1971   "An interdisciplinary investigation into the
            comparative causes of societal stability and
            instability: A longitudinal analysis of Great
            Britain, Germany, France, and Italy for the
            period of 1825-1965." A proposal to the
            National Science Foundation for a research
            grant. Madison, Wisconsin: The University of
            Wisconsin, Department of Sociology.

    System analysis is to be used to identify and
authenticate twenty-eight variables and their indicators
for comparative analysis of societal stability and
instability in the four countries. System analysis needs
the coordinates of the system, for this purpose the social
indicators; utilizes the scores for these indicators to
denote stable and unstable states; and examines feedback
processes to identify the causes of those that work and
which variables are involved. Three critical processes,
each involving a different domain of variables, are adjustment, adaptiveness and control. A typology of the
variables is given graphically, including basic dimensions, social inputs, social structure, control processes,
social performances and social outputs, with Figure 2
listing the indicators for each dimension.

Herrick, Neal Q. and Robert P. Quinn
    1971   "The working conditions survey as a source of
            social indicators." Monthly Labor Review
            (April):15-24.

    Presents preliminary findings from a nationwide survey
of employed persons 16 years of age and older, working a
minimum of 20 hours weekly and is concerned with workers'
attitudes toward job satisfaction and labor standards
problems.

Holmans, A. E.
    1970   "A forecast of effective demand for housing in
            Great Britain in the 1970's." Pp. 33-42 in
            Muriel Nissel (ed.), Social Trends. London:
            Her Majesty's Central Statistical Office.

    The forecast presented here is a conditional forecast
in that it is dependent on assumptions about the development of the national economy and the constancy of government housing policy in the 1970's. The article begins

with an outline of the analytical basis of the forecast;
the demographic elements are then discussed, followed by
the distribution between tenures of the demand by new
households. Flows of households between tenures are then
considered, followed by the demand by owner-occupiers for
better houses. After an account of the forecasts for the
owner-occupied sector in total and the local authority
sector, the concluding section brings together the total
forecast and its implications for the balance between the
number of households and the number of dwellings.

Johnson, Norman J. and Edward J. Ward
     1970   A New Approach to Citizen Participation: An
             Exploration Tying Information and Utilization.
             Pittsburgh, Pennsylvania: Carnegie-Mellon Uni-
             versity, School of Urban and Public Affairs.

     Some strategies in ensuring wider citizen participation
might include cooperation, consultation, education,
therapy and community power. Three defining parameters
suggested are social unit, constituency and meeting in
face-to-face encounters. A "panel information procedure"
is suggested as a method for having the information needed
at the right time, right place and with the right people
to effect change.

Jones, Kenneth J. and Wyatt C. Jones
     1970   "Toward a typology of American cities." Journal
             of Regional Science 10:217-224.

     Extension of the analysis done by Hadden and Borgatta
in "American Cities: Their Social Characteristics," by
use of factor analysis of second-order principal components. Tables showing cities' rankings on urban growth
and development factor, on the socio-economic status
factor, and arranging findings into 2x2 typology of high
and low urban growth and development, and high and low
socio-economic status.

Jones, Martin V. and Michael J. Flax
     1970   Cities Vs. Suburbs: A Comparative Analysis of
             Six Qualities of Urban Life. Washington, D.C.:
             The Urban Institute. (Preliminary Draft).

     This report deals with a comparison between 18 cities
and their suburbs on six aspects of the quality of urban
life. The aspects compared are: unemployment, poverty,
infant mortality, suicides, robberies and traffic deaths.
Suburban data is found by subtracting data for cities from
the data for metropolitan areas.

126

Kimball, Thomas L.
    1971   "Why environmental quality indices?" A paper
            presented at the Annual Meeting of the American
            Association for the Advancement of Science (De-
            cember 27-31) Philadelphia, Pennsylvania.

    The National Wildlife Federation's Environmental Quali-
ty (EQ) Index, designed to provide a comprehensive review
of published information on factors affecting environmental quality, is presented in rather simple language and
graphics readily understood by most people. First published in the fall of 1969, six natural resources were
evaluated: air, water, soil, forests, wildlife and
minerals. In 1970, a seventh item, living space, was
added. The 1971 score indicated a slippage from 57 to
55.5 EQ points. The scientific community is urged to
appoint ethics committees for the various resource
disciplines to discern scientific truths from among conflicting analyses; an advocacy role is recommended for
scientists to mold public opinion and to formulate
guidelines for improved natural environment.

Krendel, Ezra S.
    1970   "A case study of citizen complaints as social
            indicators." IEEE Transactions on Systems Sci-
            ence and Cybernetics. SSC-6 (October):265-272.

    Demonstrates the applicability of systems engineering
to urban quality of life. Conceives of social indicators
as the measure, through negative feedback loops, of the
citizenry's perception as to the gap between the goals of
an urban area's service organizations and their actual
achievements.

Lamale, Helen H. and Joseph A. Clorety, Jr.
    1959   "City families as givers." Monthly Labor Review
            82 (December):1303-1311.

    This article draws on studies of family incomes,
expenditures, and savings conducted by the Bureau of Labor
Statistics at irregular intervals since 1888. Patterns of
city family giving to religions and private welfare
organizations, particularly those of a 1950 survey, are
analyzed and presented in tabular form. The computation
of average amount and percent of income contributed to
religions and welfare organizations by families for geographic regions constitutes an early effort at quantifying
a qualitative aspect of urban life.

Land, Kenneth C.
    1970   "Some problems of statistical inference in dy-

namic sociological models." A paper presented
at the Annual Meeting of the American Statistical Association (December 27-30) Detroit,
Michigan.

Considers the requirements of model precision and rigor
as they relate to deriving valid statistical inferences
from longitudinal model analysis of multiple units. Problems presented by Heise (1969), Blalock (1970), and Wiley
and Wiley (1970) are approached with an a priori specification of the correlation processes which are assumed to
generate the observations. A Markov scheme procedure is
then developed for estimating the degree of correlation
among the measurement errors or among the disturbances via
considering a one parameter process for a set of observations. This procedure can be generalized to indicators of
several variables over time if specified conditions of parameter identity are maintained.

Lebergott, Stanley
    1967   "Three aspects of labor supply since 1900." Pp.
            172-178 in Proceedings of the Social Statistics
            Section, American Statistical Association, Wash-
            ington, D.C.

Topics covered include patterns of labor supply; the
role of the family; the decline of the entrepreneur; and
new control mechanisms. Tables of data include average
weekly hours in factories since 1900; worker rates for men
and children, by age, since 1900; female worker rates in
white and nonwhite categories, by marital status; proportion of family income contributed by husband (in urban
families); labor force and employment; manufacturing
sales; concentration of employment in factories;
employment in manufacturing; and percent of factory
workers on piece work (1890) or incentive pay (1958).

Lingoes, James C. and Martin Pfaff
    1971   "Measurement of subjective welfare and satisfac-
            tion." A paper presented at the Annual Meeting
            of the American Economic Association jointly
            with the Association for the Study of the Grants
            Economy (December 27) New Orleans, Louisiana.

Outlines a methodology to supplement previous objective
indices of social welfare by representing goods and services in terms of satisfaction perceived by the consumer
and citizen. Methodology dealt with is that of nonmetric
scaling techniques as applicable to deriving Indices of
Consumer Satisfaction and Indices of Citizen Satisfaction.
General description given of dimensional simplification

via monotone distance analysis, monotone vector analysis, and probability evaluated partitions techniques; and procedures for scaling and aggregation of responses, including the uses of optimal weighted and optimal monotone scores.

Lionberger, Herbert F. and Betty S. Heifner
    1969   Occupational Views and Decisions of Missouri
            College of Agriculture Students: A Panel Study
            of 1964 Freshmen-1968 Seniors. Research
            Bulletin 967 (August) Columbia, Missouri: Uni-
            versity of Missouri, College of Agriculture,
            Agricultural Experiment Station.

This bifurcated panel study assesses idealized expectations people have of occupations opportunities for (1) being a materialistic doer, (2) management creativity, (3) extrinsic reward and personality fulfillment and how maturation of occupational interests in a college atmosphere is effected by prior residence as measured by the Strong Vocational Interest Blank. This test was administered to freshmen in 1964 and again in 1968 as seniors. Expectations and interests are posited as having significant quality of life implications; and, while these implications were not treated, this study is importantly concerned with measuring qualitative aspects of life.

Martin, Thomas and Kenneth J. Berry
    1971   "Generalizing to individuals: Another problem
            of evidence and inference." A paper presented
            at the Annual Meeting of The Rural Sociological
            Association (August) Denver, Colorado.

The authors elaborate the problem of inference beyond the conceptions of Robinson and others considering the issue through an exhaustive delineation of types which comprise the entire set of cross level inferences. A single type - trait to individual differences - was utilized to demonstrate the futility and logical fallacy of inferring both associations and differences across any two levels of analysis in either direction. This report ought to serve both as a preventative to meaningless findings and a note of caution in drawing theoretical interpretations from cross level inference.

McDevitt, Matthew and Thomson McGowan
    1970   New York State's Central Social Environment
            Study: Social Research for Comprehensive
            Planning. Albany, New York: New York State
            Office of Planning Coordination.

This report of a study by the New York Office of
Planning Coordination describes the need and methods for
development of a monitoring system to provide continuous
information on social attitudes and problems, and to evaluate systematically the state programs which deal with
these problems and steps undertaken to meet the needs.   To
develop an impact analysis system about the programs,
questioning and evaluation is being directed to six general categories relating to the creation and maintenance of
the programs, target groups, location, access and time of
the programs.   Appendices include an overall view of the
study design, models, methods, strategies, measurement,
data collection, analysis, reliability, and graphic presentation of the study design.

Mitchell, Arnold
    1967   Alternative Futures: An Exploration of a
            Humanistic Approach to Social Forecasting.   Re-
            search Note-EPRC 6747-2.   Menlo Park,
            California: Stanford Research Institute, Educa-
            tional Policy Research Center.

The pilot forecasting study reported here utilized
Bosley's needs - concerns view of society and explores how
this humanistic approach can be exploited in examining alternative futures.   Aspects of the basic concept - a needs
heirarchy comprising five levels - are delineated and the
consequences of changing the model needs profile of a
society are considered.   This experiment was undertaken
with the purposive notion that societal forecasting should
take specific account of the influence of education on the
future and should eventually provide education policy
makers with information germane to gearing education
towards an evolving future.

Moser, C. A.
    1970   "Some general developments in social statis-
            tics."   Pp. 7-11 in Muriel Nissel (ed.), Social
            Trends.   London: Her Majesty's Central Statis-
            tical Office.

Because of the increased emphasis in the past on economic statistics, social statistics have had to take second place.   The picture is changing, however, and this
author outlines some of the major developments in social
statistics in the United Kingdom.   These include the
Office of Population Censuses and Surveys; the General
Household Survey; a system of social statistics which
brings many statistics bearing on social conditions, resources and flows of people together into a meaningful
whole and collected broadly along internationally agreed
lines; social indicators and social trends.

Ogburn, William Fielding
1946   The Social Effects of Aviation. Cambridge,
        Massachusetts: Houghton Mifflin (Riverside
        Press).

A good early discussion of the problems of predicting
social effects and the requisite measurement techniques,
(Chapters 3 and 4 of Section 1) wherein he traces nine
uses of aviation through twenty-two different 'effect'
situations.

Olson, Mancur, Jr.
1970   "An analytic framework for social reporting and
        policy analysis." The Annals of the American
        Academy of Political and Social Science 388
        (March).112-126.

Coordinating agency programs for optimal Federal effectiveness is inconceivable, Olson suggests, without a
Presidential administrative staff comparable with those of
other Federal subunits, for formulating the larger or
strategic alternatives that face the nation. A synthesis
of the structural-functionalist and problem-solving approaches, called "complex systems analysis" is suggested
as a theoretical framework for reducing agency
"suboptimization" and structuring annual social reports.

Ostrom, Elinor
1971   "Institutional arrangements and the measurement
        of policy consequences in urban areas." Urban
        Affairs Quarterly 6 (June):447-475.

Sources of error in the policy process are identified
as three: adequacy and reliability of data regularly generated; validity of interpretation given the data; and the
availability of appropriate techniques for changing institutional arrangements and knowledge concerning the effects
produced by the techniques. To avoid the gross errors
possible at each of these phases, a model is presented
that provides negative feedback mechanisms and can thus be
self-correcting for the institutions. As examples the
competitive market is considered, and the FBI Index of
Crime examined in detail, concluding that the Crime Index
is an example of Blau's "vicious circle" and should not be
considered adequate, valid or reliable. Needed are new
interpretations of the meaning of crime statistics, new
indicators for the evaluation of police services, and new
institutional arrangements for the provision of police
services. The Lakewood Plan of Los Angeles County,
California merits consideration for adaptation and/or use
elsewhere.

Patrick, Ruth
   1971   "Aquatic communities as indices of pollution."
         A paper presented at AAAS Symposium "Indicators
         of Environmental Quality" (December)
         Philadelphia, Pennsylvania.

Biological organisms, considered as constituents of
aquatic communities and multivariate ecosystems, are discussed in this article as being a means for monitoring
life quality dimensions which entail water use. Analysis
of the population structure of aquatic communities, particularly primary producers, herbivores, and carnivores,
is suggested as a technique for measuring the effect of
various types of pollution over time, which is not possible with current methods of chemical analysis.

Pelz, Donald C. and Ray E. Faith
   1970   "Some effects of causal connections in simulated
         time-series data." A paper presented at the
         American Sociological Association symposium on
         Methodological Problems in Longitudinal Studies
         (December 27) Ann Arbor, Michigan.

Concerned with the measurement of change, this work was
presented at the American Statistical Association
Symposium on Methodological Problems in Longitudinal Studies (1970). The authors generated two autoregressive
panels through computer simulation and by defining model
relations recursively. Developing a correlogram of cross-
correlations and by assuming stationary properties, procedures of path analysis were applied to derive expressions
for the simulation model. These procedures are identical
with those of Robert Lew, yet explain and convey the features of the models in terms which better describe the
feasibility of their use in constructing social indicator
monitoring programs based on time-series data analysis.

Pikul, Robert, Charles Bisselle and Martha Lilienthal
   1971   "Development of environmental indices: Outdoor
         recreational resources and land use shift." A
         paper presented to the American Association for
         the Advancement of Science (December 26) McLean,
         Virginia: The MITRE Corporation.

This paper presents concepts for developing indices for
outdoor recreational resources and for land use. Suggested are indices of recreational availability, visits, intensity and urban area recreational resources. Sources of
land use information and problems of data assessment are
discussed. The concept of a land use shift matrix is introduced; several indices with computational formulae

132

derived from such a matrix are proposed. Suggested data needs, assessment and the proposed indices are given in tabular form.

Rappaport, Carl
    1970   "A framework for evaluating the impact of the model cities program." A paper presented at the National Meeting of the Operations Research Society of America (October 28-30) Detroit, Michigan.

    Desirability of evaluating and the bases on which it should be done; lists ten areas in which the Model Cities Program is conducting or considering evaluation efforts and broad content of each: experience reports, institutional change, planning process, resident observers, surveys, citizen participation, categorical funds, evaluation institute and technical assistance, models and information systems. The model presented is designed to establish the relationships between and among conditions, problems, inputs, outputs and impacts.

Richard, Robert
    1969   Subjective Social Indicators. Chicago, Illinois: National Opinion Research Center, University of Chicago.

    This reports a methodological study of the design validation and measurement of variables comprising a social profile of "target areas". This social profile section was developed for inclusion as a chapter of the Household Survey Handbook, a Bureau of the Budget publication. The profile is meant to serve the needs of policy-making and social-action agencies involved in PP&E research. The applicability and validity of the subjective (attitudinal) social indicators obtainable using the profile will depend on adapting it to the research, hypotheses, resources, and circumstances of a specific community survey through professional guidance.

Rochberg, Richard, Theodore J. Gordon and Olaf Helmer
    1970   "The use of cross-impact matrices for forecasting and planning." (April) Middletown, Connecticut: Institute for the Future, Riverview Center.

    Future developments through computer simulation using 1) estimated probabilities that certain events will occur, and 2) estimates of the effect that the occurrence of any of these events would be expected to have on the likelihood of occurrence of each of the others. Presents an appendix of the computational method emphasizing the advantages, disadvantages and the implications of computer simulation.

Rummel, Rudolph J.
    1969   "Indicators of cross-national and international
            patterns." American Political Science Review 63
            (March):127-147.

Devises an analytic conceptual scheme through factor
analysis to account for major patterns of variation between nations. Suggests certain criteria for variables as
indicators. Divides international relations into two
kinds of data, defined by two matrices; nations by attributes, and behavior between nations. Mathematics are then
used to locate the largest independent patterns of relationships in each space.

Russett, Bruce M.
    1970   "Indicators for America's linkages with the
            changing world." The Annals of the American
            Academy of Political and Social Science 388
            (March):82-96.

Views the major problem of a world social indicators
project as deciding among the infinity of indicators which
will serve as measures of variables that are theoretically
important. Lists current variables on which data is
available and outlines the categories into which
indicators might be classified as being: national-
attribute data, value achievement/aspiration differentials, and indicators of international linkage. Asserts
the present research climate and the varieties of present
information are such that this strategy would optimize the
efficiency of individual scholars in filling gaps in and
encouraging others to use testable models of international
phenomena.

Shinn, Allen M., Jr.
    1971a "Magnitude estimation: Some applications to
            social indicators." A paper presented at the
            Annual Meeting of the American Political Science
            Association (September) Chicago, Illinois.

Introduces a scaling method which has been applied for
some thirty years in psychophysics. Shinn describes this
methodological approach in considerable detail arguing
that, where precise measurement is required, a magnitude
scale is also required since category scales are limited
by their essentially ordinal nature. The significant, yet
few, applications of magnitude estimation to the study of

social status, crime, power, and housing and
transportation norms demonstrate the usefulness of its
weighting techniques and suggests that magnitude
estimation may serve as a unique approach to the problems
encountered in developing social indicators, notably those
of aggregating data at different analytical levels.

1971b "Measuring the utility of housing:
Demonstrating a methodological approach."
Social Science Quarterly (June):88-102.

This is an attempt to demonstrate the usefulness of the
"magnitude estimation" technique for measuring "utility
functions." Ascertaining utility functions for all important groups in a society will require isolating important
variables first. To know how well society is "doing" will
be virtually impossible without such measures, otherwise
no rational way exists for considering variable trade-
offs. The ability of "magnitude estimation" to measure
subjective utilities, largely non-quantifiable, suggests
it bears promise for solutions to major social problems
and developing social indicators.

Shults, Wilbur D. and J. Beauchamp
1971 "Statistically based air quality indices." A
paper presented at the Annual Meeting of the
American Association for the Advancement of Science (December 27) Philadelphia, Pennsylvania.

Most air quality index systems developed so far have
been mathematical statements, which, while having some desirable attributes, also have serious deficiencies. Presented in this paper is the rationale for a statistical
index, one of the more important advantages being that the
potential hazard from some pollutant or combination of
pollutants is usually indicated statistically, by the frequency of effect. A statistical index assumes, however,
that the necessary data is available, which is not always
so; that valid standards have been set, which isn't necessarily the case; and that an adequate and effective distribution can be identified. Discussed are weighting
factors, scaling for individual pollutant values, combination of individual indices, and future work needed. Data
used as examples are for carbon monoxide, nitrogen
dioxide, sulfur oxide and oxidant, for normal and log normal distributions for Denver, Philadelphia, Cincinnati,
Chicago and St. Louis.

Terleckyj, Nestor
1970 "Measuring possibilities of social change."
Looking Ahead (Publication of the National
Planning Association) 18 (August):1-11.

As Director of National Priorities Study, he presents
the preliminary results of research directed toward questions as 1) how best to achieve national goals; 2) how to
measure progress toward objectives; 3) what kinds of priority choices do we have; 4) how to do more with given resources; and 5) how to relate efforts toward various goals
to each other. Tables: I, largely illustrative, showing
effect of certain activities on goal output indicators,
1970-1980; II, estimates of maximum potentials for social
change and their costs, 1970-1980; III, sensitivity analysis of projections of resources available for undertaking
'new' activities, 1971- 1980 by subperiod; and IV, comparison of output results of allocating $1.5 trillion in var-
ious ways, 1971-1980.

Thompson, Jean
    1970   "The growth of population to the end of the
            century." Pp. 21-32 in Muriel Nissel (ed.),
            Social Trends. London: Her Majesty's Central
            Statistical Office.

    Each year population projections covering the period up
to forty years ahead are carried out by the Government
Actuary's Department. Each year the methods used in the
projections are subject to review but have remained essentially unchanged. The object of the article is to examine
some of the main features of the current (1969 based)
projections and to illustrate how they set the background
for considering future developments in the social and economic field in particular. Discussion centers on the
nature and reliability of population projections, the
changing population both nationally and regionally, the
age and sex ratio, and the implications of the projections
for social services. Finally a chart showing the size of
the total population of the United Kingdom is included in
an annex.

Todd, Seldon P.
    1970   "Data sources for computing a system of social
            indicators for the aged." A paper prepared for
            the Administration on Aging by the Operations
            Research and Policy Systems Division.
            Minneapolis, Minnesota: American Rehabilitation
            Foundation.

    The American Rehabilitation Foundation has taken the
responsibility of developing and collecting the needed information to assess the quality of life of the elderly.
This task is relying on the results of one-time surveys.
For maximum utilization of information, it is desirable to
obtain data sources that are part of a constant on-going
system. Data sources suggested in this document to pro-

vide information about the elderly are classified under
the general headings of indicators for attitudes, housing,
social relations, economic well-being and health.

Todd, Seldon and Jacqueline Anderson
    1970   "A system of social indicators for the aged."   A
            paper prepared for the Administration on Aging
            by the Operations Research and Policy Systems
            Division. Minneapolis, Minnesota: American Re-
            habilitation Foundation.

    Part 2 of a study by the American Rehabilitation Foun-
dation for the Administration on Aging. Two criteria were
used to decide whether or not a social indicator should be
included in the system for the aged; what was thought the
social indicator should measure and the availability of
statistics and data to compute the indicator once it was
defined. Five major social indicators are presented with
suggestions for operationalization of the concepts: attitudes (toward life satisfaction, present financial,
housing, health and social relationships), housing
(comfort, privacy and neighborhood desirability), social
relations (isolation and alienation), income (disposable
income, adequacy, economic welfare and security), and
health (life expectancy, non-chronic life expectancy,
probable age of onset of disability and illness). Also
contains a detailed Appendix of medical care.

United Nations
    1963   Compendium of Social Statistics: 1963.   New
            York: United Nations.

    This is an international compendium comprising tables
dealing with statistical indicators of the international
level of living components. Organized into eight sections, the Compendium describes the major aspects of the
social situation in the world by nation and regions indicating trends or changes in the levels of living over the
decade ended 1960. Data was contributed and the
Compendium was prepared under the auspices of the Inter-
Agency Working Party on Statistics for Social Programmes
by United Nations organizations, the International Labour
Office, the Food and Agricultural Organization, and the
World Health Organization.

United Nations, Department of Economic and Social Affairs
    1964   Handbook of Household Surveys. New York:
            United Nations.

    This Handbook was designed as a practical guide for
persons concerned with general (multi-subject) sample

household surveys aimed at measuring aspects of a populations level of living. Part 1 is concerned with defining these and ancillary substantive aspects relevant to such household surveys. Part 2 is devoted to the theory and methods for taking a sample survey including sample design, frame, estimation and errors. Design of questionnaires, interviews, data processing and organizational operation are also discussed. In Annex 1, a questionnaire is presented for obtaining level-of-living information on demographic, health food consumption, housing, educational employment, and economic characteristics of households.

United Nations, Department of Social Affairs
    1967   "Statistics needed for educational planning."
            Pp. 118-150 in Conference of European
            Statisticians: Statistical Standards and Studies No. 11. ST/CES/11, Vol 2. New York:
            United Nations.

Outlines the various types of statistical data needed for educational planning at the national level, as this affects resource allocation and assessment of educational programmes. Presents an inventory of both "basic" and "supplementary" statistics requisite while recognizing the interrelationship and integration between educational development and general social and economic progress for a country. Preliminary inventory of information needed for adequate planning at national level is subdivided into basic data and supplementary data. Specific categories are demographic, labor force, economic and financial, educational institutions, teachers and educational personnel, classes, pupils, school buildings and equipment, testing and vocational guidance, health and feeding of pupils, out-of-school education and costs.

United Nations Research Institute for Social Development
    1971   "Proposal for a research project on the measurement of real progress at the local level." Unpublished manuscript. New York: United
            Nations. UNRISD/72/C.10.

Proposes exploratory research on the hypothesis that by systematic examination of real progress at the local level, that is, in specific small towns, villages and city districts, aspects of social change, the nature of change, and the interrelations between economic and social factors can be better observed and assessed. Reviews three limitations of national "aggregates" as indicators and proposes local observations to correct and supplement national indicators. Emphasizes use of local data to aid in national development policy and planning and proposes systematic comparative research in selected industrialized

and developing countries. Outlines past work at the
Institute on development indicators and details the project's organization, research methods and timing for
accomplishing the proposed research on three basic questions: What to observe at local level? How to gather the
information? How to analyze and present to form part of
the national system of development measurement?

Voight, Robert B.
1970   "Costs, response rates, and other aspects of
        data collection in the 1970 census." A paper
        presented at the Annual Meeting of the American
        Statistical Association (December 28) Detroit,
        Michigan.

A paper designed to present a brief overview of the
Nineteenth Decennial Census of the United States. Procedures discussed include the manner in which names and addresses were obtained for the mail out questionnaires,
problems encountered in conducting such a complicated
task, availability of census tapes and the response rate.
Two types of questionnaires were used in the 1970 Census
consisting of a short form and a long form. The actual
percent of mail response exceeded the expected with 87%
returns compared to an expected rate of 82%.

Wheeler, David N.
1971   "The measurement of job relatedness for
        vocational program evaluation." Minneapolis,
        Minnesota: University of Minnesota, Minnesota
        Research Coordinating Unit for Vocational Educa-
        tion.

Factors involved in measuring job relatedness are considered in this paper. The percentage of graduates
initially employed is held to be a less viable indicant of
vocational program evaluation now that "accountability"
and "relevancy" are beginning to influence educator's
values. Hence, a framework for program evaluation is
forwarded that can measure the degree to which an individual's program is related to his employment situation, a
program corresponds with its objectives, or two or more
programs compare.

Wheelock, Gerald
1969   "National agricultural structure and its rela-
        tion to agricultural productivity: A Cross
        National Study." Unpublished manuscript.
        Ithaca, New York: Cornell University, Depart-
        ment of Rural Sociology.

Emphasizing one sector of our national economy to the neglect of another, e.g., industry and agriculture, tends to bring about the stagnation of the economy as a whole. This study does not focus on the interdependencies but on the institutional structures emerging from those interdepencencies, designated as "structural differentiation." This structural differentiation is shown to be a powerful predictor of productivity, based on a study of 87 nation-states interdependent by 1960. Nations are ranked by a Guttman scale on the basis of cumulative structural aspects; analysis of the data is by rank order correlation, factor analysis and multivariant analysis. Indicators of the structural differentiation variable are identified as fertilizer production, membership in international organizations, farm machinery manufacturing, plant breeding expertise, pesticide production and agricultural related education.

Whitehead, F. E.
    1971   "Trends in certificated sickness absence."
            Social Trends No. 2:13-23.

Examines data on upward trends during the past decade in the level of sickness and absence from work. Describes how records of claims for national insurance sickness benefits, analyzed over a number of years, illustrates a general increase in certified sickness absence or incapacity for work.

Widdison, Harold A. and James K. Skipper, Jr.
    1971   "The use of an interval scale technique with
            occupational prestige rankings." A paper pre-
            sented at the Annual Meeting of the American
            Sociological Association (August 30-September 2)
            Denver, Colorado.

Respondents were to indicate by placement on a series of 20 cm. lines, labeled with logical extremes, the relationship felt to exist between the occupations being rated and the extremities of the lines. Eight dimensions of occupational prestige as independent variables and two of general prestige as dependent variables were related. In analyzing, comparisons were made between the kind and value of information when treating the responses as ordinal and as interval data. Although neither seemed superior in prediction of general prestige, several values and relationships, such as the relative saliency of some of the prestige dimensions, were indicated on the interval analysis that were not apparent through ordinal interpretation.

Wilber, George L.
1971   "Determinants of poverty." A paper prepared for
        the joint session of the American Sociological
        Association and the Rural Sociological Society
        (August 30) Denver, Colorado.

Develops five mathematical statements relating poverty
properties as function of resources and mobilization; two
listings of these items: 1) poverty properties, basic resources and resource mobilization over the life cycle of
the individual, and 2) poverty properties for areas and
collectivities of people.

Wilcox, Leslie D. and Ralph M. Brooks
1971   "Social indicators: An alternative approach for
        future research." A paper presented at the
        Annual Meeting of the Rural Sociological Society
        (August) Denver, Colorado.

Suggests a possible empirical approach to the development of a system of social indicators, conceived as one
alternative that may offer greater promise than the current discussions and research that focus initially on
macro-models for urban or national systems. The paper
presents, as an alternative to the macro-model approach, a
more inductive approach to social indicator research with
three methodological phases representing increasing levels
of methodological sophistication. These steps are:
conceptualizing social indicators that reflect the human
meaning of societal change and development by examination
of the life experience of people at the nonmetropolitan
community level; working inductively toward the macro-
level by combining these empirical indicators into more
abstract indicators that provide relational models of
community systems; and drawing causal inferences by the
use of controlled indicators designed to measure the
social effects of major demographic changes as one
strategic force in societal change.

Yoesting, Dean R., Richard D. Warren and Dan L. Burkhead
1971   "Leisure orientation scale--replication and
        measurement analysis." A paper presented at the
        Annual Meeting of the Rural Sociological Society
        (August) Denver, Colorado.

Eleven-item Burdge scale used with two independent Iowa
samples, one primarily urban, one rural. Through use of
certainty method, both reliability and validity of scale
found to be consistent though increased by use of only
five of the original 11 items.

Alberts, David S.
   1971   "An operations research approach to measuring
          the performance of social programs." A paper
          presented at the Annual Meeting of the Ohio
          Valley Sociological Society (April 22-24)
          Cleveland, Ohio.

Based on operations research, this paper presents a
conceptual framework with which to evaluate social programs. Discusses reconciliation of both societal needs
and individualistic needs suggesting possible performance
measurements. Relationship between program evaluation and
program change is examined in light of reaction time; suggested steps to formulate "fast" objective functions; research needs to be directed toward development and testing
of indicants used in fast objective functions.

Alpbach European Forum
   1969   "The structure of society must change." Futures
          1 (December):478.

Brief summary of 1969 Alpbach European Forum, organized
by the Austrian College Society. Forum stressed the
future as an integrated system, that present problems too
often seen through insufficient egocentric views must be
viewed as part of world problems; subgroups explored relationships between values, norms, institutions and
instrumentalities; felt society should become more dynamic
through conscious decisions resulting from creative examination of value systems. Rough timetable given for some
of the world's major problems to reach explosive proportions.

Anderson, Claire M., Edward E. Schwartz and Narayan
Viswanathan
   1970   "Approaches to the analysis of social service
          systems." Pp. 42-51 in Edward E. Schwartz
          (ed.), Planning-Programming-Budgeting Systems
          and Social Welfare. Chicago, Illinois: The
          University of Chicago, The School of Social
          Service Administration.

This paper is a description of the content of program
analysis out of which PPBS has developed. Since PPBS has
only been a rather recent development, this article attempts to outline the development and usefulness of other

142

analytic approaches to administrative management and analysis to be applied to the field of social welfare. Some light analytical techniques - periodic statistical reporting, time study, cost accounting, cost analysis, performance budgeting, evaluation research, cost-benefit analysis, and PPBS - are described from the point of view of each's contribution toward an increasingly fuller analysis of the various components going into an open systems view of organizations, but particularly the input, throughput, output, and outcome components.

Andrade, Preston
    1970   "Pilot research projects in rural growth
            centers." Unpublished manuscript. New York:
            The Ford Foundation.

    Objectives and organization of a program initiated by the government in India to accelerate and guide rural development. Specific goals are to build a social, economic and physical infrastructure to support continued modernization of agriculture, diversify economic opportunities, improve social progress and quality of life for rural people, and new and more suitable patterns of urbanization.

Area Analysis Branch
    1970   An Economic Analysis of the Iowa Rural Renewal
            Area. Agricultural Economic Report No. 181.
            Washington, D.C.: Economic Research Service,
            U.S. Department of Agriculture.

    Two counties in southern Iowa provided the data in this study to aid the Farmers' Home Administration in planning a development program for the area. The counties were deficient in comprehensive medical services, public water and sewage disposal systems and the ability to generate nonfarm jobs. Based on an index to measure economic growth, it is suggested that the growth rate in the 1970's must be double that of the 1960's in order to provide future economic opportunities. Two possible approaches are suggested to reach this goal: (1) expansion of nonfarm industry and (2) a multicounty approach in planning programs to stimulate employment growth and to upgrade community services and facilities.

Barnard, Robert C. (ed.), Lynn D. Patterson, Elizabeth L. Diffendal, David C. Miller, Grace E. Miller and Melissa Garman
    1970   The Regional Quality of Puget Sound Life: First
            Steps in Its Measurement and Report. Seattle,
            Washington: Puget Sound Governmental
            Conference, Research Division.

First year developmental work by the Puget Sound
Governmental Conference to adapt social indicator tools
for the Puget Sound region is reported, with the preconference reports, data sources survey summary, seminar
reportage, typical indicators and a summary abstract of
directions for the future in the appendices. In addition
to the background and direction of social indicators for
the Puget Sound region, one chapter surveys social
indicators and social accounting in general, and discusses
the relevant critical issues in definition of terms and
concepts, measurement of social trends, consensus, development strategy, criteria selection, and data requirements, transferability and deficiency. Prototype
indicators for education and health are suggested. Dr.
Marvin B. Katzman served as consultant for the conference.
Selected bibliography unclassified, relating to both
Puget Sound and to indicators nation-wide.

Bauer, Raymond A.
    1967   "Societal feedback." The Annals of the American
            Academy of Political and Social Science 373
            (September):180-192. (Reprinted in Bertram M.
            Gross (ed.), 1969 Social Intelligence for
            America's Future. Boston: Allyn and Bacon).

Explores the problems involved in the use of more and
better information as it relates to a potential societal
information system. The breadth, complexity and unique
problems of an entire society of actors and evaluators for
such a system, particularly when no consensus exists on a
feasible model, make it highly reliant on rapid feedback
because of the weakness it would exhibit in providing anticipation of the full range of causal relations between
actions or changes and their consequences. Feedback and
ad hoc analytic research will be crucial to bridging gaps
of inference in such a system.

Beals, Ralph L.
    1970   "Who will rule research? The big problem on the
            far side of the dry spell in funding." Psychol-
            ogy Today (September):45-47, 75.

Tracing the development of government supported social
science research, some very basic questions are asked.
Included for discussion in this paper are these issues:
How shall social research be used?, To what ends?, Are
government agencies using social research in appropriate
ways?, Are there areas where it should be used but is
not?, Are there areas where it should not be and is
(invasion of privacy)?, Who makes the decisions to use or
not to use?, On what basis?, What monitoring system of the

funding and use of social research should be set up?, Who
operates the monitoring system?, What criteria should be
used for the decisions?, Who decides the criteria?, How
about the qualifications of the staffs of organizations
contracting for government research? No easy answers to
these are given, but suggestions are worth consideration.

Becker, Harold S. and Raul de Brigard
    1970   "Considerations on a framework for community
            action planning." Working Paper WP-9.
            Middletown, Connecticut: The Institute for the
            Future. May.

This paper describes and formulates a framework for a
program known as Community Development Action Plans, created by the Connecticut Department of Community Affairs,
for the purpose of strengthening local government's
ability to improve the conditions of community life. This
framework is directed towards investigating methods which
could improve what communities use for determining needs,
and within which action programs can be formulated. The
higher order goals of a community is an improvement of its
quality of life. Twelve components of quality-of-life--
education, housing, health, recreation, social services,
economic development, public utilities, public safety,
transportation, culture, inter-personal communication, and
local government--are described in detail, tentative goal
statements are established, and potential areas of need
are established for each component. These twelve components are subsumed within a three way categorization of
quality-of-life into physical, social and economic.

Bell, Daniel
    1969   "The idea of a social report." The Public
            Interest 15 (Spring):72-84.

The author points out that the "idea" of a social
report is one whose time has come and that the publication
of a Social Report should be an established feature of
public policy analysis. He reviews the idea of social
costs, social trends, the lag in indicators of a nation's
progress, and the new impetus being given by a number of
authors to social indicators. Finally he endeavors to
point out what social indicators are and the next steps
involved in institutionalizing a social report.

Bennis, Warren G.
    1970   "The failure and promise of the social scienc-
            es." Technology Review (October-
            November):38-43.

Concern with the implementation gap in the social sciences, between the men who have knoweldge and lack power and those with power who lack knowledge, is examined in three examples, Project Camelot, the M.I.T. Center for International Studies and its office and work in New Delhi, and a sociological study of the Air Force. Identified are four primary causes for failure: sponsorship, clearance, communication and collaboration. Recommendations focus on deeper mutual understanding between scientists and policy-makers; a more developed science of utilization; a loud, clear and useful voice of social science; wider, more vigorous support to social science by the public; a need for social scientists to be social as well as scientific; and re-examination and modification of the value system of social scientists.

Biderman, Albert D.
  1963   National Goals and Statistical Indicators.
          Washington, D.C.: Bureau of Social Science Research, Inc.

This paper, the forerunner of his chapter in Bauer's Social Indicators, explores the ways in which our space efforts may produce major social change, and the need to consider those effects in policy-making decisions about the scope and nature of the space program. Evaluates our ability to formulate effective indicators related to consensual goals, such as the National Goals stated by the President's Commission; tables present this evaluation in relationship to the Statistical Abstract of the United States, Historical Statistics of the United States, Space Goals, Economic Indicators and HEW Trends. Discusses briefly problems of quality and acceptability of indicators.

  1966   "Social indicators and goals." Pp. 68-153 in
          Raymond A. Bauer (ed.), Social Indicators.
          Cambridge, Massachusetts: The Massachusetts
          Institute of Technology Press.

This contribution to Bauer's "Social Indicators" presents forcefully our deficiencies in trying to use current data series and statistics to assess our society, whether relating to the nature of the system or to the state of the system. Analyzes the factors that determine which series will be developed, the biases in the selection, and the selectiveness of use. Discusses technical obstacles to adequate consensual system of social indicators as invalidity, inaccuracy, conflicting indicators, lack of data, incompatible models, and value consensus. As an example of problems of indicator quality and social change, the generating and usage of crime statistics is illustrative. Appendix shows in table form the

specific goals and goal areas of the President's
Commission on National Goals; corresponding goals of the
1933 statement of President Hoover's Commission; and
indicators from five sources: 1) Statistical Abstract of
the U.S., 1962; 2) Historical Statistics, Colonial Times
to 1957; 3) Economic Indicators; 4) HEW Trends; and 5)
Gendell and Zetterberg's "Sociological Almanac".

Blaisdell, Thomas C., Jr.
    1954   "Problems of evaluating the effectiveness of de-
           velopment measures." Economic Development and
           Cultural Change 2 (January):286-297.

    In a recent review of the United Nations and the
Specialized Agencies, the questions of "what is economic"
and of priority were considered. This paper presents some
of the issues from that discussion. Standards of priority
used in allocating funds were: 1) to increase food production and distribution; 2) increased production and distribution of other necessities of life; and 3) projects to
broaden technical knowledge itself. Technical project
criteria too often are based on operational efficiency
rather than fundamental results. Discusses national
income (as defined in the U.S. by Gross National Product)
as the economic measure of evaluation, as both result and
process. Program evaluation rests on: 1) awareness of
the impact of the technical changes and tension created;
2) potential increase of productivity and capital resources; and 3) consideration of the ratios between
consumption and production goods (capital), and among land
capital, power, communication, manufacturing and
commerce.

Boucher, Wayne, I.
    1971   "The future environment for technology assess-
           ment." In M. J. Cetron and B. Bartocha (eds.),
           Technological Assessment in Perspective. Paris,
           France: Hermann Press.

    Trends intrinsic to technology assessment (TA) seem to
be: increasing recognition that the basic idea of TA has
been overstated; rapid development of methods, criteria
for problem choices, and professional standards; increasing funds for TA; and the emergence of centers primarily
or exclusively for TA. Pressures for change external to
the movement may include the rapid growth of new
technologies; absence of short term change in how TA
users, especially government, cope with issues raised by
technology; no change in TA usage by decision makers; increased usage and efforts to effect reforms in many areas
of interest to TA; gradual shift in public values that may
make some TA concerns irrelevant. Turbulence in the

future of TA is seen as many of these pressures are at cross purposes, both conceptually and institutionally. The most basic problem is the formidable accumulation of literature, mostly by those with no working knowledge of TA itself.

Brady, Edward L. and Lewis M. Branscomb
1972   "Information for a changing society." Science 175 (March):961-966.

    To ensure that changing societies make wise decisions, information, social analysis, well-informed decision-makers and appropriate institutions are needed. Reviews extensively the report entitled Information for a Changing Society, prepared by the Organization for Economic Cooperation and Development. Recognizes four communities as users of information: the science specialist (the researcher), the industrial engineer (the applier), the planner, the policy maker, the decision-maker, the manager (the innovators and guiders) and the public (the consumer, beneficiary, and victim). Summarizes the report's formulated set of four goals for a national policy on information, set of eight governmental objectives to meet the four broader goals and the report's conclusions and recommendations which are also conveniently summarized.

Bryan, C. Hobson and Alvin L. Bertrand
1970   Propensity for Change Among the Rural Poor in the Mississippi Delta: A Study of the Roots of Social Mobility. Agricultural Economic Report No. 185. Washington, D.C.: Economic Research Service, U.S. Department of Agriculture.

    Generally, low rates of social participation and considerable fatalism are common among the rural poor in the Mississippi Delta. However, in this study neither factor appears to be related to the propensity for change to achieve upward social mobility. Socio-demographic factors which do seem to be related include: small household size, education beyond the 6th grade, married status and being under 45 years of age.

Burke, Edmund M.
1965   "The road to planning: An organizational analysis." Social Science Review 39 (September): 261-270.

    Structural change in health and welfare planning agencies is discussed with three broad levels of structural organization identified. Originally there were the "councils of social agencies" designed to coordinate the

148

service programs of the cooperating agencies. These
gradually evolved into "community welfare councils" with a
wider membership base, including unaligned citizens.
Emerging now are "citizens associations for health and
welfare planning", which minimize or abolish agency representation. Questions of who the participants are, and
what incentives for participation are offered, if any,
and, if so, how adequate are those incentives, are examined in relation to each type of structural organization
involved.

Byrnes, James C.
     1970   The Quantity of Formal Instruction in the United
             States. Syracuse, New York: Syracuse Universi-
             ty Research Corporation.

     Charts and data on the growth and development of ele-
mentary, secondary and post-secondary education, including
community colleges and the proportion of educational com-
pletions at these various levels. A quantitative model is
presented with two possible alternatives of continuous
growth for policy stability.

Campbell, Donald T.
     1969   "Reforms as experiments." American Psychologist
             24 (April):409-429.

     The author posits that administrators have so committed
themselves in advance to the efficacy of any given reform
that they cannot stand the hard-headed scrutiny and honest
evaluation so often needed. Specific reforms are
advocated as though they were certain to be successful.
With the scope and complexity of issues facing us, we
should support experimental administrators willing to implement a policy for a period of time, as five years, with
the understanding that if evaluation at that time indicates ineffectiveness, that Policy B will be tried. Identified and discussed are nine threats to internal validity
and six to external validity. Interrupted time series
designs, control series designs, regression discontinuity
designs, randomized control group experiments, allocation
of scarce resources by lottery, the use of staged
innovation and pilot projects are all administrative
decisions which might preclude the difficulties involved
with "known outcomes" of reform measures.

Canada Department of Regional Economic Expansion
     1970   Development Plan for Prince Edward Island.
             Ottawa, Canada: Queen's Printer for Canada.

     Presents the enabling legislation (agreement) for the

development plan, a memorandum of implementation, and the development strategy in regard to the current situation, strategy, regional implications, phasing, Indians and expected effects. Outlines program areas in resource adjustment and development (integrated land management, development of land based resource sectors, fisheries); social development (education, adult education and vocational training, housing and urban services and development, health and welfare services); resource supporting and commercial services (transportation, power, industrial waste disposal and water supply, manufacturing and processing, market development and short term credit); and implementation (plan management, provincial government organizational and staff development, public participation and involvement, evaluation), administration and finance.

Central Statistical Office
　　1971　　Social Trends. No. 2. A publication of the Government Statistical Service, Muriel Nissel (ed.). London, England: Her Majesty's Stationery Office.

Opening with a series of articles on social services manpower, trends in certificated sickness absence, and social indicators (health), there follows a series of tables and charts emphasizing regional material and statistics relating to the United Kingdom as a whole. There is also a section on social services manpower resources which complements and extends the information on financial resources already included in issue No. 1 of Social Trends in the section on public expenditure. Another new section pertains to the environment. A set of tables and charts covers these topics: population, employment, leisure, personal income and expenditure, social security, welfare, health, education, housing, environment, justice and law, public expenditure, manpower and international (comparisons).

Chaiklin, Harris
　　1970　　"Evaluation research and the planning-programming-budgeting system." Pp. 27-34 in Edward E. Schwartz (ed.), Planning-Programming-Budgeting Systems and Social Welfare. Chicago, Illinois: The University of Chicago, The School of Social Service Administration.

Chaiklin presents one social work educator's view of the relationship of PPBS to the formulation of social policy. The argument of this short paper is that, although PPBS provides a structure that will permit social welfare evaluation research, neither PPBS nor evaluation

research will be of any use unless we really want to find
the answers to hard questions about how best to advance
the welfare of all people. The paper discusses the PPBS
analyst from the perspective of evaluation research, the
relationship between politics, science and the truth, and
the prospects for PPBS within this framework.

Christakis, Alexander N.
    1970   "Regional economic development futures: A meth-
            odological review and study design." A paper
            based on a report prepared for the Special
            Assistant to the Secretary of Commerce for
            Regional Economic Coordination, Washington,
            D.C., December 31.

Focus of this paper, prepared for the Special Assistant
to the Secretary of Commerce, is on a study design aimed
at incorporating futures research into regional planning
so that the planner may have presented to him as many
social desirable alternatives as possible, as well as
evaluating alternative policies for goal achievement.
Perhaps the most difficult question is how best the
planner can assist the decision-maker in assigning values
to the choices and consequences. Recommends a multi-level
approach, estimation of impacts and evaluation of alternatives.

Clague, Ewan
    1963   "Economics and public welfare." A paper pre-
            sented at the Southeastern Regional Conference,
            American Public Welfare Association (September
            27) Asheville, North Carolina. BLS Report No.
            238-4.

Drawing upon findings of the 1960-1961 Survey of
Consumer Expenditures, support is generally given for the
adage, "the rich get richer and the poor get poorer."
Discussed is the interrelationship of low income, low education and high unemployment with the implications for
welfare policy and unemployment insurance. Findings indicated a substantial rise in real income for the large
majority of American families in the middle and upper
class ranges but a disproportionately smaller rise for the
disadvantaged. With technological changes and earlier
retirement, the clustering of people at the lower edge of
our economy who were not sharing in the general prosperity
seemed to be growing larger, with an increasing disparity
between the lowest and the middle class groups.

Colm, Gerhard
    1966   "On goals research." Pp. 1-16 in Leonard A.

Lecht, Goals, Priorities and Dollars: The Next
Decade. Glencoe, Illinois: The Free Press.

This book is a contribution of the National Planning
Association to the field of goals research. The book is a
beginning or first attempt at estimating dollar costs of
our aspiration goals. It covers many fields including
consumer expenditures and savings, private plant and
equipment, urban development, social welfare, health, education, transportation, defense, housing research and development, natural resources, international aid, space,
agriculture, manpower, and area redevelopment.

Davidson, Frank P.
   1968   "Macro-engineering: A capability in search of a
          methodology." Futures 1 (December):153-161.

Broader methods than systems analysis techniques are
needed for policy-makers concerned with major projects.
To achieve macro-engineering may require expertise from
many disciplines with additional emphasis on national and
international study groups. One example might be an international joint venture project for mass transportation
needs.

de Brigard, Raul and Olaf Helmer
   1970   Some Potential Societal Developments--1970-2000.
          Middletown, Connecticut: Institute for the
          Future, Riverview Center.

Thirty-four experts in numerous disciplines
participated in a series of three questionnaires through
the Delphi process to parallel for the social future the
similar study done for the physical and biomedical areas
in an earlier report. Classified into the ten broad areas
of: urbanization, the family, leisure and the economy,
education, food and population, international relations,
conflict in society and law enforcement, national
political structure, values, and impact of technology on
government and society. Each area is presented in terms
of current trends, future developments, implications of
technology and societal indicators. Included in section
10 on technology are the breakthroughs considered in the
study done on physical and biomedical potentials, this
time rated and ranked by social scientists. Tables and
graphs accompany the narrative for each section, with
upper and lower quartile ranges and medians given; date
estimates for the expectations; and strength ratings from
very important to unimportant for the potential developments.

de Neufville, Judith I.
   1972   Social Indicator Design and Use: An Interactive
           Process. Unpublished Doctoral Dissertation.
           Cambridge, Massachusetts: Massachusetts
           Institute of Technology.

   Focus on the development of social indicators has nor-
mally been on how the indicators should be structured,
what new or reinterpreted data is needed, whether the
indicator measures what it purports to measure, or what
sort of institutions to set up for them. This description
of a thesis attempts to identify the critical factors
which both motivate and shape the design and utilization
of social indicators. The major difficulty seems to be
that the development of a useful indicator is seldom
thought of as a process wherein actual and potential uses,
public conceptions, values, pragmatic and political considerations all make demands and impose constraints, a
process highly interactive with the environment and
continuing as long as the indicator has a role in that environment. The thesis examines the development of
indicators of the employment rate, a standard budget, and
the poverty line, the first being relatively complete, the
latter two in progress.

Discussion at Delos
   1969   "The scale of settlements and the quality of
           life." Ekistics 28 (October):277-281.

   A discussion which calls for a new approach when
considering the settlements of man. One which advocates
viewing of total environment as a series of systems operating within and around society. Quality of life is included in this reordering of thinking toward social
planning.

Duhl, Leonard J.
   1968   "Planning and predicting: Or what do you do
           when you don't know the names of the variables."
           Pp. 147-156 in Daniel Bell (ed.), Toward the
           Year 2000. Boston: Houghton Mifflin Company.
           (Also in Daedalus 96 (Summer):779-788, 1967).

   This paper is an attempt to define the role and function of a planner, to suggest his methods of operation and
how best he can fulfill his function as an agent of
change. Must involve process as a constantly changing but
definable variable, always interacting with specific and
general goals. Sees two basic planning problems 1) inadequate tools with which to plan with scientific accuracy
and no systematic way of developing them and 2) not under-

standing that all involved in planning must be sensitive
to process.

Duncan, Otis Dudley
    1967   "Discrimination against Negroes." The Annals of
            the American Academy of Political and Social
            Science 371 (May):85-103. (Reprinted in Bertram
            M. Gross (ed.), 1969 Social Intelligence for
            America's Future. Boston: Allyn and Bacon).

    To measure progress in reducing discrimination, it is
necessary to distinguish between the type of handicaps -
general societal or status specific - and have methods,
models and comprehensive time series suited to the analysis of causal sequences. Circumvention of specified statistical hazards will be a must to reliable inference and
realistic proposals; this will depend upon the availability of research funds (statistical), agency cooperation,
investigative latitude, and improved analytical and
interpretive models.

Economic Council of Canada
    1971   Design for Decision-Making: An Application to
            Human Resources Policies. Eighth Annual Review
            (September) Ottawa, Canada: Information Canada.

    This annual review of the Economic Council of Canada is
about government decision-making. It is concerned with
the processes of such decision-making rather than with the
outcomes of such decisions. Emphasis is placed on the
need for a more comprehensive framework, covering a
broader range of goals and their interrelationships,
within which policy objectives can be considered and appropriate priorities chosen. Chapter 2 discusses briefly
the increasing role of government in affecting policy.
Chapters 2 through 5 are devoted to an examination of the
major aspects of government decision-making processes and
presents a framework for governmental decision-making.
Chapters 6 through 8 seek to illustrate this theme with
reference to the main programs of federal manpower policy:
training, mobility, job placement. Chapter 9 treats a
major policy area in the provincial sphere of jurisdiction
- education. Chapter 10 sets out a few conclusions and
recommendations relating to the main theme of the report.

Engquist, Carlton L.
    1970   "PPBS: An operating agency view." Pp. 14-26 in
            Edward E. Schwartz (ed.), Planning-Programming-
            Budgeting Systems and Social Welfare. Chicago,
            Illinois: The University of Chicago, The School
            of Social Service Administration.

One of the earliest and most instructive experiences in applying PPBS to welfare programs at the operating level has been that of a Federal Agency - the Veterans Administration which is the largest employer of social workers in the country. This discussion is oriented to: the reasons for the agency's decision to adopt this approach, the content of its particular application of PPBS, the extent to which the agency has been able to make the application as planned, problems involved and ways of dealing with them, and a general evaluation of the utility of PPBS.

Fedkiw, John
    1969   "Social costs and benefits of timber program al-
            ternatives for meeting national housing goals."
            A paper presented at a conference on Assessment
            of Social Costs of Federal Programs (June 16)
            Washington, D.C.

Meeting the national housing goals for new units and for assisted rehabilitations of units for low income people entails a 46% increase of softwood lumber and plywood supplies from the 1968 level to 1978, and an 84% increase in the following decade to 1988. Recent increased timber demand has brought greatly increased prices contributing disproportionately to inflation pressures on the general economy. A Major Program Issue paper on timber was developed from an analytic study that projected demands under three alternative price assumptions, estimating budget impacts and social costs of supply alternatives. Impact of the alternatives on sustained yield and multiple use constraints was also considered. Highlights of the analysis of social costs and impact is presented in tabular form.

Fontaine, Andre
    1967   "The mass media--a need for greatness." The
            Annals of the American Academy of Political and
            Social Science 371 (May):72-84. (Reprinted in
            Bertram M. Gross (ed.), 1969 Social Intelligence
            for America's Future. Boston: Allyn and
            Bacon).

Explores the notion that media, to be great, must illuminate the values of American life and serve to instruct, guide and lead people to a more rewarding way of living. To achieve this will entail improving credibility, information access, editorial power, and the knowledge of audience impact; this will require systematic measures to indicate both progress and the efficacy of raising more difficult questions.

Galnoor, Itzhak
    1971   "Social information for what?" The Annals of
            the American Academy of Political and Social
            Science 393 (January):1-19.

    Galnoor defines "social indicators," "social account-
ing," "social reporting," and "social information" in the
context of their development. Their use is related to the
emergence of social problems in economically developed
countries. He makes a plea for better information so that
"development" will include social as well as economic
models. The lack of any model of societal
industrialization for which measurements could be developed is pointed out. Development and developing countries
are discussed and a new conceptualization of development
is urged. Different kinds of social information are
needed in "developed" and "developing" situations. Some
major approaches to social information are touched upon
and are related to their possible use by developing
countries.

Glaser, Daniel
    1967   "National goals and indicators for the reduction
            of crime and delinquency." The Annals of the
            American Academy of Political and Social Science
            371 (May): 104-126. (Reprinted in Bertram M.
            Gross (ed.), 1969 Social Intelligence for
            America's Future. Boston: Allyn and Bacon).

    Suggests types of research required to establish valid
indicants of progress in achievement of crime control
goals. The data required makes it imperative to establish
a national research agency, perhaps a bureau of the Department of Justice operating under an advisory board representing the major academic, professional and public
service groups concerned with crime control, to insure
that data will be collected, coordinated and fully interpreted in terms of national and local crime problems.

Gordon, Theodore J.
    1971   "Future machines and human values: The role of
            coincidence." A paper presented at the Annual
            Meeting of the American Association for the
            Advancement of Science (December 27)
            Philadelphia, Pennsylvania.

    The exploration of and techniques for indicating value
coincidences are presented as critical to exploiting the
points of "change sensitivity" which they prescribe.
Among the "value coincidences" cited by the author are:
1) covert war coincidence, 2) education-memory drug

coincidence, 3) women's lib coincidence, and 4) criminality/rehabilitation coincidence. These points specify regions of confluence or define the loci of effective policy which is where actions or inactions can produce results disproportionate to effort.

Gordon, Theodore J. and Robert H. Ament
    1969   Forecasts of Some Technological and Scientific
            Developments and Their Societal Consequences.
            Middletown, Connecticut: Institute for the
            Future, Riverview Center.

Four questionnaires were used with the Delphi process examining possible developments and their physical and biomedical consequences for the future. Successive questionnaires developed major trends in areas of biomedical techniques, control of behavior, increased automation, environmental control and space exploration. Consequences were explored; more than twice as many seemed favorable as unfavorable. For selected consequences appearing either very favorable or very unfavorable, the experts delineated possible ways of either expediting, delaying or avoiding the results in each case. Some of the drawbacks of the Delphi process are discussed. Forecasts consensus and time of occurrence presented in figures; complete list of some 200 consequences are in the appendix.

Gross, Bertram M.
    1965   "Planning: Let's not leave it to the
            economists." Challenge (September-
            October):30-33.

The interest in national planning since World War II has given the economists a major role at the expense of other social scientists. Understanding the noneconomic aspects of economic policies is becoming increasingly more important and it has been suggested that we strive for a system of social indicators to complement the highly organized economic indicators. Gross suggests that a necessary step would be to develop an ordered set of concepts to provide guidance for such a system of social indicators. He contributes to this conceptualization task by presenting a structure-performance model of society at the level of the nation state.

    1968   "Some questions for presidents." Pp. 308-350 in
            Bertram M. Gross (ed.), A Great Society? New
            York: Basic Books, Inc.

Gross addresses himself to the role of the President in today's society; a role which is to provide a center of creative stability in the midst of turbulent change. The

President must first be a truth teller, one requisite
being a source of intelligence gleaned from available data
in our culture which is underdeveloped in social
technology. The President must also be peace-maker;
champion of justice, especially social justice; humanist,
in employment, a city of man, and a new economics; and a
learner, employing synergic statesmenship in tasks often
improbable.

Grosse, Robert H.
    1970   "The planning, programming and budgeting system
            in the federal government: A planner's view."
            Pp. 1-13 in Edward E. Schwartz (ed.), Planning-
            Programming-Budgeting Systems and Social
            Welfare. Chicago, Illinois: The University of
            Chicago, The School of Social Service Adminis-
            tration.

    Robert Grosse, an economist and planner in the office
of the Secretary of the Department of Health, Education
and Welfare, outlines in some detail the Planning, Programming and Budgeting System. He reviews President
Johnson's full and enthusiastic support of PPBS as a comprehensive approach to planning and administrations, as
well as his order that it be adapted by all federal departments. He fully describes the primary requirements of
PPBS, its relationship between information and decisions
in program analysis and continuity of decision-making in
planning, its purpose in program evaluation, and its
impact on management processes.

Haas, J. Eugene, E. J. Bonner and Keith S. Boggs
    1971   "Science, technology and the public: The case
            of planned weather modification." A paper pre-
            sented at the Annual Meeting of the American
            Sociological Association (August 30) Denver,
            Colorado.

    Brief report of snow modification experiments in rural
areas in three states in 1968-69; conducted by scientists,
not commercial operators; financed by public funds; discussion of who accepts the new technology and factors associated with acceptance; raises a number of pertinent
questions of decision making, public interest, etc.

Harland, Douglas G.
    1971   Social Indicators: A Framework for Measuring
            Regional Social Disparities. Ottawa, Canada:
            Department of Regional Economic Expansion.
            (July 1, Second Draft).

The Canada Department of Regional Economic Expansion
has been established to ameliorate certain regional social
economic disparities in Canada. This report presents an
analytical typology for planning and evaluating social adjustment strategies in collaboration with other federal
departments. The concept of quality-of-life, including
the components of a social system, is presented in an analytical model in terms of level, standard, and norm-of-
living and its axes of analysis-unit, type, subject and
level-of-analysis. This typology leads to an elaborate
discussion of social indicators in terms of goal specification, measurement of goal attainment and the construction of social indicator indices within a social development framework leased on a social reporting paradigm for
social policy accounting. Finally the report reviews work
in progress and directions of future work in this area by
the Social and Human Analysis Branch of the Canada Department of Regional Economic Expansion.

Harris, Fred R.
    1967   "National social science foundation: Proposed
            congressional mandate for the social sciences."
            American Psychologist 22 (November):904-910.

    In this article Senator Harris presents the major argu-
ments for and fields relevant objections to a National
Social Science Foundation. The relative state of development between the natural and social sciences is cited as
demonstrating an imbalance which is unrealistic in terms
of the answers being sought from the social sciences to
national problems. A NSSF would be a strong corrective
mandate and legislative/administrative base in the
councils of government for developing innovative approaches to combating poverty, ignorance, crime, and the
vast international challenges we face.

Hauser, Philip M.
    1949   "Social science and social engineering." Phi-
            losophy of Science 16 (July):209-218.

    Addresses the issues raised by the outline for research
advocated by Merton into the role of applied social science in the formation of policy. Disagrees with Merton's
fundamental assumption about this role and elaborates various areas of importance to framing the proposed study.
Develops a case for making a distinction between the
diverse functions of conducting research and giving advice
which would regard these as best achieved through a division of labor, the former by the social scientist and the
latter by the social engineer.

    1967   "Social goals as an aspect of planning." Pp.

446-454 in Hearings before the Subcommittee on
Government Research of the Committee on Government Operations, U.S. Senate, 90th Congress, 1st
Session on S.843 Full Opportunity and Social Accounting Act, Part 3 (July 28).

Specifies the general goal is to provide opportunity
for the optimal development of each person, with discussion and subgoals in categories of education, health, environment, employment and income, family maintenance,
justice, governance, cultural and economic development,
and in world order.

1971   "Political implications of social indicators."
        A paper presented at the Annual Meeting of the
        American Political Science Association (Septem-
        ber) Chicago, Illinois.

Use of social indicators is not just a matter of
technical skills but of values, interest, policies,
politics. Four areas where political implications are
operative regarding data: 1) definition 2) gathering 3)
reporting 4) use; a case study illustrating political
decisions at work in each of four areas is provided.

Horowitz, Irving Louis and Lee Rainwater
    1967   "Comment: Social accounting for the nation."
            Transaction (May):2-3.

Among the potential functions of the Council of Social
Advisers proposed in Mondale's Social Accounting Bill
could be a more systematic assessment of the social implications of various government actions, introduction into
policy making process of the kinds of social considerations now usually ignored, facing some of the now unrecog-
nized consequences of government actions, and forcing us
to address as policy issues various social problems which
factual ignorance now often conceals. Seen as equally
encouraging is Ribicoff's plan for an Office of
Legislative Accounting and Harris' proposal for a National
Social Science Foundation.

Ink, Dwight A.
    1971   "Statement of Dwight A. Ink, Assistant Director
            for Office of Management and Budget." In U.S.
            Congress. Senate. The Full Opportunity and
            National Goals and Priorities Act. Committee on
            Labor and Public Welfare on S.5.

Compares the machinery proposed by S.5 to the Executive
Branch's present processes for receiving social advice,

goal setting, and priority determination asserting that
the Domestic Council is more effective, since its members
are agents of government agencies, than a "Council of
Social Advisors" could be. Relates OMB social indicator
work to the feasibility of "Social Report to the Nation"
and an "Office of National Goals and Priorities."

Institut National de la Statistique et des Etudes
Economiques
    1971   Social Indicators. Unpublished manuscript.
            Paris, France: Social Statistics Group. (June)

This document, divided into three parts, basically
defines the role of social indicators and attempts to
justify their use in research. The first part defines the
role of social indicators as (1) the representation of
social reality and its development and (2) as the action
in view of modifying the conditions of social development.
In this first part, social indicators are to describe,
compare, explain and predict social evolution and development. Also, social indicators are to determine what
action must be taken by governmental agencies to modify
social development and to attain a certain social state.
The second part of the document focuses on the analysis of
the domain in determining the significance of social
indicators. It suggests a need for research to discuss
the possible methods and the various types of needed
social indicators. The third and last part of the paper
pertains to the role of the National Institute in relation
to social indicators.

Iowa Development Commission
    1970   "Iowa, a place to grow: 10 year targets to
            2001." Findings from the Conference for Planned
            Economic Development, sponsored by the Iowa De-
            velopment Commission (April 13-14) Ames, Iowa:
            Iowa State University.

A report of the 1970 Conference for Planned Economic
Development specifying goals and needs in federal, state
and local government. In addition, the service sector,
business climate, leisure time activities, education and
quality of life are reviewed as potential areas of future
growth for Iowa.

Jantsch, Erich
    1969   "Integrative planning for the 'joint systems' of
            society and technology--the emerging role of the
            university." Ekistics 28:371-380.

The author examines the functions of the university,

the education function, the research function, and the
service function, and recommends a new purpose for the
university of the future. At present, progress through
university is from generalization to specialization. He
proposes university life to proceed from generalization to
specialization and back to generalization and recommends a
15 year planning horizon to accomplish it.

Johnson, Helen W.
    1971   "Toward-balanced development." A paper present-
            ed at the Annual Meeting of the Rural
            Sociological Society (August 27) Denver,
            Colorado.

Suggested prototype for balanced development program
for initial four-county area in Nebraska, to be expanded
later to eight and then twelve county-area; includes consideration of factors of population distribution, income
and employment opportunity in the area; negates rural or
urban crisis. She posits interrelatedness of rural and
urban problems.

Kaplan, Max
    1968   "Leisure as an issue for the future." Futures
            1:91-99.

Leisure, as a "clue" to observers of quality of life,
is examined in terms of the increasing awareness on the
part of industrialized nations as to its potential impact
on future society.

Keyserling, Leon H.
    1967   "Employment and the 'new economics'." The
            Annals of the American Academy of Political and
            Social Science 373 (September):102-119.
            (Reprinted in Bertram M. Gross (ed.), 1969
            Social Intelligence for America's Future.
            Boston: Allyn and Bacon).

Presents a case for synthesizing the aggregate and
structural approaches to full employment. To bring the
aims of optimal economic growth and resource allocation
into line with the real order of societal priorities, a
ten year "freedom budget" under the Employment Act (1946)
is needed. This would ensure that public policy will move
more effectively to address national priorities which require optimal personal development under full-employment
conditions.

Krieger, Martin H.
    1970   "Six propositions on the poor and pollution."
            Policy Sciences 1:311-324.

With limited funds, relative priorities must be decided
for spending on environmental problems and on problems of
the poor. Environmental problems are, in most cases,
issues for the nonpoor; questioning the incidence of poor
environmental quality and the distribution of its
betterment leads to Proposition I: the quality of environment available is proportional to the socioeconomic
status. Proposition II indicates that environment improvement will likely increase the disparities of Proposition I. That resolution of these inequities will increase
the discontentment about the environment is stated in
Proposition III. The 4th suggests that federal environmental policy is such that the rich get richer and the
poor poorer. A coalition of forces concerned with poverty
and environmental programs can be the most effective for
actuating change for both is given in Proposition V; the
sixth insists man's centrality in our culture must guide
solutions to environmental issues that will be equitable.
Supporting logic and examples are given for all six propositions.

Lamson, Robert W.
    1969   "The future of man's environment." The Science
            Teacher 36 (January):25-30.

    Identified and briefly discussed in this article are
three critical environmental questions for the United
States. Denoted first are the trends and conditions
confronting the United States: population growth and distribution, supply and use of resources, waste output,
growth of technological and organizational power, and the
changing proportions of natural and manmade aspects of the
environment. The range of alternative future environments
is surveyed, then the question of how to control or influence the trends identified above is considered. The relationship between management of environmental trends and
personal and political values places emphasis on the role
of education to teach preservation of the values of
freedom, privacy, autonomy of personality, dispersal of
power, and pluralism, within the necessary management and
control minimals for survival.

    1970a   "Federal action for population policy--what more
            can we do now?" BioScience 20 (August):854-857.

    Categorizing the three means of limiting population
growth as the physical limits of war, famine and disease,
repression, and voluntary limitations, this paper presents
the resources presently available to implement the third
alternative of voluntary limitations, if or when we decide

to take advantage of them. A chart presents the research
categories listed by the Ad Hoc Group on Population Research, with the planning, operations, goals and options
in a framework for analysis of federal action for population policy.

1970b "Policy considerations for environmental
       management." Pp. 267-283 in Alfred Blumstein,
       Murray Kamrass and Armand Weiss (eds.), Systems
       Analysis for Social Problems. Washington, D.C.:
       Washington Operations Research Council.

An attempt to define more adequately environmental
problems and policy issues is made through exploration of
five questions: 1) what is the problem we are trying to
solve? 2) what is meant by "environmental management"?
3) what objects in our environment should we try to
manage? 4) values, goals, and principles, and by means of
what activities, techniques and institutions.

1971a "Policy and futures research--Some important
       questions, principles and issues." Pp. 127-134
       in Japan Society of Futurology (ed.), Challenges
       from the Future: Proceedings of the Interna-
       tional Future Research Conference, Vol. II.
       Kodansha, Ltd. (also in Technology Assessment -
       1970, Hearings before the Subcommittee on Sci-
       ence, Research, and Development of the Committee
       on Science and Astronautics, U.S. House of Rep-
       resentatives, 1970. Pp. 235-239).

From the assumption that man now has the power to manipulate consciously most aspects of his natural and man-
made environment, his society and himself, to what extent
and for what values, goals and interests should this power
be used? Questions of perception, evaluation and control
of effects relating to nature and the environment, man and
society are raised; issues discussed include power distribution in society, the role of the analyst, the tendency
for some futures analysts to neglect the need to evaluate
and control the perceived future, and the treatment of
projections as goals.

1971b "Research on the population problem." Statement
       of Dr. Robert W. Lamson before the Subcommittee
       on Human Resources Committee on Labor and Public
       Welfare, United States Senate. (October 5)

This statement concerns the problems of and needs for
population research. It suggests questions and criteria
which Executive and Legislative Branches should consider
in addressing the population problem and particularly for
more effective management of research resources. Contends
that more research is required on policy alternatives to

appraise or realize the goal of population stabilization.
This research will have to rely and possibly develop
indicants for the analysis of population
growth/distribution, technological development/use, economic growth, supply/use of resources/ services, waste
production/disposal, and alternative programs/laws.

MacDonald, Gordon J.
    1971   "Remarks by Dr. Gordon J. MacDonald." Presented
           at the American Association for the Advancement
           of Science Symposium (December 27) Philadelphia,
           Pennsylvania.

Using the example of the use of potentially harmful
chemicals, particularly possible substitutes for
phosphates in detergents, this paper illustrates both the
needs and the gaps of information in the formulation of
environmental policy. Development of adequate data and
indices must: 1) result in a form easily understood by
the users; 2) be representative of the area and time
period they're intended to cover; 3) be reliable; 4) be
relatively easy to gather, both the data directly representative and that which is not, correlating these and
processing into the index. The Council on Environmental
Quality is currently at work in developing indices in the
six areas of air pollution, water pollution, land use,
wildlife, recreation and pesticides. The function of the
Environmental Protection Agency is also examined.

Maimon, Zvi
    1971   "Second-order consequences - a presentation of a
           concept." Detroit, Michigan: Center for Urban
           Studies, Wayne State University.

Argues the need for new approaches for planning and
policy initiation to anticipate the secondary consequences
as well as primary goals. Brief survey of present methods
such as cost and time analyses. Offers a framework for
analysis; some comments on measurement and anticipation.

Manley, Vaughn Porter
    1967   Iowa's Human and Community Development Re-
           sources. Des Moines, Iowa: Iowa State Manpower
           Development Council, Office of the Governor.

Designed to help local communities, this report suggests the necessary planning and development procedures
for effective action. The logical order to prepare for
action would include problem assessment, needs, general
goals, proposed program content and specific goals. Specific areas are; 1) health and welfare services, 2) educa-

tional, training and counseling services, 3) general
social and economic services, 4) other aids for community
development, and 5) state responses. All of these specific areas are discussed in terms of resources available,
state and local contacts and type of services offered.

Markley, O. W.
      1970   Alternative Futures: Contexts in which Social
              Indicators Must Work. Research Note-EPRC
              6747-11. Menlo Park, California: Stanford Re-
              search Institute, Educational Policy Research
              Center.

    A "morphological" method for projecting a set of alter-
native future histories is presented, and interim results,
which serve as a set of contexts, are described.
Normative social indicators for guiding national policy
should have alternative scoring procedures according to
what embracing societal context is assumed. That is, any
set of social indicators must reflect what this author
terms the "macro problem", be positive indicants of well-
being and fulfillment of human life, and serve to monitor
cultural changes which would illuminate the problems inherent in all plausible future histories.

Mead, Margaret
      1970   "What Margaret Mead told the congressmen about
              urban growth." Nation's Cities 8 (Janu-
              ary):24-26.

    Testimony before a Congressional Subcommittee on Urban
Growth. Emphasizes the stress on the human values and on
the need to consider human beings as persons, in planning
done with them rather than for them; suggests that the man
on the street can and should participate in the major
value decisions that will affect him, to help construct a
system of both trusting and monitoring the experts. Other
remarks relevant to developing a sense of community, on
technological revolution and the generation gap, urban development and the urban future.

Michigan Office of Planning Coordination, Bureau of
Policies and Programs
      1970   Social Reporting in Michigan: Problems and
              Issues. January. Lansing, Michigan: Wayne
              State University Center for Urban Studies.

    This report examines how the State provides leadership
in the development of a comprehensive system of social reporting. The first three sections of the report deal with
the need for regular public reporting associated with

166

quality of life, while the major section is devoted to six substantive areas of high priority policy significance: demographic indicators, health indicators, economic indicators, lawful behavior indicators, education indicators, and environmental quality indicators. Finally the last two sections of the report provide recommendations relative to the State of Michigan.

Mondale, Walter F.
    1967   "Some thoughts on stumbling into the future."
           American Psychologist 22 (November):972-973.

    Senator Mondale, as author of the Full Opportunity and Social Accounting Act, herein describes its purpose of bringing social data and the knowledge of its scientists together in forecasts of future behavior which will help public officials appreciate, understand and supervise change and facilitate application of social information to the pressing problems of American Society. Thus this Act's provisions for a Council of Social Advisors, annual Social Report, and joint Congressional Committee are specifically designed to provide a rigorous, reliable and verifiable accounting of progress and possibilities in the social arena.

    1970a   Full Opportunity Act. 91st Congress, 2nd Session, Senate (July 1) Hearings before the Special Subcommittee on Evaluation and Planning of Social Programs. Report No. 91-998. Washington, D.C.: U.S. Government Printing Office.

    A favorable report from the Committee on the Act, with a proposed amendment to establish within the Congress an Office of Goals and Priorities Analysis. The function would be to draw data and evaluations from the Council of Social Advisers, and submit an annual report to Congress: 1) an analysis of the budgeted programs submitted by the President and in the Economic and Social Reports; 2) examination of national resources, foreseeable costs and benefits of the proposed programs and of the alternatives and 3) recommendations concerning spending priorities. Section by section analysis is given; some of the more important and relevant testimony is included and summarized from the Hearings on the bill.

    1970b   "Social advisers, social accounting, and the Presidency." Law and Comtemporary Problems (Summer):496-504.

    With the question not whether, but which and when, new units should be established within the Executive Office, this paper presents the rationale and urgency for the creation of a Council of Social Advisers, as recommended

in the Full Opportunity Act, S.5. Details the need for
social accounting and the ways in which the Council could
meet these needs; discusses the need for structural change
within the Executive Office to meet the needs of our
people more effectively and efficiently.

1971a "Behavioral scientists urge establishment of
       council of social advisers." U.S. Senate,
       Congressional Record (August):S13107-S13113.

Comments by Senator Mondale, Raymond A. Bauer, Professor of Business Administration, N. J. Demerath III, Executive Officer of the American Sociological Association and
Sol M. Linowitz, Chairman, National Urban Coalition in
support of establishing a social accounting mechanism in
the government. Bauer states that much of what is important to the decency and dignity of Americans does not fall
in the mandate of existing federal agencies and he gives
his support with the others for the establishment of a
Council of Social Advisers.

1971b "S.5--Introduction of the full opportunity and
       national goals and priorities act." U.S.
       Senate, Congressional Record 117 (January
       25):S119-S127.

Outlines rationale for Title I and Title II of this
bill. Title I, establishing full social opportunity as a
national goal, discusses: declaration of policy, social
report of the President, and Council of Social Advisers to
the President. Title II--National Goals and Priorities
discusses: declaration of purpose, establishment, functions, powers of the office (proposes Office of a Director
of Goals and Priorities Analysis), and payment of
expenses. Also printed in the Record are excerpts from
the Report of the National Commission on the Causes and
Prevention of Violence: summary and major recommendations, the scope of the behavioral and social sciences,
behavioral and social science research in and outside the
university, and outlook for the behavioral and social sciences.

1971c "Social advisers, social accounting, and the
       presidency." U.S. Senate, Congressional Record
       117 (August 6):S13437-S13439.

Introductory remarks and a request by Senator Nelson
that the article "Social Advisers, Social Accounting and
the Presidency" by Senator Walter F. Mondale be read into
The Congressional Record. The article discusses what a
Council of Social Advisers would do, the need for a Social
Accounting System and the need for structural change
within the Executive Office. Principal concern of the article is the inter-relationship between a proposed federal

mechanism for improving social policymaking and the Office
of the President of the United States.

Morrison, Denton E., Kenneth E. Hornback and W. Keith
Warner
    1971   "The environmental movement: Some preliminary
            observations." A paper presented at the Annual
            Meeting of the Rural Sociological Society
            (August) Denver, Colorado (Forthcoming in
            William Burch, Neil Cheek and Lee Taylor (eds.),
            Social Behavior, Natural Resources and the Envi-
            ronment, New York: Harper and Row.

    Presented are the organizations involved, nature of
their concerns, changes they seek, strategies and modes of
organization, demographic and attitudinal characteristics;
and from public sources; some data from a national survey
of the mailing list of the organization coordinating Earth
Day, 1970.

National Goals Research Staff
    1970   Toward Balanced Growth: Quantity with Quality.
            (July 4) Washington, D.C.: U.S. Government
            Printing Office.

    NGRS established by President Nixon for public report
on key choices and possible consequences of those
decisions for US; neither a goal-setting nor a planning
function, but rather defines questions, analyzes debates
and examines alternative sets of consequences for comprehensive long-range view of policy in six areas; population
growth and distribution; environment; education; basic
natural science; technology; and consumerism. Useful appendix of charts for trends and projections to 1985.

Nixon, Richard M.
    1971a   The First Annual Report on Financial Assistance
            to Rural Areas, Pursuant to Title 9 of the
            Agricultural Act of 1970. 92nd Congress, 1st
            Session, House Document No. 92-147. July 26.
            Washington, D.C.: U.S. Government Printing
            Office.

    Some of the social and economic trends of recent years
and current relative status of non-metropolitan population
are outlined: employment, income, community assets, education, health, housing, electricity and telephone service. Reviews program availability in rural areas and
efforts to expand availability of Federal programs to
rural people. Appendix includes discussion of the source
(Federal Information Exchange System) and nature of the
information upon which this report is based.

1971b   The First Annual Report on Government Services
         to Rural America, Pursuant to the Agricultural
         Act of 1970. 92nd Congress, 1st Session, House
         Document No. 92-55. March 1. Washington, D.C.:
         U.S. Government Printing Office.

Financial programs considered are limited to credit
programs of major significance in rural areas for purposes
of establishing or expanding (a) private farm and nonfarm
business or enterprises, (b) community public facilities
and (c) other assets in rural development such as housing;
other financial assistance directly related to the purposes of credit programs; and those programs which are
"folded into" the proposed revenue sharing for rural development. Kinds, amounts and purposes of financial
assistance, with the selected present programs are discussed in relation to major rural target groups. Recommendations are made on Federal financial assistance in relation to national objectives of improving the quality of
life in rural America and achieving better geographical
balance in economic growth and population through rural
development, with recommendations stressing rural credit
policy rather than individual programs.

1972   "Problems of population growth." Pp. 249-255 in
         Rex R. Campbell and Jerry L. Wade (eds.),
         Society and Environment: The Coming Collision.
         Boston, Massachusetts: Allyn and Bacon, Inc.).

Proposes a Commission on Population Growth and the
American Future to create the machinery necessary for
acquiring an understanding of demographic change and
applying it to public policy through inquiry and recommendations on: 1) the probable demographic developments, 2)
the public resources required to serve these developments,
and 3) ways that population growth may affect governmental
activities. Better indicants and interpretive analysis of
the implications present information holds will facilitate
the Commission's dual educational and investigative functions. This will require increased research, more people
trained for, expanded and better articulated family
planning programs.

O'Connell, Harold J.
    1972   Toward a Social Policy Model: Methodology and
            Design. Unpublished M.S. Thesis. Ames, Iowa:
            Iowa State University.

This thesis is a derivation of a quantitative social
decision-making policy model within a developmental framework for purposes of planning and evaluation of social

170

policy. The model is an adaptation of Jan Tinbergen's
quantitative economic policy model to a social system, integrated with a social indicator typology, and is constructed to measure the performance of a social system
with respect to its general welfare. The social system
chosen as the empirical referent for the theoretical
equational relationships is the Province of Prince Edward
Island, Canada. Consisting of twenty-one equations in
forty-eight variables, the model is constructed to depict
relationships within seven social components or sectors of
the province - education, housing, health, social services, employment, income, and population. Also included
in the paper is a short discussion of the limitations and
. potential of such a model in the design and evaluation of
public policy along with an appendix which lists a set of
social accounts for the estimation of the policy model for
the province.

Orlans, Harold
    1971   "Social science research policies in the United
            States." Minerva 9 (January):7-31.

    Though titled "in the United States", this paper deals
primarily with the relationship of the social sciences to
the federal government, its departments and agencies, and
the various councils as through the Office of the
President. Compared to the financial support given the
natural sciences, the social sciences come off a poor second; explored here are some of the reasons and factors,
the historical background of this present situation, government policy toward social science, the intractability
of special interests, and some of the unstated functions
of social research.

Pardee, Frederick S., Nake M. Kamrany, Joseph L. Midler
and Charles T. Phillips
    1971   "Developing tools for regional environmental as-
            sessment: A study design." A report prepared
            for Special Assistant to the Secretary for
            Regional Economic Development, U.S. Department
            of Development, Washington, D.C. Los Angeles,
            California: The Institute for Analysis.

    Suggests an appropriate approach to developing a
systematic environmental assessment technique. An initial
exploratory effort is prescribed as necessary for
proceeding toward the goal of comprehensive regional environmental assessment. Such an exploratory study would be
useful towards developing an interim procedure of environmental assessment which would lay the groundwork for more
extensive formal modeling in that it could combine operational results with requirements for further development.

Phillips, Derek L.
    1971   "Sociologists and their knowledge." American
            Behavioral Scientist 14 (March-April):563-582.

Analyzing the field and role of sociology, this paper
delineates the agreement among sociologists that the
profession possesses a unique and valuable body of "knowledge" and expertise, and the disagreements center about
whether or not this knowledge should be put to work, and
if so, for whom. Questions are then raised of how good
sociological knowledge really is, (the author sees no body
of sociological knowledge unique to sociology); on the accuracy of data, its validity for explanation or prediction.

President's Commission on National Goals
    1960   "The commission report." Pp. 1-23 in Goals for
            Americans. New York: Prentice-Hall.

The Report of the President's Commission on National
Goals requested by President Eisenhower; broad outline of
coordinated national policies and goals for future implementation, covering fifteen areas, eleven within the
United States and four abroad; non-partisan commission
with no government connection, finance from private
sources; discussion based on 1) to guard the rights of the
individual; 2) to ensure his development; and 3) to
enlarge his opportunity.

Ratajczak, Rosalinda
    1969   "Problems in the evaluation of poverty pro-
            grams." Working paper. Santa Monica,
            California: Systems Development Corporation.

An SDC working paper which examines concepts of income
and economic well-being with suggested ways to detect
poverty and its frequency distribution; indicates the
context for evaluation of programs, and the importance of
the interactions of such programs with each other and with
other societal forces. In-depth discussion of measures of
income and poverty, income maintenance, income supplement,
public assistance and negative income tax proposals, with
tables and graphs illustrating the salient points.

Rosenthal, Robert A. and Robert S. Weiss
    1969   "Problems of organizational feedback processes."
            Pp. 302-340 in Raymond A. Bauer (ed.), Social
            Indicators. Cambridge, Massachusetts:
            Massachusetts Institute of Technology Press.

172

Defining feedback as the total information process
through which primary and second-order effects of organization actions are fed back to the organization and compared with desired performance, this paper then discusses
the problems involved in terms of organizational survival;
estimating the feedback requirements; feedback from both
external and internal sources and the effects on policy;
potential dangers; and research in maintaining feedback.
Specific illustrations are given from NASA's experiences.
Recommends further development of social science receptor
roles within NASA and other government and non-government
organizations to operate interorganizationally, for more
effective evaluation and utilization of second-order consequences, to reduce some of the wasteful incoherence of
social action.

Samuelson, Robert J.
    1967   "Council of social advisers: New approach to
            welfare priorities?" Science 157
            (July-August):49-50.

    Brief critical remarks regarding Senator Mondale's
"Full Opportunity and Social Accounting Act of 1967"; difficulties of 1) "channel vision" of executive agencies and
congressional committees to concentrate on own projects
and responsibilities; and 2) limits of research findings -
"could agencies, communities and executive office admit a
program was ineffective and scrap it?"

Schmid, A. Allan
    1969   "Developing community spending priorities." A
            paper presented at Central Michigan Leadership
            Program (December 4) Mount Pleasant, Michigan.

    Given here are some of the difficulties in determining
budget allocations and priorities, trade-offs, and
priorities and intergovernmental fiscal relationships, illustrated through tabled budget figures for Isabella
County, Michigan. Local communities should begin to ask
if the ratios of public products and services are in line
with their priorities; whether counties get their share of
state and federal services in useful combinations; the
relative value of some items of lower priorities that
might be exchanged for others; and whether some functions
could better be provided by being shifted to a different
level of government. Budget information is not now available in a form to provide answers; such information is
needed.

Schwartz, Arthur
    1970   "PPBS and evaluation and research: Problems and

promises." Pp. 35-41 in Edward E. Schwartz
(ed.), Planning-Programming-Budgeting Systems
and Social Welfare. Chicago, Illinois: The
University of Chicago, The School of Social
Service Administration。

This paper centers cn the relationship, present and potential, between PPBS and evaluation research. The author
states that the PPBS requires research as a basis for
rational decision-making in the allocations of limited resources and the setting of program priorities.
Accordingly, the PPBS system is looked at as a system and
a goal-model, useful in cost-benefit analysis, and makes
program objectives more specific. Finally, the complexity, limitations, and potentials of PPBS to social welfare
are discussed.

Schwartz, Edward E. (ed.)
   1970   Planning-Programming-Budgeting Systems and
           Social Welfare. Chicago, Illinois: The Univer-
           sity of Chicago, The School of Social Service
           Administration.

This short booklet is a compendium of five papers by
seven authors. These papers were presented at the
Workshop in Evaluating the Delivery of Social Welfare
Services in 1968 at San Francisco. The collection of
papers introduced here describe the PPBS system as introduced by the Federal Government, the potentials and limitations of PPBS in its application to social welfare programs, and concrete applications of the relationship of
PPBS to the formulation of Public Policy. The idea of
linking planning to budgeting through programming based on
comparative analysis is shown to be the vital essence of
PPBS.

Sheldon, Eleanor Bernert
   1971   "Social reporting for the 1970's." Pp. 403-435
           in Volume II, Federal Statistics: A Report of
           the President's Commission. Washington, D.C.:
           U.S. Government Printing Office.

At the request of the President's Commission on Federal
Statistics, the author along with Raymond Bauer, Kenneth
Land and several other contributors suggest one alternative to the future development of a long-term program in
social indicators. To decide whether or not a substantive
area should be added or deleted, they recommend using
acknowledged social goals, emerging social goals and the
potentiality for change as possible criteria. An overview
of what has been done in selected areas of public safety
and legal justice, health, social mobility and youth pro-

vides an assessment of what has been done and recommendations for future development in each of the areas. A
paradigm is presented relating institutional sponsorship
(government or cther) with type of indicator (problem-
oriented or descriptive-analytical). Some general recommendations: federal agencies - review existing series of
social data to determine where we are and what we have,
facilitated by developing subject area panels to view content areas such as socio-economic welfare, social participation and alienation, use of time, consumption behavior
and aspirations, satisfactions and morale; private sector
- NSF and HEW to encourage and fund developmental work on
new statistical series emphasizing subjective areas. Also
they recommend the development of testable explanatory
models at the subsystem levels.

Smith, Courtland L. and Thomas C. Hogg
    1971   "Cultural aspects of water resource development
            past, present, and future." Water Resources
            Bulletin 7 (August):652-660.

Water resources definition and use in the American West
has changed from the settlement period of a stimulus for
population and economic growth, to the present as being
necessary to keep up with growth. The incipient third
stage can be seen as a means of controlling or managing
both the location and extent of population and economic
growth. Cultural functions important for planning are
adaptation to the environment, gaining of subsistence, development of a meaningful community, enhancement of communication and the stimulation of innovation are discussed.
Cited as examples are the California Water Plan, the Central Arizona Project and Willamette (Ore.) Basin Comprehensive Plan.

Springer, Michael
    1970   "Social indicators, reports, and accounts:
            Toward the management of society." The Annals
            of the American Academy of Political and Social
            Science 388 (March):1-13.

Argues that a system of social indicators and accounts
should be developed using models of democracy, as well as
rational management, and based on a social science developed to serve the needs of the poor and unorganized as
well as the rich and powerful. In Springer's view, this
is necessitated by the fact that the two most fully developed conceptions of social accounting (those offered by
Bertram Gross and Mancur Olson) differ on their notions of
what would be a rationally managed social order.

Stagner, Ross
    1970   "Perceptions, aspirations, frustrations, and
            satisfactions: An approach to urban
            indicators." Ekistics 30 (September):197-199.
            (Also in Bertram Gross and Michael Springer
            (eds.), The Annals: Political Intelligence for
            America's Future 388 (March):59-68).

    Expresses that socio-psychological orientations in
urban systems planning for humans are the irreducible
units of the author's feedback system depicted. Thus,
this paper asserts that cities exist to provide satisfactions for their citizens and proposes a series of social
indicators based on systemic output of citizen-
satisfaction. Types of analysis are delineated for find-
ing latent dissatisfaction variables which specify where
social action might make a difference with the view that
satisfaction is relative to the level of aspiration and
the reference groups which spawn individual percepts of an
urban situation.

Sundquist, James L.
    1970   "Where shall they live?" The Public Interest 18
            (Winter):88-100.

    Approximately 60% of the United States population is
confined to four megalopolises--Boston to Washington,
D.C., base of the Great Lakes region, San Francisco to
Mexican border and Florida. A rationale for the development of a national policy on population distribution is
presented with a request for broad outlines of alternative
programs.

Tenbruck, Friedrich H.
    1970   "Limits of planning." A paper presented at the
            Seventh World Congress of Sociology (September
            14-19) Varna, Bulgaria.

    Examines several assumptions of the social sciences
that our knowledge will continue to progress, that more
knowledge leads to better planning, better planning increases societal control, and increasing control generates
greater happiness. He finds these assumptions to be
faulty and suggests a need to specify the limits of
planning for use in sociology.

United Nations Social Development Division
    1969   "Social policy and the distribution of income in
            the nation." Ekistics 28 (December):399-405

Recounts some of the historical development of thought
about economic equality, productivity and wages, redistribution of income, guaranteed annual income and elimination
of poverty. Discusses more recent economic views that
both need and productivity must be considered as criteria
in determining income distribution. Much of present
disagreement has shifted from aims and policies to how
best to achieve the aims.

U.S. Department of Agriculture
    1969   "Rural development program." (November 7) Wash-
            ington, D.C.: Office of the Secretary, U.S. De-
            partment of Agriculture.

    Gives the Department's policies and structure for im-
plementation of The President's Task Force on Rural Development of November, 1969. Refers specifically to efforts
to expand farm and nonfarm employment, income
opportunities and more attractive living conditions in
nonmetropolitan areas. Suggests available agencies and
resources, and channels of cooperation.

U.S. President, Research Commission on National Goals
    1960   Goals for Americans: Programs for Action in the
            Sixties. Englewood Cliffs, New Jersey:
            Prentice-Hall.

    This commission, having no connection with government,
was requested to "develop a broad outline of coordinated
national policies and programs" and to "set up a series of
goals in various areas of national activity." This resulting document covers many fields including fundamental
American values, goals at home, and goals abroad. It is a
document intended to be renewed every ten years for the
purpose of reevaluating broad American goals.

U.S. Senate
    1969   "Full opportunity and social accounting act."
            House of Representatives Bill #10116, 91st
            Congress 1st Session (April).

    Introduced by Mr. Diggs, this bill states that it is
the continuing policy and responsibility of our government
to promote and encourage such conditions as will give
every American the opportunity to live in decency and
dignity. Provides for an annual Social Report to Congress
by The President, a Council of Advisers to The President,
and a Joint Senate-House Committee on the Social Report.

United States Senate, Committee on Public Welfare
    1970   Full Opportunity Act. Hearings before the Spe-

cial Subcommittee on Evaluation and Planning of
Social Programs, on S.5, 91st Congress, 1st and
2nd Session.

These hearings on S.5, The Full Opportunity Act, cover
six days of testimony before the subcommittee and much additional information presented in written form to the
subcommittee. The Appendix includes an extended annotated
bibliography, subdivided into: social science policy;
social accounting; social scientists and policy-making;
professional concerns; interdisciplinary social science
research; social and political forecasting; Department of
Defense military sponsored social science research;
National Academy of Sciences; National Foundation for the
Social Sciences; National Science Foundation; and
periodicals dealing with the social sciences and public
policy.

Verba, Sidney
     1967   "Democratic participation." The Annals of the
            American Academy of Political and Social Science
            373 (September):53-78. (Reprinted in Bertram M.
            Gross (ed.), 1969 Social Intelligence for
            America's Future. Boston: Allyn and Bacon).

Elaborates the conceptual dimensions of democratic participation by focusing on participation vis-a-vis
governmental decision-makers. Discusses the complicated
process of arriving at social indicators in terms of the
multiplicity of forms of participation and the complexity
of political goals; guidelines are suggested for
developing indicators of participation and access to it
which will encompass a meaningful perspective of its relevance to decision-making.

Waterston, Albert
     1965   "What do we know about planning?" International
            Development Review 7 (December):2-10.

The article reports on a study by a small group within
the World Bank who have been assembling, classifying and
analyzing planning data of countries throughout the world.
The attempt was to determine when, how, and why planning
has been successful and unsuccessful, and to draw relevant
lessons of wide applicability from the experience of
countries which have been more or less systematically
planning their development.

Wilcox, Leslie D. and Ralph M. Brooks
     1971   "Toward the development of social indicators for
            policy planning." A paper presented at the

178

Annual Meetings of the Ohio Valley Sociological
Society (April 22-24) Cleveland, Ohio.

This paper offers a perspective to reassess the role
and potential of social indicators, critiques various definitions and suggests the next steps in research. Examines social indicator claims for descriptive reporting,
program evaluation, planned development and societal control; finds some claims unrealistic, others excessive.

Wilensky, Harold L.
1967   Organizational Intelligence: Knowledge and
        Policy in Government and Industry. New York:
        Basic Books.

Intelligence is defined by Wilensky as "the problem of
gathering, processing, interpreting, and communicating the
technical and political information needed in the
decision-making process." Wilensky is concerned with the
organizational use or misuse of this intelligence. This
problem is becoming more acute due to the knowledge
explosion and organizational revolution, which "makes an
understanding of the use of intelligence indispensable for
the proper conduct of adminstrative life and the effective
pursuit of the public interest." He cites the Council of
Economic Advisers as an example of a social science
discipline, economics, that is successful in the application of reason to public affairs. He argues that all
sociologists, even those labelled theoretical, have been
concerned with policy-oriented problems in the broad
sense. He thus argues for a more encompassing breadth of
view by the "technologists who produce this intelligence.
. . as a requisite for effective policy advice, especially
when social science is to be incorporated into decision-
making."

1970   "Intelligence in industry: The uses and abuses
        of experts." The Annals of the American Academy
        of Political and Social Science 388
        (March):46-58.

Describes structural roots of intelligence failures and
irrational policy decisions. Hierarchy, specialization
and centralization are cited as being universal sources of
intelligence, distortion and blockage in any complex
social system. Obtaining quality intelligence typically
requires circumvention of typical ranking systems and
measures which expedite the free flow of rival
perspectives. Devices which have served these needs are
noted and emphasize that without eliminating certain
sources of intelligence blockage and distortion a system
of social indicators may merely contribute to the chaos of
information overload and not rational policy planning.

Williams, Robin M., Jr.
    1967   "Individual and group values." The Annals of
            the American Academy of Political and Social
            Science 371 (March):20-37. (Reprinted in
            Bertram M. Gross (ed.), 1969 Social Intelligence
            for America's Future. Boston: Allyn and
            Bacon).

    Presents a case for the general usefulness and
feasibility of bringing systematic knowledge of operative
value standards into societal diagnoses and planning.
More explicit definition and analysis of value problems
ought to enhance effectiveness of goal achievement, widen
the scope of awareness in decision-making, and refine
capacities for sensing limits and hazards in current
societal trends and policies.

Winthrop, Henry
    1969   "Social costs and studies of the future."
            Futures 1 (December):488-499.

    This paper is concerned with the relative neglect of
social costs by many writers about the future. Uses
systems analysis with nuclear power as an example of the
indifference to and the need for systematic treatment of
social costs. Two tables of the costs (insults) to the
physical and social environment.

Wright, Christopher
    1969   "Some requirements for viable social goals."
            Pp. 194-197 in R. Jungk and J. Galtung (eds.),
            Mankind-2000. London: Allen and Unwin.

    The author discusses the many meanings of social goals
in terms of specific goals (landing a man on the moon),
less specific goals (commitments to extent of life span),
and general goals (advancemnnt of well being of mankind
throughout the world). He examines the concept of goals
in three sections: Understanding the means-goals relationships, clarifying choices among goals, and generating
viable new goals.

APPLICATION

AFL-CIO American Federationist
    1970   "Crime in America Part I: A national concern;
            Part II: Profile of the offender; Part III:
            The root causes." American Federationist
            77:6-13.

This article is excerpted from the final report of the
National Commission on the Causes and Prevention of
Violence. It gives a historical overview of crime in
America as a national concern; an analysis of the offender
such as age, sex, socio-economic status, and his victim
characteristics; and finally the root causes of violence
from a standpoint of race, home, family and neighborhood
life, the school, and the job.

Aiken, Michael and Robert R. Alford
    1970   "Community structure and innovation: The case
            of public housing." The American Political Sci-
            ence Review 64 (September):843-864.

Examines 646 communities seeking variables which have
had significant impact upon participation in federal
public housing programs. Previous studies of innovation
have not considered issues which involved substantial external resources, sponsorship or legitimization by a
community organization, or low degrees of citizen participation. Findings suggest a model which conceives of a
community as the key unit of analysis, considers organizations as the key actors, and views their interrelationships and degree of coordination as critical to better
explain policy outcomes for issues with these features.
Variables studied were: availability and application for
federal urban renewal funds, ethnicity, income, voting behavior, political structure, industrial character, educational level, city age and size, unemployment, migration,
housing and nonwhite composition. Theoretical
shortcomings of political culture, political power
centralization, community differentiation or continuity,
and community integration perspectives are discussed. An
alternative theory is proposed which assumes that the accumulation of experience and information is crucial to
innovative structural differentiation and the coordinative
capacity created by interorganizational networks of
"interfaces" between centers of power.
Alford, Robert R.
    1972   "A critical evaluation of the principles of city
            classification." Chapter XII in Brian Berry
            (ed.), Classification of Cities: New Methods

and Evolving Uses. New York: Wiley and Sons, Inc.

Evaluates some assumptions underlying factor analysis of city characteristics, and assesses their utility in creating city classifications. The empirical relationships of six selected variables are considered. Some suggestions are forwarded for taking a wider range of characteristics into account in city classifications, not only for national but for cross-national studies as well.

Anderson, Jacqueline, Eugene Lourey and Seldon Todd
    1969   "Preliminary social indicator concepts: American Rehabilitation Foundation study to develop a social indicator system for the aging." Minneapolis, Minnesota: Institute for Interdisciplinary Studies, American Rehabilitation Foundation.

Preliminary report for the Administration on Aging prepared for the White House Conference on Aging (November, 1971). The discussion of social indicators is in reference to aging with specific attention given to definitions on social indicators, functions, problems in construction, review of relevant literature, proposed social indicators in life satisfaction (attitudes), income, health, shelter (housing) and socialization. The concept of social indicators is developed as giving a clear picture of the social conditions of older Americans. The document does not assign normative values to indicators. The Appendix includes a "Comparative Analysis of National Indicators" by Lourey, an examination of precision of present indicators, some examples, validity, awareness, effects, interpretation and ultimate use of indicators.

Anderson, James G.
    1971   "Social indicators and second-order consequences: Measuring the impact of innovative health and medical care delivery systems." Research Memorandum No. 71-7. Lafayette, Indiana: School of Industrial Engineering, Purdue University.

Developing a model to be used with innovative health care system in seven-county area in southern New Mexico; considerations of population, nonhuman resources, subsystems, internal and external relations in the system structure; inputs and outputs of the system performance; path analysis diagram; tables of intercorrelation of several health indices from National Health Interview Survey, for all of New Mexico.

Andrews, Frank M. and George W. Phillips
    1970   "The squatters of Lima: Who they are and what
            they want." The Journal of Developing Areas 4
            (January):211-223.

    Presents the results of a sample survey of barriada residents in 1967 to determine priorities for urban development projects wherever squatter settlements have occurred. Attitudes toward twenty-six public and private services were measured and descriptive data obtained to serve as benchmarks for assessing subsequent changes. Services which ranked high on both indexes, extent and intensity, of dissatisfaction were: location of medical services, water, sewers, lights, street paving, postal service and police protection. Relative importance of services was found to be quite stable across various subgroup classifications.

Baster, Nancy and Wolf Scott
    1969   Levels of Living and Economic Growth: A Comparative Study of Six Countries 1950-1965. Geneva,
            Switzerland: United Nations Research Institute
            for Social Development.

    This volume reports findings of a project designed to examine the relation of specific social factors to specific forms of economic growth from 1950 to 1965 in Morocco, Chile, Jamaica, Mexico, Ceylon, and Malaysia. In particular, the influence of education and health on the economic growth of these countries is examined and a set of hypotheses is developed to account for findings. Emphasis is given in the report to the ways social factors may influence economic growth and their effect upon the responsiveness of the economic system and their role in the mediation of stimuli from one economic sector to another.

Bayer, Alan E. and Robert F. Boruch
    1969   "Black and white freshmen entering four-year
            colleges." Educational Record 50
            (Fall):371-386.

    In reporting a study of 83,000 college freshmen in the fall of 1968, answers were sought for the background and characteristics for black men and women and white men and women, in 4-year colleges both predominantly black and predominantly white. Data presented in tabular form, weighted to approximate national population estimates, includes proportion of black students among all college freshmen, demographic data, average aptitude test scores, SES by race and sex. Findings include the proportionate underrepresentation of black students; that the proportion has changed but little in the last few years; that the overwhelming majority of institutions enroll only a minute proportion of black students, that underrepresentation will likely continue through the next generation; that most of the predominantly black colleges are unable to compete for superior students.

Becker, Catherine and Rabel J. Burdge
  1971 "The effects of familism, traditionalism and socio-economic status on attitude toward reservoir construction in an eastern Kentucky county." A paper presented at the Annual Meeting of the Rural Sociological Society (August 27) Denver, Colorado.

Value orientations of familism and traditionalism considered as intervening variables are found to have no direct influence on the attitudes studied; socio-economic status and flood damage is significantly associated; a conceptual model is examined; table of correlation matrixes is given; and some implications for water resource development research are presented.

Becker, Harold S. and Raul de Brigard
  1971a A Framework for Community Development Action Planning. Volume I: An Approach to the Planning Process. Report R-18. Middletown, Connecticut: Institute for the Future.

In cooperation with the Connecticut Community Development Action Plan and using the Delphi process, the Institute for the Future generated check lists of goals or objectives, needs, social indicators and possible actions for each of 13 areas of municipal development concern: education, housing, health, recreation, social services, economic development, public utilities and services, public protection, transportation and circulation, culture, interpersonal communication, general municipal government, and natural resources. A format is given for relating goals and objectives, actions and indicators; appendices give the check lists for planning all 13 areas.

  1971b A Framework for Community Development Action Planning. Volume II: Study Procedure, Conclusions, and Recommendations for Future Research. Report R-19. Middletown, Connecticut: Institute for the Future.

184

Continuing the summary of the work of the Institute for the Future, in cooperation with the Connecticut Community Development Action Plan, this volume details the study flow including alternative community objectives, and the study conclusions with the format for relating goals and objectives, actions, and indicators, and the limitations of the study results. The Delphi process is delineated with the instructions, questions and responses used in each of its three rounds. Additional research suggestions are given. An analysis and evaluation of five Connecticut communities using the plan indicated weaknesses and needs for improvement in the techniques used, without discounting their value.

Bell, Daniel
    1968   "The measurement of knowledge and technology."
            Pp. 145-246 in Eleanor B. Sheldon and Wilbert
            Moore (eds.), Indicators of Social Change: Con-
            cepts and Measurements. New York: Russell Sage
            Foundation.

This essay attempts first to delineate the fundamental structural trends in society as they affect knowledge and technology in respect to an emerging and distinct structural change leading to post-industrial society. Five dimensions of the post-industrial society are outlined and discussed. An analysis of some of the problems in the measurement of knowledge and technology was presented from the point of view of patterns and limits of growth. Finally, the present and future dimensions of the educated and technical class of the country, are presented using tables and graphs of data trends.

Bender, Lloyd D., Bernal L. Green and Rex R. Campbell
    1971   "The process of rural poverty ghettoization:
            Population and poverty growth in rural regions."
            A paper presented at the Annual Meeting of the
            American Association for the Advancement of Sci-
            ence (December) Philadelphia, Pennsylvania.

The proposition here examined is that once poverty becomes concentrated in a region, the economic and social systems of the nation operate to further intensify poverty rather than provide any kind of automatic self-correction. Poverty is generated by the same social and economic system which produces affluence. Data for this research comes from study since 1965 in the rural Ozarks region. From the initial economic stress, three sub-processes are identified and discussed: a) intergenerational familial poverty; b) class selective migration; and c) changes in the productivity of social and economic institutions, from all of which are derived policy implications.

Blumenthal, Monica D.
    1971   "Alienation and violence for social change."   A
            paper presented at the 13th Canadian-American
            Seminar Program (November 19) Windsor, Ontario,
            Canada.

    Using Seeman's conceptualization of alienation as
powerlessness, isolation and normlessness, this paper discusses how various groups feel about the use of property
damage and personal injury as tolls for producing change.
An Index for Violence of Social Change is developed and
used as an instrument with a representative control
sample, university student protesters, a group of mostly
young Chicano dissenters in Los Angeles and prisoners in a
minimum security prison. Findings include the expected
relationship between violent behavior and attitudes toward
violence, with discussion of the implications of that relationship.

Blumenthal, Monica D. and Frank M. Andrews
    1970a   "Resentment and suspicion."   Ann Arbor,
            Michigan: The University of Michigan, Institute
            for Social Research.

    Using items originally used by Buss and Durkee, this
paper forwards an index measuring resentment and
suspicion. This index is conceived as an indicant of attitudes toward violence based on the linkage between these
attitudes and threatened feelings. Items were chosen on
the basis of data collected in several small populations,
and the index was constructed from those items showing
stable inter-relationships across a variety of demographic
groups. The measure was inversely correlated with a measure of trust and increasing resentment and suspicion was
found to be associated with decreasing social class and
status, with blacks scoring considerably higher than
whites.

    1970b   "Values: Retributive justice, self defense,
            kindness." Ann Arbor, Michigan: The University
            of Michigan, Institute for Social Research.

    This paper identifies three main problems of values
defining values as attitudes that include affective, cognitive and motivational contents in relation to some
object or target, and further, which contain the property
of "oughtness" for oneself and for others. The first
problem deals with the type value, the second with the
strength of adherence, and third, the place of the value
in the individual's hierarchy of values. Measures are
presented to develop indices for retributive justice,
kindness and self-defense. Data is analyzed in relation

186

to numerous demographic variables: education, religion, race, marital status, foreign backgrounds, age, regional differences, and social class. Tables summarize the findings and correlations.

Blumenthal, Monica D., Robert L. Kahn and Frank M. Andrews
    1971   "Attitudes toward violence." Ann Arbor,
            Michigan: The University of Michigan, Institute
            for Social Research. (Reprinted in part in Science News 100:14-15).

    Data from a national representative sample of American men is presented and analyzed. Discussed are: the measurement of attitudes toward violence for social change and for social control; definitions of violence by the sample; values and attitudes; dissent and dissenters; and the demographic variables on the attitudes. Findings include: that a high proportion of American men will tolerate high levels of violence by police, the most important explanatory factor being basic values held. The summary suggests a real need to develop mechanisms for social change through nonviolent means, and cites the danger of labelling all protest as "violent" because of the effect on the public's attitudes. Twenty-eight tables present the data in summary form.

Boruch, Robert F. and John A. Creager
    1972   "A note on stability of self-reported protest
            activity and attitudes." Measurement and Evaluation in Guidance 5 (July)

    More than 200 college freshmen were surveyed twice (test-retest interval of one week), reporting their attitudes toward and behavior in military, racial and administrative protests. Data suggest small changes occur in the responses from one survey to the next, both for the participation in the protests and the attitudes toward them; degree of correlational stability depends on nature of the protest. Attitudes polled were self-ratings on liberalism, toward college control of student activism, regulation of off-campus students, student publications, college veto power on campus speakers, and on administrative laxity in dealing with student protesters. Statistics reported are means, standard deviations, differences and the correlations for tests one and two.

Brackett, Jean C.
    1969   "New BLS budgets provide yardsticks for measuring family living costs." Monthly Labor Review
            92 (April):3-16.

The Bureau of Labor Statistics provides budgets for three levels of living for a family of four, based on spring, 1967 figures for 39 cities grouped regionally, with comparable amounts for nonmetropolitan areas for each region and for urban U.S. as a whole. Tables summarize both the amounts and indexes of comparative costs.

1971   "The application of discriminant analysis in distinguishing between the crime profiles of large and small metropolitan areas." Unpublished manuscript. Washington, D.C.: The Urban Institute.

Using a discriminant analysis of the data for the seven index crimes of the FBI Uniform Crime Report for 1965 and 1969, this analysis identifies a profile (defined as a linear combination of major crimes) that significantly differentiates between large and small metropolitan areas, the single most important category being that of murder and non-negligent manslaughter. Findings discussed also indicate (as summarized in tables) metropolitan areas with profiles uncharacteristic of their population size class, shifts that occurred between the 1965-1969 reports, primarily large areas assuming profiles typical of small areas which indicate a reduction in the relative weight of murder and non-negligent manslaughter. Size differentiation is at the 250,000 mark; 202 metropolitan areas were included in the study. Additional indications suggest population size is a poor indicator of the crime profile for a metropolitan area: there were significant different distributions of metropolitan areas based on population size to those based on the crime profile.

Bryce, Herrington J.
1972   Are Regional Rates of Poverty Among Whites and Nonwhites Subject to the Same Determinants? Working Paper No. 1206-3. Washington, D.C.: The Urban Institute.

Further testing of Thurow's hypothesis and findings that the variables which determine white poverty also determine nonwhite poverty and with the same weights, this study partially accepts that hypothesis. With a model using the variables of dependency ratio, high school completion, male unemployment rate, female unemployment rate and an index of relative concentration in low paying industries, it was found that the same determinants are operant, but that the weights and interaction of the determinants are markedly different. Among whites, the single most important cause of poverty is male unemployment; among nonwhites it is lack of education.

Bush, J. W., Milton M. Chen, Ann S. Bush and Christopher
B. Karlene
    1971   "The quantitative analysis of issues in medical
            malpractice claims." A paper presented at the
            Conference on Medical Malpractice (September
            1-3) Center for the Study of Democratic Institu-
            tions, Santa Barbara, California.

A mathematical model for use in medical malpractice
cases is presented where probability is used to determine
the causality of cases and thus determine damages.
Damages are measured in part by health status and
function-time. To properly determine damages, an
administrative agency is proposed which collects and evaluates all a nation's data on medical damages to individuals. The reasons for this agency are presented along with
its advantages and disadvantages.

Bush, J. W. and S. Fanshel
    1970   "Basic concepts for quantifying health status
            and program outcomes." A paper supported by the
            National Center for Health Services Research and
            Development and by contracts with the New York
            State Health Planning Commission. Unpublished
            manuscript. San Diego, California: University
            of California.

A numerical description of health status is developed
and applied to a tuberculin testing program. Each member
of the population can be on several levels of function
from well-being valued at 1.0 through various states of
dysfunction to death valued at 0.0. A method is proposed
for assigning social values to the intermediate status of
dysfunction, and a set of utility numbers thus assigned
between 0 and 1 is called the Health Status Index. Comparison among health programs for different diseases is
computed in terms of output.

Cebotarev, E. A. and E. J. Brown
    1971   "On community resource development." A paper
            presented at the Annual Meeting of the Rural
            Sociological Society (August) Denver, Colorado.

Analysis of two basic change strategies in CRD: 1)
"process" (and psychological development sequence); and 2)
"task" oriented (and sociological development sequences);
and one auxiliary strategy, the "social chain sequence."
Failure to distinguish between the two major orientations
in the Extension Service Organizations studied (Maryland,
Pennsylvania, Missouri) caused ineffectiveness and difficulties in Extension in operation.

189

Citizens Advisory Committee on Environmental Quality
    1971   Report to the President and to the Council on
            Environmental Quality. Washington, D.C.: Exec-
            utive Office of the President.

This report summarizes the findings and recommendations
of six subcommittees of the Advisory Committee which had
the responsibility of making a depth study of specific environment problems. Problems covered are: people and
land, energy production and use, pollution abatement, environmental education and citizen responsibility. Recommendations calling for increased financing, greater priority and joint industry-government programs are indicated
for dealing with the environment.

Demerath, N. J. III
    1968   "Trends and anti-trends in religious change."
            In Eleanor B. Sheldon and Wilbert Moore (eds.),
            Indicators of Social Change. New York: Russell
            Sage Foundation.

This chapter indicates that hard data on religious
change are in scarce supply, unreliable, and
unilluminating. The goal is to raise a host of issues
concerning major processes and trends in 20th century
American religion. This is done by looking at the issues
and data surrounding religious revival in America, the
extent of religious belief, the changes in its organizational aspects, and the spirit of ecumenism in contemporary times.

Deutsch, Karl W., John Platt and Dieter Senghaas
    1971   "Conditions favoring major advances in social
            science." Science 171 (February):450-459.

Major advances in social science since 1900 were
analyzed as to their: identifiability, field, nature,
innovator(s) characteristics, institutional or geographic
origin, socio-political conditions and time from
conception to impact. Sixty-two advances were readily
discernible, contributed by either individuals or teams
from few geographic centers. Impact lag was indicated to
be decreasing with delay presently between 10-15 years;
programs at favorable locations might optimize the
advances in social science knowledge and applications.

Drewnowski, Jan and Muthu Subramanian
    1970   "Social aims in development plans." Part II in
            Studies in the Methodology of Social Planning.
            Report No. 70.5. Geneva , Switzerland: United

Nations Research Institute for Social Development.

Examining 61 National Development Plans, only 14 had
the minimum data for formulation of a methodology to
derive the preference weights assumed for three social
factors: nutrition as indicated by daily per capita
caloric intake as a percent of requirement; health denoted
by the percent of population with access to medical care;
and education, comparing primary school enrollments to
percent of population aged 5-14 years. These three
factors were the only quantified ones common to any of the
plans. Preference weights attached to the three sectors
seem to be proportional inversely to the level of that
sector at that point of time. Social aims seem to be more
related to the development level of a country than to any
specific characteristics.

Duncan, Beverly
  1968   "Trends in output and distribution of
          schooling." Pp. 601-672 in Eleanor B. Sheldon
          and Wilbert E. Moore (eds.), Indicators of
          Social Change. New York: Russell Sage Founda-
          tion.

Duncan, in this chapter, attempts to identify the basic
data sets that bear on twentieth century trends in output
and distribution of schooling in America. The author indicates that the value of information collected in different surveys is considerably enhanced when it is compiled
for a cohort i.e., a group of people having in common an
event, such as birth, which defines their membership.
From this perspective, the output and duration of
schooling, the distribution of schooling in the population, and the quality of the schooling received become important considerations.

Elazar, Daniel J.
  1966a "State aid and local action." Pp. 194-195 in
          Daniel J. Elazar (ed.), American Federalism: A
          View from the States. New York: Thomas Y.
          Crowell Company.

Local governmental services depend on state aid which
is given contingent on how receptive the state is to local
requests. Availability of resources is most important;
however, cultural factors influence a state's willingness
to spend. Local communities must take advantage of
opportunities available from state and federal governments.

  1966b "The civil community and the state." Pp.
          173-176 in Daniel J. Elazar (ed.), American

Federalism: A View from the States. New York:
Thomas Y. Crowell Company.

The close connection between the state and its local
subdivisions is emphasized. Three central factors are
noted which aid localities in their ability to exercise
control over the governmental services and activities provided, the emphasis being on organization.

1966c   "Variations in state-local relations." Pp.
         180-186 in Daniel J. Elazar (ed.), American
         Federalism: A View from the States. New York:
         Thomas Y. Crowell Company.

The following seven variables 1) political culture, 2)
general culture, 3) sectionalism, 4) urban-rural, 5)
metropolitan-nonmetropolitan, 6) localism, and 7)
intermetropolitan are presented in a table demonstrating
the extent to which they are present in each of the fifty
states.

Farley, Reynolds
    1971   "Indicators of recent demographic change among
            blacks." A paper presented at the Annual
            Meeting of the American Sociological Association
            (August 30-September 2) Denver, Colorado.

This paper presents and analyzes data taken from the
U.S. Census Bureau reports and from the Census of Population, 1970, to examine the hypothesis that the
socioeconomic status of blacks, relative to whites, has
improved in recent decades. Background statistical information is given of the growth rates of the black and white
population, the changing residential distribution of
blacks, and regional and city-suburban growth rates.
Demographic data concerning education, occupation and
income are then examined, with the conclusion that some
progress was made in the 1960's, just as in previous
decades; that the gains were somewhat greater among blacks
than among whites; and that most indicators of racial
differentiation declines. Nevertheless, at the present
rates of growth there will still be large differences at
the end of the 1970's, and blacks will still be at a distinct disadvantage.

Ferriss, Abbott L.
    1969   "Indicators of trends in American education."
            New York: Russell Sage Foundation.

Continuing the Russell Sage Foundation series on
Indicators of Social Change, statistical time series on

educational trends are given. Each of the chapters on enrollment, teachers, quality of education, graduates,
trends in educational organization and finance, and educational attainment is extensively illustrated with tables
and figures, with detailed notes and the statistical
series in the appendices. Discussed also are the interpretation of trends, aggregated and disaggregated measures, criteria for the selection of an indicator, and
types of statistical series. Major sources of data are
the U.S. Bureau of the Census and the U.S. Office of Education. The President's Commission on National Goals
(1960) included 25 specific goals and other subordinate
objectives for education; thirteen of these are examined
and the extent of achievement illustrated through the time
series or through other data.

> 1971   Indicators of Trends in the Status of American
>   Women. New York: Russell Sage Foundation.

Building on the framework presented in the Foundation's
first volume Indicators of Social Change (1968), Abbott
Ferriss has collected, analyzed and assessed data on a
particular subject matter bearing on social trends.
Focusing on the changing status of women in the United
States, he asks whether changes in the objective status of
women might account for the rise of protest movements and
related feminist endeavors. The vast array of trend data
presented cover a variety of life situations in which
women are involved: education; marital status and
fertility; labor force status; employment and income;
health and recreation. On the data themselves he finds
little cause for the reemergence of feminists' activities
and refers to other plausible hypotheses.

Finsterbusch, Kurt
    1971   "The recent rank ordering of nations in terms of
            level of development and rate of development."
            A revision of a paper presented at the Seventh
            World Congress of Sociology of the International
            Sociological Association, September 14-19, 1970
            (Varna, Bulgaria).

This paper is concerned with measurement of national
development. Defined as the increase of a nation's
ability to control and process its resources and environment, several methods are judged satisfactory for measuring a nation's level of development. However, extant
measures of rate are described as unreliable, failing to
adequately account for the multiple dimensions of change.
A multivariate index, combining ten rates, is developed
and its merits relative to the GNP are discussed.

Fitzgerald, Sherman
   1970   Multi-County Regions in Utah.   Salt Lake City,
           Utah: The Bureau of Community Development, Uni-
           versity of Utah.

   Purposes of this study were generally to investigate
approaches to delimiting regional boundaries in Utah by
the collection and analysis of empirical data by counties.
The relative capacity of each county to provide the major
social and economic needs for its population was examined
to indicate: 1) "service areas", 2) intrastate organizational classifications of regions, 3) areas for State and
Federal decentralization of departmental services, and 4)
multi-county regions which would coincide with existing
intercounty activities and affiliations.

Flax, Michael J.
   1970   Selected White/Non-White Socioeconomic Compari-
           sons: An Experiment in Racial Indicators.   Pre-
           liminary Draft Paper: 136-5.   Washington, D.C.:
           The Urban Institute.

   This report elaborates several approaches for improving
the compilation and presentation of racial indicators.
Data depicting socio-economic white/non-white differences
and projected relative rates of change with regard to
indicators of employment, family stability, and 14 other
indicators is used to demonstrate that alternate interpretations may be valid.   Data on white/non-white population
and income distribution for 1960 and 1968 is compared and
implications for progress toward racial equality are discussed with suggestions for research toward developing
more useful racial indicators.

Garn, Harvey A. and Michael J. Flax
   1971   "Urban Institute indicator program."   Working
           Paper 1206-1 (July 14).   Washington, D.C.:   The
           Urban Institute.

   Describes the research program in social and urban
indicators at the Urban Institute.   The incremental approach taken by the Institute and its completed studies
are discussed.   These are related to the broader issues in
the development of social and urban indicators.   The
Institute will continue to address these issues by
undertaking to update past work where relevant, conduct
five additional operational studies, and a summary methodological report covering the Institute's indicator research over the period 1969 to 1972.

194

Gitter, A. George and Robert R. Peterson
   1970   Toward a Social Indicator of Education--A Pilot
           Study. Communication Research Center. Report
           No. 44. Boston: Boston University.

This pilot study represents an effort to devise an aggregate index to be used as a social indicator of education. Methods of constructing two types of factor analytical indicators--factor scores and basic variables--were
developed and shown to apply in aggregating multivariate
education data. Procedures for computing both state and
national indicators for both a base year, and any subsequent one, were described. State and national indicators
of education for 1960 were computed.

Goode, William J.
   1968   "The theory of measurement of family change."
           Pp. 295-347 in Eleanor B. Sheldon and Wilbert
           Moore (eds.), Indicators of Social Change: Con-
           cepts and Measurements. New York: Russell Sage
           Foundation.

This chapter is an attempt to carefully analyze the
present difficulties in the development of an adequate
theory of family change and in achieving precise measurement of change over time. This attempt is made by
enumerating the main types of theoretical questions to be
answered and determine which kinds of data are required
for each. Suggestions, as to how to better utilize existing time data for measuring change, and the kinds of
units within which data should be compiled, are indicated.

Gordon, David M.
   1969   "Income and welfare in New York City." The
           Public Interest 13 (Summer):64-88.

Attuned to "hold the line on taxes" of taxpayers, and
to the cries of neglect by the poor, this study attempts
more meaningful interpretations of the distribution of
wealth, income levels of living, the welfare crisis, etc.
Supported by statistics from the Census Bureau, among
others, tables of comparison for incomes at different
levels for different size families, minority groups, are
presented which indicate support for these findings: 1)
New York City's great corporate wealth is
disproportionately distributed; 2) complaints of both
white and minority groups about their level of income seem
justified; and 3) the cause of the "welfare crisis" is
simply widespread poverty, not chiseling, or welfare
rights organizations, or liberal administrative policies.
Further, income inequities have not declined in over 20

years; the tax system is unfairly loaded on those poor or
of modest incomes; the movement to the suburbs of the more
affluent families with children will continue or
accelerate; and the structure of income earnings, the
initial cause of inequality of income, is unlikely to
change.

Gottehrer, Barry
    1967   "Urban conditions: New York City." The Annals
            of the American Academy of Political and Social
            Science 371 (May):141-158. (Reprinted in
            Bertram M. Gross (ed.), 1969 Social Intelligence
            for America's Future. Boston: Allyn and
            Bacon).

    Considers the political aspects of urban indicators.
As assistant to the mayor of New York City, Gottehrer
makes a proposal for "State of the City" reports which go
beyond the present fiscal and departmental situation to
describe the "quality of life" in urban areas. These
reports would stem from defining governmental programs
actively in terms of evaluating alternative ways to reach
program objectives in terms of meaningful social
indicators.

Hawes, Mary H.
    1969   "Measuring retired couples' living costs in
            urban areas." Monthly Labor Review 92
            (November):3-16.

    A less detailed summary of the Bureau of Labor Statis-
tics' report of a low, medium and high budget for a
retired couple (BLS 1570-6, 1969) includes a summary of
component cost levels and how the figures were derived for
39 metropolitan and 4 nonmetropolitan areas in the United
States. Indexes of comparative costs on the three levels
are given as well as the dollar figures. A summary table
of the three levels and distribution by major components
is given for a younger, four person family and for the
retired couple, for convenient comparisons.

Holden, Constance
    1971   "Corporate responsibility: Group rates company
            social performance." Science 171 (February):
            463-466.

    Redirection of corporate priorities is described as the
objective of the Council on Economic Priorities (CEP).
This article gives an overview of CEP's history, organizational makeup, and major projects. CEP is concerned with
developing information on what companies are doing in four

196

areas of social responsibility: pollution control,
minority employment policies, foreign investments, and involvement in war materials production. The Council has
issued two major reports. One contains 105 corporate
profiles describing each company's antipersonnel weapons
contracts and the other concerns the efforts of 24 paper
producers and 131 mills to combat their pollution.

Hunt, H.
    1969   "Forecasting the need for research and develop-
           ment." Futures 1 (September):382-390.

Describes methods used to forecast research and development needs of de-salination process, including market
analysis, technological forecasting, and price-trend
forecasting; synthesis of optimum research and development
program. Graphic presentation of world total installed
capacity, anticipated market, anticipated capital costs,
sensitivity of returns to 1988 from different strategies,
analysis of two and three firm competition and penetration
of market.

Huttman, E. D.
    1971   "Diminished social inequality through programs
           of housing assistance: International compari-
           sons." A paper presented at the Annual Meeting
           of the American Sociological Association
           (August) Denver, Colorado.

One approach to decreasing social inequality may be
through government housing expenditures designed to increase class mix or social balance. The assumption proposed by the author is that families of different class
background living in the same housing indicates a greater
degree of social equality than a low degree of class mix.
The data comes from research conducted in England, Norway,
Sweden, Holland and North America. It appears that government programs in Britain, Holland, Sweden and Norway
tend to increase the degree of equality between the upper-
lower class and middle-middle class workers. In North
America the groups most likely to benefit from government
aid are the lower middle class. Current programs for
lower class appear to increase instead of decrease
inequality.

Iowa State Department of Health, Records and Statistics
          Division
    1970   Measures of Health Status for Counties and
           Regions in Iowa 1965-1969. Des Moines, Iowa:
           Office of Comprehensive Health Planning.

The purpose of this report is to present several health indicators and an overall summary measure (or index) of health status for each county and region in Iowa, so that comparisons between areas and progress toward achieving higher levels of health can be made. The work of Johnson and Franzen in their report on health Levels in Kansas Counties was the mathematical model used as a basis for this study. Mortality, morbidity, illegitimacy, poverty and immunization become the indicators of health status and each variable is weighted in terms of its contribution to the model.

Jackson, Edward Neill
1970   A Factor Analysis of Small Community Develop-
        ment. Unpublished master's thesis. Manhattan,
        Kansas: Kansas State University.

All communities, whether growing or declining, have problems; leaders need information on different aspects of community growth, on both strengths and weaknesses. Using a statistical factor analysis model to aggregate 37 economic, social and geographic variables into sixteen factors for 66 Kansas communities, this thesis analyzes community growth during the 1960-1970 period to determine factors of Kansas communities which can be compared and to provide guidelines for community leaders. Findings indicate that size is not the sole determining factor, that individual communities do have some control over their future development, and that smaller communities without the needed resources in themselves can promote multicounty or area cooperation to provide the needed economic, social and geographic sources. Data presented in tables for community population and size, individual factor scores for each community, weighted factor score sums, community rank, complete regression results, and weighted factor score sums for comparison with a similar study done for the 1950-1960 period.

Jones, Martin V. and Michael J. Flax
1970   The Quality of Life in Metropolitan Washington
        (D.C.). Washington, D.C.: The Urban Institute.

Working paper from the Urban Institute on urban indicators and conditions in fourteen "quality of life" areas. These include income, unemployment, poverty, housing, education, health, mental health, air pollution, public order, traffic safety, racial equality, community concern, citizen participation and social disintegration. Charts and summary tables using secondary data sources are presented with Washington, D.C. ranked among seventeen large metropolitan cities in relation to current status in the fourteen quality areas. Delineates several criteria for indicators, presents a detailed example for education and suggests possible new indicators from existing city records and from a telephone survey.

Josowitz, Aaron
    1970   "Housing changes in metropolitan areas--
            Preliminary findings." A paper presented at the
            American Statistical Association Meeting (Decem-
            ber 28) Detroit, Michigan.

U.S. Census Bureau preview of findings from 1970 Census; broad percentages on national housing available; partial figures on trends, mostly from less populated states.

Kaplan, H. Roy and Bhopinder S. Bolaria
    1971   "Income, ideologies and health care with special
            reference to the rural poor." A paper presented
            at the Annual Meeting of the American
            Sociological Association (August) Denver,
            Colorado.

Utilization of selected health care services in 1,044 households in 15 rural Maine communities; part of a study of Maine Regional Medical Association research and evaluation service. Services reported included cancer pap smear for women, medical and dental visits preventive or symptomatic, interval between dental visits, and indications of stigma attached to receiving medical care under any of the public assistance programs.

Lamale, Helen H.
    1965   "Levels of living among the poor." A paper pre-
            sented at the UCLA Seminar on Poverty (April 2)
            Los Angeles, California. BLS Report No. 238-12.

A brief historical statement on levels of living the mid-1930's through the gains of the 1950's gives perspective on the levels and patterns of the 1960's. Tables give comparisons for measurement by value of consumption, food expenditures, the basics of shelter and clothing, discretionary spending, and use of credit and insurance.

    1968   "Workers' wealth and family living standards."
            Monthly Labor Review 91 (June):676-686. BLS
            Report No. 238-1.

Information from the Bureau of Labor Statistics from the Survey of Consumer Expenditures for 1960-61 is given in tabular form, with indications that during the 1950's

greater purchasing power and financial resources enabled
city workers' families to consume and save more and to
build these improvements into their living standards.
Discussed are changing patterns relative to more leisure,
participation in community activity, emphasis on education, and working wives. An appendix gives a short description of the Survey of Consumer Expenditures, 1960-61.

Lamson, Robert W.
    1969   "Framework of categories for science policy
           analysis and technology assessment." (November)
           Washington, D.C.: Office of Planning and Policy
           Studies, National Science Foundation.

This framework is presented in outline form as a working tool for use by science policy and technology analysis. Some questions are asked; most material is presented
topically in its relevant area. Tables of categories and
flow charts are given for use in examining specific
aspects of the problems, stages of development, types of
research, needed functions and elements of a solution,
inputs, science policy content, process and values,
actions, programs, institutions, goals and controls.

    1971a "Science policy--Needed research." (August)
           Washington, D.C.: Science Policy Research Sec-
           tion, Social Science Division, National Science
           Foundation.

Perceiving many of today's major problems as arising
from misuse or misunderstanding of our scientific knowledge and technology, this article calls for the creation
and implementation of wise scientific policies. Presents
a framework of categories for analyzing scientific policy,
with questions that must be answered in such analysis.
Specific research questions to be answered and implemented
are categorized under systems, uses, resources, policy
process, institutions and interaction in Table I; Table II
includes problem areas, values, goals, principles, means,
evaluation, and communication.

    1971b "Science policy research--A suggested structure
           to link national problems, goals and means."
           (March 17) (Draft) Washington, D.C.: Plans and
           Analysis Office, National Science Foundation.

A structure of suggested questions for policy research
and analysis is given. Areas for evaluation include: 1)
systems, alternate futures, goals and means; 2) uses, outputs, effects and goals; 3) support; 4) policy process;
and 5) institutions. Categories 2 to 5 are to be related
to science, technology and the universities.

Land, Kenneth C.
1971   "Some exhaustible poisson process models of
        divorce by marriage cohort." Journal of Mathe-
        matical Sociology 1:213-232.

A one parameter exhaustible Poisson process model is
formulated to represent the cumulative divorce trajectory
of marriage cohorts. The model has two possible modifica-
tions, (1) with an assumption that the longer the couples
remain married the smaller their probability of divorce,
or (2) with an assumption that a marriage cohort can be
divided into two groups one of which is subject to risk of
divorce while the other is not. The latter model being
better, Land suggests its use to construct a theory of
divorce differertials and changes in the divorce condition
over time.

Law Enforcement Assistance Administration, U.S. Department
of Justice
1971   Criminal Justice Agencies in the United States
        1970. Washington, D.C.: National Institute of
        Law Enforcement and Criminal Justice, Statistics
        Division.

This statistical summary was compiled from the 1970
National Criminal Justice Directory survey by the Bureau
of the Census. Included are all state, county, city,
township and special district governments with a 1960 population of 1,000 or more persons. Agencies for which
figures are given are enforcement agencies, courts,
prosecutor's offices, defender's offices, adult and
juvenile correction agencies, probation offices, and other
agencies; given for each state by level of government.
Individual names and addresses by sectors for each state
are to be published later; a follow-up study of the court
sector is due in 1972.

Law Enforcement Assistance Administration, U.S. Department
of Justice and Bureau of the Census
1970   Expenditure and Employment Data for the Criminal
        Justice System: 1968-69. Washington, D.C.:
        U.S. Government Printing Office.

Thirty tables present the data in this report of
financial and employment data on the criminal justice activities of federal, state and local governments. The
local government data are estimates derived from a sample
of counties, cities and townships; additional local data
is included for the 55 largest individual counties and the
43 largest cities. This edition of the report also
includes expenditure and employment data on prosecution

and indiginent defense activities of the various
governmental levels. The text also discusses expenditure
and employment by level of government, sources and limitations of the data and definition of the terms.

Lebergott, Stanley
    1968   "Labor force and employment trends." Pp. 97-114
            in Eleanor B. Sheldon and Wilbert Moore (eds.),
            Indicators of Social Change: Concepts and Meas-
            urements. New York: Russell Sage Foundation.

This paper is an attempt to review some of the most
striking changes in labor supply and employment since
1900. The paper contains five sections, the first of
which is addressed to the role of the family in labor
force supply. Secondly, status changes in the labor
market, from the decline of the entrepreneur to labor
supervision, addresses itself from labor management.
Trends in the distribution of employment, from both an
industry and occupation perspective, occupy the third section while the fourth section is donated to stability and
change in the labor market. Finally, data compilation by
government is classified by market skills, occupational
classifications, productivity and education.

Lipscomb, David M.
    1971   "Indicators of environmental noise." A paper
            presented at the Annual Meeting of the American
            Association for the Advancement of Science (De-
            cember 27) Philadelphia, Pennsylvania.

A wide variety of individual responses to loud sound
seems to defy simplistic notions that one or two
indicators can determine environmental quality from an
acoustic perspective. "The noise problem" cannot thus be
reduced to a definable entity. Briefly examined are suggested physical indicators including various scaling
methods for quantification of loudness perception;
physiologic indicators directed to: "Is noise a
stressor?"; and auditory and vestibular indicators, such
as hearing threshold shifts, cochlear cell damage, inter-
ruption of cochlea and vestibular blood supply and the
mechanism of noise damage. Further areas worthy of attention are education, safety, psychological, social,
political and economic indicators of noise.

Little, Dennis and Richard Feller
    1970   "Stapol: A simulation of the impact of policy,
            values, and technological and societal develop-
            ments upon the quality of life." Working Paper
            WP-12. (October) Middletown, Connecticut:
            Institute for the Future.

This paper describes an effort to bring together parts
of the Institute's research into a simulation game ("state
policy" or STAPOL) for analysis of the impact of government policy, social values, and technological and societal
developments upon the quality of life in a hypothetical,
highly industrialized, two-party, New England state. This
paper serves as a general overview for use by participants
in the simulation but also could be of interest to the
student, researcher, or public administrator interested in
policy analysis or planning.

Lowe, Jay
    1966   "Prediction of delinquency with an attitudinal
            configuration model." Social Forces 45
            (Summer): 106-113.

Attitudinal data concerning high school students' perceptions of parental and peer expectations for delinquency
were analyzed in accordance with cognitive dissonance
theory by an Attitudinal Configuration Model. Cross-
tabulations with a situational measure of behavior, the
Hye scale, supported the efficiency of the ACM. Comparisons of the ACM with a measure of internalized attitudes,
the Glueck social factors scale, and the So scale of the
California Test of Personality indicated the ACM could
indeed predict juvenile delinquency as determined by a
situational scale of the delinquency.

McGranahan, Donald V.
    1971   "Analysis of socio-economic development through
            a system of indicators." The American Academy
            of Political and Social Science 393
            (January):65-81.

This paper approaches the definition and measurement of
development viewing socio-economic factors as interdependent aspects of an evolving system not macro level causes
or effects. Using 1960 data, the U.N. Research Institute
for Social Development has selected a group of priority
indicators on an empirical basis and interrelated them by
a method of analysis called correspondence analysis. This
type of analysis provides the basis for showing how development varies for different kinds of countries and a means
of constructing a synthetic indicator or general development index.

McIntosh, William Alex
    1971   "Social indicators and social change: An
            interpretive essay." Unpublished paper. De-

partment of Sociology. Ames, Iowa: Iowa State
University.

Role and function of a change agent, and value of using
social indicators in a country other than the United
States, e.g., Laos; emphasis that indicators need to be
developed within each nation, involving the people of that
nation, considering their values and needs rather than
imposing concepts of change and choice of indicators from
a different country.

Mitchell, Joyce M. and William C. Mitchell
   1968   "The changing politics of American life." Pp.
        247-294 in Eleanor B. Sheldon and Wilbert Moore
        (eds.), Indicators of Social Change: Concepts
        and Measurements. New York: Russell Sage Foun-
        dation.

In a summary view of what happens within a broadly
formulated conception of the changing American political
system, the authors outline the formal political structures and processes, policy and policy-making, the
changing political activities of citizens, changing
governmental activities, the impact of policy on society,
and some further research needs if the measurement of the
political component of society in the sense of social
indicators can become a reality.

Moriyama, Iwao M.
   1968   "Problems in the measurement cf health status."
        Pp. 573-599 in Eleanor B. Sheldon and Wilbert
        Moore (eds.), Indicators of Social Change: Con-
        cepts and Measurements. New York: Russell Sage
        Foundation.

In an excellent discussion of the incidence and
prevalence of health status, Moriyama pursues a major discussion of indicators of health and the construction of
indices of health status. Indicating the general
inadequacy of mortality rates for measuring change in
health status among the population, the author elaborates
on the need to develop indicators of health status from
morbidity data, especially disability data, and the general limitations of such data under present collection procedures.

Moser, Claus A.
   1957   The Measurement of Levels of Living with Special
        Reference to Jamaica. Colonial Research Study
        No. 24. London, England: Her Majesty's
        Stationery Office.

With the UN Report on International Definition and
Measurement of Standards of Living as a background, this
study concentrates on the four components of nutrition,
education, health and housing, with some general considerations of income, expenditure and consumption. Other
topics discussed are: levels vs. standards of living definitions, classification of indicators, combination of
indicators and of components, and international and
intertemporal considerations; some general comments and
recommendations for future work both specifically in
Jamaica and elsewhere.

Moss, Milton
    1968   "Consumption: A report on contemporary issues."
            Pp. 449-523 in Eleanor B. Sheldon and Wilbert
            Moore (eds.), Indicators of Social Change: Con-
            cepts and Measurements. New York: Russell Sage
            Foundation.

Moss focuses on three broad issues from the perspective
that these are unsolved problems rather than clear-cut
goals. The American economy is discussed from the assumption that growth will continually occur; thus, assessing
the severity of economic disadvantage and the extent to
which it is charging becomes the first issue. Secondly,
developments which tend to broaden and restrict consumer
choice are outlined at length and statistical measurements
of a limited number of changes are provided. Finally, the
chapter briefly discusses the effect of consumer behavior
on the economy especially the timing of consumer's
investment decisions and anticipated oscillations in
consumer behavior.

Murphy, Kathryn R.
    1964   "Contrasts in spending by urban families."
            Monthly Labor Review 87 (November):1249-1253.
            BLS Report No. 238-8.

Based on the Survey of Consumer Expenditures 1960-61,
broad trends since 1950 in the income, spending and saving
of urban families as a whole are analyzed. Part II summarizes the distinct patterns of spending for families with
differing characteristics of income level and place of
residence.

    1965   "Spending and saving in urban and rural areas."
            Monthly Labor Review 88 (October):1169-1176.
            BLS Report No. 238-14.

Farm and nonfarm families exhibit contrasting spending
patterns irrespective of income level. Degree of dependence on the automobile, residential real estate values

and housing quality are more influential than income in
forming buying habits. Tables present: 1) family
expenditures, income and savings, all families in United
States, 1960-61 by urbanization and location inside and
outside metropolitan areas; 2) the expenditures in selected income classes by urbanization; and 3) the comparison
in the urban, rural nonfarm and rural farm categories.

Pfaff, Anita B.
    1971   "An index of consumer satisfaction." A paper
            presented at the Annual Meeting of The American
            Economic Association jointly with the Associa-
            tion for the Study of the Grants Economy (Decem-
            ber 27) New Orleans, Louisiana.

    The Consumer Price Index measures variations in the
prices of a general "market basket." This paper reports
an attempt to develop a subjective Index of Consumer Satisfaction to complement the CPI cost measure with a benefit measure. Models are developed to express as an index
or profile of indices the benefits consumers receive or
the satisfactions they experience from the operation of
the market. Items included houses or cars as attributes
for the husbands, food or clothing as breakfast cereals,
luncheon meats, women's cloth, food-general, and
appliances for the wives. A set of optimal scores derived
through Multivariate Analysis of Contingencies is the
basis for the indices. Tables present the data for the
profile of indices; the questionnaire is given in an Appendix.

Price, Daniel O. and Melanie M. Sikes
    1971   "Rural-urban migration and poverty: A synthesis
            of research findings, with a look at the litera-
            ture." A paper presented at the Annual Meeting
            of the American Sociological Association (August
            30-September 2) Denver, Colorado.

    With the assumption of labor mobility to meet differen-
tial needs in our society has gone also the assumption of
rural-urban migrants as being uneducated, poor, black, and
moving in order to get higher welfare payments. This
search of relevant studies indicates these assumptions of
migrant characteristics are all false: most rural-urban
migrants are white; recent black migrants are as well
educated as native urban blacks; relatively small proportions of migrants are on welfare; and the migrants are
earning about the same average incomes as the nonmigrants.
Discusses also motivation and decision to migrate,
migrant characteristics in areas of origin, migrant adjustment in urban areas, return migration, and the effects
of migration on both rural and urban areas.

Ridley, Clarence E. and Herbert A. Simon
    1938   Measuring Municipal Activities: A Survey of
            Suggested Criteria and Reporting Forms for
            Appraising Administration. Chicago, Illinois:
            The International City Managers' Association.

    This is an early attempt to develop measurement
techniques applicable for local governments and to suggest
some next steps for measurement of municipal activities.
The activities discussed, one per chapter, include: fire,
police, public works, public health, recreation, public
welfare, public education, public libraries, personnel in
public administration, municipal finance and city
planning. An appendix is included with suggested report
forms to accumulate the requisite information for the
evaluation of municipal activities.

Rokeach, Milton and Seymour Parker
    1970   "Values as social indicators of poverty and race
            relations in America." The Annals of the Ameri-
            can Academy of Political and Social Science 388
            (March):97-111.

    Explores the use´uiness of various terminal and
instrumental values as social indicators of underlying
societal problems by determining the extent and nature of
cultural differences between groups differing in socio-
economic status and race. Using the Rokeach Value Survey
to evaluate a national sample, authors infer that considerable differences distinguish rich from poor but not
Negroes from Whites when socio-economic position is controlled.

Roterus, Victor
    1946   "Effects of population growth and non-growth on
            the well-being of cities." American
            Sociological Review 11 (February):90-97.

    A comparative review of non-growth, classified
declining, and urban communities which demonstrates the
complementary effect of non-economic factors and their
requisite interdependence with economic factors in the
general "well-being" of cities.

Russett, Bruce M. and Robert Bunselmeyer
    1964   World Handbook of Political and Social
            Indicators. New Haven: Yale University Press.

    The authors compare 133 countries using as criteria the
fundamental human rights proclaimed in the Universal Dec-

laration of Human Rights. Data are presented for the
areas of human resources, government and politics, communications, wealth, health, education, family and social
relations, distribution of wealth and income and religion.

Sametz, A. W.
    1968   "Production of goods and services: The measure-
            ment of economic growth." Pp. 77-96 in Eleanor
            B. Sheldon and Wilbert E. Moore (eds.),
            Indicators of Social Change: Concepts and Meas-
            urements. New York: Russell Sage Foundation.

    Commenting on the accuracy of Gross National Product in
measuring economic growth or welfare, Sametz indicates
that the basic time-series data collected and portrayed by
the national income and product accounts needs to be
revised and augmented by basic data for use in analysis of
problems in growth and development and for measuring
changes in economic welfare. He suggests that allowance
should be made for population and price changes in
arriving at real per capita GNP. In addition, allowance
should be taken into account for quality of both output
and input in terms of goods and services and various
nonmarket production costs of industrialization to give a
better understanding of contributions to social welfare.

Sanders, Barkev S.
    1964   "Measuring community health levels." American
            Journal of Public Health 54 (July):1063-1070.

    Sanders suggests that the increased prevalence of vari-
ous chronic diseases is an indication of better medical
care since less people die from these diseases. Thus the
present morbidity rate is inadequate. Measurement of the
efficiency of health care should be made in terms of its
contribution to increasing the productive man-years from a
given cohort.

Scammon, Richard M.
    1967   "Electoral participation." The Annals of the
            American Academy of Political and Social Science
            371 (May):59-71. (Reprinted in Bertram M. Gross
            (ed.), 1969 Social Intelligence for America's
            Future. Boston: Allyn and Bacon).

    Describes and includes partial tabular findings of the
Kennedy Commission on Registration and Voter Participation
and other data as factual indicators of voter participation. Suggests that, rather than to consider voter participation as a goal in itself, it should be the goal of
our modern American democracy to maximize access to the
polls.

Schwartz, Mildred A.
   1967   Trends in White Attitudes toward Negroes.
           Chicago, Illinois: National Opinion Research
           Center, The University of Chicago.

   This is a topical exposition of white attitudes towards
the civil rights of Negroes with regard to education,
housing, jobs, transportation, public services, and future
prospects. Examines opinion trends on these issues in relation to two characteristics - region of residence and
level of education. Response trends of white respondents
for the total sample on eleven questions and for regional
and educational subgroups on six questions are presented,
both in graphs and tables, as least squares regression
lines.

Sewell, William H.,   Leonard A. Marascuilo and Harold W.
Pfautz
   1967   "Review symposium." American Sociological
           Review 32 (June):475-483.

   This is a review of the nationwide survey ordered by
the Civil Rights Act of 1964 of the U.S. Office of Education to survey inequalities in educational opportunities
for major racial, ethnic and religious groups in the
United States. The study was entitled "Equality of Educational Opportunity" under the direction of James S.
Coleman et al. Coleman had the major responsibility for
the design, administration and analysis of the survey of
public schools, and the reviewers have high praise for the
quality of the work done. Survey considered: 1) extent
of segregation; 2) equality of opportunities offered; 3)
extent of variation of performance on standardized
achievement tests; and 4) extent to which these differences are related to family and school influences.
Reviewer William H. Sewell considers the most serious
defect to be administrative - no schools nor students are
identified so that no longitudinal study is possible;
Marascuilo felt too little explanation of the methods of
statistical analysis were given and that a subsequent
technical report would be helpful; Pfautz calls it
admirable but pedestrian, thoughtful but thoughtless. All
reviewers agree that even with its limitations, it is an
important survey and report.

Sheldon, Eleanor B. and Wilbert E. Moore
   1968   "Monitoring social change in American society."
           Pp. 3-26 in Eleanor B. Sheldon and Wilbert Moore
           (eds.), Indicators of Social Change: Concepts

and Measurements. New York: Russell Sage Foundation.

In their introduction to the edition of Indicators of
Social Change, Sheldon and Moore discuss major structural
change and its measurement. They propose four major
rubrics for examining structural changes in American
society and its constituent features: (1) the demographic
base, giving an indication of aggregative population
trends, its changing composition and distribution across
the nation's surface; (2) major structural components of
society of the ways in which a society produces goods, or-
ganizes its knowledge and technology, reproduces itself,
and maintains order; (3) distributive features of the
society, looking at how the products of society - people,
goods, services, knowledge, values and order - are
allocated across the several sectors; (4) aggregative features of the society, suggesting how the system as a whole
changes in terms of its social welfare.

Simon, Rita James
    1971   "Public attitudes toward population and
            pollution." The Public Opinion Quarterly 35
            (Spring):93-99.

This survey of Illinois residents indicates the degree
of interest, knowledge and concern of the respondents
toward national priorities of population and pollution
problems and possible solutions. The questionnaire was
also designed to see if and how the respondents assessed
responsibility for solutions. Findings indicate a high
level of concern when asked specific questions, a much
lower level when questions did not give specific cues.
Asked for reasons and possible solutions, very few (5 and
2 percent) made any connection between population and
pollution; respondents neither perceived people as a cause
of, nor reason for, pollution, nor did they recommend any
form of population control as possibly alleviating the
pollution problems.

Smith, David Horton and Alex Inkeles
    1966   "The OM scale: A comparative socio-
            psychological measure of individual modernity."
            Sociometry 29 (December):353-377.

Attempts to derive a simple, comparative, overall measure of the modernity of individuals using a subset of 119
attitudinal items taken from a larger set of interview
items. This larger set, of over 150 items, was administered to 5,500 men from six developing countries:
Argentina, Chile, India, Pakistan, Israel and Nigeria.
Defined as a set of attitudes, beliefs, behavior, etc.

characterizing persons in highly urbanized,
industrialized, and educated social settings, "modernity"
is operationalized by three types of Overall Modernity
(OM) measures. One measure uses item analysis methods; a
second uses criterion group methods; and the third is a
short OM scale meeting both selection procedures
simultaneously.

State of Iowa Office for Planning and Programming
    1971   The Quality of Life in Iowa: An Economic and
            Social Report to the Governor for 1970. Des
            Moines, Iowa: State Capitol.

    Purpose of the report is to assess economic and social
developments in Iowa in 1970 to assist public and private
officials in decision making. On the premise that economic indicators do not tell enough about the well-being of
the citizenry, there are sections on qualitative changes
in environment, care of aged, health, leisure time activities, lawful behavior and education; as well as quantitative change in agriculture, manufacturing, public,
wholesale and retail trade, construction, transportation,
communication, public utilities, and finance and
insurance. Tables and figures used to summarize data in
each section.

Sulc, Oto
    1969   "Interactions between technological and social
            changes." Futures 1 (September):402-407.

    The Delphi technique is used to obtain forecasts from
which a model is constructed relating the interactions of
technological and organizational change to the impact of
technological innovations. Two panels, one of computer
scientists, and one of industrial management executives,
made the forecasts. Tabular presentation of the findings.

Taeuber, Conrad
    1968   "Population: Trends and characteristics." Pp.
            27-76 in Eleanor B. Sheldon and Wilbert E. Moore
            (eds.), Indicators of Social Change: Concepts
            and Measurements. New York: Russell Sage Foun-
            dation.

    Growth of United States in terms of population is de-
scribed in this paper by Taeuber from a macro national or
regional approach over a long term trend period. Population growth since 1790 is documented by use of graphs and
tables from census data. A note is added on the sources
and limitations of such data. Characteristics of the population are discussed from the point of view of age, sex,

race, ethnic origin, religion, education, economic activity, migration, households, and various other macro vital statistics. Finally a brief discussion on future data needs is outlined.

Ulrich, Gary
      1969   "Indicators of equal opportunity for social
              mobility in the occupational structure." Unpub-
              lished manuscript. Ann Arbor, Michigan: School
              of Social Work, University of Michigan.

      From the framework of Duncan's Index of Occupational Socio-economic Status is presented the data needs and policy implications for a more meaningful index of social mobility. Suggestions are made for reassessment of job training, employment needs, and value consensus relating to goals, social mobility, and equality of opportunity.

United Nations
      1968   Compendium of Social Statistics: 1967.   New
              York: United Nations.

      This is a revised and up-dated edition of the 1963 Compendium. Like its predecessor, it comprises basic statistical indicators required for describing the major aspects of world and regional social situations as well as changes and trends in the levels of living over the decade ending in 1964. A total of sixty-two tables are included comprising analytical rates, index numbers, and ratios which are organized into eight sections paralleling the international definition and components for measurement of levels of living.

United Nations Research Institute for Social Development
      1970   Contents and Measurement of Socio-Economic De-
              velopment: An Empirical Enquiry.   Report No.
              70.10.   Geneva, Switzerland: United Nations Re-
              search Institute for Social Development.

      The central purpose of the study described in this report was to examine the nature of development - particularly the interrelations of its social and economic aspects through cross-national comparative analysis using social and economic indicators available as of 1960.   Data on a set of 73 development variables for 115 countries with populations over 1,000,000 were incorporated in a data bank.   Variables were reduced to 18 core indicators; the interrelationships of which were studied by a system of "correspondence analysis." General index of socio-economic development was subsequently developed combining these 18 indicators.

212

U.S. Department of Agriculture, Economic Development Division
1971   Rural Development Chartbook. March. Washington, D.C.: U.S. Department of Agriculture, Economic Development Division, Economic Research Service.

Graphic presentation of statistics concerning nonmetropolitan areas, compared with metropolitan areas. Comparisons are made on population change, income, incidence of poverty, physicians and hospital beds, per capita expenditures by local governments for services and employment gains for industry groups by metropolitan residence.

U.S. Department of Commerce, Bureau of the Census
1968   Report on National Needs for Criminal Justice Statistics. (August) Washington, D.C.: U.S. Department of Commerce.

Three major conferences on law enforcement, courts and correction were convened in 1967-68 to identify data users, uses and needs for criminal justice statistics. Part I of this report includes the detailed list of desirable data items identified by the conferences. Part II describes the long range research efforts needed to resolve serious conceptual and methodological problems involved in creating a comprehensive statistics program.

1971a   Environmental Quality Control: Expenditure for Selected Large Governmental Units: Fiscal Year 1968-69. State and Local Government Special Studies No. 57. Washington, D.C.: U.S. Government Printing Office.

Following brief introductory remarks on the background, sources and limitations of the data and definition of terms and history, this report presents in tabular or graphic form the expenditures of selected large governmental units for water quality control, solid waste management, and air quality control for fiscal 1968-69. Governmental units evaluated were federal, state, 43 large city and 55 large counties' total expenditures for the three areas, and the expenditures by 38 large standard metropolitan statistical areas for water quality control and solid waste management.

1971b   National Data Needs: Fire Service Statistics. Washington, D.C.: U.S. Department of Commerce.

Under the direction of the Bureau of the Census, this analysis followed a two-day conference called to discuss

needs for statistical data describing available fire services, possible uses of such data by the fire service and
other governmental agencies, to make the Bureau's data
collection and presentation on state and local governments
more responsive to those who use the data and particularly
to those whose needs are not being presently met by any
source.   Extensive data are currently available from the
National Fire Protection Association, and the Municipal
Year Book of the International City Management Association, but small city, county and rural data are noticeably
absent.   Content is summarized and presented in outline
form, under organization study, financial data, personnel
data and fire incident and loss data, with data users and
uses, gathering problems and needs considered under each
topic.

U.S. Department of Health, Education, and Welfare
    1970   Social Indicators for the Aged. (October)
            Minneapolis, Minnesota: Quantitative Social
            Planning Division, Institute for Interdiscipli-
            nary Studies, American Rehabilitation Founda-
            tion.

    Developed by the Institute on Interdisciplinary Studies
for the Administration on Aging, primarily for use of
state agencies but can be used also by smaller
geographical units; areas of housing, social relations;
life satisfaction; health; nutrition; economic; degree of
independence; complete questionnaire, information for its
use, for computations, card scoring and sampling procedures.

U.S. Department of Labor, Bureau of Labor Statistics
    1970   Three Budgets for a Retired Couple in Urban
            Areas of the United States 1967-68. Bulletin
            1970-6. Washington, D.C.: U.S. Government
            Printing Office. (Supplement included).

    Based on data from the 1960-61 Survey of Consumer
Expenditures, the three sets of budget figures for high,
medium and low budgets are given for each of 39
metropolitan and four nonmetropolitan regions.   Discussed
are the budget concepts, the manner in which the lists of
goods and services were derived, and brief analyses of the
component cost levels and intercity differences.   Detailed
tables present the item costs and totals for each urban
area; appendices include the average annual quantities of
items used in determining the cost levels; the specifications used to collect or estimate prices for the lower and
higher budgets; and the population weights for aggregating
the 43 regions to United States urban averages.

U.S. Department of Labor/Workplace Standards Administration
1970   State Economic and Social Indicators. Workplace
        Standards Administration, Bureau of Labor Stan-
        dards, Bulletin 328. Washington, D.C.: U.S.
        Government Printing Office.

Data drawn from published reports of the major national
collection agencies directed to States and to various
civic and labor-management organizations working to improve labor legislation and other programs concerned with
the status of the wage earner. State rankings for data
series in following categories; population and labor
force, economic base, income and earnings, social
indicators, state government finance, and public
employment with explanation of terms. Includes a "do-it-
yourself" outline for a state to compile its own socio-
economic profile.

Wayman, Morris
1971   "Socio-ecologic analysis in industrial
        enterprise development planning." A paper pre-
        sented at the Conference on Environmental
        Studies-The Role of the University (May 19-21)
        Toronto, Canada.

In planning industrial development, Wayman proposes
that in addition to conventional profitability, economic
risk and secondary benefit cost analyses, an analysis of
the social and ecological benefits, costs and risk must
also be initiated. The social impact could be measured by
social indicators were these available on a national
basis.

Williams, Faith M.
1956   "Standards and levels of living of city-worker
        families." Monthly Labor Review 79
        (September):1-9. Bureau of Labor Statistics
        Reprint No. 2204.

Tabulation of expenditures of large city wage earners
and clerical workers in 1950 provided a comparison of
those money disbursements with those of employed workers
in 1934-36, and enabled a comparison to be made in terms
of changes in standards of living, incomes and employment
patterns.

Wilson, John O.
1969   Quality of Life in the United States: An
        Excursion into the New Frontier of Socio-

Economic Indicators. Kansas City: Midwest
Research Institute.

Identifying the inadequacies in the economic indicators
currently used for many studies in social welfare, this
study develops social indicators for nine of the eleven
basic domestic goals included in the Report of the
President's Commission on National Goals. Using the
states as units of analysis, indicators are developed for:
individual status, individual equality (racial equality),
state and local government, education, economic growth,
technological change, agriculture, living conditions and
health and welfare, with the states then ranked according
to these nine indicators. The models and techniques used
to develop the specific indices for racial equality and
for education are discussed in detail, as examples. An
appendix lists the components of all nine indices.

Abt, Clark C.
  1970   "An approach to methods of combined
          sociotechnological forecasting." Technological
          Forecasting and Social Change 2:17-22.

    It is argued that technological forecasting alone is
inadequate for effective research and development
planning, and that social forecasting is a necessary
complement. The greater complexity of social forecasting
makes it important to distinguish first-order from second-
order consequences, to narrow the field for analysis.
Needed is a more disaggregated approach, the basis of
which might be functional (health, education, recreation,
housing, etc.), or industrial (chemical, electronic,
metallurgical, etc.), or disciplinary (economics, sociology, psychology, engineering, etc.), or by
consumption/production functions. Discussed and evaluated
are four methods of social forecasting: judgment, and
various manipulations of it (e.g. Delphi); extrapolation,
linear or of distributions; speculation, including
scenario generation and decomposition; and analysis,
including building of analytical models. The
food/chemical industry serves as an example for the
methods. A seven-step procedure for social forecasting is
suggested.

Alford, Robert R.
  1970   "Data resources for comparative studies of urban
          administration." Social Science Information
          9:193-203.

    A report on an exploratory session of persons concerned
professionally with improving the data available and relevant to problems of urban administration. Held at the
U.N., which co-sponsored the meeting with a subcommittee
of the American Society for Public Administration,
participants considered: needs for and problems involved
in creating or obtaining international urban data, the
feasibility of a "director" of inter and intra national
agencies and an "inventory" of the data holdings maintained by them, establishing working committees to advise
on the data needs of agencies and scholars and to
establish agendas and priorities for tasks.

American Psychological Association
  1967   "Special issue: Congress and social science."
          American Psychologist 22 (November).

A special issue devoted to the recent interest in the
underdeveloped social and behavioral sciences. Various
leaders in the social sciences presented statements before
Congress regarding the new arrangements "for the Federal
support of these disciplines and for the utilization of
social and behavioral science knowledge and methods in
public policy formulation." Selected articles include
Kenneth E. Boulding, "Dare We Take the Social Sciences
Seriously;" Donald N. Michael, "Social Engineering and the
Future Environment;" Fred R. Harris, "National Social Science Foundation: Proposed Congressional Mandate for the
Social Sciences;" Walter F. Mondale, "Some Thoughts on
stumbling into the Future;" and Andrew Kopkind, "The
Future-Planners."

Association for Public Program Analysis
    1970   The Role of Analysis in Establishing Program
            Priorities. Proceedings of the APPA Symposium.

An edited compilation of the symposium papers. The
symposium design was to assist decision-makers, formulate
goals, assign priorities, and plan, design and evaluate
their programs in terms of these goals. The priorities of
consideration were: transportation, urban, pollution, and
the military budget.

Bauer, Raymond A.
    1963   "Data needs of a science for solving social
            problems." An address to the 1968-1969 Seminar
            Series, The Travelers Research Center, Inc. (No-
            vember 7) Hartford, Connecticut.

An address made at The Traveler's Research Center, Inc.
which concentrates on the more recent manifestations of
the concern for a set of "social indicators" or form of
"social accounting." Dimensions of system structure and
performance would be gauged by the model proposed by
Bertram Gross which Bauer relates to the issue of whether
data should index benefits conferred or treat citizens as
resources and measure capacities for producing, performing
and sharing in our culture. The matters of privacy,
costs, fadism, utility, model consensus, and
disaggregating data are also assessed.

    1966   "Social indicators and sample surveys." Public
            Opinion Quarterly 30:339-352.

The author makes a strong plea for greater use of
sample surveys to collect a greater variety of basic
social statistics. He traces present dissatisfactions

with the current state of social statistics and proposals
for better social statistics.

1968   "Social indicators: or, Working in a society
        which has better social statistics." P. 237-258
        in Stanford Anderson (ed.), Planning for
        Diversity and Choice: Possible Futures and
        Their Relations to the Man-Controlled Environ-
        ment. Cambridge, Massachusetts: Massachusetts
        Institute of Technology Press.

Relates the need and anticipation of improved social
statistics to architectural opportunities. Deficiencies
of our present social statistics--validity, usefulness,
applicability, adequacy and systematic coherence--are described. A brief history of the emergent field of social
statistics is set in the anticipatory context of
"inventing the future." Forces--such as privacy and
technical difficulties which will act against the development of social statistics--are contrasted to factors
favoring their development. In conclusion, it formulates
a number of suggestions for anticipating what such data
will mean for the architect.

1969   "Detection and anticipation of impact: The
        nature of the task." Pp. 1-67 in Raymond A.
        Bauer (ed.) Social Indicators. Cambridge,
        Massachusetts: The Massachusetts Institute of
        Technology Press.

Broad overview of the fundamental problem, felt to be
the lack of measures of whether things are getting better
or worse with many issues and topics on which social
critics and researchers must express opinions and
formulate studies. Discusses origin of social indicator
concept in concern over second-order consequences of NASA,
with the inherent difficulties of 1) assessing causal relations, 2) impacts, and 3) too-prevalent practice of
irresponsible inferences. Differentiates between prediction: indentifying the most probable of conceivable
futures, and anticipation: the consideration of reason-
ably probable and important alternatives. Sees the need
for anticipatory function of social indicators. Summarizes and comments on other articles in the book.

Bauman, Zygmunt
   1971   "Uses of information: When social information
           becomes desired." The American Academy of
           Political and Social Science 393 (Janu-
           ary):20-31.

One of the tasks of social information, for Bauman, is
to study and obtain conditions which make the system open

to the kind of information necessary to promote socio-
economic growth. Contra to the organic analogy, society -
as a system - must be more than interested in absorbing
"all available" information for the information generated
is always selective and the product of power considerations.

Beal, George M. and Gerald E. Klonglan
    1970   "Needed research themes in rural sociology--
            social indicators." A paper presented at the
            Rural Sociological Society Meetings (August)
            Washington, D.C.c.

An argument presenting the unique contribution that
rural sociologists can make in the study of social
indicators for non-metropolitan territorialities or
ecological areas.

Beal, George M., Gerald E. Klonglan, Leslie D. Wilcox and
Ralph M. Brooks
    1971   "Social indicators and public policy: Toward an
            alternative approach." A paper presented at the
            Annual Meeting of the American Sociological As-
            sociation (September) Denver, Colorado.

The increased interest in social indicators has come
about through a need for better information regarding current societal conditions and future decision-making. A
major unresolved problem is the meaning(s) of the concept
social indicators. Furthermore, the movement has not
solidified into one definite strategy for the development
of social indicators to be used in planning for public
policy. Alternative strategies are needed. The authors
of this paper have been guided by three major research
interests. First, there seems to be interest in human resource development, community development, or the more
general social and economic development. Yet, there does
not appear to be consensus as to what constitutes these
types of development. Second, how does one develop reliable and valid measures of these concepts? Third, the
rapid increase of population brings to mind the question
of population redistribution and the concern that
nonmetropolitan areas may play a key role in the future
growth of our society. The authors suggest that the
"community ecosystem" which contains the elements of population, environment, social organization and the cultural
system might provide a framework for the development of a
system of interrelated social indicators that will allow
them to understand the concepts of development, how to
measure them and address themselves to the question of
population redistribution.

220

Bell, Daniel
    1970   "The post-industrial society: Technocracy and
            politics." A paper presented at the Seventh
            World Congress of Sociology (September 14-19)
            Varna, Bulgaria.

    A theoretical analysis of past paradigms of the
industrial society and how they are inadequate today. A
gross paradigm of today's societal flux in which new
hierarchical positions and relationships among societal
concepts and institutions are emerging. The recognition
of value and political choice as at least deserving co-
equal attention with technical expertise in 'rational'
societal problem solving is demonstrated.

Biderman, Albert D.
    1966   "Anticipatory studies and stand-by research ca-
            pabilities." Pp. 272-301 in Raymond A. Bauer
            (ed.), Social Indicators. Cambridge,
            Massachusetts: The Massachusetts Institute of
            Technology Press.

    The use of regular and continuous trend statistics as
social indicators leaves untouched important research
needs for particular events that may be of very limited
relevance to the entire population, as well as for events
that may only be dimly anticipated if at all. To fill
this gap, the author of this paper explores the
feasibility of before-during-after studies and stand-by
research designs, and concludes that institutional factors
are the main reasons for the present neglect of fruitful
anticipatory studies, rather than the inability to foresee
future targets deserving research attention. He proposes
a pilot study of stand-by research capability designed to
minimize institutional difficulties, and discusses it in
terms of the prediction phase, research staff preparatory
work, field associates and cost estimates.

    1969   "Information, intelligence, and enlightened
            public policy: Functions and organization of
            societal feedback." A paper presented at the
            65th Annual Meeting of the American Political
            Science Association. (September 6) New York.
            (Also in 1970 Policy Sciences 1:217-230).

    The author considers the properties of social statis-
tics which make them useful as social indicators. Two
functions of social organizations, that of information and
administration, are well served by the present state of
social statistics but the two other functions, of formation of broad social policy and enlightenment of the
public on general conceptions of the social world, are not

well served by the present data base. Social indicators
when fully developed should strive to fulfill all four
functions. Levels of social statistics vary from "information" at the lowest level, through "intelligence" in intermediate bureaucratic level, through "public knowledge"
for formation of social policy, to "enlightenment," general social conceptions held by the public; functions change
at each level; limitations of usage of social indicators
between levels.

　　1971　"A proposed general measure of interpersonal
　　　　　violence." Unpublished manuscript. Washington,
　　　　　D.C.: Bureau of Social Science Research, Inc.

A proposal is set forth for developing a method to
circumvent the normative selectivity and thus improve current statistical indicators of the incidence of interpersonal violence. The proposal involves two parts: the
first deals with the practicability of running a validity
check on a relevant facet of the National Criminal
Victimization Survey; the second discusses the theoretical
issues which arise from the proposal's basic idea that the
approach of vital and health statistics can afford a means
of circumventing the present normative bias of
criminological survey methods.

Boulding, Kenneth E.
　　1967　"Dare we take the social sciences seriously."
　　　　　American Psychologist 22 (November):879-887.

This is the text of the Vice Presidential Address presented to the American Association for the Advancement of
Science in 1966. Queries whether the present structure of
disciplinary departmentalization does not prevent the development of a general social theory for integrating the
specialized focuses of abstraction, which are presently
inadequate for taking the sociosphere and its complexity
seriously. Suggests that the sociosphere might be viewed
as a four dimensional structure, three dimensions of space
and of time, consisting of random elements but perceivable
nonrandom patterns.

Bowman, R. T., Alexander Gall and Israel Rubin
　　1960　"Social statistics: Present conditions, future
　　　　　needs and prospects." Pp. 74-81 in Proceedings
　　　　　of the Social Statistics Section, American Sta-
　　　　　tistical Association. Washington, D.C.

The authors in this article suggest factors to be taken
into account in the formulation of a program to rectify
existing deficiencies in social statistics. Their discussion of those factors are organized under three major

headings as follows: special aspects of the collection and dissemination of social statistics, present federal social statistics evaluated, prospects for the future.

Brolin, K. G.
    1967   "Statistics needed for education planning." Pp.
            60-96 in Proceedings of the Conference of
            European Statisticians, Statistical Standards
            and Studies. Statistics of the Educational
            System. New York: United Nations. ST/CES/10
            Sales No. 67, II E/mim 10.

This is a broad inventory of statistics needed for educational planning for the purpose of presenting the total
framework from a world-wide perspective. Included in the
paper are topics on educational planning in general, the
importance and role of statistics in educational planning,
and the types of statistical data needed for educational
planning including demographic statistics, labor force
statistics, economic and financial statistics, and a host
of endogenous educational institutional statistics on such
things as teachers, classes, pupils, etc.

Cabello, Octavio
    1959   "The use of statistics in the formulation and
            evaluation of social programmes." Pp. 206-215
            in Proceedings of the Social Statistics Section,
            American Statistical Association, Washington,
            D.C.

Social statistics are defined as those required for
social programs with a social program defined as the
scheme of public or private activities which have a direct
bearing on a particular aspect of living conditions. The
need and uses of statistics are illustrated from the field
of housing, estimating of economic resources for the program, indicators for measurement of living conditions,
estimation of social needs, e.g. "dwellings," testing of
consistency of social and economic needs, human and material resources and adoption of goals for programs consistent with expected resources. Author is in the Statistical
Office of the United Nations.

Campbell, Rex R. and Jerry L. Wade
    1972a   "A perspective." Pp. 1-8 in Rex R. Campbell and
            Jerry L. Wade (eds.), Society and Environment:
            The Coming Collision. Boston, Massachusetts:
            Allyn and Bacon, Inc.

Introduces the crucial dimensions and magnitude of
man's struggle for survival discussing particularly the

223

social context of increasing consumption rates reflected
in the growing yearly air pollutant tonnage and the
results being predicted. By using a quantitative measure
of pollution it becomes more than an implicit assumption
that indicants of resource consumption and socio-
ecological conditions will be necessary to pursue any of
the three humanly viable alternatives posited: 1) the
rest of the world cannot be permitted to rise to our
(U.S.) level of consumption, 2) we must lower our
consumption rate and 3) a combination of these.

> 1972b Society and Environment: The Coming Collision.
> Boston, Massachusetts: Allyn and Bacon, Inc.

This book gathers a comprehensive selection of works to
convey a broad ecological perspective to the concerned
person which includes both the biological and social
aspects of the current environmental situation. Readings
emphasize often neglected social consequences of our alternatives for human viability. Central as quality of
life implications are to the social indicator movement
this work may instrumentally serve to alter individual attitudes towards population and consumption or at least
orient readers to the pervasive effects of their own behavior on the consequences at issue.

Carey, Charles B. and Kenneth W. Yarnold
> 1966   "America '75 conference." (September 28) Santa
> Monica, California: Systems Development
> Corporation.

A working paper which examines concepts of income and
economic well-being, with suggested ways to detect poverty
and its frequency distribution. Indicates the context for
evaluation of programs, and the importance of the interaction of such programs with each other and other society
forces. In-depth discussion of measures of income and
poverty, income maintenance, income supplement, public
assistance and negative income tax proposals. Tables indicating income, income needs, household units, Lorenz
curve for spending units, Gini coefficients for types of
income and units, incidence of poverty by family type,
employability and results of negative income tax on after-
tax income are included.

Carnegie Endowment Study Group
> 1960   "Needs and resources for social investment."
> International Social Science Journal 12:409-433.

This international group examines the utility of social
outlays as investment within an economy, focusing on
health, services, education, subsidized housing, and

workers' welfare programs. The uniqueness of social
outlays to productive outlays in terms of their
alienability, marketability, and divisibility is contrasted. The measurement of social development has been examined under three aspects; (1) as a pattern of technically
defined levels, e.g. patterns of living levels; (2) as a
structure of stocks, e.g. the main elements of a nation's
wealth measured on a per capita basis; and (3) as a balance of expenditure, the increments to human capital, to
compare opportunity costs of the various inputs in an
economy. Also the authors discuss the assessment of both
direct and indirect returns of particular social
investments as they would relate to an economy and the
nation-state.

Carter, Genevieve W.
    1971   "Social indicators: A perspective of the social
            indicators movement." A paper presented at the
            Annual Meeting of the Western Conference on the
            Uses of Mental Health Data (October 20-22)
            Newport Beach, California.

    Reviews the origins and characteristics of the social
indicators "movement" and includes an annotated bibliography of literature useful for this examination. Describes
the "movement" as attempting to make a hook-up with a number of useful techniques, methods, theory building, good
social statistics, and systems concepts. Concludes that
this hook-up, conceived as a "societal public policy approach," does an injustice to the parts which are linked
to the whole; but if the social indicators movement
results in increased funds for improving social statistics, there is then a practical purpose to consider.

Center for Community Studies and the Nashville Urban
Observatory
    1970   Social Change and Quality of Life. A report on
            a conference held in (May 7-9) Nashville,
            Tennessee.

    Summary accounts of a 1970 conference at the Center for
Community Studies in Nashville, Tennessee, indicate the
difficulties and complexities of relating the inclusive
concept of social indicators to the local level. Concerned with the three areas of housing, education, and
health and mental health, this report presents the essence
of the issues confronted, methodological concerns, and
some relevant indicators within that metropolitan area.
Appendices include preconference papers from consultants
David M. Heer, Ardie Lubin and David Pearson, and a summary statement and overview from the Conference.

Clausen, A. W.
    1971   "Toward an arithmetic of quality."   Conference
            Board Record 8 (May):9-13.

    Measurement of factors and elements involved in
assessing the "quality of life" is considered. The question of why our progress toward developing this concept
has been delayed is answered in three parts: by
detractors who say it can't be done, by those who say it
has been done, and those who say it should not be done.
The paper speaks to all three approaches.

Clavel, Pierre and Paul Eberts
    1971   "The organization of data for public policy."   A
            paper presented at the Annual Meeting of the
            Rural Sociological Society (August 29) Denver,
            Colorado.

    This paper explores some data organization problems
with social indicators and social accounting. Sees one
critical area as the decision regarding the unit of analysis; their choice is for communities or counties. Develops an intercorrelation matrix based on three sets of variables: indicators of better population welfare, of major
manipulatable policy options and of community structures.

Cohen, Wilbur J.
    1967   "Education and learning."   The Annals of the
            American Academy of Political and Social Science
            373 (September):79-101.   (Reprinted in Bertram
            M. Gross (ed.), 1969 Social Intelligence for
            America's Future.   Boston: Allyn and Bacon).

    Describes why indicators should account for both quan-
titative and qualitative dimensions, definitions, and
emphases of society's numerous educational goals.   Asserts
that new indicators relating to educational opportunities,
the quality of education, fundamental human behavior, and
politico-economic behavior would have a powerful influence
on change and modernization in the educational system.

    1968   "Social indicators: Statistics for public
            policy."   The American Statistician 22
            (October):14-16.

    Cohen calls for the development of social statistics
along two lines. The first of those he calls social
indicators and would deal with present conditions in our
society, the magnitude of social problems and their rate
of change. The second type would give a sense of problems

which exist and suggest the cost and effectiveness of alternative means of resolving these problems.

Coleman, James S.
1969   "The methods of sociology." Pp. 86-114 in
        Robert Bierstedt (ed.), A Design for Sociology:
        Scope, Objectives, and Methods. Monograph 9.
        Philadelphia: The American Academy of Political
        and Social Science.

Coleman discusses new developments and accompanying problems in sociological research methods, one of these being social indicators. To be of value, social indicators: (1) must not be aggregated; (2) should recombine data from several indicators; (3) should be controlled, that is, show only a part of a given condition so it can be attributed to a single cause; (4) should have controlled indicators for the combined conditions; and (5) are the first step in a conversion process which operates upon resources. Coleman believes present methodology can handle large social problems and urges more research on social change.

Cummings, Gordon J.
1970   "Community resource development--how extension
        workers perceive the job." July, ESC-568.
        Washington, D.C.: U.S. Department of
        Agriculture, Extension Service.

The report of a national survey of Cooperative Extension staff members working in Community Resource Development, vis-a-vis characteristics, competencies, perceptions of community and areas problems, etc. Explains how the author concludes that Cooperative Extension can begin to identify itself as a potential contributor to the goal of building more "livable" communities.

Day, Lincoln H. and Alice Taylor Day
1969   "Family size in industrialized countries: An
        inquiry into the social-cultural determinants of
        levels of childbearing." Journal of Marriage
        and the Family 31 (May):242-251.

Outlines a framework for studying socio-cultural determinants of family size in twenty low mortality countries of controlled natality. Two broad hypotheses are proposed: 1) Family size will vary inversely with alternatives to need satisfaction through children. 2) Family size is smallest where social setting a) maximizes an individual's expectations that his interests and those of his children will be satisfied and b) minimizes this expectation. Representative social indicators for making

227

the necessary international comparisons are enumerated,
and steps towards their construction discussed.

1970   "The social setting of low natality in
        industrialized countries." A paper presented at
        the Annual Meeting of the International
        Sociological Association (August) Varna,
        Bulgaria.

A progress report on a six-nation study taking a macrosociological approach in analyzing the relation between
natality and socio-cultural living conditions. It is
hoped that measures relating the change over time in
demographic conditions to social attributes can be developed. Observations will be required for all of the twenty
nations proposed for the study before any conclusions can
be made concerning the hypothesis that: natality will be
lowest under polar conditions where either social needs
are met externally in abundance or where the sparse means
of meeting needs in scarcity largely prohibit procreation.

Dial, O. E.
    1970   "Notes on the prospects for social indication."
            A paper presented at the Annual Meeting of the
            American Political Science Association (Septem-
            ber) Los Angeles, California.

Reviews and analyzes recent efforts in developing
systems of social indicators. Classified current research
into four schools; quality of life, goals, social movement
and social statistics. Each is useful to the other and
the current greatest need is for more qualified
researchers to apply their expertise in the field of
social indicators.

Drewnowski, Jan
    1966   Social and Economic Factors in Development -
            Introductory Considerations on their Meaning,
            Measurement and Interdependence. Report No. 3.
            February. Geneva, Switzerland: United Nations
            Research Institute for Social Development.

This paper is intended as an introduction to studies
addressing the problems of adequately defining social concepts connected with development, quantification of these
concepts, and investigating the interrelated roles of
social and economic elements in the development process.
General approaches to quantifying social concepts, particularly "level of living" and "level of welfare", are discussed.

228

Duncan, Otis Dudley
1961   "From social system to ecosystem." Sociological
        Inquiry (Spring):140-149.

An exposition on the concept ecosystem and criticism of
its use by sociologists. A summation definition advanced:
"ecosystem...refer(s) to a community together with its
habitat."

Ellickson, Katherine Pollak
1959   AFL-CIO "Discussion" of the Cabello and
        Stringham papers. Pp. 222-223 in Proceedings of
        the Social Statistics section, American Statis-
        tical Association. Washington, D.C.

A discussion of the text of the two articles
emphasizing that more effort should be made to develop estimates of "unmet needs" and estimates of social strain
and personal maladjustment, in any effective social programming.

Fisher, Joseph L.
1967   "The natural environment." The Annals of the
        American Academy of Political and Social Science
        37 (May):127-140. (Reprinted in Bertram M.
        Gross (ed.), 1969 Social Intelligence for
        America's Future. Boston: Allyn and Bacon).

Treats various indicators of environmental quality and
proposes that social welfare be measured in terms of net
social benefits; but, where estimates of benefits seem impossible, the concept of "environmental problem shed"
which entails minimizing a given measure of societal costs
might integrate problems and indicators. This would
promote research needed on the process of formulating
standards and programs; thus illuminating where statistical indicators are necessary for measuring direction,
rates of change, and trends in environmental population
and its qualitative effect on people.

Flax, Michael J.
1971   "Future prospects for the development of addi-
        tional social and urban indicators." Working
        Paper No. 1206-2. Washington, D.C.: The Urban
        Institute.

In this working paper, definitions of social and urban
indicators are suggested, and examples of current
indicator works are described. Prospects given include
characteristics of some needed indicators; political, in-

stitutional and psychological barriers to the indicator concept are discussed; future utilization and effect are considered. Bibliography: 1) background; 2) general social indicator theory; 3) examples of the "doing" of indicators; 4) general research philosophy and techniques.

Fox, Karl A.
    1970   "Population redistribution among functional eco-
            nomic areas: A new strategy for urban and rural
            America." A paper presented at the Annual
            Meeting of the American Association for the
            Advancement of Science (December 30) Chicago,
            Illinois.

A discussion of the proposal to form the nation into functional economic areas as systems of governing bodies for economic planning and political decision-making to promote an optimal redistribution of the population.

    1971   "Combining economic and noneconomic objectives
            in development planning: Problems of concept
            and measurement." Unpublished manuscript.
            Ames, Iowa: Department of Economics, Iowa State
            University.

An economist's proposal to include the social into the economic model of assessing GNP, resulting in what the author refers to as a Gross Social Product. Suggests using Roger Barker's theory of behavior settings as the bridge from estimates of gross economic product to estimates of gross social product at the level of the small town.

Gastil, Raymond D.
    1970   "Social indicators and quality of life." Public
            Administration Review 30 (November-December):
            596-601.

Cautions against uncritical use of statistics and pinpoints some confusions which may result from combining input and output statistics. He recommends working out in detail the meaning and comparability of less aggregated social statistics with clear separation of input and output. "Releasing statistics already gathered, such as those in education, to make possible further meaningful comparisons and analyses should be as important a goal as the gathering of new data."

Gerbner, G.
    1970   "Cultural indicators: The case of violence in
            television drama." The Annals of the American

Academy of Political and Social Science 388
(March):69-81.

Develops the notion that a culture's message system
cultivates conceptions of life relevant to socialization
and public policy. Periodic analysis of trends and
systematic indicators of the changing symbolic environment
would reflect structural-functional attributes of
transmitting institutions and is specified as being cen
tral to informed policy-making. While the terms for such
analysis are suggested by previous studies of T.V.
violence, they also demonstrate the need for more comprehensive, cumulative and comparative information on mass
cultural trends and configurations.

Goldman, Nathan
    1967   "Social breakdown." The Annals of the American
            Academy of Political and Social Science 373
            (September):156-179. (Reprinted in Bertram M.
            Gross (ed.), 1969 Social Intelligence for
            America's Future. Boston: Allyn and Bacon).

The inability of society to mobilize an attack on situations deemed undesirable; family breakdown, suicide,
addiction, sexual deviance, mental disorder and others is
testimony that we should consider these problems as
indicators of strain and improve data collection. This
requires standardization of the criteria for a social
problem and increased scope and accuracy of data. Coordination at the national level is needed for developing a
set of social indicators which will adequately describe
the state of the nation.

Gross, Bertram
    1966a   "Let's have a real state of the union message."
            Challenge 14 (May-June):8-10.

Gross calls for a state of the union message which
would be developed as a unified "package." A Social
Report should complement the Economic Report and the
Budget Message, and the State of the Union Message would
encompass all three.

    1966b   "The state of the nation: Social systems ac-
            counting." Pp. 154-271 in Raymond A. Bauer
            (ed.), Social Indicators. Cambridge,
            Massachusetts The Massachusetts Institute of
            Technology Press.

Presents the view that social systems accounting must
be based on integrated relevant concepts from economics,
political science, sociology, anthropology, psychology and

social psychology. From this he develops a social systems
model of two multi-dimensional, interrelated elements:
the system structure (the internal relations among the
system's parts) and the system performance (the acquiring
of inputs and their transformations into outputs). The
model then can be adapted to any country of any stage of
development or politics; both quantitative and qualitative
expression of national purposes and the extent to which
they're being achieved; or to any organization or
subelement. Cautions against a "new Philistinism": the
use of monetary units as the common denominator of the important things in human life.

Identifies two areas of resistance to development and
use of social indicators: inertia, and the unending
struggle for adequate resources. Controversy develops
over: 1) whether social system accounting should be done,
2) selectivity-comprehensiveness paradox, and 3)
abstraction-specificity ladder.

Proposes 1) that the President's State of the Union
Message to Congress or his Economic Report should be
broadened (or else a Social Report also presented) to
include the major aspects of social structure and performance, 2) that the State of the World surveys of the United
Nations should also be broadened and 3) that the United
Nations could develop model social reports for a pilot set
cf countries to be used as examples by other nations.
Recognizes that progress in whole area will be slow and
uneven, that maturation of social accounting concepts will
likely take many decades. Tabular presentation of elements of system structure, national structure, system performance, and national performance abstractions: grand
and intermediate.

> 1967a "The city of man: A social systems reckoning."
> Pp. 136-156 in William R. Ewald, Jr. (ed.), En-
> vironment for Man: The Next Fifty Years.
> Bloomington, Indiana: Indiana University Press.

An article oriented to planners, especially city
planners, to "shock" them into greater consideration of
the "human" aspect of their planning. Specifically, the
potentialities (and dangers) in social systems accounting
for urban areas.

> 1967b "The coming general systems models of social
> systems." Human Relations 20 (Novem-
> ber):357-374.

Gross reviews the historical aspects of social accounting and the shift from economic to social accounting. He
delineates three approaches to 'social accounting," i.e.
micro, macro-residual, and social system analysis, and
opts for a general systems model, which he explicates in
Bauer's Social Indicators.

Gross, Bertram M. and Michael Springer
    1967a "A new orientation in American government." The
           Annals of the American Academy of Political and
           Social Science 371 (May):1-19. (Reprinted in
           Bertram M. Gross (ed.), 1969 Social Intelligence
           for America's Future. Boston: Allyn and
           Bacon).

    Introduces the issues which have arisen with the rapid
proliferation of social indicators. The authors describe
historical sources of approaches taken, key points in the
social indicator information explosion and our
unsystematic national data system. A table of "Indicator
Suggestions" adopts various proposals to the context of
demands which the authors specify are being made upon data
gathering agencies.

    1967b "New goals for social information." The Annals
           of the American Academy of Political and Social
           Science 373 (September):208-218. (Reprinted in
           Bertram M. Gross (ed.), 1969 Social Intelligence
           for America's Future. Boston: Allyn and
           Bacon).

    Proposes that rational consideration of policy is
impeded by a domestic "intelligence gap." A dimension of
this gap is "concept lag" and its remedy is the concern
for the table of Indicator Suggestions which concentrates
on conceptual innovation for upgrading obsolescent data
and devising new social information which involves the
complex relationship between indicators and goals in terms
of the normative questions involved in the selection of
indicators; their underpinnings, in concepts, theories and
values; the need for both quantitative and qualitative information; and the possible consequences of this new orientation for American government.

    1968   A Great Society? New York: Basic Books, Inc.

    The Great Society proposed by President Johnson is
appraised by Gross and others of the university community.
Gross answers five specific questions suggested by
President Johnson. Eleven other authors from various
fields examine social processes. The authors include
Daniel Bell, Kenneth E. Boulding, Bertram M. Gross,
Herbert Marcuse, Michael Marien and Robin M. Williams, Jr.
among others. The authors take stands on matters of
public policy to encourage future cooperation of government and academia.

Hackes, Peter
    1971   "The uncommunicative scientist: The obligation

of scientists to explain environment to the public." A paper presented at the Annual Meeting of The American Association for the Advancement of Science (December 27) Philadelphia, Pennsylvania.

This is a popular presentation of the need for better communication and for the willingness of scientists to communicate in understandable language to the public. The emphasis here is for environmental indices. The author recognizes that there is not a single, complete right answer, but that still the public is entitled to know the issues and the facts. Scientists have a duty and obligation to present those issues and facts.

Harris, Fred R.
    1970   "A strategy for the social sciences." Pp. 1-11 in Fred R. Harris (ed.), Social Science and National Policy. Chicago, Illinois: Aldine Publishing Company.

The introduction deals with the history of social sciences in relation to governmental policy and their subsequent diminishing stature during World War II. Some specific social science problems that are covered in articles included in the book are segregation and poverty, rural to urban population shift, and the effects on individuals who are the subjects or clients of any policy program. The last section deals with some possible legislative proposals designed to encourage the development of a strategy for the social sciences, specifically a National Social Science Foundation.

Hauser, Philip M.
    1946   "Are the social sciences ready?" American Sociological Review 11 (August):379-384.

Asks whether social scientists are ready for the opportunity and challenge of providing enough knowledge to prevent the suicidal anachronism represented by our social institutions and practices. Viewed the debate over the advisability of including a Division of Social Sciences in the National Science Foundation as a symptom of the prevalent state of social disorganization. Highlights considerations which should figure heavily in blueprints drawn for foundations sponsored research. Such projects will test whether the social sciences are ready with carefully-planned, well-designed, far-reaching and significant research objectives.

    1967   "Social accounting." Pp. 423-446 in Hearings before the Subcommittee on Government Research

of the Committee on Government Operations,
United States Senate, 90th Congress, first ses-
sion on Senate Bill S.843, the Full Opportunity
and Social Accounting Act. Part 3 (July 28).
(Also Pp. 839-875 in Paul F. Lazarsfeld, William
H. Sewell, Harold Wilensky (eds.), The Uses of
Sociology. New York: Basic Books.)

Traces the historical development of accounting procedures, pointing to the expansion of statistics in the U.S.
as in the world as a function of social change, a product
of the increasing complexity and interdependence of the
social order. Assigns the significant role to sociology
in interpreting and understanding both the development and
the function of social accounting; sociology is active in
several census areas: 1) real differentiation; 2)
nativity, race and ethnic classification; 3) household and
family; 4) socio-economic differentiation; 5) demography;
6) labor force; 7) housing; 8) current statistics; 9)
methodology; and 10) monographs. Its vital role in many
noncensus areas also listed, as well as in relationship to
policy and administration.

Hauser, Philip M., Alvin W. Gouldner, Charles P. Loomis
and Kenneth Lutterman
    1970   "Review symposium." American Sociological
            Review 35 (April):329-341.

Hauser, Loomis and Lutterman generally find much of
merit in these books; Gouldner reviews only "Sociology,"
sees it as a plea for increasing support for the
Sociological Establishment without rocking the "American
Welfare-Warfare State" boat. Hauser felt the Committee
report was more inclusive, far-reaching and innovative,
though both should be "must" reading. Loomis felt "Sociology" tried to reach too broad an audience, thus losing
some of its potential effectiveness; wished for greater
emphasis in the Committee report on development of general
theory. Lutterman cites inadequate or absent data and inadequate resources as limiting what both books set out to
do; comments also on the primitive organization of social
sciences in that this is the first comprehensive attempt
to assess their development.

Henriot, Peter J.
    1970a   "Political questions about social indicators."
            The Western Political Science Quarterly 23
            (June):235-255.

Traces the development of the concept social indicator,
discusses its potential value in society and suggests
reservations regarding the safeguards, dangers and ulti-

mate impact indicators might have in politics. He inter-
prets social indicators as more than how to gather and
correlate data; they are basically a matter of values,
interests and policies.

> 1970b "Social indicators: Some practical politics."
> A paper presented at the Annual Meeting of the
> American Association for Public Opinion Research
> (May 20) Pasadena, California.

Presents the strong political implications of the
social indicator movement, based on the concept that more
is involved than just gathering and correlating data,
i.e., matters of values, interests, policies - politics.
The political premises from which he views the movement
are: 1) concern for "quality of life" is eminently
political; 2) commitment to social indicator work springs
from an identifiable political position; 3) the generation
and utilization of social indicators occur with a
political environment. Examines four areas of political
issues with cases illustrating the politics of definition,
gathering, reporting and use.

Hoos, Ida R.
1971 "Information systems and public planning."
Management Science 17 (June):B-658 - B-671.

Deals with questions needed for more detailed information systems; and raises the fear of accumulation of
computerized data as encroachment on the individual's
right to privacy.

Horowitz, Irving Louis
1968 "Social indicators and social policy." Pp.
328-339 in Irving L. Horowitz, Professing Sociology: Studies in the Life Cycle of Social Science. Chicago: Aldine Publishing Company.

The author examines four questions, which, when
satisfactorily resolved would form the core of any serious
discussion of the worth of social indicators and a Council
of Social Advisors. He argues for more involvement on the
part of social scientists in shaping the national policy.

Howard, William A.
1969 "City-size and its relationship to municipal efficiency: Some observations and questions."
Ekistics 28 (November):312-315.

The author reviews two sides of the problem of city
size and municipal efficiency. On the one hand consider-

able research, but very little consensus, has been reached
on the optimum size of the city and, on the other hand,
relatively little research has gone into the quality of
service provided by urban areas. He suggests more and
better formulation of methods of analysis in such areas as
the institutional make-up, economic development, and
socio-political characteristics.

Ikle, Fred Charles
   1971   "Social forecasting and the problem of changing
           values with special reference to Soviet and East
           European writings." Futures 3 (June):142-150.

     Changes in values influence the future as much as
changes in technology. It is, therefore, important for
forecasters and decision-makers to work from a structure
of preferences concerning alternatives and for them to
understand their own current values which affect their selection of predictions. There is a need to separate
forecasting function and planning function distinctly to
offer as many opportunities for the future as possible.

Institut de Recherche Economique et de Planification
   1971   "Recherche sur l'integration des indicateurs
           sociaux dans les modeles de changement social."
           Unpublished manuscript. (September) Grenoble,
           France: University of the Social Sciences of
           Grenoble.

     Research undertaken by the Economic Research and
Planning Institute of Grenoble and the Institute of
Political Studies of Grenoble following a six month
contract with the Service of Social Affairs of the
Commissioner of Planning. The duration of the research is
18 months beginning January 1972. The paper is not designed to present the results of the research, but while
keeping in mind the goal of the research, is to indicate
the great amount of work already effected as well as indicate the perspectives yet to come in social indicator research.

Institut National de la Statistique et des Etudes
Economiques
   1971   "Presentation des travaux francais." Unpub-
           lished manuscript. Paris, France: Commissariat
           General du Plan d'Equipment et de la
           Productivite. (November)

     This is a presentation of the results of studies made
of existing social indicators. The object of the research
is to examine the current long-term studies in the social

domain and to evaluate their effectiveness. The first
section of the paper is a response to the call by
administrators for such a study. The second section
treats the objectives and some of the first results of
that study.

Johnston, Denis F.
    1970   "Forecasting methods in the social sciences."
            Technological Forecasting and Social Change 2
            (July):173-187.

    Identifying present types of outlook statements as pre-
diction, projections or forecasts, this paper suggests a
different classification may be more realistic and
helpful. Proposed are two broad subgroupings of
exploratory and normative, each of which is further
subdivided into quantitative and qualitative. Discussed
are some of the present methods in each of the four categories, with their strengths and weaknesses. An improved
social science methodology requires forecasting methods to
fulfill a dual function, that of advance warnings and that
of explorations of the possible. Social indicators may
offer hope for the needed convergence of the qualitative
and quantitative by realization that data manipulation involves value judgments, that typical social problems
cannot readily be solved by the techniques of the physical
sciences or by technology, and by emphasizing that
decision makers need more than a statistical model, however elegant, to provide the deeper sense of social values
and derived goals essential for meaningful action.

    1971   "Social indicators and social forecasting."
            Cahiers du Centre de Recherches Science et Vie
            (Paris) No. 2 (September):41-83.

    After tracing the developing concept of social
indicators, this paper then moves to a comprehensive presentation of alternative directions for further development of social indicators. Following Springer's rough
consensus of five functions of a social accounting system,
within which a similar framework social indicators must be
analyzed, several developmental paradigms are evaluated:
a system of descriptive categories; an organizational
framework relating to normative adequacy involving
national goals and priorities; social systems model which,
at least theoretically, can measure the impact of particular inputs and trace their consequences; and finally, a
"prognostics" framework in the context of Dennis Gabor's
Inventing the Future. Differentiating among prediction,
projection and forecasting provides the basis for describing the use of social indicators within a prognostics
framework of analysis, and the specification of somewhat
different requirements for social indicators to provide
that framework with its empirical content.

238

Judge, Anthony J. N.
    1971   "Information systems and inter-organizational
            space." The American Academy of Political and
            Social Science 393 (January):47-64.

    Maintains that a worldwide information collection
system is required which, to be viable, cannot be dependent on any central administration if it is to facilitate
interaction between groups which are currently isolated
geographically or by specialization. To facilitate communication across jurisdictional boundaries and/or within
organizational structures, the technique of "computer interactive graphics" should be developed for depicting the
recognized conceptual complexity of social processes.

Jungk, Robert
    1968   "Human Futures." Futures 1 (September):34-39.

    The author discusses the importance of devising a
system of human forecasting as an essential part of
futures research. Accordingly he discusses in his article
technology, passivity, 'participative' democracy, and information as important concepts to be considered in human
forecasting. He closes by saying that goals must become a
serious preoccupation of humanistic futures research.

King-Hele, Desmond
    1970   "The quality of living." Pp. 134-171 in Desmond
            King-Hele, The End of the Twentieth Century.
            New York: St. Martins Press.

    In this article the author discusses ways of improving
the environment so as to improve the quality of life. In
this treatment he deals with such topics as pollution,
better town planning, the idea of misgovernment, and
planning for leisure. By recognizing the social costs and
benefits of these parts of the environment, the author
feels that a better quality of living can be prepared.

Konvitz, Milton R.
    1967   "Civil liberties." The Annals of the American
            Academy of Political and Social Science 371
            (May):38-58. (Reprinted in Bertram M. Gross
            (ed.) 1969 Social Intelligence for America's
            Future. Boston: Allyn and Bacon).

    Deals with the philosophy of values which attends the
issue of civil liberties. Asserts that, while watchdogs
are built into our political system, there still remains a
need for an independent civil liberties research agency to

assure that the guardians of our goals will have factual
indicators of the degree to which American life approxi-
mates its ideals.

Kopkind, Andrew
    1967   "The future-planners." American Psychologist 22
            (November):1036-1041. (Also in New Republic,
            February 25:19-23.)

    Considers the attitudes and research of Bell, Moynihan,
Harrington and others as suggesting the emergence of an
ideology of technical problem solving. Argues that future
formulators' theories may be used to manipulate the attitudes of the society they are pretending to serve as
disinterested technicians and that Gross, Bauer, and
Biderman have admitted this possibility. Kopkind's position that "elitism" may taint the theory and movement
towards social accounting is discussed in relation to current notions of "corporate state" of "post-industrialism"
as varieties of totalitarianism.

Krieger, Martin H.
    1969   "Social indicators for the quality of individual
            life." Working Paper No. 104. Berkeley,
            California: Institute of Urban and Regional De-
            velopment, University of California.

    Develops a context for considering and measuring the
concept of empathy as a quality of life dimension. It is
maintained that man's need for affective qualities will
increase as new goals emerge in the transition to beyond a
post-industrial society. A procedure for measuring the
affectivity of interpersonal relations via friendship is
proposed. This might accomplish the needed sensitization
of people to policy consequences by techniques which might
be of interest to the systems people.

Krohn, Edward
    1967   "Statistical requirements for the promotion of
            health." Pp. 151-158 in a discussion paper for
            Conference of European Statisticians, Statisti-
            cal Standards and Studies: ST/CES/11, 2.

    The author discusses the relationship between economic
status and health and suggests that plans for economic or
social development are not complete unless contributions
to improvement in health have been considered. He
recounts the epidemiological characteristics of Europe and
goes into considerable detail on statistical requirements
needed as a basis for promotion of health.

Lehman, Edward W.
    1971   "Social indicators and social problems."   Pp.
            149-176 in Erwin O. Smigel (ed.), Handbook on
            the Study of Social Problems. Chicago: Rand
            McNally and Company.

    Presenting a broad overview of the conceptual and meth-
odological problems of social indicators, this chapter
specifically speaks to the question: "How can we best
select and/or construct indicators of social problems?"
Uncritical use may lead to incorrect social diagnoses or
may generate ineffective or even harmful policy
formulation.   Discussed are aggregated data about system
members, including single-item vs. multi-item methods,
marginal characterizations vs. intrasystem variation,
reductionist vs. nonreductionist analyses; global data
relating to the kind of social system property under analysis, membership vs. nonmembership properties, collective
activities; problems of data collection and indirect measurement, congruence of system attributes and system
indicators; and supramembership properties, positional
weighting, linking indicators, and criteria ambiguities.

Levin, Lowell S.
    1969   "Building toward the future: Implications for
            health education."   American Journal of Public
            Health 59 (November):1983-1991.

    A projection of the future of health education and
services in a changing society.   Technical, distributive
and social-cultural developments as they impact health education are examined.

Lewis, Wilfred, Jr.
    1971   "Public policy and national priorities in the
            next decade."   Looking Ahead 19 (July):5-8.

    Although there has been attention to national goals and
the measurement of social progress, consensus is lacking
on what the national goals are or how to determine or
measure them.   An estimate of the value of costs and benefits of institutional change is needed.   Changes in some
federal government processes and machinery is proposed to
aid in monitoring national goals.

Linowes, David
    1971   "Accounting for social progress; Yardsticks must
            be found for public programs."   Extension of

241

remarks of the Hon. Frank E. Moss.
Congressional Record (March 29):E2369-E2370.

The author argues for the establishment of socio-
economic management councils at every level of government,
to evaluate current programs and to create programs to
provide solutions to major urban problems. Socio-economic
management is defined as "the measurement and analysis of
the social and economic consequences of governmental and
business actions on the public sector." Subsumed within
this article is the discussion of the necessity to make
more qualitative assessments of our programs.

Lompe, Klaus
      1968   "Problems of futures research in the social sci-
              ences." Futures 1 (September):47-53.

The author believes that in order to provide comprehensive future forecasts, futures research must broaden and
strengthen its methodology and coordinate information from
all branches of science. In this article he also outlines
three basic problems of futures research. One is deciding
on the rank or priority of social goals. The second problem is that of inventing the future - simulation models.
The third problem is that of forecasting on the basis of
available data. He discusses these problems and offers
some suggestions for solution.

Long, Norton E.
      1968   "Planning for social change." Pp. 67-79. Amer-
              ican Society of Planning Officials (eds.),
              Planning: 1968. Chicago: ASPO.

The author demonstrates that non-physical planning or
social planning is receiving belated and hopelessly inadequate attention in city planning. He is interested in
planning for neighborhoods where the human interaction
pattern will generate a normative structure that will
maintain social control and provide the future basis for
an effective leadership.

Madden, J. Patrick
      1970   "Social change and public policy in rural
              America: Data and research needs for the
              1970's." American Journal of Agricultural Eco-
              nomics 52 (May):308-314.

Directed to researcher and to practitioner-policy-maker
alike; broaden scope of researcher's view of potential research problems and provide practitioners with a better
basis for interpreting the results of various research

findings. Some pitfalls might be the incongruity between concept and measurement, quality versus quantity, fractional measurement, means versus ends, hardening of the categories and overgeneralization from limited or biased samples.

    1971   "Poverty data in relation to other indicators of
            social welfare." A paper presented at the
            Annual Meeting of the American Sociological
            Society (August 30) Denver, Colorado.

Current definitions and interpretations of poverty and poverty statistics are examined and found generally inadequate on both conceptual and empirical grounds. Relative and absolute deprivation are considered with support for the concept that deprivation is a continuum extending well above the defined poverty line. Other dimensions of poverty besides low income are discussed, with emphasis on hunger, health and mortality. From the premise that poverty is a multidimensional social problem, many faceted social indicators are needed to monitor the trends and provide necessary information for adequate planning for the social welfare of the nation. Statistics summarizing and supporting the findings are presented in tabular form.

Malenbaum, Wilfred
    1971   "Progress in health: What index of what
            progress?" The Annals of the American Academy
            of Political and Social Science 393
            (January):109-121.

Reports a study concerned with the importance of health variables in the analysis of economic progress in poor lands. Analysis of change in health programs in poor areas, where labor is the dominant factor of production, suggests a positive effect of health inputs on subsequent output. Concludes that a measure of health inputs might serve as an index of socio-economic progress. If so, it would call for revising the postulate of health inputs negative influence and encourage a reallocation of world health resources for meeting critical development tasks.

Mauro, John T.
    1968   "Planning as an instrument for social change."
            Pp. 59-67 in American Society of Planning
            Officials (eds.), Planning: 1968. Chicago:
            ASPO.

An analysis of seventeen years of city planning in Pittsburgh emphasizing physical planning as one method of approaching "social problems" such as housing, education facilities, jobs, transportation, parks, and playgrounds.

Emphasizes importance of city planners to understand land
and money management for planning with a social purpose.

Mayer, Lawrence A.
    1972   "U.S. population growth: Would slower be
            better?" Pp. 238-245 in Rex R. Campbell and
            Jerry L. Wade (eds.), Society and Environment:
            The Coming Collision.   Boston, Massachusetts:
            Allyn and Bacon, Inc.

    Total fertility rate is examined as a clue to future
family size and demographic prediction of the national
population.   It is described as an unreliable indicator at
any one point in time as Bogue's and Campbell's divergent
views and the findings of Bumpass and Westoff on unwanted
children are considered.   The "population" problem is
appraised in terms of density, externalized production
costs, reduced standards of consumption, adequacy of resources and eventual stability.   Projected social implications of population stability are presented raising questions about, particularly, the dire projections of Cole
and Sauvy.

McGranahan, Donald
    1972   "Development indicators and development models."
            The Journal of Development Studies.

    It is held in this article that social indicators are
not a substitute for research but a tool and would be
misapplied if used to reveal "impact" of different development factors upon each other.   Various developed models
are described and limitations of the measurement of the
use of social indicators to gauge national development are
forwarded.   Notably, indicators are asserted to be impossible to convert into a single value scale.   Concepts of
optimum patterns of development are represented as another
value aspect over and above that of single indicators and
are further complicated by system interdependency.

Meyer, John R.
    1969   "The evaluation and planning of social pro-
            grams." Testimony before the Special
            Subcommittee on the Evaluation and Planning of
            Social Programs, Senate Committee for Labor and
            Public Welfare, July 17, 1969.   A Supplement to
            National Bureau Report 5.   (December) New York:
            National Bureau of Economic Research, Inc.

    Testimony before the Senate Subcommittee on the Evalua-
tion and Planning of Social Programs.   Describes deficiencies of national income accounts.   Argues that the needs

for social indicators go beyond the measurement of the by-products of productive activity where no intellectual base for their development parallels that which gave rise to economic measurement. Hence initial evaluations may be wasteful but taking this perspective, waste may be minimized and should not prematurely discredit efforts at better social measurement which awaits the development of conceptual schemes that account for the multiorder social consequences of government programs.

Michael, Donald N.
    1967   "Social engineering and the future environment."
            American Psychologist 22 (November):888-892.

This is the author's statement at Hearings on S.68. Described the role of social science knowledge or technology in forecasting social impacts on the human environment as being problematic in that present data is inadequate for decisive answers or predictions. The impact of obtaining the data required is emphasized by examples of the types of situations which could plausibly ensue. In sum, Michael asserts that the application of social engineering will confront us with formidable dilemmas over what we want, what we believe in, and how we obtain what we want in terms of what we believe in.

Miller, S. M., Martin Rein, Pamela Roby and Bertram M. Gross
    1967   "Poverty, inequality, and conflict." The Annals
            of the American Academy of Political and Social
            Science 373 (September):16-52. (Reprinted in
            Bertram M. Gross (ed.), 1969 Social Intelligence
            for America's Future. Boston: Allyn and
            Bacon).

Attention is directed to aspects of "spiritual poverty" as well as to neglected aspects of economic living standards. Proposes six dimensions for measurement of well being which would elaborate the authors' position that a minimum approach by government in any society with significant inequalities must provide not only for rising minimum levels of income, wealth and basic services, but also self-respect and opportunities for social mobility and participation in many forms of decision-making.

Moynihan, Daniel P.
    1967   "Urban conditions: General." The Annals of the
            American Academy of Political and Social Science
            (May):159-177. (Reprinted in Bertram M. Gross
            (ed.), 1969 Social Intelligence for America's
            Future. Boston: Allyn and Bacon).

Systematically examines the array of social data to outline a starting point for constructing urban social indicators. Aspects of this process suggest that indicators should: (1) be disaggregated and correlated, (2) pan political, (3) both future and present oriented, (4) provide local, national and "best practice" comparisons, and (5) report conditions in terms of individual people, families and institutions.

    1969   "Toward a national urban policy." Appalachia (August):1-9.

A general exposition on the development of "urban" problems and the requirement for a federally integrated national "urban" policy, not a proliferation of programs. Federal integration implies that the goals are set at the national government whose scope would encompass the nation through the active recognition and involvement of all existing governments as to how their decisions influence what occurs or fails to occur in America's cities.

National Academy of Engineering, Committee on Public Engineering Policy
    1971   Priorities in Applied Research: An Initial Appraisal. Washington, D.C.: National Academy of Engineering.

Summarized are the suggestions and recommendations of the Committee on Public Engineering Policy of the National Academy of Engineering to provide the National Science Foundation resource ideas to implement its new legislative mandate to support applied research "relevant to national problems involving the public interest." General recommendations indicate: 1) support needed on a problem-oriented rather than a disciplinary basis; 2) encouragement of interdisciplinary research projects preferable; 3) that special emphasis should be on social values and goals; and 4) that reliable social and environmental indicators are long overdue. Primary efforts should be concentrated on applied research related to the biosphere, and to the interface between social and physical systems. Research on materials and on construction and transportation is next in importance and need. Recommendations for the fifth main area, electronics, are given although the area is unranked, and the Committee felt the level of private and government support was already adequate.

Nisbet, Robert A.
    1968   "The year 2000 and all that." Commentary 45 (June):60-66.

Nisbet notes that prediction of the future, especially
the year 2000, is becoming popular. One reason is the
wizardry of technology--its power to solve problems. Prediction based on technology and the extrapolation of
present statistics has its pitfalls. Any means of
predicting must always be held suspect. Events do not
multiply and small social changes do not accumulate direc-
tionally to become large social changes.

Nixon, Richard M.
    1969   "Statement by President Nixon on creating a
            National Goals Research Staff." Futures 1
            (September):458-459.

A White House Statement announcing the creation of the
National Goals Research staff to attempt social
forecasting for the future, estimating range of social
choice in terms of alternatives, measuring probable future
impact of alternative courses of action, developing and
monitoring social indicators that can reflect the present
and future quality of American life, its direction and
change, and summarizing and integrating the results of related research activities by various federal agencies,
state and local governments.

Official Summary of HEW Toward a Social Report
    1969   "A social report in practice." The Public
            Interest 15:98-105.

A summarizing report of several areas of American life,
social mobility, physical environment, income and poverty,
etc. as examples of how social reporting could elucidate
the well-being of the nation.

Organization for Economic Cooperation and Development
    1970   "Demographic accounts: A step towards social
            accounting." OECD Observer 49 (December):35-37.

A brief description of an accounting classificatory
scheme organized on the "life sequence" of an individual
showing his "inflow" and "outflow" by activity aggregated
to a "national" account profile.

Osman, John
    1969   "Alternative futures for the American city."
            Public Management 51 (September):2-3.

The author discusses the usefulness for city managers
of planning and projecting future trends and preparing
policies and programs with which to meet the conditions

created by the trends. He describes a symposium in which
32 city managers met for four days to consolidate their
thinking about management problems in different sized
American cities in two time frames: 1969-1975 and
1975-1985.

Palley, Howard A. and Marian Lief Palley
    1971   "Social policy analysis--The use of social
            indicators." Welfare in Review 9
            (March-April):8-14.

    A general statement about the need for some type of
social indicator for policy makers is presented.
Indicators are viewed as defined by HEW in Toward A Social
Report, i.e. those statistics of direct normative
interest. The example cited was the "social problem" of
racial disorders. All data was in aggregated form
principally from the U.S. Census.
    The authors found their model's variables, racial dif-
ferential in economic opportunities, educational
attainment, health services, and level of police
protection, did not explain the occurrence or non-
occurrence of racial disorders.

Perle, Eugene D.
    1970a   "Editor's introduction." Urban Affairs
             Quarterly 6 (December):135-144.

    Brief survey of the developing interest and potential
use of social indicators and urban indicators;
perspectives on some of the difficulties involved, e.g.,
aggregate forms of analysis; futurism and decision making;
what should be measured and why. This introduces the six
articles in this special issue where the new emerging
field of urban indicators is discussed. Three of the articles are primarily state of the art reports (Dueker,
Kirasian, Simmons); two are based upon original research
in progress (Boyce, Maimon); and one article is both a
review and an original research contribution (Mattila).

    1970b   "Notes on urban information systems and urban
             indicators." A paper presented at the Annual
             Meeting of the Association for Computing Machin-
             ery (September 1) New York City.

    Distinguishes between management of information and
management by information, into which latter category he
puts field of social indicators. Generally critical of
emphasis on the potential value of social indicators.

    1971   "Local societal indicators: A progress report."
            Pp. 114-120 in Proceedings of the Social Sta-

248

tistics Section, American Statistical Association, Washington, D.C.

Reviews the present interest in social indicators and
notes two general orientations. Some individuals are ex-
tremely optimistic about the possibilities of developing
social accounting systems. This orientation is supported
by public officials and academicians closely related to
the political system. Their indicators are generally
specified for nation states and represent the macro approach to the question of social indicators. Others are
optimistic but cautious in their efforts to assess the
usefulness of social indicators. This group according to
Perle consists of academics interested in the functioning
of the social system, who approach this interest at a
micro level and with a demand for greater empirical sophistication.

Urban indicators are viewed as a level below the macro
approach to the nation and Perle suggests that additional
models need to be presented and empirically verified. The
author questions the use of social indicators for the
assessment of societal performance without the specification of goals against which actual performance can be compared. Several socio-economic studies of the Detroit area
are reviewed with a discussion of findings and plans for
future social indicator pursuits.

Raymond, Robert S. and Elizabeth Richards
    1971   "Social indicators and business decisions."
           Michigan State University Business Topics
           (Autumn):42-46.

The thesis of this article is, first, that the current
emphasis on environmental and human problems should
persuade business managers to incorporate social considerations into corporate marketing and manufacturing
decisions, and second, that this can be done most effectively through the development and use of social
indicators to be collected regularly on a national basis
and conveyed through a social report. The quality of
life, measured by the objective dimensions of individual
well-being, should weigh equally with economic progress.

Riecken, Henry W.
    1969   "Social sciences and social problems." Social
           Science Information 8 (February-June):101-129.

A discussion of how the social sciences can contribute
to social problem solving particularly through its scientific and intellectual orientation. Particular problems
which would be encountered in applying social science to
social problems are discussed, such as manipulatability of

variables, the Hawthorne effect, and the defects of indirect data. The author states and discusses four requirements to improve the social sciences to make them more relevant to social problems: (1) more basic research to solve the scientific and intellectual problems of these disciplines; (2) forms of organization and funding need to be devised which are appropriate for the task; (3) impediments to utilization of social science research must be overcome; and (4) the freedom of open, continuous and honest discussion of public policy problems raised by the social sciences.

Schatz, Gerald S.
    1970   "Spectrum management: The problems of defining the public interest." National Academy of Sciences News Report 20 (October):1, 4-5.

Report of a panel study from the National Academy of Engineering's Committee on Telecommunications, originally working through the Office of Emergency Preparedness, now in the Executive Office of the President; difficulties of defining public interest: "A function cannot be simultaneously maximized for several dependent variables. The greatest good for the greatest number of people, or the greatest value for the least cost, simply does not exist;" explores the need for systematic analysis; suggests some beginning steps.

Schneier, Edward
    1970   "The intelligence of congress: Information and public policy patterns." The Annals of the American Academy of Political and Social Science 388 (March):14-29.

Depicts the congressional information environment as one which virtually precludes objective weighing of data and priorities. This system encourages vindicators instead of indicators when centralization of certain information gathering activities is a necessary precondition to eroding the autonomy of congressionally supported policy subsystems. It is particularly important to develop new intelligence systems in the executive branch and the private sector to arrive at meaningful data or indicators. These indicators may then generate new interest groups which in turn would supplement and extend the information environment within which Congress acts.

Shariff, Zahid
    1971   "Social information and government-sponsored development: A case study from West Pakistan.

The Annals of The Academy of Political and
Social Science 393 (January):92-108.

Governmental participation in economic organization,
specifically the impact of the Pakistan Industrial Development Corporation, is examined in this paper. Three dimensions of PIDC were studied to determine the justification for the application of social information to new development. PIDC's diseconomies - wasteful and inefficient
uses of resources, corruption, empire-building, and its
excessive drain on governmental fund/personnel - are contrasted against its unformidable achievements. Conclusions drawn in this study argue a need for sensitizing
ourselves to the possibility of social information's
misuse particularly in connection with the issue of
industrial expansion in developing countries.

Sheldon, Eleanor Bernert and Howard E. Freeman
    1970   "Notes on social indicators: Promises and po-
            tential." Policy Sciences 1 (April):97-111.

A critical overview of social indicator development
based on the authors' beliefs that use and value of
indicators have been oversold. Delineates three areas
where we are technically deficient and conceptually inadequate: 1) the setting of goals and priorities, 2) the
evaluation of programs, and 3) the development of a balance sheet. Suggests three strong areas of promise and
potential: 1) improved descriptive reporting, 2) analysis
of social change, and 3) prediction of future social
events and social life.

Shonfield, Andrew
    1969   "Thinking about the future." Encounter 32
            (February):15-26.

"Futurology will remain allied to fantasy if the
technologists, both physical and social, do not put some
numbers to it" is the eloquent plea of this author for a
coordinated program of carefully defined, analytically
predictive studies of future alternatives.

Sills, David Lawrence
    1971   "Unanticipated consequences of population
            policies." A paper presented at the Annual
            Meeting of the Population Association of America
            (April 24) Washington, D.C.

A provocative discussion of the relevance of social
scientists studying the unanticipated consequences of
governmental programs or policies, demonstrated through
population program example, particularly the social and

demographic effects of one governmental program to or on other interrelated and interdependent areas.

Singer, Fred S.
    1971   "Can we develop an index for quality of life?"
           Science 173 (September 24):1253-1254.

The author briefly describes the usefulness of indices, such as social indicators, in assessing and planning for "quality of life" concerns. Eight questions are posed for the symposia in defining, measuring, quantifying, and implementation of any such indices.

Smith, Courtland L. and Thomas Hogg
    1971   "Benefits and beneficiaries: Contrasting eco-
           nomic and cultural distinctions." Water Re-
           sources Research 7 (April):254-263.

Examines the social and cultural context for water re- source development decision making. Two examples from the United States and another from Africa are used to emphasize that benefit-cost methodology has limitations which might be remedied by shifting to the "people and their values" side of analysis. This would entail explication of the beneficiary-benefactor dichotomy and integration of these concepts into feasibility determined view of the benefit-cost framework as a mechanism for op- timizing cultural values instead of being objectively value-free.

Soderlind, Sterling E.
    1970   "The outlook: Appraisal of current trends in
           business and finance." Wall Street Journal 51
           (Monday, November 2) Number 14:1.

A cautious, but hopeful, presentation of social indicators and quality of life research potential.

Springer, Michael (ed.)
    1970   Political Intelligence for America's Future.
           The Annals of the American Academy of Political
           and Social Science 388 (March).

This is the third issue of The Annals devoted to the discussion of social indicators and reports. It addresses the thorny issues raised by Toward a Social Report and the commitment of the Nixon administration to the issuance of annual presidential reports on social goals and indicators which has been accompanied by substantial private and governmental research grants and considerable exploration

252

with social reporting at regional, state, and municipal
levels. Issues raised concern the focus of social reporting, definitions used for indicators developed, and the
policy implications of this social knowledge.

Stockdale, Jerry D.
    1969   "Social implications of technological change in
            agriculture." A paper presented at the Annual
            Meeting of the Rural Sociological Society
            (August 29) San Francisco, California.

A discussion in the last section of the impact of
agricultural technology on "quality and meaning of life"
for rural Americans. Focuses generally on social-
psychological variables such as alienation, satisfaction,
and cosmopolitanism.

Stringham, Luther W.
    1959   "Health, education and welfare indicators and
            trends." Pp. 216-221 in Proceedings of the
            Social Statistics Section, American Statistical
            Association, Washington, D.C.

A descriptive account of the evolution of two HEW publications, HEW Indicators and HEW Trends including a summary statement of their definition of "indicators of human
well-being," i.e. social demographic statistics.

Taeuber, Karl E.
    1970   "Toward a social report: A review article."
            The Journal of Human Resources 5
            (Summer):354-360.

The author discusses the fact that social indicators,
social accounting, a Council of Social Advisers, and
social reporting are ideas whose time has come. He compares quantitatively and qualitatively the 1933 report of
Recent Social Trends in the United States with the recent
report Toward a Social Report, and indicates that the time
has indeed come for regular social reporting. An attempt
is made to clarify the definition of social indicators by
defining it as a statistic of direct normative interest
about the major aspects of society.

Terleckyj, Nestor E.
    1970a   "Data systems for measuring social change." A
            paper presented at the Annual Meeting of the
            American Statistical Association (December 27)
            Detroit, Michigan.

Discusses the present inadequacies of existing statistic systems for policy making, measurement and analysis of social change in the United States. The supply of and demand for social statistics developing along separate lines is presented with a listing of important data deficiencies in various categories of social statistics; health, crime, education, income distribution, housing and urban environment, pollution, recreation and leisure.

1970b "Measuring progress towards social goals: Some possibilities at national and local levels." Management Science 16 (August):B765-B778.

Stresses both the need for further development of social indicators and national goals, and the inadequacy of much of the data, with several large gaps noted; summary list of 6 major areas of national goals with corresponding principal indicators of goals output.

Thomas, William A.
    1971   "Indicators of environmental quality." Science 174 (October 22):437-438.

Viewed as a scientific necessity, Thomas expands the restricted physical notion of "environment" to include biological and sociocultural elements. The complexity of constructing social indicators where values are assigned to qualitative aspects of life are more challenging since a complete understanding is not possible for even the quantitative definition of "environment." Of necessity, the problem is interdisciplinary and must assume a processual orientation towards developing environmental indices which allow conceptual reduction that minimizes components and maximizes information content.

Toffler, Alvin
    1967   "The art of measuring the arts." The Annals of the American Academy of Political and Social Science 373 (September):141-155. (Reprinted in Bertram M. Gross (ed.), 1969 Social Intelligence for America's Future. Boston: Allyn and Bacon).

Advocates a cultural data system to provide information for rational policy-making in terms of cultural consequences; also a tentative model for monitoring quanti-qualitative aspects of cultural change on society. Fifteen cultural "quality indicators" are suggested which are dimensions of the model and may be aggregated to form an index of a nation's cultural health. Ways are proposed by which changes in these variables can be statistically measured.

254

Tweeten, Luther G.
  1969   "Causes of rural poverty." Ekistics 28
          (December):395-398.

A discussion of how two current theories of economics,
settlement theory and matrix-location theory, fail to
explain poverty. A general theory of economic stagnation
is advanced which recognizes the effects of "area environment," public services and resultant social costs, i.e.
the effects of non-economic factors and their salience to
a "healthy" economic environment.

United Nations, Report of the Secretary General
  1970   "Problems of the human environment." Ekistics
          29 (April):225-231.

Accelerated population growth, increased urbanization,
and an expanded and efficient new technology, with their
associated increase in demands for space, food, and natural resources, have, over time, led to a considerable
deterioration of the human environment. To overcome these
problems which are outlined in the article carefully
planned and vigorous action at all levels is required.
The article concludes by outlining 5 purposes of the "1972
United Nations Conference on the Problems of the Human Environment."

U.S. Senate
  1967   Hearings before the 90th Congress - 1st Session.
          Congressional Record 113 (February 6, June 19).

Introduction to The Full Opportunity and Social Ac-
counting Act of 1967 by Senator Mondale with supplementary
comments by Senator Harris. Also included are editorials:
"A Social Accounting," by Joseph Kraft in the Washington
Post and "Crime and Our Loss of Trust in Human Beings," by
Max Lerner in the Washington Star. Introduction of The
Full Opportunity and Social Accounting Act as a House Res-
olution by Congressman Fraser of Minnesota along with in-
clusion of an article from the May issue of Trans-Action,
"Social Accounting for the Nation."

  1968   Hearings before the 90th Congress - 2nd Session.
          Congressional Record 114 (May 8, June 3).

Reintroduction of the 1967 Full Opportunity Act by Rep-
resentative Conyers of Michigan with detailed explanation
of each section. Also includes a telegram from Dr. Martin
Luther King, Jr. and a Washington Post editorial by
William Raspberry "District March Now Dilemma of King's
Aides." A statement of support by Senator Nelson includes

the entire June 1968 Trans-action article by Senator
Mondale, "Reporting on the Social State of the Union."

    1969   Hearings before the 91st Congress - 1st Session.
                Congressional Record 115 (January 15, 22, 23,
                February 4, 7, 25, March 4, 24-27, October 27,
                December 16).

Introduction of the Full Opportunity Act of 1969 by
Senator Mondale. Also included are the texts of Daniel
Bell's "The Art of Forecasting Social Change," the Depart-
ment of Health, Education, and Welfare's "Toward a Social
Report" under the editorship of Wilbur Cohen, and the
National Academy of Sciences and the Social Science Re-
search Council's "Behavioral and Social Sciences: Outlook
and Needs." Other statements of congressional support of
the bill, social accounting, and the proposed council of
social advisors were made by Senators Harris, McGovern and
Javits and Representatives Yarborough of Ohio, Pepper of
Florida, and Gilbert of New York.

United States Senate, Committee on Labor and Public
           Welfare
    1971   Full Opportunity and National Goals and
                Priorities Act. Hearings before the Special
                Subcommittee on Evaluation and Planning of
                Social Programs, on S.5, 92nd Congress, 1st Ses-
                sion.

In addition to statements by Raymond Bauer, Nicholas
Demerath III, Dwight Ink, David Linowes, Sol Linowitz and
William Proxmire, this report of the hearings includes
statements from varicus governmental offices and agencies
expressing their support or rejection of the bill: GAO,
Council of Economic Advisers, Departments of Agriculture
and Treasury, Equal Employment Opportunity Commission,
National Science Foundation and the Office of Management
and Budget. This bill calls for a Social Report by the
President, a Council of Social Advisers, and a
Congressional Office of Goals and Priorities Analysis. An
appendix gives an annotated bibliography on social science
policy, social accounting, policy making, interdisciplinary research, forecasting and relevant foreign area research.

United States Senate, Subcommittee on Government Research
of the Committee on Government Operations
    1967   Full Opportunity and Social Accounting Act -
                Seminar. Hearings before the Subcommittee on
                Government Research of the Committee on Govern-
                ment Operations, 90th Congress, 1st Session on
                S.843. Washington, D.C.: U.S. Government
                Printing Office.

Complete statements concerning this bill are presented
from Gerhard Colm, Bertram Gross, Preston Wilcox, Irving
Horowitz, Howard Bowen, Joseph Cooper and S. M. Miller.
Other participants included Raymond Bauer, Francis Keppel,
Joseph Kraft, Harvey Perloff, Nelson Polsby, Lawrence
Speiser, Charles Backstrom and Mancur Olson. Senator Fred
R. Harris (Oklahoma) was the committee chairman. This
bill contained the request for the annual Social Report by
the President, a Council of Social Advisers and the Joint
Committee on the Social Report.

The Urban Institute
    1971   "Developing urban indicators: Some first
            steps." Search/A Report from The Urban
            Institute 1 (May-June):3-6.

    Brief summary of the work of the Urban Institute; one
study of urban quality of life mentioned, showing Washington, D.C.'s ranking with 18 metropolitan areas; another
comparing indicators in suburbs and central cities; points
up two problems: inadequate concepts of what is important, and inadequate data with which to work; limitations
noted that indicators do not answer the "why," but serve
to bring issues into the open for discussion and decision.

Vandermark, E. H.
    1970   "Measuring the quality of urban environment."
            Australian Journal of Social Issues 5:179-200.

    Australian economist exploring development of social
indicators in the United States and concern with second-
order consequences; notes some mileposts in American
progress; HEW's involvement; some comments on methodology;
concludes with some reservations about over-reliance on
indicators.

Wasson, K. William and Harold J. O'Connell
    1971   "Social indicators: The bibliographic review as
            a first step toward scientific inquiry." Unpub-
            lished paper. Department of Sociology. Ames,
            Iowa: Iowa State University.

    Rationale of need for development of taxonomy and bib-
liography in field of social indicators. Classification
into seven headings of: 1) theory, 2) concept, 3) definition, 4) methodology, 5) application, 6) criticism and the
state of the art, and 7) policy and planning; with suggested basic readings in each of the areas.

Wiles, Peter
    1971   "Crisis prediction." The Annals of the American
            Academy of Political and Social Science 393
            (January):32-39.

    Wiles believes the importance of the social sciences
has been much exaggerated. Social scientists are poor at
prediction, so rapid social change produces many
"surprises." Although surprises can be reduced by
improving information, Wiles discusses reducing surprises
by reducing change, e.g. by controlling new technological
development in rich countries. Poor countries need better
information on their slower technology. Information to
predict crises has no source except perhaps the government
which is influenced by political power. Social prediction
is now meager, but its improvement might abolish
democracy.

Williams, Robin M.
    1968   "A model of society--the American case." Pp.
            32-57 in Bertram M. Gross (ed.), A Great
            Society? New York: Basic Books, Inc.

    Williams examines American society as a social system
and its various models. To build a "national system of
social accounts", a detailed model of the social system
must be made, filling it with yet to be developed
strategic sets of data. Next the economic, political,
psychological, and sociological models must be integrated
into one. He notes that all societies are held together
by the processes of 1) interdependence, 2) authority and
power, 3) consensus, and 4) cathexis, all of which must be
inventoried. American society is changing and needs to
adapt; yet there are five doctrines which retard adaptive
changes. The "greatness" of a society will be best measured by socio-analysis.

Winthrop, Henry
    1968   "The sociologist and the study of the future."
            The American Sociologist 3 (May):136-145.

    Considers the current emphasis on, major contributions
to, and the utopian thinking about future forecasting.
Early precautions about projecting the future are described as arising from inadequate methodologies which are
presently being replaced with ones which are adequate for
such purposes. Hence, value-free positions are regarded
as obsolete and the integration of social philosophy and
information has become an adjunct to the responsibility
social scientists have for dealing with emerging social
problems. This follows the postulate that value-free

258

methodologies are inadequate for conceptualizing future
social systems.

Agocs, Carol
    1970   "Social indicators: Selected readings." The
            Annals of the American Academy of Political and
            Social Science 388 (March):127-132.

    A selection of readings, the majority 1965 or later,
which illustrates the interdisciplinary nature of the
social accounting movement. Representative sources from
the various areas of the social indicator movement are included to outline theoretical developments in the field
and illustrate attempts to develop social indicators and
reports.

Andrzejewski, Norm
    1970   "Social indicators and accounting: Bibliography
            and work in progress." Unpublished manuscript.
            Ithaca, New York: Cornell University, Depart-
            ment of Rural Sociology.

    This report lists some of the published materials, some
of the individuals involved and their research projects,
and annotates a few selected readings. Bibliography
headings: 1) background; 2) critiques of social comment
and evaluation; 3) social indicators and social reports;
4) anticipation and prediction; and 5) the specific areas
of the urban situation, education, religion, crime and
delinquency, health, politics and participation,
employment and communication.

Beal, George M., Ralph M. Brooks, Leslie D. Wilcox and
Gerald E. Klonglan
    1971   Social Indicators: Bibliography I. Sociology
            Report No. 92. (January) Ames, Iowa: Iowa
            State University, Department of Sociology and
            Anthropology.

    This work contains an extensive author listing of lit-
erature on social indicators. Most of these sources have
appeared within the past eight years and reflect the
interest in the prospects of developing social indicators
to monitor changes in society.

Bonjean, Charles M., Richard J. Hill and S. Dale McLemore
    1967   Sociological Measurement: An Inventory of
            Scales and Indices. San Francisco, California:
            Chandler Publishing Company.

A compilation and classification by seventy-eight
conceptual classes of measures most frequently used by
social scientists in the 1954 to 1965 time period.
Bibliographic references are given for the measures of
each conceptual class. Forty-seven specific measures for
forty-seven different conceptual classes are discussed in
some detail.

Brady, Henry
    1970   "Social indicators: Report and bibliography."
            Washington, D.C.: National Science Foundation,
            Division of Social Sciences.

    Citing the reliance of many social indicator advocates
on the past successes of economic indicators as the justification for social indicators, Part I of this report
explores this analogy between social and economic
indicators, concluding that a successful system of social
indicators require much more than just the collecton,
collation and analysis of relevant statistics and the
issuance of a social report. Part II examines such areas
as social goals and values, the publics and their use of
social indicators, effects of increased dissemination of
social statistics, the feasibility of a social report
soon, and the possible role of the National Science Foundation. Detailed footnotes; extensive bibliography.

Gebert, Gordon A.
    1972a   "Environmental indicators: A selected and
            annotated bibliography." New York: City Col-
            lege of the City University of New York, School
            of Architecture and Environmental Studies, Urban
            Research Group.

    A listing of books, papers, reports and articles
relating to research in environmental indicators.
Annotation for most entries is chapter, section or other
divisional titles as used by the author. Some listings
considered to be of key importance include reviews by
U.R.G. staff members.

    1972b   "Environmental indicators: Selected readings."
            New York: City College Environmental Studies,
            Urban Research Group.

    An article in preparation describing the key readings
available for environmental indicator research. To be
published in early 1972.

Harland, Douglas G.
  1971a   The Content, Measurement and Forecasting of
          Quality of Life: Volume I - The Literature.
          (October) Ottawa, Canada: Social and Human
          Analysis Branch, Canadian Department of Regional
          Economic Expansion.

Represents a compilation of 250 articles, papers,
reports, journals and books collected by the author over a
two year period. These are listed alphabetically within
sections with three additional sections devoted to documents generated by the Canadian Government, United States
Government and the United Nations.

  1971b   The Content, Measurement and Forecasting of
          Quality of Life: Volume II - Index to the Lit-
          erature. (November) Ottawa, Canada: Social and
          Human Analysis Branch, Canadian Department of
          Regional Economic Expansion.

This is an index for "The Content, Measurement and
Forecasting of Quality of Life, Volume I, The Literature"
designed primarily to aid the Department of Regional and
Economic Expansion Task Force on Social Indicators. The
index is divided into four sections; 1) persons associated
with social indicators, 2) governments, institutes,
societies and universities, 3) subject matter index, and
4) chronological index.

Institut National de la Statistique et Des Etudes
Economiques
  1971   Inventaire Bibliographique. Unpublished
          manuscript No. 320/1163 prepared by the Social
          Statistics Group. Paris, France: Institut
          National de la Statistique et Des Etudes
          Economiques.

This French survey and bibliography consists of two
major sections. The first, Exact Studies, has two
chapters: social accounts, and works other than social
accounts which include statistical works relative to the
social domain (for France, foreign and international organizations) and social indicators, including leisure and
vacations, housing, education, higher learning, work conditions, immigration, social action and cultural development. The second major section, global studies, is similarly divided into works other than social accounts with
references from France, America, England and international
organizational sources, including J. Delors' report, and
social accounts with the socio-demographic accounts section including Stone's model and its use.

262

Knezo, Genevieve J.
    1971a   Social Science Policies: An Annotated List of
            Recent Literature. (July 8) (71-167 SP) Wash-
            ington, D.C.: Science Policy Research Division,
            Congressional Research Service, Library of
            Congress.

Twelve additional listings to the Social Science
Policies annotated bibliography of July 1971 by the same
editor. No classification into categories.

    1971b   Social Science Policies: An Annotated List of
            Recent Literature--Addendum. (August 4) Wash-
            ington, D.C.: Science Policy Research Division,
            Congressional Research Service, Library of
            Contress.

This bibliography of July 1971 updates the one of June
1970, recognizing trends in the development of social science policies through increased interest from the National
Science Foundation, efforts of the Office of Statistical
Policy Analysis, Office of Management and Budget, to develop a Social Indicator publication and state and local
governments among other groups. Categories included are:
social science policy (national and international); social
accounting; social scientists and policy-making (professional concerns); interdisciplinary social science research (general and science, technology and the environment); social and political forecasting; foreign area
social and behavioral science research.

Marien, Michael D.
    1971   Alternative Futures for Learning: An Annotated
           Bibliography of Trends, Forecasts, and Propos-
           als. Syracuse, New York: Educational Policy
           Research Center, Syracuse University Research
           Corporation.

Categories of general; elementary and secondary; higher
education; other educating institutions; planning and
plans; miscellaneous with pre-1960 forecasts, new and relevant periodicals and bibliographies not classified
elsewhere; and addenda for the five major groupings.
Fewer than half the entries are critically annotated;
publishers advertisements are given for a number of
entries; approximately 1/5 of the items are cited as "recommended." Major focus (over 80%) is on books or book-
length documents. Discussed are generalizations on
quantity and quality of the literature, major themes and
major omissions, and relationship of educational futures
literature to other futures literature, with recommendations for further work. Indexes by major author, organization, selected subject, and of bibliographies.

Sloan, Helen W.
    1970   Social Change, Quality of Life, and Urban
            Affairs: A Selective Bibliography of Current
            Popular Literature. (April) Nashville,
            Tennessee: Center for Community Studies.

This bibliography was compiled at the Center for
Community Studies in Nashville for a 1970 Conference held
there. The extensive listing for the period January, 1969
to February, 1970 is done only alphabetically by author.
A subject index was to be made available in late 1971.

Tugac, Ahmet
    1971   "Social indicators and social prediction in
            planning process: A review of literature and
            bibliography." State Planning Organization Pub.
            No. DPT:1124--SPD:243. Ankara, Turkey: Devlet
            Planlama Teskilati, Bakanliklar.

Develops a conceptual model of social prediction in the
planning process, discusses the necessity of developing
reliable social indicators for social prediction, examines
problems and techniques of forecasting, and speculates on
possible utilities of social indicators and social prediction for short-range and long-range planning.

Wilcox, Leslie D., Ralph M. Brooks, George M. Beal and
Gerald E. Klonglan
    1972   "Social indicators: Recent trends and select
            bibliography." Sociological Inquiry 42
            (Winter):37-50.

A brief overview of the rationale and historical development of the social indicator movement with some of the
most influential leaders and writings in the field
specifically mentioned. An abridgement of a more extensive bibliography, this is intended to provide basic readings and is divided into broad areas of general theory,
methodology (conceptual and definitional), empirical research and data resources, criticism and the state of the
art, policy planning and application, and related general
articles.

Bevan, William
      1971   "The topsy-turvy world of health-care delivery."
             Science 173 (September 10):985.

      Senator J. Glenn Beall, Jr. in a recent speech, dis-
cussed the need for the establishment of a National
Institute of Health-Care Delivery. From the proliferation
of organizations and individuals, both public and private,
actively involved, it would appear that the U.S. is providing the world's best health care, but in fact we are
not. He is calling for a central forum or clearinghouse
to collect data on health care and evaluation research on
its delivery.

Bratt, Elmer C.
      1971   "Economic growth and fluctuations." The Annals
             of the American Academy of Political and Social
             Science (January):121-131.

      Argues that, since fluctuaticns generally represent de-
viations from growth according to econometric explana-
tions, production functions remain the dominant proposal
for examining growth; but we are still at a stalemate in
choosing between alternative functions. It is concluded
that a differentiation needs to be made between equilibrium forces and the influences making for fluctuation. This
might be facilitated by the observation that the current
momentum of change tor many variables is more closely related to successive change in economic fluctuations than
to equilibrium change.

Dodd, Stuart C.
      1971   "The tetramatrix for modeling macrosociology."
             A paper presented at the Annual Meeting of the
             American Sociological Association (August
             30-September 2) Denver, Colorado.

      The author presents an organization schema for treating
substantively the domain of macrosociology in terms of a
four cell matrix which include: the planning, the
systemed, the stochastic, and the cybernetic matrices.
Each cell is carefully defined as to appropriate input and
output, explained in terms of the mathematical description
each type generates. The author also relates each of his
cells to the four aims of science, description, explanation, prediction, and control.

Elazar, Daniel J.
    1970   Cities of the Prairie. New York: Basic Books,
            Inc.

    Elazar studies the civil communities of midwestern
urban areas with their accompanying local political
systems. He concentrates on recent developments in these
communities and shows that these communities are the basis
for solving problems which occur in developing areas.

Hage, Jerald and Robert Dewar
    1971   "The prediction of organizational performance:
            The case of program innovation." A paper pre-
            sented at the Annual Meeting of the American
            Sociological Association (August) Denver,
            Colorado.

    The authors use time-series data to predict organiza-
tional innovation, using structural, resource, and the attitude of elites as variables. A good methodological example of examining organizations as to how they acquire
new or different jobs/clients.

Hogg, Thomas C. and Marlin R. McComb
    1969   "Cultural pluralism: Its implications for edu-
            cation." Educational Leadership (Decem-
            ber):235-238.

    Although lip service is given to a perspective of
America as a culturally pluralistic society, our approach
in reality has been to assume a proper melting-pot effect
to the end that American society should be, and therefore
is, a homogeneous cultural system. Cultural pluralism and
its attendant conflicts are increasing; the educational
system must adapt to this new view, accept the premise of
individual cultural worth beyond just a reflection of cultural diversity. To prepare youth adequately for a
culturally pluralistic life, society must become a major
and clearly articulated goal for the educational process.

Law Enforcement Assistance Administration, U.S. Department
of Justice
    1971   1970 National Jail Census. National Criminal
            Justice Information and Statistics Service,
            Series SC-No. 1. Washington, D.C.: U.S. Gov-
            ernment Printing Office.

    Textual discussion in this report includes juveniles in
adult institutions, inmates by types of retention - adults
and juveniles, facilities available and age of cells,

overcrowding, jails by type of retention authority, employment, expenditures and planned construction; method of data collection; definition of terms used; and reliability of data. Detailed tables present the data summarized in the text.

Mather, William G.
     1971   "The continuing involvement of rural
            sociologists with public policy." A paper pre-
            sented at the Annual Meeting of the Rural
            Sociological Society (August 27) Denver,
            Colorado.

Brief account of beginning concern with rural sociology; founding fathers; origin of Rural Sociological Association; examines need for, role of, and future function of rural sociologists in continuing concern for people.

Morgan, James N. and James D. Smith
     1969   "Measures of economic well-offness and their
            correlates." The American Economic Review,
            Proceedings and Papers 59 (May):450-462.

The author posits a function of economic well-offness that includes non-money components of income and non-economic activities, e.g. needs standard, measured by a ratio of food consumption to estimated food requirements, leisure, and a quality of housing and neighborhood index.

Shultz, James and Marge Shultz
     1970   "An annotated review of the literature on
            volunteering." (October) Washington, D.C.:
            Center for a Voluntary Society, NTL Institute
            for Applied Behavioral Science.

The Center for a Volunteer Society collaborates with other action, research and training organizations in building a body of knowledge of voluntary action through the review, synthesis and application of relevant knowledge. Major categories in this briefly annotated bibliography are, 1) volunteers, philosophical and historical, and evaluative statements, 2) program settings, 3) functional aspects of volunteer programs, 4) manpower pools for volunteer work, 5) voluntary associations, and 6) resource inventories.

Snelling, W. Rodman, Robert F. Boruch and Nancy B. Boruch
     1971   "Science graduates of private and selective
            liberal arts colleges." College and University
            46 (Spring):231-244.

This research was designed to evaluate the quality of
education and motivation of science graduates of liberal
arts colleges, enrollment range primarily of 1,000-2,499.
Sample group comprised 16,395 graduates who majored in
biology, physics, chemistry, mathematics and premedicine.
Data presented include social and economic background of
entering students, scores of freshmen on national
normative tests of academic performance, college
achievement, vocational and extraprofessional accomplishments of graduates. Findings indicate the 49 private,
high prestige, liberal arts colleges included in this
study are functioning effectively with regard to their
science graduates.

Stockdale, Jerry D. and Steven Aronson
    1970   Technology and Societal Change: Selected
            Sources with Emphasis on Resource Allocation.
            Ithaca, New York: Cornell University.

Bibliography concerned with the impact of technology on
patterns of societal organization, especially resource allocation and decision making, changes in the economic and
political systems, with the future of capitalism and
democracy.

Tait, John L. and Arthur H. Johnson
    1971   Iowa Population Trends. Ames, Iowa: Iowa State
            University of Science and Technology,
            Cooperative Extension Service.

This report is a current summation of the 1970 census
for the state of Iowa with the following statical presentations: birth and death rates, rural and urban residence, population by race, age structure, rural and urban
area population trends, i.e. by county and by multi-county
grouping, and migration. The data are presented to reflect changes in the last ten or twenty years and some
comparisons are made to the national averages. A summary
of Iowa population trends, per 1970 census, is also included.

U.S. Department of Health, Education, and Welfare
    1963   New Directions in Health, Education, and
            Welfare. Washington, D.C.: U.S. Government
            Printing Office.

"New Directions" incorporates papers which contributed
to the development and better understanding of public programs in HEW during a 1961-1963 analysis of needs and programs within the department. Each of the papers defines
the problem, presents statistics and facts, summarizes

efforts both public and private, and anticipates future
needs. All are amplified with relevant tables and graphs.
Part I, entitled New Directions for Nation and Community,
includes a section on community and needs and goals for
community services; Part II concerns changing population
and changing needs. Current and emerging issues and
opportunities in the three major departmental areas comprise Part III. Discussed for Health are environmental,
illness, manpower and facilities, and costs and insurance;
for Education are enrollments for 1962 and 1963, educational attainment and family background, library services,
and the National Defense Education Act; three areas presented under Welfare concern the older population,
juvenile delinquency, and efforts toward work-
rehabilitation and training programs.

U.S. Department of Housing and Urban Development
    1968   Urban and Regional Information Systems: Support
            for Planning in Metropolitan Areas. Washington,
            D.C.: U.S. Government Printing Office.

This report from the System Development Corporation was
prepared for the Department of Housing and Urban Development to consider how the availability and accessibility of
information can be improved by automatic data processing.
Part I, Support for Planning in Metropolitan Areas, provides both long and short range guidelines for planning,
with use and implementation of the Urban and Regional Information Systems. Three main sections are an introduction, data base management and data processing systems,
with four appendices. Part II is a selected bibliography,
both a stratified section and an author listing. Part III
provides an index to Part I. Part IV presents case studies of nine major areas and their experiences in the development of urban and regional information systems.

AFL-CIO American Federationist
 * 1970   "Crime in America; Part I: A National Concern;
           Part II: Profile of the Offender; Part III:
           The Root Causes." American Federationist
           77:6-13. (A)

Aaker, D. A.
    1970   "A new method to evaluate stochastic models of
           brand choice." Journal of Marketing Research
           (August).

Abel-Smith, Brian
 * 1970   "Public expenditure on the social services."
           Pp. 12-20 in Muriel Nissel (ed.), Social Trends.
           London: Her Majesty's Central Statistical
           Office. (M, A)

Abelson, Philip H.
    1972   "Limits to growth." Science 175 (March
           17):1197.

Abrams, Mark
 * 1968   "Britain: The next 15 years." New Society 7
           (November):670-673. (C, P)

Abt, Clark C.
 * 1970   "An approach to methods of combined
           sociotechnological forecasting." Technological
           Forecasting and Social Change 2:17-22. (CS, M)

Acierto, Pedro R., Pedro F. Hernandez and George S. Tracy
    1971   "Rural change agents: Factors associated with
           levels of work performance." A paper presented
           at the Annual Meeting of the Rural Sociological
           Society (August 27) Denver, Colorado.

Adams, Robert F.
    1965   "On the variation in the consumption of public
           services." Review of Economics and Statistics
           47:400-405.

Adelman, Irma and Cynthia T. Morris
    1967   Society Politics and Economic Development: A
            Quantitative Approach. Baltimore, Maryland:
            The Johns Hopkins Press.

    1970   "The derivation of cardinal scales from ordinal
            data: An application of multidimensional scal-
            ing to measure levels of national development."
            September 8. Northwestern University and Ameri-
            can University.

Agency for International Development
    1971   Summary Economic and Social Indicators 18 Latin
            American Countries: 1960-1970. Washington,
            D.C.: Office of Development Programs, Bureau
            for Latin America.

Agocs, Carol
  * 1970   "Social indicators: Selected readings." The
            Annals of the American Academy of Political and
            Social Science 388 (March):127-132. (B)

Aiken, Michael and Robert R. Alford
  * 1970a   "Community structure and innovation: The case
            of public housing." The American Political Sci-
            ence Review 64 (September):843-864. (A, GT)

    1970b   "Community structure and innovation: The case
            of urban renewal." American Sociological Review
            35 (August):650-665.

Alberts, David S.
  * 1970   A Plan for Measuring the Performance of Social
            Programs. New York: Praeger Publishers. (M,
            A)

  * 1971   "An operations research approach to measuring
            the performance of social programs." A paper
            presented at Annual Meeting of the Ohio Valley
            Sociological Society (April 22-24) Cleveland,
            Ohio. (P, C)

Albuquerque Urban Observatory
  * 1971   Social Reporting for Albuquerque: Development
            of a Social Indices System. Albuquerque, New
            Mexico: Albuquerque Urban Observatory. (M)

271

Alexander, Robert M.
* 1971   "Social aspects of environmental pollution."
          Agriculture Science Review 9 (First Quar-
          ter):9-18.   (C)

Alford, Robert R.
* 1970   "Data resources for comparative studies of urban
          administration." Social Science Information
          9:193-203.   (CS)

* 1972   "A critical evaluation of the principles of city
          classification." Chapter XII in Brian Berry
          (ed.), Classification of Cities: New Methods
          and Evolving Uses. New York: Wiley and Sons,
          Inc. (A)

Alker, Haywood and Bruce Russett
     1966   "Indices for comparing inequality." Pp. 349-372
             in Richard Merritt and Stein Rokkan, Comparing
             Nations. New Haven: Yale University Press.

Allardt, Erik
     1971   "Individual needs, social structure and
             indicators of national development." Unpub-
             lished manuscript. Helsinki, Finland: Univer-
             sity of Helsinki.

Almond, Gabriel and Sidney Verba
     1963   The Civic Culture. Princeton, New Jersey:
             Princeton University Press.

Alpbach European Forum
* 1969   "The structure of society must change." Futures
          1 (December):478.   (P)

Alvarez, Jose Hernandez
     1966   "A demographic profile of the Mexican
             immigration to the United States, 1910-1950."
             Journal of Inter-American Studies 8:471-496.

American Academy of Arts and Sciences
     1967   "Toward the year 2000: Work in progress."
             Daedalus 96:639-1002.

The American Academy of Political and Social Science
     1967a   Social Goals and Indicators for American

Society: Volume I. The Annals of the American
Academy of Political and Social Science 371
(May).

1967b   Social Goals and Indicators for American
Society: Volume II. The Annals of the American
Academy of Political and Social Science 373
(September).

1970   Political Intelligence for America's Future.
The Annals of the American Academy of Political
and Social Science 388 (March).

1971   Social Science and the Federal Government. The
Annals of the American Academy of Political and
Social Science 394 (March).

1972   The Nation's Health: Some Issues. The Annals
of the American Academy of Political and Social
Science 399 (January).

American Country Life Association
1967   Achieving Quality Life in the Countryside.
Proceedings of the Forty-Sixth Conference of the
American Country Life Association, Inc. (July
11-12) Ames, Iowa, Iowa State University.

American Psychological Association
* 1967   "Special issue: Congress and social science."
American Psychologist 22 (November). (CS, P)

Anderson, Claire M., Edward E. Schwartz and Narayan
Viswanathan
* 1970   "Approaches to the analysis of social service
systems." Pp. 42-51 in Edward E. Schwartz
(ed.), Planning-Programming-Budgeting Systems
and Social Welfare. Chicago, Illinois: The
University of Chicago, The School of Social
Service Administration. (P, A, C)

Anderson, Jacqueline
1970   "A framework for social indicators." A paper
presented at the 38th National Meeting of the
Operations Research Society of America (October
28-30) Detroit, Michigan.

Anderson, Jacqueline, Eugene Lourey and Seldon Todd
* 1969   "Preliminary social indicator concepts: Ameri-

can Rehabilitation Foundation study to develop a
social indicator system for the aging."
Minneapolis, Minnesota: Institute for Interdisciplinary Studies, American Rehabilitation Foundation. (A, M, D)

Anderson, James G.
* 1970a   "Causal models and the evaluation of health
           service systems." Working paper No. 43.
           Lafayette, Indiana: Institute for the Study of
           Social Change, Department of Sociology, Purdue
           University. (M, A)

* 1970b   "Social indicators and second-order conse-
           quences: Measuring the impact of intercultural
           health programs." Las Cruces, New Mexico: New
           Mexico State University Research Center. (GT,
           M, A)

* 1971a   "Path analysis: A new approach to modelling
           health service delivery systems." A paper pre-
           sented at the Joint National Conference on Major
           Systems, National Meeting of the Operations Re-
           search Society of America (October 27-29)
           Anaheim, California. (M)

* 1971b   "Social indicators and second-order conse-
           quences: Measuring the impact of innovative
           health and medical care delivery systems." Re-
           search Memorandum No. 71-7. Lafayette, Indiana:
           School of Industrial Engineering, Purdue Uni-
           versity. (A)

Anderson, Stanford (ed.)
   1968   Planning for Diversity and Choice: Possible
           Futures and Their Relations to the Man-
           Controlled Environment. Cambridge,
           Massachusetts: MIT Press.

Andrade, Preston
* 1970   "Pilot research projects in rural growth
           centers." Unpublished manuscript. New York:
           The Ford Foundation. (P, A)

Andrews, Frank M. and George W. Phillips
* 1970   "The squatters of Lima: Who they are and what
           they want." The Journal of Developing Areas 4
           (January):211-223. (A, P)

Andrzejewski, Norm
 * 1970   "Social indicators and accounting: Bibliography
           and work in progress." Unpublished manuscript.
           Ithaca, New York: Cornell University, Depart-
           ment of Rural Sociology. (B)

Angel, R. B.
   1967   "Discussion-explanation and prediction: A plea
           for reason." Philosophy of Science 34
           (Summer):276- 282.

Antoine, Jacques
   1970   "Role des indicateurs sociaux dans la
           planification." Chronique Sociale de France
           78:19-31.

Applied Urbanetics, Inc.
 * 1968   Social Maps, District of Columbia Population and
           Social Problems Characteristics: 1968, Data by
           Census Tract. Washington, D.C.: Applied
           Urbanetics, Inc. (M)

Area Analysis Branch
 * 1970   An Economic Analysis of the Iowa Rural Renewal
           Area. Agricultural Economic Report No. 181.
           Washington, D.C.: Economic Research Service,
           U.S. Department of Agriculture. (P, A)

Arndt, Johan
   1968   Insights into Consumer Behavior. Boston,
           Massachusetts: Allyn and Bacon, Inc.

Arnfield (ed.)
   1969   Technological Forecasting. Edinburgh:
           Edinburgh University Press.

Association for Public Program Analysis
 * 1970   The Role of Analysis in Establishing Program
           Priorities. Proceedings of the APPA Symposium.
           (CS)

Austin, Charles J.
 * 1971   "Selected social indicators in the health
           field." American Journal of Public Health 61
           (August): 1507-1513. (GT, A, P)

Avison, N. H.
    1972   "Criminal statistics as social indicators." In
            Andrew Shonfield and Stella Shaw (eds.), Social
            Indicators and Social Policy. London, England:
            Heinemann Educational Books Limited. (In press)

Babb, Christopher T.
    1971   "Housing quality: Measurement and assessment."
            In Working Papers on Rural Community Services
            compiled by S. M. Leadley, Department of
            Agricultural Economics and Rural Sociology, The
            Pennsylvania State University for the National
            Workshop on Problems of Research on Delivery of
            Community Services in Rural Areas (December
            13-16) Lincoln, Nebraska.

Babcock, Lyndon R., Jr. and Niren L. Nagda
  * 1971   "Indices of air quality." A paper presented at
            the Annual Meeting of the American Association
            for the Advancement of Science (December 27)
            Philadelphia, Pennsylvania. (M, C)

Banks, S. and Robert B. Textor
    1962   A Cross-Polity Survey. Cambridge,
            Massachusetts: Massachusetts Institute of
            Technology Press.

Barnard, Robert C. (ed.), Lynn D. Patterson, Elizabeth L.
Diffendal, David C. Miller, Grace E. Miller and Melissa
Garman
  * 1970   The Regional Quality of Puget Sound Life: First
            Steps in Its Measurement and Report. Seattle,
            Washington: Puget Sound Governmental
            Conference, Research Division. (P, CS)

Baster, Nancy and Wolf Scott
  * 1969   Levels of Living and Economic Growth: A Compar-
            ative Study of Six Countries 1950-1965. Geneva,
            Switzerland: United Nations Research Institute
            for Social Development. (A, GT)

Bauer, Raymond A.
  * 1963   "Data needs of a science for solving social
            problems." An address to the 1968-1969 Seminar
            Series, The Travelers Research Center, Inc. (No-
            vember 7) Hartford, Connecticut. (CS)

276

1966a   "Detection and anticipation of impact: The nature of the task." In Raymond A. Bauer (ed.), Social Indicators. Cambridge, Massachusetts: The Massachusetts Institute of Technology Press.

* 1966b   Social Indicators. Cambridge, Massachusetts: The Massachusetts Institute of Technology Press. (GT, M)

* 1966c   "Social indicators and sample surveys." Public Opinion Quarterly 30:339-352. (CS)

* 1967   "Societal feedback." The Annals of the American Academy of Political and Social Science 373 (September):180-192. (Reprinted in Bertram M. Gross (ed.), 1969 Social Intelligence for America's Future. Boston: Allyn and Bacon). (P, C)

* 1968   "Social indicators or working in a society which has better social statistics." Pp. 237-258 in Stanford Anderson (ed.), Planning for Diversity and Choice: Possible Futures and Their Relations to the Man-Controlled Environment. Cambridge, Massachusetts: Massachusetts Institute of Technology Press. (CS)

* 1969a   "Detection and anticipation of impact: The nature of the task." Pp. 1-67 in Raymond A. Bauer (ed.), Social Indicators. Cambridge, Massachusetts: The M.I.T. Press. (CS)

1969b   Second-Order Consequences. Cambridge, Massachusetts: The Massachusetts Institute of Technology Press.

Bauer, Raymond A. and Alice H. Bauer
* 1960   "America, 'mass society' and mass media." The Journal of Social Issues 16:3-66. (GT, CS, C, M)

Baum, Ranier C.
1970   "French trends toward 'consociational plannocracy' as a remedy for America's social ills." Sociological Inquiry 40:122-125.

Bauman, Zygmunt
* 1971   "Uses of information: When social information becomes desired." The American Academy of Political and Social Science 393 (January):20-31. (CS)

Bayer, Alan E. and Robert F. Boruch
* 1969   "Black and white freshman entering four-year
          colleges." Educational Record 50
          (Fall):371-386. (A)

Beal, George M. and Gerald E. Klonglan
* 1970   "Needed research themes in rural sociology--
          social indicators." A paper presented at the
          Rural Sociological Society Meetings (August)
          Washington, D.C. (CS)

Beal, George M., Ralph M. Brooks, Leslie D. Wilcox and
Gerald E. Klonglan
* 1971   Social Indicators: Bibliography I. Sociology
          Report No. 92. (January) Ames, Iowa: Iowa
          State University, Department of Sociology and
          Anthropology. (B)

Beal, George M., Gerald E. Klonglan, Leslie D. Wilcox and
Ralph M. Brooks
* 1971   "Social indicators and public policy: Toward an
          alternative approach." A paper presented at the
          Annual Meeting of the American Sociological As-
          sociation (September) Denver, Colorado. (CS)

Beale, Calvin L.
  1971   "Population and migration trends in rural and
          nonmetropolitan areas." Testimony before Gov-
          ernment Operations Committee, U.S. Senate, 92nd
          Congress, 1st Session, April 27. Washington,
          D.C.: U.S. Government Printing Office.

Beals, Ralph L.
* 1970   "Who will rule research? The big problem on the
          far side of the dry spell in funding." Psychol-
          ogy Today (September):45-47, 75. (P)

Becker, Catherine and Rabel J. Burdge
* 1971   "The effects of familism, traditionalism and
          socio-economic status on attitude toward
          reservoir construction in an eastern Kentucky
          county." A paper presented at the Annual
          Meeting of the Rural Sociological Society
          (August 27) Denver, Colorado. (A)

Becker, Harold S. and Raul de Brigard
* 1970   Considerations on a Framework for Community

Action Planning. (Working Paper WP-9)
Middletown, Connecticut: The Institute for the
Future. (P, A, GT)

* 1971a A Framework for Community Development Action
Planning. Volume I: An Approach to the
Planning Process. Report R-18. Middletown,
Connecticut: Institute for the Future. (A, C)

* 1971b A Framework for Community Development Action
Planning. Volume II: Study Procedure Conclu-
sions, and Recommendations for Future Research.
Report R-19. Middletown, Connecticut:
Institute for the Future. (A, C)

Beckman, Norman
1971 "Congressional information processes for
national policy." The Annals of the American
Academy of Political and Social Science
(March):84-99.

Behavioral and Social Sciences Survey Committee
1969 The Behavioral and Social Sciences: Outlook and
Needs. Washington, D.C.: National Academy of
Sciences.

Bell, Daniel
1964 "Twelve modes of prediction-a preliminary
sorting of approaches in the social sciences."
Daedalus 93 (Summer):845-880.

1967a "Notes on the post-industrial society (I)." The
Public Interest 6 (Winter):24-35.

1967b "Notes on the post-industrial society (II)."
The Public Interest 7 (Spring):102-118.

1967c "The year 2000--the trajectory of an idea."
Daedalus 96 (Summer):639-651.

1968a "Coda: Work in further progress." Pp. 378-381
in Daniel Bell (ed.), Toward the Year 2000.
Boston: Houghton Mifflin Company.

* 1968b "The adequacy of our concepts." Pp. 127-161 in
Bertram M. Gross (ed.), A Great Society? New
York: Basic Books, Inc. (C, GT)

* 1968c "The measurement of knowledge and technology."
Pp. 145-246 in Eleanor B. Sheldon and Wilbert

Moore (eds.), Indicators of Social Change: Concepts and Measurements. New York: Russell Sage Foundation. (A, P)

   1968d Toward the Year 2000. Boston: Houghton Mifflin Company.

* 1969 "The idea of a social report." The Public Interest 15 (Spring):72-84. (P, A)

* 1970a "The commission on the year 2000." Futures 2 (September):263-269. (C, M)

* 1970b "The post-industrial society: Technocracy and politics." A paper presented at the Seventh World Congress of Sociology (September 14-19) Varna, Bulgaria. (CS, GT)

Belshaw, Cyril S.
   1970 The Conditions of Social Performance. New York: Schocken Books.

Bender, Lloyd D., Bernal L. Green and Rex R. Campbell
* 1971 "The process of rural poverty ghettoization: Population and poverty growth in rural regions." A paper presented at the Annual Meeting of the American Association for the Advancement of Science (December) Philadelphia, Pennsylvania. (A, P)

Benjamin, Bernard
   1971 "Some aspects of model building in the social and environmental fields." Social Trends No. 2:24-30.

Bennett, M. K.
* 1937 "On measurement of relative national standards of living." Quarterly Journal of Economics (February):317-335. (M, C, D)

Bennis, Warren G.
   1969 "Post-bureaucratic leadership." Trans-Action 6 (July-August):44-51, 61.

* 1970 "The failure and promise of the social sciences." Technology Review (October-November):38-43. (P, CS)

Berelson, Bernard
    1964   The Behavioral Sciences Today. New York:
            Harper and Row, Harper Torchbooks.

Berkowitz, Leonard
    1962   Aggression: A Social Psychological Analysis.
            New York: McGraw-Hill

Berry, Brian J. L. and Jack Meltzer
    1967   Goals for Urban America. Englewood Cliffs, New
            Jersey: Prentice-Hall.

Bestuzhev-Lada, Igor
  * 1969   "Forecasting--an approach to the problems of the
            future." International Social Science Journal
            21:526-534. (D, C)

Bettman, James R.
  * 1971   "Measuring individuals' priorities for national
            goals: A methodology and empirical example."
            Policy Sciences 2:373-390. (M, A)

Bevan, William
  * 1971   "The topsy-turvy world of health-care delivery."
            Science 173 (September 10):985. (R)

Biderman, Albert D.
  * 1963   National Goals and Statistical Indicators.
            Washington, D.C.: Bureau of Social Science Re-
            search, Inc. (P, CS)

  * 1966a   "Anticipatory studies and stand-by research ca-
            pabilities." Pp. 272-301 in Raymond A. Bauer
            (ed.), Social Indicators. Cambridge,
            Massachusetts: The Massachusetts Institute of
            Technology Press. (CS, C, A, M)

  * 1966b   "Social indicators and goals." Pp. 68-153 in
            Raymond A. Bauer (ed.), Social Indicators.
            Cambridge, Massachusetts: The Massachusetts
            Institute of Technology Press. (P, A)

    1967   "Surveys of population samples for estimating
            crime incidence." The Annals of the American
            Academy of Political and Social Science 374
            (November):16-33.

* 1969a   "Information, intelligence and enlightened public policy: Functions and organization of societal feedback." A paper presented at the 65th Annual Meeting of the American Political Science Association (September 6) New York. (Also in 1970 Policy Sciences 1:217-230). (CS, C)

1969b   "On the influence, affluence and congruence of phenomena in the social sciences." American Sociologist 4:128-130.

* 1970   "The municipal social indicator leagues." Washington, D.C.: Bureau of Social Science Research, Inc. (C, P, A)

* 1971a   "A proposed general measure of interpersonal violence." Unpublished manuscript. Washington, D.C.: Bureau of Social Science Research, Inc. (CS)

* 1971b   Kinostatistics for Social Indicators. Washington, D.C.: Bureau of Social Science Research, Inc. (M, C, CS)

* 1971c   "Notes on the value selectivity of environment-allocating institutions." (April 29) Washington, D.C.: Bureau of Social Science Research, Inc. (GT)

Biderman, Albert D. and Albert J. Reiss, Jr.
1967   "On exploring the 'dark figure' of crime." The Annals of the American Academy of Political and Social Science 374 (November):1-15.

Bixhorn, Herbert J.
* 1971   "Cluster analysis: An application to typology of urban neighborhoods." A paper presented at the Annual Meeting of the American Statistical Association (August) Fort Collins, Colorado. (M, A)

Blaisdell, Thomas C., Jr.
* 1954   "Problems of evaluating the effectiveness of development measures." Economic Development and Cultural Change 2 (January):286-297. (P, GT)

Blau, Peter and Otis Dudley Duncan
1967   The American Occupational Structure. New York: Wiley.

Blumenthal, Monica D.
* 1971   "Alienation and violence for social change." A
          paper presented at the 13th Canadian-American
          Seminar Program (November 19) Windsor, Ontario,
          Canada. (A)

Blumenthal, Monica D. and F. M. Andrews
* 1970a   "Resentment and suspicion." Ann Arbor,
          Michigan: The University of Michigan, Institute
          for Social Research. (A, M)

  1970b   "The trust index." Ann Arbor, Michigan: The
          University of Michigan, Institute for Social Re-
          search.

* 1970c   "Values: Retributive justice, self defense,
          kindness." Ann Arbor, Michigan: The University
          of Michigan, Institute for Social Research. (A,
          C)

Blumenthal, Monica D., R. L. Kahn, F. M. Andrews and K. B.
Head
  1970   Justifying Violence: Attitudes of American Men.
          Ann Arbor, Michigan: The University of
          Michigan, Institute for Social Research.

* 1971   "Attitudes toward violence." Ann Arbor,
          Michigan: The University of Michigan, Institute
          for Social Research. (Reprinted in part in Sci-
          ence News 100:14-15). (A, C)

Blumstein, Alfred
  1967   "Systems analysis and the criminal justice
          system." The Annals of the American Academy of
          Political and Social Science 374 (Novem-
          ber):92-100.

Bonjean, Charles M., Richard J. Hill and S. Dale McLemore
* 1967   Sociological Measurement-An Inventory of Scales
          and Indices. San Francisco, California:
          Chandler Publishing Company. (B)

Boruch, Robert F.
* 1971a   "Assuring confidentiality of response in social
          research: A note on strategies." American
          Sociologist 6 (November):308-311. (M)

1971b "Educational research and the confidentiality of
data: A case study." Sociology of Education 44
(Winter):59-85.

* 1971c "Maintaining confidentiality of data in educational research: A systematic analysis." American Psychologist 26:413-430. (M)

Boruch, Robert F. and J. E. Dutton
1970 "A program for testing hypotheses about correlation arrays." Educational and Psychological
Measurement 30 (Autumn):719-721.

Boruch, Robert F. and John A. Creager
* 1972 "A note on stability of self-reported protest
activity and attitudes." Measurement and Evaluation in Guidance 5 (July). (A)

Boruch, Robert F., John D. Larkin, Leroy Wolins and Arthur
C. MacKinney
* 1970 "Alternative methods of analysis: Multitrait-
multimethod data." Educational and Psychological Measurement 30 (Winter):833-853. (M)

Boruch, Robert F. and Leroy Wolins
1969 "Quasi-experimental design: Further
explorations." Proceedings of the Social Statistics Section, American Statistical Association, Washington, D.C.

* 1970 "A procedure for estimation of trait, method,
and error variance attributable to a measure."
Educational and Psychological Measurement 30
(Autumn): 547-574. (M)

Boucher, Wayne I.
* 1971a "Futures research and national priorities." New
Priorities Vol. 1, Number 1. (M, GT)

* 1971b "The future environment for technology assess-
ment." In M. J. Cetron and B. Bartocha (eds.),
Technological Assessment in Perspective. Paris:
Hermann Press. (P, CS)

Boulding, Kenneth E.
1964 The Meaning of the Twentieth Century: The Great
Transition. New York: Harper and Row.

* 1967a "An economist looks at the future of sociology."
         et al. 1 (Winter):1-7. (GT)

* 1967b "Dare we take the social sciences seriously."
         American Psychologist 22 (November):879-887.
         (CS)

Bowman, R. T., Alexander Gall and Israel Rubin
* 1960   "Social statistics: Present conditions, future
         needs and prospects." Pp. 74-81 in Proceedings
         of the Social Statistics Section, American Sta-
         tistical Association, Washington, D.C. (CS)

Box, G. E. P. and G. M. Jenkins
  1971   Statistical Models for Forecasting and Control.
         San Francisco: Holden Day, Inc.

Boyce, David E.
  1970   "Toward a framework for defining and applying
         urban indicators in plan-making." Urban Affairs
         Quarterly 6 (December):145-172.

Brackett, Jean C.
* 1969   "New BLS budgets provide yardsticks for measur-
         ing family living costs." Monthly Labor Review
         92 (April):3-16. (A)

Bradburn, Norman M. and David Caplovitz
  1965   Reports on Happiness: A Pilot Study of Behavior
         Related to Mental Health. Chicago: Aldine
         Publishing Company.

Brady, Edward L. and Lewis M. Branscomb
* 1972   "Information for a changing society." Science
         175 (March):961-966. (P)

Brady, Henry
* 1970   "Social indicators: Report and bibliography."
         Washington, D.C.: National Science Foundation,
         Division of Social Sciences. (B, CS)

Bratt, Elmer C.
* 1971   "Economic growth and fluctuations." The Annals
         of the American Academy of Political and Social
         Science (January):121-131. (R)

Brayfield, Arthur H.
    1967   "Inquiry on Federally Sponsored Social Re-
            search." American Psychologist 22
            (November):893-903.

Breton, Albert
    1965   "Scale effects in local and metropolitan govern-
            ment expenditures." Land Economics 41:370-372.

Broady, Maurice
  * 1970   "The sociology of the urban environment."
            Ekistics 29 (March):187-190.   (C)

Broel-Plateris, Alexander
    1964   "Association between marriage disruption,
            permissiveness of divorce laws, and selected
            social variables." In Ernest W. Burgess and
            Donald J. Bogue (eds.), Contribution to Urban
            Sociology. Chicago: University of Chicago
            Press.

Brolin, K. G.
  * 1967   "Statistics needed for education planning." Pp.
            60-96 in Proceedings of the Conference of
            European Statisticians, Statistical Standards
            and Studies. Statistics of the Educational
            System. New York: United Nations. ST/CES/10
            Sales No. 67 II E/mim 10.   (CS, A, P)

Bromley, Daniel W.
    1971   "Rural development for whom: A market failure
            approach." A paper presented at the Annual
            Meeting of the Rural Sociological Society
            (August 27) Denver, Colorado.

Brooks, Ralph M.
    1971   Social Indicators for Community Development:
            Theoretical and Methodological Considerations.
            Unpublished Ph.D. Dissertation. Ames, Iowa:
            Iowa State University.

Brooks, Ralph M., Leslie D. Wilcox, George M. Beal and
Gerald E. Klonglan
  * 1971   "Toward the measurement of social indicators:
            Conceptual and methodological implications."
            Proceedings of the Social Statistics Section,

American Statistical Association, Washington,
D.C. (GT, C, M)

Brown, Harrison, James Bonner and John Weir
   1957   The Next Hundred Years. New York: The Viking
          Press.

Brown, Robert M., Nina I. McClelland, Rolf A. Deininger
and Michael F. O'Connor
 * 1971   "A water quality index - Crashing the psycholog-
          ical barrier." A paper presented at the Annual
          Meeting of the American Association for the
          Advancement of Science (December 28)
          Philadelphia, Pennsylvania. (M, C, A)

Bryan, C. Hobson and Alvin L. Bertrand
 * 1970   Propensity for Change Among the Rural Poor in
          the Mississippi Delta: A Study of the Roots of
          Social Mobility. Agricultural Economic Report
          No. 185. Washington, D.C.: Economic Research
          Service, U.S. Department of Agriculture. (P, A)

Bryce, Herrington J.
 * 1971a "Income and general welfare: An identification
          of the socio-economic gaps between low and high
          income regions." Unpublished manuscript. Wash-
          ington, D.C.: The Urban Institute. (M)

 * 1971b "The application of discriminant analysis in
          distinguishing between the crime profiles of
          large and small metropolitan areas." Unpub-
          lished manuscript. Washington, D.C.: The Urban
          Institute. (A)

 * 1972   Are Regional Rates of Poverty Among Whites and
          Nonwhites Subject to the Same Determinants?
          Working Paper No. 1206-3. Washington, D.C.:
          The Urban Institute. (A)

Brzezinski, Zbigniew
 * 1968   "America in the technetronic age." Encounter
          (January):16-26. (C, P)

Bulmer-Thomas, Ivor
   1967   "So, on to the great society." Twentieth
          Century 175:12-13.

Bureau of Labor Statistics, U.S. Department of Labor
    1971   Handbook of Labor Statistics 1971. Washington,
            D.C.: U.S. Government Printing Office.

Burke, Edmund M.
  * 1965   "The road to planning: An organizational analy-
            sis." Social Science Review 39 (September):261-
            270. (P)

Burkhead, Danny L.
  * 1971   "Leisure: A taxoncmic approach." Unpublished
            paper. Department of Sociology. Ames, Iowa:
            Iowa State University. (C, A)

Burr, Robert N.
    1970   "Recent developments in Latin American history."
            The Annals of the American Academy of Political
            and Social Science (March):133-144.

Bush, J. W. and M. M. Chen
  * 1972   "Markovian analysis of disease history and the
            problem of equilibrium." American Journal of
            Public Health (forthcoming). (GT, A)

Bush, J. W., Milton M. Chen, Ann S. Bush and Christopher
B. Karlene
  * 1971   "The quantitative analysis of issues in medical
            malpractice claims." A paper presented at the
            Conference on Medical Malpractice (September
            1-3) Center for the Study of Democratic Institu-
            tions, Santa Barbara, California. (A, GT)

Bush, J. W. and S. Fanshel
  * 1970   "Basic concepts for quantifying health status
            and program outcomes." A paper supported by the
            National Center for Health Services Research and
            Development and by contracts with the New York
            State Health Planning Commission. Unpublished
            manuscript. San Diego, California: University
            of California. (A, M, P)

Byrnes, James C.
  * 1970   The Quantity of Formal Instruction in the United
            States. Syracuse, New York: Syracuse Universi-
            ty Research Corporation. (P, C)

Cabello, Octavio
* 1959   "The use of statistics in the formulation and
          evaluation of social programmes." Pp. 206-215
          in Proceedings of the Social Statistics Section,
          American Statistical Association, Washington,
          D.C. (CS, D, P)

Calder, Nigel
* 1967   "Future research." New Statesman 74 (Septem-
          ber): 399-400. (C, P)

Caldwell, Catherine
* 1970   "Social science as ammunition." Psychology
          Today (September):38-41, 72-73. (C, A, P)

Campbell, Alan K. and Philip Meranto
  1966   "The metropolitan education dilemma: Matching
          resources to needs." Urban Affairs Quarterly
          2:42-63.

Campbell, Angus
  1971   White Attitudes Toward Black People. Ann Arbor,
          Michigan: Institute for Social Research.

Campbell, Angus and Philip E. Converse
* 1970   "Monitoring the quality of American life." A
          proposal to the Russell Sage Foundation. Ann
          Arbor, Michigan: University of Michigan, Survey
          Research Center. (C, M)

  1972   The Human Meaning of Social Change. New York:
          Russell Sage Foundation.

Campbell, Donald T.
* 1969   "Reforms as experiments." American Psychologist
          24 (April):409-429. (P, M)

* 1971   "Methods for the experimenting society." Pre-
          liminary draft of a paper delivered in abbrevi-
          ated form to the Eastern Psychological Associa-
          tion (April 17) and to the American Psychologi-
          cal Association (September 5) Washington, D.C.
          (M)

Campbell, Rex R. and Jerry L. Wade
* 1972a   "A perspective." Pp. 1-8 in Rex R. Campbell and

Jerry L. Wade (eds.), Society and Environment:
The Coming Collision. Boston, Massachusetts:
Allyn and Bacon, Inc. (CS)

* 1972b   Society and Environment: The Coming Collision.
Boston, Massachusetts: Allyn and Bacon, Inc.
(CS)

Canada Department of Regional Economic Expansion
* 1970   Development Plan for Prince Edward Island.
Ottawa, Canada: Queen's Printer for Canada.
(P)

Cantril, Hadley
1966   The Pattern of Human Concerns. New Brunswick,
New Jersey: Rutgers University Press.

Carey, Charles B. and Kenneth W. Yarnold
* 1966   "America '75 conference." (Spetember 28) Santa
Monica, California: Systems Development
Corporation. (CS, D)

Carlisle, Elaine
1972   "The conceptual structure of social indicators."
In Andrew Shonfield and Stella Shaw (eds.),
Social Indicators and Social Policy. London,
England: Heinemann Educational Books Limited.

Carnegie Endowment Study Group
* 1960   "Needs and resources for social investment."
International Social Science Journal 12:409-433.
(CS)

Carruthers, Garrey and N. Scott Urquhart
1971   "Some methodological considerations for rural
community services research." In Working Papers
on Rural Community Services compiled by S. M.
Leadley, Department of Agricultural Economics
and Rural Sociology, The Pennsylvania State University for the National Workshop on Problems of
Research forDelivery of Community Services in
Rural Areas (December 13-16) Lincoln, Nebraska.

Carter, Genevieve W.
* 1971   "Social indicators: A perspective of the social
indicators movement." A paper presented at the
Annual Meeting of the Western Conference on the

Uses of Mental Health Data (October 20-22)
Newport Beach, California. (CS)

Cassidy, Michael W. A.
 * 1970   "Social indicators: Accidents and the home en-
          vironment." Working Paper No. 132. Berkeley,
          California: Institute of Urban and Regional De-
          velopment, University of California. Berkeley.
          (C, M, CS, P)

Cazes, Bernard
     1970   "Que peut-on attendre des indicateurs sociaux?"
            Chronique Sociale de France 78:5-17.

     1971   "Quelques publications recentes sur les
            indicateurs sociaux." Analyse and Prevision
            11:351-363.

     1972   "The development of social indicators: A
            survey." In Andrew Shonfield and Stella Shaw
            (eds.), Social Indicators and Social Policy.
            London, England: Heinemann Educational Books
            Limited.

Cebotarev, E. A. and E. J. Brown
 * 1971   "On community resource development." A paper
          presented at the Annual Meeting of the Rural
          Sociological Society (August) Denver, Colorado.
          (A)

Center for Agricultural and Economic Development
     1970   Policy Choices for Rural People. Ames, Iowa:
            Iowa State University, Center for Agricultural
            and Economic Development.

Center for Community Studies and the Nashville Urban
Observatory
 * 1970   Social Change and Quality of Life. A report on
          a conference (May 7-9) Nashville, Tennessee.
          (CS, C)

Central Statistical Office
 * 1970   Social Trends. No. 1. A publication of the
          Government Statistical Service, Muriel Nissel
          (ed.). London, England: Her Majesty's
          Stationery Office. (M, A)

 * 1970   Social Trends. No. 2. A publication of the
          Government Statistical Service, Muriel Nissel

(ed.). London, England: Her Majesty's
Stationery Office. (P, C)

Centre National de la Recherche Scientifique
* 1971 "Etat d'avancement de la recherche sur des
indicateurs sociaux des conditions de travail."
Unpublished manuscript. Paris, France:
Laboratoire d'Econcmie et Sociologie du Travail.
(November) (C)

Cerha, Jarko
* 1969 "The fourth power." Futures 1 (September):427-439. (C, P)

Chaiklin, Harris
* 1970 "Evaluation research and the
planning-programming-budgeting system." Pp.
27-34 in Edward E. Schwartz (ed.),
Planning-Programming-Budgeting Systems and
Social Welfare. Chicago, Illinois: The University of Chicago, The School of Social Service
Administration. (P, M, C)

Chamberlain, N.
1965 Public and Private Planning. New York: McGraw-
Hill.

Chapin, F. S.
1968 "Activity systems and urban structure: A working schema." Journal of the American Institute
of Planners 34 (January):11-18.

Chapin, F. Stuart and Shirley F. Weiss
1962 Urban Growth Dynamics in a Regional Cluster of
Cities. New York: Wiley.

Chen, M. M. and J. W. Bush
* 1971 "A mathematical programming approach for
selecting an optimum health program case mix."
A paper presented at the meeting of the Operations Research Society of America (October
27-29) Anaheim, California. (GT, A)

Chiang, C. L.
* 1965 An Index of Health: Mathematical Models.
Public Health Service Publication No. 1000,

Series 2, No. 5. Washington, D.C.: National
Center for Health Statistics. (GT, A)

Christakis, Alexander N.
* 1970   "Regional economic development futures: A meth-
          odological review and study design." A paper
          based on a report prepared for the Special
          Assistant to the Secretary of Commerce for
          Regional Economic Coordination, Washington,
          D.C., December 31. (P)

Citizens' Advisory Committee on Environmental Quality
* 1971   Report to The President and to The Council on
          Environmental Quality. Washington, D.C.: Exec-
          utive Office of the President. (A, GT)

City Club of New York
   1965   Goals for New York: A Challenge to Greatness in
          the Life of our City. New York: City Club of
          New York.

Clague, Ewan
* 1963   "Economics and public welfare." A paper pre-
          sented at the Southeastern Regional Conference,
          American Public Welfare Association (September
          27) Asheville, North Carolina. BLS Report No.
          238-4. (P, A)

Clark, Margaret
   1959   Health in the Mexican-American Culture.
          Berkeley: University of California Press.

Clark, Terry N.
   1968   Community Structure and Decision-Making: Com-
          parative Analyses. San Francisco: Chandler
          Publishing Company.

* 1971   "Citizens' values and preference revelation:
          Notes on a proposal for operationalization."
          (August) Working draft. Chicago, Illinois:
          University of Chicago, Department of Sociology.
          (M)

Clausen, A. W.
* 1971   "Toward an arithmetic of quality." Conference
          Board Record 8 (May):9-13. (CS, C)

Clavel, Pierre and Paul Eberts
* 1971   "The organization of data for public policy." A
          paper presented at the Annual Meeting of the
          Rural Sociological Society (August 29) Denver,
          Colorado. (CS, M)

Cohen, Wilbur J.
  1966   "Social policy for the nineteen seventies."
          Health, Education and Welfare Indicators. Wash-
          ington, D.C.: U.S. Department of Health, Educa-
          tion and Welfare. (May):8-19.

* 1967   "Education and learning." The Annals of the
          American Academy of Political and Social Science
          373 (September):79-101. (Reprinted in Bertram
          M. Gross (ed.), 1969 Social Intelligence for
          America's Future. Boston: Allyn and Bacon).
          (CS, P)

  1968   "Social indicators: Statistics for public
          policy." The American Statistician 22
          (October):14-16.   (CS)

Cohn, Edwin J.
* 1971   "Social criteria for project and sector
          lending." Revised draft, PPC/PDA, CP, June 28.
          Washington, D.C.: Agency for International De-
          velopment. (C, P)

Coleman, A. Lee
  1971   "Rural development and the quality of life in
          the rural south: Concepts and indicators in the
          S-79 regional project." In Working Papers on
          Rural Community Services compiled by S. M.
          Leadley, Department of Agricultural Economics
          and Rural Sociology, The Pennsylvania State Uni-
          versity for the National Workshop on Problems of
          Research on Delivery of Community Services in
          Rural Areas (December 13-16) Lincoln, Nebraska.

Coleman, James S.
* 1969   "The methods of sociology." Pp. 86-114 in
          Robert Bierstedt (ed.), A Design for Sociology:
          Scope, Objectives, and Methods. Monograph 9.
          Philadelphia: The American Academy of Political
          and Social Science. (CS, A)

  1970   "Social inventions." Social Forces 49
          (December):163-173.

294

* 1971a   A Flow Model for Occupational Structures.
Report No. 101. Baltimore, Maryland: The Johns
Hopkins University, Center for Social Organiza-
tion of Schools. (C, M)

* 1971b   Resources for Social Change: Race in the United
States. New York: Wiley-Interscience. (GT,
CS)

Coleman, James S., Ernest Q. Campbell, Carol J. Hobson,
James McPartland, Alexander M. Mood, Frederick D. Winfield
and Robert L. York.
     1967   "Review symposium." American Sociological
Review 32 (June):475-483.

Colm, Gerhard
* 1966   "On goals research." Pp. 1-16 in Leonard A.
Lecht, Goals, Priorities and Dollars: The Next
Decade. Glencoe, Illinois: The Free Press.
(P)

Converse, Philip E.
     1969   "Survey research and the decoding of patterns in
ecological data." Pp. 459-485 in Mattei Dogan
and Stein Rokkan (eds.), Quantitative Ecological
Analysis in the Social Sciences.

Coombs, H. C.
     1970   "The fragile pattern." P. 54 in The Boyer
Lectures. Sydney, Australia: Australian
Broadcasting Corporation.

Copa, George
     1971   "Identifying inputs toward production function
application in education." Minneapolis,
Minnesota: University of Minnesota, Minnesota
Research Coordinating Unit for Vocational Education.

Cornblit, Oscar, Torcuato S. Di Tella and Ezequiel Gallo
* 1968   "A model for political change in Latin America."
Social Science Information 7:13-48. (M, GT)

Corning, Peter A.
* 1970   "The problem of applying Darwinian evolution to

political science." A paper presented at the
VIIIth World Congress of the International
Political Science Association (August 31-Septem-
ber 5) Munich, Germany. (GT, C)

* 1971   "Can we develop an index for quality of life?"
A paper presented at the Annual Meeting of the
American Association for the Advancement of Sci-
ence (December) Philadelphia, Pennsylvania. (C,
CS)

Council of Economic Advisers
    1964   Economic Report of the President. Washington:
U.S. Government Printing Office.

Coward, E. Walter, Jr., George M. Beal and Ronald C.
        Powers
    1971   "Domestic development: Becoming a post-
industrial society." In George M. Beal, Ronald
C. Powers and E. Walter Coward, Jr. (eds.),
Perspectives on Domestic Development. Ames,
Iowa: Iowa State University Press.

Cowhig, James D. and Calvin L. Beale
* 1965   "Levels of living among whites and non-whites."
Pp. 11-20 in the U.S. Department of Health, Education, and Welfare Indicators. Washington,
D.C.: U.S. Government Printing Office. (C, M)

Crawford, Charles O.
    1971   "Some relevant concerns and issues in research
on personal health delivery systems with special
emphasis on nonmetropolitan areas." In Working
Papers on Rural Community Services compiled by
S. M. Leadley, Department of Agricultural Eco-
nomics and Rural Sociology, The Pennsylvania
State University for the National Workshop on
Problems of Research on Delivery of Community
Services in Rural Areas (December 13-16)
Lincoln, Nebraska.

Culyer, A. J., R. J. Lavers and Alan Williams
* 1971   "Social indicators--health." Social Trends No.
2:31-42. (C, M)

    1972   "Health indicators." In Andrew Shonfield and
Stella Shaw (eds.), Social Indicators and Social
Policy. London, England: Heinemann Educational
Books Limited.

Cummings, Gordon J.
* 1970   "Community resource development--how extension
          workers perceive the job." July, ESC-568.
          Washington, D.C.: U.S. Department of
          Agriculture, Extension Service. (CS)

Czamanski, S.
   1966   "Effects of public investments on urban land
          values." Journal of the American Institute of
          Planners 32 (July):204-216.

D'Agostino, Ralph B.
* 1971   "Social indicators: A statistician's view." A
          paper presented in the Symposium on Social
          Indicators at the Annual Meeting of the American
          Psychological Association (September). Boston,
          Massachusetts: Boston University, Department of
          Mathematics. (M)

Dahl, Robert A.
   1963   Modern Political Analysis. Englewood Cliffs,
          New Jersey: Prentice-Hall.

   1967   "The city in the future of democracy." American
          Political Science Review 61:953-970.

David, Henry
* 1970   "Assumptions about man and society and histori-
          cal constructs in futures research." Futures 2
          (September):222-230.   (C)

David, Paul T.
   1969   "Index numbers of party strength: National,
          state, and local." A paper presented to the
          Sixty-fifth Annual Meeting of the American
          Political Science Association. New York.

Davidson, Frank P.
* 1968   "Macro-engineering--a capability in search of a
          methodology." Futures 1:153-161. (P, C)

   1969   "Forecasting and inventing the future." Pp.
          98-102 in American Society of Planning Officials
          (eds.), Planning: 1969.

Davis, Joe H.
   1971   "Suggested health sector social indicators."

U.S. Government Memorandum--Internal working
paper, TA/Health, September 27. Washington,
D.C.: Agency for International Development.

Day, Lincoln H. and Alice Taylor Day
 * 1969   "Family size in industrialized countries: An
           inquiry into the social-cultural determinants of
           levels of childbearing." Journal of Marriage
           and the Family 31 (May):242-251. (CS, A)

 * 1970   "The social setting of low natality in
           industrialized countries." A paper presented at
           the Annual Meeting of the International
           Sociological Association (August) Varna,
           Bulgaria. (CS, A)

 * 1971   "Indicators of social conditions related to
           natality differentials among developed
           countries." A paper presented at the Annual
           Meeting of the Population Association of America
           (April 22-24) Washington, D.C. (M)

Day, Virgil B.
 * 1971   "Management and society: An insider's view."
           Address presented at the Conference on
           Management and Public Policy, SUNY (May 21)
           Buffalo, New York. (C, P)

de Brigard, Raul and Olaf Helmer
 * 1970   Some Potential Societal Developments--1970-2000.
           (April) Middletown, Connecticut: Institute for
           the Future, Riverview Center. (P, M)

De Jong-Gierveld, Jenny
   1971   "Social isolation and the image of the
           unmarried." Sociologia Neerlandica 7:1-14.

deJouvenel, Bertrand
   1965   "Utopia for practical purposes." Daedalus 94
           (Summer):437-453.

 * 1966   "A letter on predicting." American Behavioral
           Scientist 9 (June):51. (M, CS)

Delors, Jacques
   1971   Les Indicateurs Sociaux. Paris, France:
           SEDEIS.

Demerath, N. J. III
 * 1968   "Trends and anti-trends in religious change."
           In Eleanor B. Sheldon and Wilbert Moore (eds.),
           Indicators of Social Change. New York: Russell
           Sage Foundation. (A, P)

de Neufville, Judith I.
 * 1972   Social Indicator Design and Use: An Interactive
           Process. Unpublished Doctoral Dissertation.
           Cambridge, Massachusetts: Massachusetts
           Institute of Technology. (P, CS)

De Sola Pool, Ithiel
   1968   "The international system in the next half
           century." Pp. 318-326 in Daniel Bell (ed.),
           Toward the Year 2000. Boston: Houghton Mifflin
           Company.

Deutsch, Karl W.
   1966   The Nerves of Government: Models of Political
           Communication and Control. New York: The Free
           Press, Macmillan Company.

Deutsch, Karl W., John Platt and Dieter Senghaas
 * 1971   "Conditions favoring major advances in social
           science." Science 171 (February):450-459. (A,
           P)

Dial, O. E.
 * 1970   "Notes on the prospects for social indication."
           A paper presented at the Annual Meeting of the
           American Political Science Association (Septem-
           ber) Los Angeles, California. (CS, C)

Dietz, Stephen K.
   1971   "Social indicators in the nation's capital."
           Rockville, Maryland: Westat Research, Inc.

Dillman, Don A. and James A. Christenson
 * 1971   "Towards the assessment of public values." Un-
           published manuscript. Pullman, Washington: De-
           partment of Sociology, Washington State Univer-
           sity. (GT, M, P)

Dirasian, Henry A.
    1970   "Water quality: The state of the art." Urban
            Affairs Quarterly 6 (December):199-212.

Discussion at Delos
  * 1969   "The scale of settlements and the quality of
            life." Ekistics 28 (October):277-281. (P, D)

Dixon, John
    1965   Man the Measure: Human Processes and National
            Policies. Working staff paper. Washington,
            D.C.: Office of Planning, National Institute of
            Mental Health.

Dluhy, Milan
  * 1969   "Housing and social indicators." Unpublished
            manuscript. Ann Arbor, Michigan: School of
            Social Work, University of Michigan. (C, M)

Dobzhansky, Theodosius
    1955   Evolution, Genetics and Man. New York: John
            Wiley & Sons.

Dodd, Stuart C.
  * 1971   "The tetramatrix for modeling macrosociology."
            A paper presented at the Annual Meeting of the
            American Sociological Association (August
            30-September 2) Denver, Colorado. (R)

Dorfman, Robert
    1965   Measuring Benefits of Government Investments.
            Washington, D.C.: Brookings Institution.

Drewnowski, Jan
  * 1966   Social and Economic Factors in Development -
            Introductory Considerations on their Meaning,
            Measurement and Interdependence. Report No. 3.
            February. Geneva, Switzerland: United Nations
            Research Institute for Social Development. (CS)

  * 1970   Studies in the Measurement of Levels of Living
            and Welfare. Report No. 70.3. Geneva,
            Switzerland: United Nations Research Institute
            for Social Development. (M, A)

300

* 1971   "The practical significance of social informa-
          tion." The Annals of the American Academy of
          Political and Social Science 393 (Janu-
          ary):82-91.   (GT)

Drewnowski, Jan and Muthu Subramanian
* 1970   "Social aims in development plans." Part II in
          Studies in the Methodology of Social Planning.
          Report No. 70.5 Geneva, Switzerland: United
          Nations Research Institute for Social Develop-
          ment.   (A, C)

Drewnowski, Jan, Muthu Subramanian and Claude Richard-
Proust
* 1970   "A planning model for social development." Part
          I in Studies in the Methodology of Social
          Planning. Report No. 70.5.   Geneva,
          Switzerland: United Nations Research Institute
          for Social Development.   (C, M)

Drewnowski, Jan and Wolf Scott
  1968   "The level of living index. Report No. 14, Sep-
          tember 1966." Programme 11.   Geneva,
          Switzerland: United Nations Research Institute
          for Social Development.

Dror, Yehezkel
* 1969   "The prediction of political feasibility."
          Futures 1 (June):282-288.   (C, P, M)

Dubin, Robert
* 1971   "Causality and social systems analysis." A
          paper presented at the Annual Meeting of the
          American Sociological Association (August
          30-September 2) Denver, Colorado.   (GT, M)

Dubos, Rene
  1968   So Human An Animal. New York: Scribner Press.

  1969   Future Oriented Science in Perspectives of
          Planning, OECD. Paris: OECD.

Dueker, Kenneth J.
  1970   "Urban information systems and urban
          indicators." Urban Affairs Quarterly 6
          (December):173-178.

Duhl, Leonard J.
 * 1968   "Planning and predicting: Or what do you do
           when you don't know the names of the variables."
           Pp. 147-156 in Daniel Bell (ed.), Toward the
           Year 2000. Boston: Houghton Mifflin Company.
           (Also in Daedalus 96 (Summer):779-788, 1967).
           (P, C)

Duncan, Beverly
 * 1968   "Trends in output and distribution of
           schooling." Pp. 601-672 in Eleanor B. Sheldon
           and Wilbert E. Moore (eds.), Indicators of
           Social Change. New York: Russell Sage Founda-
           tion. (A, P)

Duncan, Otis Dudley
    1949   An Examination of the Problem of Optimum City
           Size. Unpublished Ph.D. dissertation. Chicago,
           Illinois: Department of Sociology, University
           of Chicago.

   1961a   "A socioeconomic index for all occupations."
           Pp. 109-138 in Albert J. Reiss, Jr. et al., Oc-
           cupations and Social Status. New York: The
           Free Press.

 * 1961b   "From social system to ecosystem." Sociological
           Inquiry (Spring):140-149. (CS)

   1964a   "Social mobility of the American Negro." Report
           to the Public Affairs Program of the Ford Foun-
           dation (June) Ann Arbor, Michigan: University
           of Michigan.

   1964b   "Social trends." In William F. Ogburn, Culture
           and Social Change. Chicago: University of
           Chicago Press.

 * 1967a   "Discrimination against Negroes." The Annals of
           the American Academy of Political and Social
           Science 371 (May):85-103. (Reprinted in Bertram
           M. Gross (ed.), 1969 Social Intelligence for
           America's Future. Boston: Allyn and Bacon).
           (P, M, A)

   1967b   "Measuring the trend in social stratification."
           Pp. 171-172 in Proceedings of the Social Statis-
           tics Section, American Statistical Association,
           Washington, D.C.

 * 1968   "Social stratification and mobility: Problems

302

in the measurement of trend." Pp. 675-719 in
Eleanor Bernert Sheldon and Wilbert E. Moore
(eds.), Indicators of Social Change: Concepts
and Measurements. New York: Russell Sage Foundation. (C, M)

* 1969a "Human ecology and population studies." Pp.
678- 716 in Philip M. Hauser and Otis Dudley
Duncan (eds.), The Study of Population: An
Inventory and Appraisal. Chicago: University
of Chicago Press. (C, GT)

1969b "Inheritance of poverty or inheritance of race?"
In Daniel P. Moynihan (ed.), On Understanding
Poverty. New York: Basic Books, Inc.

1969c "Social forecasting: The state of the art."
The Public Interest 17:88-118.

1969d Toward Social Reporting: Next Steps. Paper
Number 2 in Social Science Frontiers Series.
New York: Russell Sage Foundation.

Duncan, Otis Dudley and Beverly Duncan
1955 "A methodological analysis of segregation
indexes." American Sociological Review
20:210-217.

Dunlap, Riley and Richard P. Gale
1971 "Student recruitment into the environmental
movement: A test of a reformulation of 'mass
society' theory." A paper presented at the
Annual Meeting of the Rural Sociological Society
(August) Denver, Colorado.

Dyck, Harold J. and George J. Emery
* 1970 Social Futures: Alberta 1970-2005. Edmonton,
Canada: Human Resources Research Council of
Alberta. (M, P)

Easton, D.
1965a A Framework for Political Analysis. New York:
Prentice-Hall.

1965b A Systems Analysis of Political Life. New York:
Prentice-Hall.

Eberts, Paul R.
1970 "Toward a general model of macro-system social
change: Some answers to questions people are

asking." A paper presented at the Annual
Meeting of the Rural Sociological Society
(August 25-29) Washington, D.C.

Eckstein, Harry
    1963   "Internal war: The problem of anticipation."
            In Ithiel de Sola Pool, et al., Social Science
            Research and National Security. Washington,
            D.C.: Smithsonian Institution.

Economic Council of Canada
    1971   Design for Decision-Making: An Application to
            Human Resources Policies. Eighth Annual Review
            (September) Ottawa, Canada: Information Canada.
            (P, A, GT)

Economic Development Division
    1971a   Developing Rural Communities. Economic Research
            Service Report No. 465. Washington, D.C.: U.S.
            Department of Agriculture.

    1971b   The Economic and Social Condition of Rural
            America in the 1970's. Committee Print, Part I.
            Prepared for Committee on Government Opera-
            tions, U.S. Senate, 92nd Congress, 1st Session
            (May). Washington, D.C.: U.S. Government
            Printing Office.

Edwards, Clark and Robert Coltrane
  * 1972   "Economic and social indicators of rural devel-
            opment from an economic viewpoint." A paper
            presented at the Annual Meeting of the Southern
            Agricultural Economics Association (February
            14-16) Richmond, Virginia. (M, A)

Eisenstadt, Samuel
    1970   "Obstacles and reinforcements of development."
            A paper presented at the Seventh World Congress
            of Sociology (September 14-19) Varna, Bulgaria.
            (GT, C)

Eisner, Robert
  * 1970   "Socioeconomic accounting: Comment." (Working
            Paper) Northwestern University and National
            Bureau of Economic Research. (C, D)

Elazar, Daniel J.
  * 1966a   American Federalism: A View from the States.

New York: Thomas Y. Crowell Company.

* 1966b "State aid and local action." Pp. 194-195 in
    Daniel J. Elazar (ed.), American Federalism: A
    View from the States. New York: Thomas Y.
    Crowell Company. (A)

* 1966c "The civil community and the state." Pp.
    173-176 in Daniel J. Elazer (ed.), American
    Federalism: A View from the States. New York:
    Thomas Y. Crowell Company. (A)

* 1966d "Variations in state-local relations." Pp.
    180-186 in Daniel J. Elazer (ed.), American
    Federalism: A View from the States. New York:
    Thomas Y. Crowell Company. (A)

* 1970 Cities of the Prairie. New York: Basic Books,
    Inc. (R)

Eldridge, Eber
    1970 "Community resource and human development." A
    paper presented at the AAEA Annual Meeting
    (August 16, 1971) Carbondale, Illinois. (GT)

Ellickson, Katherine Pollak
* 1959 AFL-CIO "Discussion" of the Cabello and
    Stringham papers. Pp. 222-223 in Proceedings of
    the Social Statistics Section, American Statis-
    tical Association. Washington, D.C. (CS)

Emery, F. E.
* 1967 "The next thirty years: Concepts, methods and
    anticipations." Human Relations
    (August):199-237. (GT, C, M)

Engen, Trygg
* 1971 "Use of the sense of smell in determining envi-
    ronmental quality." A paper presented at the
    Annual Meeting of the American Association for
    the Advancement of Science (December 26-31)
    Philadelphia, Pennsylvania. (M)

Engquist, Carlton L.
* 1970 "PPBS: An operating agency view." Pp. 14-26 in
    Edward E. Schwartz (ed.), Planning-Programming-

Budgeting Systems and Social Welfare. Chicago,
Illinois: The University of Chicago, The School
of Social Service Administration. (P, M, C)

Ennis, Philip
  * 1968   "The definition and measurement of leisure."
            Pp. 525-571 in Eleanor B. Sheldon and Wilbert
            Moore (eds.), Indicators of Social Change: Con-
            cepts and Measurements. New York: Russell Sage
            Foundation. (C, M)

Erickson, Erik H.
    1968   "Memorandum on youth." Pp. 228-238 in Daniel
            Bell (ed.), Toward the Year 2000. Boston:
            Houghton Mifflin Company.

Etzioni, Amitai
  * 1970a   "Consensus and reforms in the 'Great Society'."
            Sociological Inquiry 40:113-122.   (C)

  * 1970b   "Indicators of the capacities for societal
            guidance." The Annals of the American Academy
            of Political and Social Science 388
            (March):25-34.   (C, A)

Etzioni, Amitai and Edward W. Lehman
  * 1967   "Some dangers in 'valid' social measurement."
            The Annals of the American Academy of Political
            and Social Science 373 (September):1-15.
            (Reprinted in Bertram M. Gross (ed.), 1969
            Social Intelligence for America's Future.
            Boston: Allyn and Bacon). (M, A, CS)

Fabricant, Solomon
    1952   The Trend of Government Activity in the United
            States Since 1909. New York: National Bureau
            of Economic Research.

Farley, Reynolds
  * 1971   "Indicators of recent demographic change among
            blacks." A paper presented at the Annual
            Meeting of the American Sociological Association
            (August 30-September 2) Denver, Colorado. (A)

Featherman, David
  * 1971   "Achievement orientations and socioeconomic
            career attainments." A paper presented at the

306

Annual Meeting of the American Sociological
Association (August 30-September 2) Denver,
Colorado. (C)

Fedkiw, John
* 1969   "Social costs and benefits of timber program al-
          ternatives for meeting national housing goals."
          A paper presented at a conference on Assessment
          of Social Costs of Federal Programs (June 16)
          Washington, D.C. (P)

Feierabend, Ivo K. and Rosalind L.
   1966   "Aggressive behaviors with polities, 1948-1962:
          A cross-national study." Journal of Conflict
          Resolution 10:249-271.

Ferratori, Franco
   1970   "A short note on the uses of sociology in
          developing societies." A paper presented at the
          Seventh World Congress of Sociology (September
          14-19) Varna, Bulgaria.

Ferriss, Abbott L.
* 1969   Indicators of Trends in American Education. New
          York: Russell Sage Foundation. (A, C)

   1970   Indicators of Change in the American Family.
          New York: Russell Sage Foundation.

* 1971   Indicators of Trends in the Status of American
          Women. New York: Russell Sage Foundation. (A,
          P, D)

   1972   Indicators of Trends in Health Status. New
          York: Russell Sage Foundation.

Finsterbusch, Kurt
* 1971a "Dimensions of nations: Inductively and
          deductively developed and propositionally relat-
          ed." A paper prepared for the Conference on
          Methodological Problems in Comparative
          Sociological Research of the Institute for Com-
          parative Sociology (April 8-9) Bloomington,
          Indiana. (GT)

* 1971b "The recent rank ordering of nations in terms of
          level of development and rate of development."
          A revision of a paper presented at the Seventh
          World Congress of Sociology of the International
          Sociological Association (September 14-19, 1970)
          Varna, Bulgaria. (A, CS, C)

* 1971c   "The sociology of nation states: Dimensions, indicators and theory." (September) Washington, D.C.: American Sociological Association. (GT, M)

Fisher, Joseph L.
* 1967   "The natural environment." The Annals of the American Academy of Political and Social Science 37 (May):127-140. (Also Pp. 455-471 in Bertram M. Gross (ed.), Social Intelligence for America's Future: Explorations in Societal Problems. Boston: Allyn and Bacon.) (CS, C)

Fitzgerald, Sherman K.
* 1970   Multi-County Regions in Utah. Salt Lake City, Utah: The Bureau of Community Development, University of Utah. (A)

Flacks, R.
  1969   "On the uses of participatory democracy." Pp. 82-87 in Philip Ehrensaft and Amitai Etzioni (eds.), Anatomies of America: Sociological Perspectives. London: Macmillan.

Flash, Edward S., Jr.
  1971a   "Macro-economics for macro-policy." The Annals of the American Academy of Political and Social Science (March):46-56.

  1971b   "The obligations of American social scientists." The Annals of the American Academy of Political and Social Science (March):13-27.

Flax, Michael J.
* 1970a   Selected Education Indicators for Twenty-one Major Cities: Some Statistical Benchmarks. Preliminary Draft Paper: 136-4. Washington, D.C.: The Urban Institute. (M, A, C)

  1970b   "Selected white/non-white socio-economic comparison: An experiment in racial indicators." Preliminary Draft Paper: 136-5. Washington, D.C.: The Urban Institute.

* 1971a   "Future prospects for the development of additional social and urban indicators." Working Paper No. 1206-2. Washington, D.C.: The Urban Institute. (CS, B)

1971b   Urban Institute Indicator Program. Working
         Paper No. 1206-1. (July 14) Washington, D.C.:
         The Urban Institute.

1972a   A Second Look at the "Quality of Life" in
         Metropolitan Washington, D.C. Including Some
         Statistical Benchmarks of City/Suburban Differ-
         ences. 136-1 Revised January 3.

1972b   A Study in Comparative Urban Indicators: Condi-
         tions in 18 Large Metropolitan Areas. Washing-
         ton, D.C.: The Urban Institute.

Flora, Cornelia Butler and Jan L. Flora
 * 1971   "Macro-model variables relevant to social ac-
           counting." Contribution No. 34. Manhattan,
           Kansas: Kansas State University, Population Re-
           search Laboratory, Agricultural Experiment
           Station. (M)

Fontaine, Andre
 * 1967   "The mass media--a need for greatness." The
           Annals of the American Academy of Political and
           Social Science 371 (May):72-84. (Reprinted in
           Bertram M. Gross (ed.), 1969 Social Intelligence
           for America's Future. Boston: Allyn and
           Bacon). (P, CS)

Fontela, E.
 * 1969   "Introducing sociological forecasting into eco-
           nomic models of the future." Futures 1
           (September):380- 381. (M, C)

Ford, Joseph B.
 * 1971a   "Contextual content analysis: A link between
           micro-social and macro-social research." A
           paper presented at the Annual Meeting of the
           American Sociological Association (August
           30-September 2) Denver, Colorado. (GT, A)

   1971b   Environmental Quality Control: Expenditure for
           Selected Large Governmental Units: Fiscal Year
           1968-69. State and Local Government Special
           Studies No. 57. Washington, D.C.: U.S. Govern-
           ment Printing Office.

Form, William H. and Joan Huber
 * 1971   "Sociological theory and occupational rewards:
           An approach to income inequality." A paper pre-

sented at the Annual Meeting of the American
Sociological Association (August 30-September 2)
Denver, Colorado.   (GT)

Forrester, Jay W.
    1967   "Engineering education and engineering practice
            in the year 2000." A paper presented to the
            National Academy of Engineering (September 21)
            Ann Arbor, Michigan, University of Michigan.

    1969   Urban Dynamics. Cambridge, Massachusetts: The
            M.I.T. Press.

  * 1971   "The computer and social catastrophe."
            Intellectual Digest 2 (November):57-60.   (M)

Foster, George M.
    1958   Problems in Intercultural Health Programs.   New
            York: Social Science Research Council.

Fox, Karl A.
  * 1969a   "A new strategy for urban and rural America."
            Appalachia (August):10-13.   (C, P)

  * 1969b   "Operations research and complex social
            systems." Chapter 9, Pp. 452-467 in Jati K.
            Sengupta and Karl A. Fox, Economic Analysis and
            Operations Research: Optimization Techniques in
            Quantitative Economic Models. Amsterdam:
            North-Holland Publishing Company. (GT, M, C)

  * 1969c   "Toward a policy model of world economic devel-
            opment with special attention to the
            agricultural sector." Pp. 95-126 in Erik
            Thorbecke (ed.), The Role of Agriculture in Eco-
            nomic Development. New York: Columbia Univer-
            sity Press.   (GT, M, C)

  * 1970   "Population redistribution among functional eco-
            nomic areas: A new strategy for urban and rural
            America." A paper presented at the Annual
            Meeting of the American Association for the
            Advancement of Science (December 30) Chicago,
            Illinois.   (CS)

  * 1971   "Combining economic and noneconomic objectives
            in development planning: Problems of concept
            and measurement." Unpublished manuscript.
            Ames, Iowa: Iowa State University, Department
            of Economics. (CS)

Fox, Karl and Paul Van Moeseke
    1972   "A scalar measure of social income." Unpub-
            lished manuscript. Ames, Iowa: Iowa State Uni-
            versity.

Frank, Lawrence K.
    1968   "The need for a new political theory." Pp.
            177-184 in Daniel Bell (ed.), Toward the Year
            2000. Boston: Houghton Mifflin Company.

Frederiksen, Harald
    1967   "Profiles of relative development." Interna-
            tional Development Review 9 (December):27-30.

Freeman, David M.
  * 1971   "Sociological intelligence, social conflict, and
            technology assessment in developmental change."
            A paper presented at the Annual Meeting of the
            Rural Sociological Society (August) Denver,
            Colorado. (C, CS)

Friedly, Philip H.
  * 1969   "Welfare indicators for public facility
            investments in urban renewal areas." Socio-
            Economic Planning Science 3:291-314.   (M, C, D)

Friedly, P. H., J. Rothenberg, J. E. Burkhardt and J. L.
Hedrick
    1968   Benefit-Cost Applications in Urban Renewal: A
            Feasibility Study. Washington, D.C.: U.S. De-
            partment of Housing and Urban Development.

Fromm, Erich
  * 1970   "Humanistic planning." Pp. 59-78 in The Crisis
            of Psychoanalysis. New York: Holt, Rinehart
            and Winston. (GT, P, CS)

Fromm, Gary
    1965   "Civil aviation expenditures." In Robert
            Dorfman (ed.), Measuring Benefits of Government
            Investment. Washington, D.C.: Brookings Insti-
            tution.

311

Fuguitt, Glenn
    1971   "The places left behind: Population trends and
            policy in rural America." A paper presented at
            the Annual Meeting of the Rural Sociological
            Society (August 27) Denver, Colorado.

Fundacia Foesse Euramerican
    1969   Informa Sociologico Sobre la Situacion Social de
            Espagna. Volume I. Madrid, Spain: Fundacia
            Foesse Euramerican.

    1970a   Informa Sociologico Sobre la Situacion Social de
            Espagna. Volume II. Madrid, Spain: Fundacia
            Foesse Euramerican.

    1970b   Tres Estudios Para Un Sistema de Indicadores
            Sociales. Madrid, Spain: Fundacia Foesse
            Euramerican.

Gabor, Dennis
    1963   Inventing the Future. London: Martin Secker &
            Warburg.

Galbraith, John Kenneth
    1967   The New Industrial State. Boston: The Houghton
            Mifflin Company.

Galle, Omer R. and Karl E. Taeuber
    1966   "Metropolitan migration and intervening
            opportunities." American Sociological Review 31
            (February):5-13.

Galnoor, Itzhak
  * 1971   "Social information for what?" The Annals of
            the American Academy of Political and Social
            Science 393 (January):1-19.   (P)

Garn, Harvey A. and Michael J. Flax
  * 1971   "Urban Institute indicator program." Working
            Paper 1206-1 (July 14). Washington, D.C.: The
            Urban Institute. (A, CS, M)

Gastil, Raymond D.
    1970a   "Should 'regional cultures' shape public
            policy." Freedom at Issue 4 (November-
            December):12ff.

* 1970b "Social indicators and quality of life." Public
Administration Review 30 (November-December):
596-601. (CS, M)

1971 "Homicide and a regional culture of violence."
American Sociological Review 36 (June):412-427.

1972 "The relationship of regional cultures to educational performance." Sociology of Education.
(Forthcoming)

Gebert, Gordon A.
* 1972a "Environmental indicators: A selected and
annotated bibliography." New York: City College of the City University of New York, School
of Architecture and Environmental Studies, Urban
Research Group. (B)

* 1972b "Environmental indicators: Selected readings."
New York: City College of the City University
of New York, School of Architecture and Environmental Studies, Urban Research Group. (B)

Geiger, H. Kent
1971 "Societal development: Notes on the vestments
of a concept." In George M. Beal, Ronald C.
Powers, and E. Walter Coward, Jr. (eds.),
Perspectives on Domestic Development. Ames,
Iowa: Iowa State University Press.

Gellhorn, Walter
1966 When Americans Complain. Cambridge,
Massachusetts: Harvard University Press.

General Electric
* 1970 "A case study of a systems analysis approach to
social responsibility programs: General
Electric's commitment to progress in equal
opportunity and minority relations." Corporate
Industrial Relations ERC-49 (10M)8-70. New
York, New York. (M, P)

Gerbner, G.
* 1970 "Cultural indicators: The case of violence in
television drama." The Annals of the American
Academy of Political and Social Science 388
(March):69-81. (CS, D)

Gessaman, Paul H. and Gordon D. Rose
    1971   "Problems cf measurement and assessment of the
            adequacy of community services: A naive
            viewpoint." In Working Papers on Rural
            Community Services compiled by S. M. Leadley,
            Department of Agricultural Economics and Rural
            Sociology, The Pennsylvania State University for
            the National Workshop on Problems of Research on
            Delivery of Community Services in Rural Areas
            (December 13-16) Lincoln, Nebraska.

Gilb, Corinne
    1969   "Can we measure beauty?" A paper presented at
            the Sixty-fifth Annual Meeting of the American
            Political Science Association. New York.

Girardeau, Catherine
  * 1971   "Elements for a social statistical system." Un-
            published manuscript. Paris, France: Institut
            National de la Statistique et des Etudes
            Economiques. (C)

Gitter, A. George
  * 1970   Factor Analytical Approach to Indexing
            Multivariate Data Communication Research Center.
            Report No. 43. Boston: Boston University.
            (M)

    1971   The Nature and Function of Social Indicators.
            Communication Research Center, Report No. 53.
            Boston: Boston University.

Gitter, A. George and E. Knoche
  * 1971   Importance Ratings of Sixteen Aspects of Life.
            Communication Research Center. Report No. 59.
            Boston: Boston University. (M, A)

Gitter, A. George and Robert R. Peterson
  * 1970   Toward a Social Indicator of Education--A Pilot
            Study. Communication Research Center. Report
            No. 44. Boston: Boston University. (A, M)

Gitter, A. George and S. Franklin
  * 1971   Subjective Quality of Life Indicators of Sixteen
            Aspects of Life. Communication Research Center.
            Report No. 58. Boston: Boston University.
            (C, GT)

Gitter, A. George and S. Lewis
* 1971   Toward a Social Indicator of Crime--A Pilot
          Study. Communication Research Center. Report
          No. 51. Boston: Boston University. (C, M)

Glaser, Daniel
* 1967   "National goals and indicators for the reduction
          of crime and delinquency." The Annals of the
          American Academy of Political and Social Science
          371 (May): 104-126. (Reprinted in Bertram M.
          Gross (ed.), 1969 Social Intelligence for
          America's Future. Boston: Allyn and Bacon).
          (P, CS)

  1969   "Crime and delinquency." Pp. 405-433 in Bertram
          M. Gross (ed.), Social Intelligence for
          America's Future: Explorations in Societal
          Problems. Boston: Allyn and Bacon.

Glock, C. Y. and F. M. Nicosia
  1964   "Uses of sociology in studying 'consumption' be-
          havior." Journal of Marketing 28 (July):51-54.

Goldhammer, Herbert and A. W. Marshall
  1953   Psychosis and Civilization: Studies in the Fre-
          quency of Mental Disease. Glencoe, Illinois:
          The Free Press.

Goldman, Nathan
* 1967   "Social breakdown." The Annals of the American
          Academy of Political and Social Science 373
          (September):156-179. (Reprinted in Bertram M.
          Gross (ed.), 1969 Social Intelligence for
          America's Future. Boston: Allyn and Bacon).
          (C, S)

Goldstein, Gerald
  1971   "Biochemical indicators of environmental
          pollution." Oak Ridge, Tennessee: Oak Ridge
          National Laboratory, Analytical Chemistry Divi-
          sion.

Goldstein, Sidney and Kurt Mayer
* 1964   "Population decline and the social and
          demographic structure of an American city."
          American Sociological Review 29 (Febru-
          ary):48-54. (M)

Goode, William J.
1966   "Family disorganization." Pp. 390-458 in Robert
        K. Merton and Robert A. Nisbet (eds.), Contempo-
        rary Social Problems. New York: Harcourt,
        Brace and World Company.

* 1968   "The theory of measurement of family change."
        Pp. 295-347 in Eleanor B. Sheldon and Wilbert
        Moore (eds.), Indicators of Social Change: Con-
        cepts and Measurements. New York: Russell Sage
        Foundation. (A, P)

Gordon, Andrew C., Donald T. Campbell et al.
* 1970   "Recommended accounting procedures for the eval-
        uation of improvements in the delivery of state
        social services." Preliminary draft. Evanston,
        Illinois: Northwestern University, Center for
        Urban Affairs. (M)

Gordon, David M.
* 1969   "Income and welfare in New York City." The
        Public Interest 13 (Summer):64-88. (A, P)

Gordon, Theodore J.
* 1971   "Future machines and human values: The role of
        coincidence." A paper presented at the Annual
        Meeting of the American Association for the
        Advancement of Science (December 29)
        Philadelphia, Pennsylvania. (P, C)

Gordon, Theodore J. and Robert H. Ament
* 1969   Forecasts of Some Technological and Scientific
        Developments and Their Societal Consequences.
        (September) Middletown, Connecticut: Institute
        for the Future, Riverview Center. (P, M)

Gottehrer, Barry
* 1967   "Urban conditions: New York City." The Annals
        of the American Academy of Political and Social
        Science 371 (May):141-158. (Also Pp. 472-494 in
        Bertram M. Gross (ed.), Social Intelligence for
        America's Future. Boston: Allyn and Bacon).
        (A, P)

1969   "A human information system for the governing of
        New York City." A paper presented at the Sixty-
        fifth Annual Meeting of the American Political
        Science Association. New York.

Government of France
    1969   "French experience in respect of social
            indicators." Government of France, Seventh
            Meeting of Senior Economic Advisers to ECE Gov-
            ernments, Economic Commission for Europe, United
            Nations (November 17-22) Geneva, Switzerland
            (mimeo).

Graubard, Stephen R.
    1968   "University cities in the year 2000." Pp.
            185-190 in Daniel Bell (ed.), Toward the Year
            2000. Boston: Houghton Mifflin Company.

Greeley, Andrew M. and Paul B. Sheatsley
    1971   "Attitudes toward racial integration." Scien-
            tific American 225 (December):13-19.

Gross, Bertram M.
  * 1965a   "Planning: Let's not leave it to the
            economists." Challenge (September-
            October):30-33.   (P)

    1965b   "The social state of the union." Trans-action
            3:5-11.

    1965c   "What are your organization's objectives? A
            general systems approach to planning." Human
            Relations 18:195-216.

    1966a   "A historical note on social indicators." In
            Raymond A. Bauer (ed.), Social Indicators.
            Cambridge, Massachusetts: Massachusetts
            Institute of Technology Press.

  * 1966b   "Let's have a real state of the union message."
            Challenge 14 (May-June):8-10.   (CS)

  * 1966c   "The state of the nation: Social systems ac-
            counting." In Raymond A. Bauer (ed.), Social
            Indicators. Cambridge, Massachusetts: The
            Massachusetts Institute of Technology Press.
            (CS, C, P, GT)

  * 1966d   The State of the Nation: Social Systems Ac-
            counting. New York: Tavistock Publications.
            (GT, M, D)

    1967a   Action Under Planning: The Guidance of Economic
            Development. New York: McGraw-Hill.

* 1967b   "The city of man: A social systems reckoning."
         Pp. 136-156 in William R. Ewald, Jr. (ed.), En-
         vironment for Man: The Next Fifty Years.
         Bloomington, Indiana: Indiana University Press.
         (CS)

* 1967c   "The coming general systems models of social
         systems." Human Relations 20 (Novem-
         ber):357-374. (CS)

* 1968a   A Great Society? New York: Basic Books, Inc.
         (CS, P)

* 1968b   "Some questions for presidents." Pp. 308-350 in
         Bertram M. Gross (ed.), A Great Society? New
         York: Basic Books, Inc. (P)

  1969a   Social Intelligence for America's Future:
         Explorations in Societal Problems. Boston:
         Allyn and Bacon.

  1969b   "The new systems budgeting." Public Administra-
         tion Review 29 (March-April):113-137.

  1969c   "Urban mapping for 1976 and 2000." Urban
         Affairs Quarterly 5:121-142.

  1970   "Societal indicator development." A paper pre-
         sented at the 38th National Meeting of the Oper-
         ations Research Society of America (October
         28-30) Detroit, Michigan.

  1971   "Learning about planned development." In George
         M. Beal, Ronald C. Powers, and E. Walter Coward,
         Jr. (eds.), Perspectives on Domestic Develop-
         ment. Ames, Iowa: Iowa State University Press.

Gross, Bertram M. and Michael Springer
* 1967a   "A new orientation in American government." The
         Annals of the American Academy of Political and
         Social Science 371 (May):1-19. (Reprinted in
         Bertram M. Gross (ed.), 1969 Social Intelligence
         for America's Future. Boston: Allyn and
         Bacon). (CS)

  1967b   "New goals for social information." The Annals
         of the American Academy of Political and Social
         Science 373 (September):208-218. (Reprinted in
         Bertram M. Gross (ed.), 1969 Social Intelligence
         for America's Future. Boston: Allyn and
         Bacon).

  1969   "Developing social intelligence." In Bertram M.
         Gross (ed.), Social Intelligence for America's

Future: Explorations in Societal Problems. Boston: Allyn and Bacon.

1970 "Political intelligence for America's future." The Annals of the American Academy of Political and Social Science 388 (March):1-194.

Grosse, Robert H.
* 1970 "The planning, programming, and budgeting system in the federal government: A planner's view." Pp. 1-13 in Edward E. Schwartz (ed.), Planning-Programming-Budgeting Systems and Social Welfare. Chicago, Illinois: The University of Chicago, The School of Social Service Administration. (P, C)

Grove, Robert D.
1968 "Vital statistics for the Negro, Puerto Rican, and Mexican populations: Present quality and plans for improvement." Pp. 100-117 in David M. Heer (ed.), Social Statistics and the City. Cambridge, Massachusetts: MIT - Harvard Joint Center for Urban Studies.

Gurin, Gerald, Jospeh Veroff, and Sheila Feld
1960 Americans View Their Mental Health: A Nationwide Interview Survey. New York: Basic Books.

Gurr, Ted
* 1968 "A causal model of civil strife: A comparative analysis using new indices." American Political Science Review 62 (December):1104-1124. (M, C)

Gurr, Ted and Charles Ruttenberg
1967 The Conditions of Civil Violence: First Tests of a Causal Model. Princeton: Center of International Studies, Princeton University. (Research monograph Number 28).

1968 "Psychological factors in civil violence." World Politics 20:245-278.

Guttman, Louis
* 1971 "Social problem indicators." The Annals of the American Academy of Political and Social Science 393 (January):40-46. (M, C, D)

Haas, J. Eugene, E. J. Bonner and Keith S. Boggs
  * 1971   "Science, technology and the public: The case
            of planned weather modification." A paper pre-
            sented at the Annual Meeting of the American
            Sociological Association (August 30) Denver,
            Colorado. (P, A)

Hackes, Peter
  * 1971   "The uncommunicative scientist: The obligation
            of scientists to explain environment to the
            public." A paper presented at the Annual
            Meeting of the American Association for the
            Advancement of Science (December 27)
            Philadelphia, Pennsylvania. (CS)

Hackett, J. and A. Hackett
    1963   Economic Planning in France. Cambridge,
            Massachusetts: Harvard University Press.

Hadden, Jeffrey K., Louis H. Masotti and Calvin J. Larson
    1967   Metropolis in Crisis. Itasca, Illinois: F. E.
            Peacock Publishers, Inc.

Hage, Jerald
  * 1971   "An interdisciplinary investigation into the
            comparative causes of societal stability and
            instability: A longitudinal analysis of Great
            Britain, Germany, France, and Italy for the
            period of 1825-1965." A proposal to the
            National Science Foundation for a research
            grant. Madison, Wisconsin: The University of
            Wisconsin, Department of Sociology. (M)

Hage, Jerald and Robert Dewar
  * 1971   "The prediction of organizational performance:
            The case of program innovation." A paper pre-
            sented at the Annual Meeting of The American
            Sociological Association (August) Denver,
            Colorado. (R)

Hagen, Everett E. and Stephanie F. T. White
    1966   Great Britain: Quiet Revolution in Planning.
            Syracuse, New York: Syracuse University Press.

Hahn, Erich
  * 1970   "Sociological system conception and social
            prognosis." A paper presented at the Seventh
            World Congress of Sociology (September 14-19)
            Varna, Bulgaria. (GT)

Hanushek, Erik A.
* 1970   "Developing local educational indicators--the
          priorities." (August) Santa Monica, California:
          The Rand Corporation.   (C)

Harbison, Frederick, J. Marawski and J. Resnick
    1970   Quantitative Analysis of Modernization.
            Princeton, New Jersey: Labor Institute of the
            Department of Economics.

Harland, Douglas G.
* 1971a   Social Indicators: A Framework for Measuring
          Regional Social Disparities. (July 1, Second
          Draft) Ottawa, Canada: Department of Regional
          Economic Expansion. (P, A, GT)

* 1971b   The Content, Measurement and Forecasting of
          Quality of Life: Volume I - The Literature.
          (October) Ottawa, Canada: Social and Human
          Analysis Branch, Canadian Department of Regional
          Economic Expansion. (B)

* 1971c   The Content, Measurement and Forecasting of
          Quality of Life: Volume II - Index to the Lit-
          erature. (November) Ottawa, Canada: Social and
          Human Analysis Branch, Canadian Department of
          Regional Economic Expansion. (B)

Harris, Fred R.
* 1967   "National social science foundation: Proposed
          congressional mandate for the social sciences."
          American Psychologist 22 (November):904-910.
          (P, CS)

* 1970   "A strategy for the social sciences." Pp. 1-11
          in Fred R. Harris (ed.), Social Science and
          National Policy. Chicago, Illinois: Aldine
          Publishing Company. (CS)

Harrison, John and Philip Sarre
    1971   "Personal construct theory in the measurement of
            environmental images: Problems and methods."
            Environment and Behavior 3 (December):351-374.

Hauser, Philip M.
 * 1946   "Are the social sciences ready?"   American
           Sociological Review 11 (August):379-384.   (CS)

 * 1949   "Social science and social engineering."   Phi-
           losophy of Science 16 (July):209-218.   (P)

   1963   "Statistics and society."   Journal of the Ameri-
           can Statistical Association 58 (March):1-12.

 * 1967a   "Social accounting."   Pp. 423-446 in Hearings
           before the Subcommittee on Government Research
           of the Committee on Government Operations,
           United States Senate, 90th Congress, first ses-
           sion on Senate Bill S.843, the Full Opportunity
           and Social Accounting Act.   Part 3, (July 28).
           (Also Pp. 839-875 in Paul F. Lazarsfeld, William
           H. Sewell, Harold Wilensky (eds.), The Uses of
           Sociology.   New York: Basic Books.)   (CS, C)

 * 1967b   "Social goals as an aspect of planning."   Pp.
           446-454 in Hearings before the Subcommittee on
           Government Research of the Committee on Govern-
           ment Operations, United States Senate, 90th
           Congress, first session on Senate Bill S.843,
           the Full Opportunity and Social Accounting Act.
           Part 3, (July 28).   (P, CS, C)

 * 1969   "The chaotic society: Product of the social
           morphological revolution."   American
           Sociological Review 34 (February):1-19.   (C)

Hauser, Philip M., Alvin W. Gouldner, Charles P. Loomis
and Kenneth Lutterman
 * 1970   "Review symposium."   American Sociological
           Review 35 (April):329-341.   (CS)

Hauser, Philip M. and Otis Dudley Duncan
   1959   The Study of Population: An Inventory and
           Appraisal.   Chicago: University of Chicago
           Press.

Havens, A. Eugene
   1971   "The quest for societal development."   George M.
           Beal, Ronald C. Powers and E. Walter Coward, Jr.
           (eds.), Perspectives on Domestic Development.
           Iowa State University Press, Ames, Iowa.

Hawes, Mary H.
* 1969   "Measuring retired couples' living costs in
          urban areas." Monthly Labor Review 92
          (November):3-16. (A)

Heady, Earl O.
* 1972   "Objectives of rural community development and
          their attainment: Consistencies and competition
          among various social and economic aggregates."
          A paper presented at the seminar on Rural
          Community Development: Focus on Iowa. Ames,
          Iowa: Iowa State University, Center for
          Agricultural and Rural Development. (GT, P)

Heberlein, Thomas A.
* 1971   "Some limitations of social science for policy-
          oriented research." Boulder, Colorado:
          Institute of Behavioral Science and Department
          of Sociology, University of Colorado. (GT, CS)

Heer, David M.
  1968   Social Statistics and the City. Cambridge,
          Massachusetts: Massachusetts Institute of
          Technology, Harvard Joint Center for Urban Stud-
          ies.

Helmers, Olaf, Theodore Gordon, and Bernice Brown
  1966   Social Technology. New York: Basic Books.

Henning, John A. and A. Dale Tussing
* 1970   "Income elasticity of the demand for public
          expenditures in the United States." (Working
          Draft, June) Syracuse, New York: Educational
          Policy Research Center, Syracuse University Re-
          search Corporation. (C, M)

Henriot, Peter J.
* 1970a   "Political questions about social indicators."
          The Western Political Science Quarterly 23
          (June): 235-255. (CS, P, C, D)

* 1970b   "Social indicators: Some practical politics."
          A paper presented at the Annual Meeting of the
          American Association for Public Opinion Research
          (May 20) Pasadena, California. (CS, P, C)

* 1971   "Political implications of social indicators."
          A paper presented at the Annual Meeting of the

American Political Science Association (September) Chicago, Illinois. (P)

1972   Political Aspects of Social Indicators: Implications for Research. In Social Science Frontiers Series. New York: Russell Sage Foundation.

Hernandez, Pedro F.
    1971   "Theoretical concerns in the measurement of adequacy of community services and how to assess them in the rural areas." In Working Papers on Rural Community Services compiled by S. M. Leadley, Department of Agricultural Economics and Rural Sociology, The Pennsylvania State University for the National Workshop on Problems of Research on Delivery of Community Services in Rural Areas (December 13-16) Lincoln, Nebraska.

Herrick, Neal Q. and Robert P. Quinn
  * 1971   "The working conditions survey as a source of social indicators." Monthly Labor Review (April):15-24. (M, A)

Hill, Morris
    1968   "A goals-achievement matrix for evaluating alternative plans." Journal of the American Institute of Planners 34 (January):19-29.

Hirsch, Abraham M.
    1971   "A schematic approach to social indicators." Internal working paper, AID, TA/PM/M. Task Force on Social Indicators, pp. 1-3. Washington, D.C.: Agency for International Development.

Hirsch, W. Z.
    1959   "Expenditure implications of metropolitan growth and consolidation." Review of Economics and Statistics 41:232-241.

Hirsch, W. Z. and E. W. Segelhorst
    1965   "Incremental income benefits of public education." Review of Economics and Statistics 47:392-399.

Hofferbert, Richard I.
    1971   "State and community policy studies: A review

of comparative input-output analyses."
Political Science Annual IV. Edited by James A.
Robinson. New York, New York: Bobbs-Merrill
and Co.

Hogg, Thomas C.
* 1966   "Toward including ethnological parameters in
          river basin models." In Water Resources and Ec-
          onomic Development of the West. Report No. 15.
          Conference Proceedings Committee on the Econom-
          ics of Water Resources Development of the
          Western Agricultural Economics Research Council.
          (GT, M)

Hogg, Thomas C. and Marlin R. McComb
* 1969   "Cultural pluralism: Its implications for edu-
          cation." Educational Leadership (Decem-
          ber):235-238.   (R)

Holden, Constance
* 1971   "Corporate responsibility: Group rates company
          social performance." Science 171
          (February):463-466.   (A, CS)

Holden, Matthew, Jr.
  1969   "Indicators of social stress and social peace."
          A paper presented at the Sixty-fifth Annual
          Meeting of the American Political Science Asso-
          ciation. New York.

Holleb, Doris
* 1968   "Social statistics for social policy." Pp.
          80-85 in American Society of Planning Officials,
          (eds.), Planning: 1968. Chicago: ASPO. (D,
          CS)

  1969   Social and Economic Information for Urban
          Planning: Vol. I: Its Selection and Use; Vol.
          II: A Directory of Data Sources. Chicago:
          Center for Urban Studies.

Holman, Mary A.
  1961   "A national time budget for the year 2000." So-
          ciology and Social Research 46:17-25.

Holmans, A. E.
* 1970   "A forecast of effective demand for housing in

Great Britain in the 1970's." Pp. 33-42 in
Muriel Nissel (ed.), Social Trends. London:
Her Majesty's Central Statistical Office. (M,
A)

Hoos, Ida R.
 * 1971   "Information systems and public planning."
          Management Science 17 (June):B-658 - B-671.
          (CS)

Horowitz, Irving Louis
 * 1968   "Social indicators and social policy." Pp.
          328-339 in Irving L. Horowitz, Professing Soci-
          ology: Studies in the Life Cycle of Social Sci-
          ence. Chicago: Aldine Publishing Company.
          (CS, P)

 * 1969   "Engineering and sociological perspectives on
          development: Interdisciplinary constraints in
          social forecasting." International Social Sci-
          ence Journal 21:546-557. (GT, C, M)

Horowitz, Irving Louis and Lee Rainwater
 * 1967   "Comment: Social accounting for the nation."
          Transaction (May):2-3. (P, CS)

Howard, William A.
 * 1969   "City-size and its relationship to municipal ef-
          ficiency: Some observations and questions."
          Ekistics 28 (November):312-315. (CS)

Hoyt, Elizabeth E.
   1956   "The impact of a money economy on consumption
          patterns." The Annals of the American Academy
          of Political and Social Science 305:12-22.

Hunt, H.
 * 1969   "Forecasting the need for research and develop-
          ment." Futures 1 (September):382-390. (A)

Huntington, Samuel P.
   1965   "Political development and political decay."
          World Politics 17:386-430.

   1968   "Political development and the decline of the
          American system of world order." Pp. 315-317 in
          Daniel Bell (ed.), Toward the Year 2000.
          Boston: Houghton Mifflin Company.

326

Huttman, E. D.
* 1971   "Diminished social inequality through programs
          of housing assistance: International compari-
          sons." A paper presented at the Annual Meeting
          of the American Sociological Association
          (August) Denver, Colorado. (A, P)

Hyman, Herbert H. and Paul B. Sheatsley
    1956   "Attitudes toward desegregation." Scientific
            American 195 (December):35-39.

    1964   "Attitudes toward desegregation." Scientific
            American 211 (July):16-23.

Ikle, Fred Charles
    1968   "Can social predictions be evaluated." Pp.
            101-126 in Daniel Bell (ed.), Toward the Year
            2000. Boston: Houghton Mifflin Company.

* 1971   "Social forecasting and the problem of changing
          values with special reference to Soviet and East
          European writings." Futures 3 (June):142-150.
          (CS, P)

Ink, Dwight A.
* 1971   "Statement of Dwight A. Ink, Assistant Director
          for Office of Management and Budget." In U.S.
          Congress. Senate. The Full Opportunity and
          National Goals and Priorities Act. Committee on
          Labor and Public Welfare on S.5. (P)

Inkeles, Alex
    1960   "The modernization of man." Pp. 138-150 in
            Myron Weiner (ed.), Modernization. New York:
            Basic Books.

Institut de Recherche Economique et de Planification
    1971   "Recherche sur l'integration des indicateurs
            sociaux dans les modeles changement social."
            Unpublished manuscript. (September) Grenoble,
            France: University of the Social Sciences of
            Grenoble.

Institut National de la Statistique et Des Etudes
Economiques
* 1971a   Inventaire Bibliographique. Unpublished
          manuscript No. 320/1163 prepared by the Social

Statistics Group. Paris, France: Institut
National de la Statistique et Des Etudes
Economiques. (B)

* 1971b "Les indicateurs sociaux dans le domaine de
l'education." Unpublished manuscript. (November) Paris, France: Commissariat General du
Plan d'Equipment et de la Productivite. (C)

* 1971c "Presentation des travaux francais." Unpublished manuscript. (November) Paris, France:
Commissariat General du Plan d'Equipment et de
la Productivite. (CS)

* 1971d Social Indicators. Unpublished manuscript.
(June) Paris, France: Social Statistics Group.
(P, CS)

   1972 Statistiques Sociales: Methodes et Sources.
No. 56 des Collections de l'I.N.S.E.E., Series C
(April) Paris, France.

Institute for Interdisciplinary Studies
   1971 Social Indicators for the Aged: A Guide for
State Agencies on Aging. American Rehabilitation Foundation. Minneapolis, Minnesota:
Institute for Interdisciplinary Studies.

Iowa Development Commission
* 1970 "Iowa, a place to grow: 10 year targets to
2001." Findings from the Conference for Planned
Economic Development, sponsored by the Iowa Development Commission (April 13-14) Ames, Iowa:
Iowa State University. (P)

Iowa State Department of Health, Records and Statistics
Division
* 1970 Measures of Health Status for Counties and
Regions in Iowa 1965-1969. Des Moines, Iowa:
Office of Comprehensive Health Planning. (A, M,
P)

Iowa State University, Center for Agricultural and Economic Development.
   1970 Policy Choices for Rural People. Ames, Iowa:
Center for Agricultural and Economic Development.

Jackson, Edward Neill
* 1970   A Factor Analysis of Small Community Develop-
          ment. Unpublished master's thesis. Manhattan,
          Kansas: Kansas State University. (A, P)

Jantsch, Erich
  1968   "Integrating forecasting and planning through a
          function-oriented approach." In James R. Bright
          (ed.), Technological Forecasting for Industry
          and Government. Englewood Cliffs, New Jersey:
          Prentice-Hall.

* 1969a "Integrative planning for the 'joint systems' of
          society and technology--the emerging role of the
          university." Ekistics 28:371-380. (P)

* 1969b "Planning and designing for the future."
          Futures 1 (September):440-444. (C, P)

Jenkins, William I. and Irving Velody
  1970   "The social sciences and government: Do the
          natural sciences show the prescribed path?"
          Social Science Information 9 (October):91-118.

Johnson, David
  1967   "Social accounting: A select annotated bibliog-
          raphy." (June) (Multilith) Washington, D.C.:
          Library of Congress, Legislative Reference Serv-
          ice.

Johnson, Helen W.
* 1971   "Toward balanced development." A paper present-
          ed at the Annual Meeting of the Rural
          Sociological Society (August 27) Denver,
          Colorado. (P)

Johnson, Lyndon B.
  1964   My Hope for America. New York: Neinemann.

Johnson, Norman J. and Edward J. Ward
* 1970   A New Approach To Citizen Participation: An
          Exploration Tying Information and Utilization.
          Pittsburgh, Pennsylvania: Carnegie-Mellon Uni-
          versity, School of Urban and Public Affairs.
          (M, P)

Johnson, Paul
  * 1969   "Social change not science will shape the
           future." New Statesman (March):438-441.   (C)

Johnston, Denis F.
  * 1970   "Forecasting methods in the social sciences."
           Technological Forecasting and Social Change 2
           (July):173-187.   (CS)

  * 1971   "Social indicators and social forecasting."
           Cahiers du Centre de Recherches Science et Vie,
           (Paris) No. 2 (September):41-83.   (CS, GT)

Jones, Kenneth J. and Wyatt C. Jones
  * 1970   "Toward a typology of American cities."   Journal
           of Regional Science 10:217-224.   (M)

Jones, Lonnie L.
    1971   "Organization of public service delivery systems
           for rural areas: Concepts and measures."   In
           Working Papers on Rural Community Services com-
           piled by S. M. Leadley, Department of
           Agricultural Economics and Rural Sociology, The
           Pennsylvania State University for the National
           Workshop on Problems of Research on Delivery of
           Community Services in Rural Areas (December
           13-16) Lincoln, Nebraska.

Jones, Martin V. and Michael J. Flax
  * 1970a   Cities vs. Suburbs: A Comparative Analysis of
           Six Qualities of Urban Life. Washington, D.C.:
           The Urban Institute. (Preliminary Draft)   (M,
           C, A)

  * 1970b   The Quality of Life in Metropolitan Washington
           (D.C.). Washington, D.C.: The Urban Institute.
           (A, C, M)

Josowitz, Aaron
  * 1970   "Housing changes in metropolitan areas--
           Preliminary findings." A paper presented at the
           American Statistical Association Meeting (Decem-
           ber 28) Detroit, Michigan.   (A)

Judge, Anthony J. N.
  * 1971   "Information systems and inter-organizational
           space." The American Academy of Political and
           Social Science 393 (January):47-64.   (CS, P)

Jungk, Robert
  * 1968   "Human futures." Futures 1 (September):34-39.
          (CS, P)

Juster, F. Thomas
    1970   "Agenda for future research: The measurement of
           social and economic performance." Preliminary
           draft. New York: National Bureau of Economic
           Research.

Kahl, Joseph A.
    1968   The Measurement of Modernism. Austin: The Uni-
           versity of Texas Press.

Kahn, Alfred J.
    1969   Theory and Practice of Social Planning. New
           York: Russell Sage Foundation.

Kahn, Herman and Anthony J. Wiener
    1967   The Year 2000: A Framework for Speculation on
           the Next Thirty-three Years. New York:
           MacMillan.

    1968   "The next thirty-three years: A framework for
           speculation." Pp. 73-100 in Daniel Bell (ed.),
           Toward the Year 2000. Boston: Houghton Mifflin
           Company.

Kahn, Robert L.
    1971   "The justification of violence: Social problems
           and social solutions." Presidential address
           presented to the Society for the Psychological
           Study of Social Issues at the 79th Annual Con-
           vention of the American Psychological Associa-
           tion (September): Washington, D.C. (C, CS, P)

Kalven, Harry, Jr.
    1968   "The problems of privacy in the year 2000." Pp.
           244-250 in Daniel Bell (ed.), Toward the Year
           2000. Boston: Houghton Mifflin Company.

Kamrany, Nake M.
  * 1968   "A note on the development of social
           indicators." Santa Monica, California: Systems
           Development Corporation. (D, CS)

1972   Economic Growth and Environmental Impact: Eval-
        uating Alternatives. (February) Los Angeles,
        California: Department of Economics, University
        of California.

Kamrany, Nake M. and Alexander N. Christakis
    1970   "Social indicators in perspective." Socio-
            Economic Planning Science 4 (June):207-216.

Kaplan, H. Roy and Bhopinder S. Bolaria
  * 1971   "Income, ideologies and health care with special
            reference to the rural poor." A paper presented
            at the Annual Meeting of the American
            Sociological Association (August) Denver,
            Colorado. (A)

Kaplan, Max
  * 1968   "Leisure as an issue for the future." Futures
            1:91-99. (P)

Kaplan, Robert, Judith Lave, Lester Lave and Samuel
Leinhardt
    1971   "Studies in the delivery of ambulatory care." A
            paper presented at the Annual Meeting of the
            American Sociological Association (August 31)
            Denver, Colorado.

Kapp, Karl William
    1950   The Social Costs of Private Enterprise.
            Cambridge, Massachusetts: Harvard University
            Press.

Katz, S. M.
    1965   A Systems Approach to Development Administra-
            tion, Paper #6. Comparative Administration
            Group, American Society for Public Administra-
            tion.

Katzman, Martin T.
  * 1968   "Social indicators and urban public policy."
            Pp. 85-94 in American Society of Planning
            Officials (eds.), Planning: 1968. Chicago:
            ASPO. (D, CS)

Keyserling, Leon H.
  * 1967   "Employment and the 'new economics'." The

Annals of the American Academy of Political and
Social Science 373 (September):102-119.
(Reprinted in Bertram M. Gross (ed.), 1969
Social Intelligence for America's Future.
Boston: Allyn and Bacon). (P)

Kimball, Thomas L.
 * 1971   "Why environmental quality indices?" A paper
            presented at the Annual Meeting of the American
            Association for the Advancement of Science (De-
            cember 26-31) Philadelphia, Pennsylvania. (M,
            A, P)

King, Mervyn A.
    1972   "Primary and secondary indicators in education."
            In Andrew Shonfield and Stella Shaw (eds.),
            Social Indicators and Social Policy. London,
            England: Heinemann Educational Books Limited.
            (In press)

King-Hele, Desmond
 * 1970   "The quality of living." Pp. 134-171 in Desmond
            King-Hele, The End of the Twentieth Century.
            New York: St. Martins Press. (CS, A, C)

Kitchen, J. W. and W. S. Hendon
    1967   Land Values Adjacent to an Urban Neighborhood
            Park. Land Economics 43:357-360.

Kitsuse, John I. and Aaron V. Cicourel
    1963   "A note on the use of official statistics."
            Social Problems 2 (Fall):131-139.

Klarman, Herbert
    1965   "Syphilis control programs." In Robert Dorfman
            (ed.), Measuring Benefits of Government
            Investments. Washington, D.C.: Brookings In-
            stitution.

Klausner, Samuel Z.
 * 1971   "Some formal theoretical components for socio-
            environmental research." A paper presented at
            the Annual Meeting of the American Sociological
            Association (August 30-September 2) Denver,
            Colorado. (GT)

Klessig, Lowell L. and Douglas A. Yanggen
    1970   Wisconsin Lakeshore Property Owners' Associa-
            tions: Identification, Description, and Percep-
            tion of Lake Problems. Research paper sponsored
            by the Inland Lake Renewal and Management Demon-
            stration Project, University Extension, Univer-
            sity of Wisconsin Department of Natural Re-
            sources, Madison, Wisconsin.

Kluckhohn, Clyde
    1956   "Toward a comparison of value-emphases in dif-
            ferent cultures." Pp. 116-132 in Leonard White
            (ed.), The State of the Social Sciences.
            Chicago: The University of Chicago Press.

Knezo, Genevieve J.
  * 1971a   Social Science Policies: An Annotated List of
            Recent Literature. (July 8) (71-167 SP) Wash-
            ington, D.C.: Science Policy Research Division,
            Congressional Research Service, Library of
            Congress. (B)

  * 1971b   Social Science Policies: An Annotated List of
            Recent Literature--Addendum. (August 4) Wash-
            ington, D.C.: Science Policy Research Division,
            Congressional Research Service, Library of
            Congress. (B)

Konvitz, Milton R.
  * 1967   "Civil liberties." The Annals of the American
            Academy of Political and Social Science 371
            (May):38-5ε. (Reprinted in Bertram M. Gross
            (ed.), 1969 Social Intelligence for America's
            Future. Boston: Allyn and Bacon). (C, S, P)

Kopkind, Andrew
  * 1967   "The future planners." New Republic (February
            25):19-23. (Also in American Psychologist 22
            (November):1036-1041). (CS)

Kormondy, Edward J.
  * 1972   "The nature of ecosystems." Pp. 40-45 in Rex R.
            Campbell and Jerry L. Wade (eds.), Society and
            Environment: The Coming Collision. Boston,
            Massachusetts: Allyn and Bacon, Inc. (GT, D,
            C)

Krendel, Ezra S.
* 1970a   "A case study of citizen complaints as social
           indicators." IEEE Transactions on Systems Sci-
           ence and Cybernetics. SSC-6 (October):265-272.
           (M, C, D)

* 1970b   "Social indicators and urban systems dynamics."
           Socio-Economic Planning Sciences 5
           (August):387-393. (GT, C, D)

Krieger, Martin H.
* 1969a   "Social indicators for the quality of individual
           life." Working Paper No. 104. Berkeley,
           California: Institute of Urban and Regional De-
           velopment, University of California. (CS, M)

* 1969b   "The life cycle as a basis for social policy and
           social indicators." Working Paper No. 106.
           Berkeley, California: Institute of Urban and
           Regional Development, University of California.
           (GT, A)

* 1970   "Six propositions on the poor and pollution."
           Policy Sciences 1:311-324. (P, C)

* 1971a   "Advice as a socially constructed activity."
           Working Paper No. 144C. Berkeley, California:
           Institute of Urban and Regional Development,
           University of California. (GT, P)

* 1971b   "Planning for an affect based society: Predic-
           tion, indicators and structure." Working Paper
           144B. Berkeley, California: Institute of Urban
           and Regional Development, University of
           California. (C, M)

* 1971c   "Social reporting for a city: A perspective and
           some problems." Berkeley, California:
           Institute of Urban and Regional Development,
           University of California. (C, M, CS, P)

Kriesberg, Louis
* 1970a   "Some observations about social conflict."
           (Working Draft, July) Syracuse, New York: Edu-
           cational Policy Research Center, Syracuse Uni-
           versity Research Corporation. (D, C, A)

* 1970b   "Toward a social science paradigm for thinking
           about futures." (Working Draft, July) Syracuse,
           New York: Educational Policy Research Center,
           Syracuse University Research Center, Syracuse
           University Research Corporation. (C)

Krohn, Edward
  * 1967   "Statistical requirements for the promotion of
            health." Pp. 151-158 in a discussion paper for
            Conference of European Statisticians, Statisti-
            cal Standards and Studies: ST/CES/11, 2.   (CS)

Kunkel, John H.
  * 1971   "Models of man and social systems analysis." A
            paper presented at the Annual Meeting of the
            American Sociological Association (August
            30-September 2) Denver, Colorado.   (GT)

Lakoff, Sanford
    1971   "Knowledge, power, and democratic theory." The
            Annals of the American Academy of Political and
            Social Science 394 (March):4-12.

Lamale, Helen H.
  * 1958   "Changes in concepts of income adequacy over the
            last century." The American Economic Review 47
            (May):291-299.   (C)

  * 1959   "Present day concepts of income adequacy." Pp.
            103-113 in The Social Welfare Forum, Official
            Proceedings, 86th Annual Forum, 1959 San
            Francisco, National Conference on Social
            Welfare.   (D, C)

  * 1965a   "Levels of living among the poor." A paper pre-
            sented at the UCLA Seminar on Poverty (April 2)
            Los Angeles, California. BLS Report No. 238-12.
            (A)

  * 1965b   "Poverty: The word and the reality." Monthly
            Labor Review 88 (July):822-827.   (D, C)

  * 1968   "Workers' wealth and family living standards."
            Monthly Labor Review 91 (June):676-686.   BLS
            Report No. 238-1.   (A)

Lamale, Helen H. and Joseph A. Clorety, Jr.
  * 1959   "City families as givers." Monthly Labor Review
            82 (December):1303-1311.   (M)

Lamson, Robert W.
  * 1969a   "Framework of categories for science policy

analysis and technology assessment." (November) Washington, D.C.: Office of Planning and Policy Studies, National Science Foundation. (A, P)

* 1969b "The future of man's environment." The Science Teacher 36 (January):25-30. (P)

* 1970a "Federal action for population policy--What more can we do now?" BioScience 20 (August):854-857. (P)

* 1970b "Policy considerations for environmental management." Pp. 267-283 in Alfred Blumstein, Murray Kamrass and Armand Weiss (eds.), Systems Analysis for Social Problems. Washington, D.C.: Washington Operations Research Council. (P, C)

* 1971a "Policy and futures research--Some important questions, principles and issues." Pp. 127-134 in Japan Society of Futurology (ed.), Challenges from the Future: Proceedings of the International Future Research Conference, Vol. II. Kodansha, Ltd. (Also in Technology Assessment - 1970, Hearings before the Subcommittee on Science, Research, and Development of the Committee on Science and Astronautics, U.S. House of Representatives, 1970. Pp. 235-239). (P, A)

* 1971b "Science policy--Needed research." (August) Washington, D.C.: Science Policy Research Section, Social Science Division, National Science Foundation. (A, C, P)

* 1971c "Science policy research--A suggested structure to link national problems, goals and means." (March 17) (Draft) Washington, D.C.: Plans and Analysis Office, National Science Foundation. (A, P)

* 1971d "Research on the population problem." Statement of Dr. Robert Lamson before the Subcommittee on Human Resources Committee on Labor and Public Welfare, United States Senate. (October 5). (P, CS)

Land, Kenneth C.

* 1970a "Social indicators." In Robert B. Smith (ed.), Social Science Methods. New York: The Free Press. (GT, M, D, P)

* 1970b "Some problems of statistical inference in dynamic sociological models." A paper presented at the Annual Meeting of the American Statisti-

cal Association (December 27-30) Detroit, Michigan. (M)

* 1971a "On the definition of social indicators." The American Sociologist 6 (November):322-325. (D, CS)

* 1971b "Some exhaustible poisson process models of divorce by marriage cohort." Journal of Mathematical Sociology 1:213-232. (A, GT)

Landsberg, Hans H.
    1964   Natural Resources for U.S. Growth. Baltimore: Johns Hopkins Press.

Landsberg, Hans H., Leonard L. Fischman and Joseph L. Fisher
    1963   Resources in America's Future: Patterns of Requirements and Availabilities, 1960-2000. Baltimore: Johns Hopkins Press.

Laumann, Edward O.
    1971   "The persistence of ethnoreligious differences in the worldly success of third and later generation Americans." A paper presented at the Annual Meeting of the American Sociological Association (August) Denver, Colorado.

Lave, Lester B.
    1966   Technological Change: Its Conception and Measurement. Englewood Cliffs, New Jersey: Prentice-Hall.

Law Enforcement Assistance Administration, U.S. Department of Justice
* 1971a 1970 National Jail Census. National Criminal Justice Information and Statistics Service, Series SC-No. 1. Washington, D.C.: U.S. Government Printing Office. (R)

* 1971b Criminal Justice Agencies in the United States 1970. Washington, D.C.: National Institute of Law Enforcement and Criminal Justice, Statistics Division. (A)

Law Enforcement Assistance Administration, U.S. Department of Justice and Bureau of the Census
* 1970   Expenditure and Employment Data for the Criminal

338

Justice System: 1968-69. Washington, D.C.:
U.S. Government Printing Office. (A)

Lear, John
   1972   "Where is society going? The search for
          landmarks." Saturday Review (April 15):34-39.

Lebergott, Stanley
 * 1967   "Three aspects of labor supply since 1900." Pp.
          172-178 in Proceedings of the Social Statistics
          Section, American Statistical Association, Wash-
          ington, D.C.   (M)

 * 1968   "Labor force and employment trends." Pp. 97-114
          in Eleanor B. Sheldon and Wilbert Moore (eds.),
          Indicators of Social Change: Concepts and Meas-
          urements. New York: Russell Sage Foundation.
          (A, P)

Lecht, Leonard H.
   1965   The Dollar Cost of National Goals. Washington,
          D.C.: National Planning Association.

Lee, Everett S.
   1968   "Needed improvements in census data collection
          procedures with special reference to the
          disadvantaged." Pp. 91-100 in David M. Heer,
          (ed.), Social Statistics and the City.
          Cambridge, Massachusetts: MIT - Harvard Joint
          Center for Urban Studies.

Lee, Philip R.
 * 1967   "Health and well being." The Annals of the
          American Academy of Political and Social Sci-
          ence 373 (September):193-207. (Reprinted in
          Bertram M. Gross (ed.), 1969 Social Intelligence
          for America's Future. Boston: Allyn and
          Bacon). (C, CS)

Lehman, Edward W.
 * 1971a "Social indicators and social problems." Pp.
          149-176 in Erwin O. Smigel (ed.), Handbook on
          the Study of Social Problems. Chicago: Rand
          McNally and Company. (CS, C)

   1971b "Toward a paradigm for the analysis of inter-
          organizational relations." A paper presented at
          the Annual Meeting of the American Sociological
          Association (August 31) Denver, Colorado.

Lerner, Daniel
    1958   The Passing of Traditional Society. New York:
            The Free Press.

Levin, Lowell S.
  * 1969   "Building toward the future: Implications for
            health education." American Journal of Public
            Health 59 (November):1983-1991. (CS)

Levitan, Sar A.
    1967   "Discussion of social indicators articles." Pp.
            187-188 in Proceedings of the Social Statistics
            Section, American Statistical Association, Wash-
            ington, D.C.

Levy, Marion J., Jr.
    1952   The Structure of Society. Princeton: Princeton
            University Press.

Lewis, Wilfred, Jr.
  * 1971   "Public policy and national priorities in the
            next decade." Looking Ahead 19 (June):5-8.
            (CS, P)

Life Sciences Panel
    1962   "Strengthening the behavioral sciences: State-
            ment by the behavioral sciences subpanel."
            President's Science Advisory Committee, Washing-
            ton, D.C. (April 20).

Lijphart, A.
    1968   The Politics of Accommodation: Pluralism and
            Democracy in the Netherlands. Berkeley,
            California: University of California Press.

Lillibridge, Robert M.
    1952   "Urban size: An assessment." Land Economics
            28:341-352.

Lingoes, James C. and Martin Pfaff
  * 1971   "Measurement of subjective welfare and satisfac-
            tion." A paper presented at the annual meeting
            of The American Economic Association jointly

with the Association for the Study of the Grants
Economy (December 27) New Orleans, Louisiana.
(M)

Linowes, David
  * 1971   "Accounting for social progress: Yardsticks must
           be found for public programs." Extension of
           remarks of the Hon. Frank E. Moss.
           Congressional Record (March 29):E2369-E2370.
           (CS)

Lionberger, Herbert F. and Betty S. Heifner
  * 1969   Occupational Views and Decisions of Missouri
           College of Agriculture Students: A Panel Study
           of 1964 Freshmen-1968 Seniors. Research
           Bulletin 967 (August) Columbia, Missouri: Uni-
           versity of Missouri, College of Agriculture,
           Agricultural Experiment Station. (M)

Lippett, Ronald
  * 1965   "The use of social research to improve social
           practice." American Journal of Orthopsychiatry
           35 (July):663-669. (C, M, A)

Lipscomb, David M.
  * 1971   "Indicators of environmental noise." A paper
           presented at the Annual Meeting of the American
           Association for the Advancement of Science (De-
           cember 27) Philadelphia, Pennsylvania. (A)

Lipsky, Michael
    1971   "Social scientists and the riot commission."
           The Annals of the American Academy of Political
           and Social Science 394 (March):72-83.

Lipson, Harry A.
    1972   "Management use of economic and/or social
           indicators in the marketing planning process."
           A paper presented at the Social Indicators
           Conference, American Marketing Association (Feb-
           ruary 18) Washington, D.C.

Lissner, Will
    1971   "Needed: An ethical code for behavioral scien-
           tists." American Journal of Economics and Soci-
           ology 30 (January):45-46.

341

Little, Alan and Christine Mabey
    1972   "An index for designation of educational priori-
            ty areas." In Andrew Shonfield and Stella Shaw
            (eds.), Social Indicators and Social Policy.
            London, England: Heinemann Educational Books
            Limited. (In press)

Little, Dennis and Richard Feller
  * 1970   "Stapol: A simulation of the impact of policy,
            values, and technological and societal develop-
            ments upon the quality of life." Working Paper
            WP-12. (October) Middletown, Connecticut:
            Institute for the Future. (A, P, M)

Liu, William T. and Robert W. Duff
  * 1971   "The structural effect of communication flows in
            a pre-industrial city." A paper presented at
            the Annual Meeting of The Ohio Valley
            Sociological Society (April 22-24) Cleveland,
            Ohio. (GT, A)

Lochhead, A.V.S.
  * 1969   "The search for measurement in social develop-
            ment." Community Development Journal 4:68-73.
            (C, M)

Lompe, Klaus
  * 1968   "Problems of futures research in the social sci-
            ences." Futures 1 (September):47-53. (CS)

Long, Norton E.
  * 1968   "Planning for social change." Pp. 67-79 in
            American Society of Planning Officials (eds.),
            Planning: 1968. Chicago: ASPO. (CS)

  * 1970   "Indicators of change in political institu-
            tions." The Annals of the American Academy of
            Political and Social Science 388 (March):35-45.
            (C, A)

Lowe, Jay
  * 1966   "Prediction of delinquency with an attitudinal
            configuration model." Social Forces 45
            (Summer):106- 113. (A)

Lyons, Gene M.
    1971a "More reading: A bibliographic note." The
            Annals of the American Academy of Political and
            Social Science 394 (March):125-128.

1971b "Social science and the federal government: An
       introductory note." The Annals of the American
       Academy of Political and Social Science 394
       (March):1-3.

1971c "The president and his experts." The Annals of
       the American Academy of Political and Social
       Science 394 (March):36-45.

MacDonald, Gordon J.
* 1971 "Remarks by Dr. Gordon J. MacDonald." Presented
        at the American Association for the Advancement
        of Science Symposium (December 27) Philadelphia,
        Pennsylvania. (P)

Mack, Ruth and Sumner Myers
    1965 "Outdoor recreation." In Robert Dorfman (ed.),
          Measuring Benefits of Government Investment.
          Washington, D.C.: Brookings Institution.

MacMillan, A. M.
    1957 "The health opinion survey: A technique for
          estimating prevalence of psychoneurotic and re-
          lated types of disorder in communities."
          Psychological Reports 111:325-339.

Madden, J. Patrick
* 1970 "Social change and public policy in rural
        America: Data and research needs for the
        1970's." American Journal of Agricultural Eco-
        nomics 52 (May):308-314. (CS, C)

* 1971a "Poverty data in relation to other indicators of
         social welfare." A paper presented at the
         Annual Meeting of the American Sociological
         Society (August 30) Denver, Colorado. (CS, D,
         A, P)

1971b "Poverty statistics: A guide to interpreta-
       tion." University Park, Pennsylvania: Depart-
       ment of Agricultural Economics and Rural Sociol-
       ogy, The Pennsylvania State University.

Maimon, Zvi
    1970 "The inner-city impact." Urban Affairs
          Quarterly 6 (December):233-248.

* 1971 "Second-order consequences - a presentation of a concept." Detroit, Michigan: Center for Urban Studies, Wayne State University. (P, M)

Malenbaum, Wilfred
* 1971 "Progress in health: What index of what progress?" The Annals of the American Academy of Political and Social Science 393 (January):109-121. (CS)

Manley, Vaughn Porter
* 1967 Iowa's Human and Community Development Resources. Des Moines, Iowa: Iowa State Manpower Development Council, Office of the Governor. (P)

Marcuse, Peter
* 1970 "Housing policy and social indicators: Strangers or siblings." Working Paper No. 130. Berkeley, California: Institute of Urban and Regional Development, University of California. (GT, CS, P)

Marie, Michel and Jose Rodriquez Dos Santos
* 1971 "Etat d'avancement de la recherche concernat la societe francaise et les travailleurs immigres." Unpublished manuscript. (December) Grenoble, France: Centre de Sociologie Economique et Politique. (C)

Marien, Michael D.
1970 "Notes on the education complex as an emerging macro-system." In Milton D. Rubin (ed.), Man in Systems. Proceedings of the 14th Annual Meeting of Sociology for General Systems Research. New York: Gordon and Breach.

* 1971 Alternative Futures for Learning: An Annotated Bibliography of Trends, Forecasts, and Proposals. Syracuse, New York: Educational Policy Research Center, Syracuse University Research Corporation. (B)

Markley, O. W.
* 1970 Alternative Futures: Contexts in which Social Indicators Must Work. Research Note-EPRC 6747-11. Menlo Park, California: Stanford Research Institute, Educational Policy Research Center. (P)

Martin, Margaret E.
  * 1971   "The current population survey as a statistical
            information system." Washington, D.C.: U.S.
            Office of Management and Budget. (C, A, P)

Martin, Thomas and Kenneth J. Berry
  * 1971   "Generalizing to individuals: Another problem
            of evidence and interference." A paper present-
            ed at the Annual Meeting of the Rural
            Sociological Association (August) Denver,
            Colorado. (M, GT)

Mather, William G.
  * 1971   "The continuing involvement of rural
            sociologists with public policy." A paper pre-
            sented at the Annual Meeting of the Rural
            Sociological Society (August 27) Denver,
            Colorado. (R)

Mattila, John M.
    1970   "Metropolitan income estimation." Urban Affairs
            Quarterly 6 (December):179-198.

Mauro, John T.
  * 1968   "Planning as an instrument for social change."
            Pp. 59-67 in American Society of Planning
            Officials (eds.), Planning: 1968. Chicago:
            ASPO. (CS)

Mayer, Lawrence A.
  * 1972   "U.S. population growth: Would slower be
            better?" Pp. 238-245 in Rex R. Campbell and
            Jerry L. Wade (eds.), Society and Environment:
            The Coming Collision. Boston, Massachusetts:
            Allyn and Bacon, Inc. (CS, A)

Mayr, Ernst
    1968   "Biological man and the year 2000." Pp. 200-204
            in Daniel Bell (ed.), Toward the Year 2000.
            Boston: Houghton Mifflin Company.

Mazlish, Bruce
    1965   The Railroad and the Space Program: An
            Exploration in Historical Analogy. Cambridge,

Massachusetts: The Massachusetts Institute of
Technology Press.

McConnell, Grant
    1966   Private Power and American Democracy. New York:
            Knopf.

McDevitt, Matthew and Thomson McGowan
  * 1970   New York State's Central Social Environment
            Study: Social Research for Comprehensive
            Planning. Albany, New York: New York State
            Office of Planning Coordination. (M)

McElveen, Jackson V. and Buddy L. Dillman
    1971   A Profile of the Rural Poor in the Northeastern
            Coastal Plain of South Carolina. Agricultural
            Economic Report No. 202. Washington, D.C.: Ec-
            onomic Research Service, U.S. Department of
            Agriculture.

McGranahan, Donald V.
  * 1971   "Analysis of socio-economic development through
            a system of indicators." The American Academy
            of Political and Social Science 393
            (January):65-81. (A, M)

  * 1972   "Development indicators and development models."
            The Journal of Development Studies. (CS, M)

McHale, John
  * 1967   "Science, technology and change." The Annals of
            the American Academy of Political and Social
            Science 373 (September):120-140. (Reprinted in
            Bertram M. Gross (ed.), 1969 Social Intelligence
            for America's Future. Boston: Allyn and
            Bacon). (GT, CS, D)

  * 1968   "Global ecology: Toward the planetary society."
            The American Behavioral Scientist 11
            (July-August):29-33. (C, P)

    1969   The Future of the Future. New York: George
            Braziller, Inc.

McIntosh, William Alex
  * 1971   "Social indicators and social change: An
            interpretive essay."
            Unpublished paper. De-

partment of Sociology. Ames, Iowa: Iowa State
University. (A, P)

McIntyre, Jennie
    1967   "Public attitudes toward crime and law
            enforcement." The Annals of the American
            Academy of Political and Social Science 374 (No-
            vember): 34-46.

McMichael, Morris Harry
    1956   A Case Study of the Taos County, New Mexico
            Cooperative Health Association. Unpublished
            Ed.D. Dissertation. East Lansing, Michigan:
            Michigan State University.

McVeigh, Thomas
    1971   Social Indicators: A Bibliography. Monticello,
            Illinois: Council of Planning Librarians.

Mead, Margaret
    1953   Cultural Patterns and Technical Change. Paris:
            UNESCO Tensions and Technology Series.

    1968   "The life cycle and its variations: The divi-
            sion of roles." Pp. 239-243 in Daniel Bell
            (ed.), Toward the Year 2000. Boston: Houghton
            Mifflin Company.

  * 1970   "What Margaret Mead told the congressmen about
            urban growth." Nation's Cities 8 (Janu-
            ary):24-26. (P, C)

Merriam, Ida C.
  * 1967   "Concepts and measures of welfare." Pp. 179-183
            in Proceedings of the Social Statistics Section
            of the American Statistical Association, Wash-
            ington, D.C. (C, M)

  * 1968   "Welfare and its measurement." Pp. 721-803 in
            Eleanor B. Sheldon and Wilbert Moore (eds.),
            Indicators of Social Change: Concepts and Meas-
            urements. New York: Russell Sage Foundation.
            (C)

Merritt, Richard L. and Stein Rokkan (eds.)
    1966   Comparing Nations: The Use of Quantitative Data
            in Cross-National Research. New Haven: Yale
            University Press.

Meyer, John R.
* 1969   "The evaluation and planning of social pro-
          grams." Testimony before the Special
          Subcommittee on the Evaluation and Planning of
          Social Programs, Senate Committee for Labor and
          Public Welfare, July 17, 1969. A Supplement to
          National Bureau Report 5. (December) New York:
          National Bureau of Economic Research, Inc. (CS)

Michael, Donald N.
   1961   Proposed Studies on the Implications of Peaceful
          Space Activities for Human Affairs. Washington,
          D.C.: U.S. Government Printing Office.

* 1967   "Social engineering and the future environment."
          American Psychologist 22 (November):888-892.
          (CS)

Michell, William C.
   1968   "The new political economy." Social Research
          35:1-77.

Michigan Office of Planning Coordination, Bureau of
Policies and Programs
* 1970   Social Reporting in Michigan: Problems and
          Issues. (January) Lansing, Michigan: Wayne
          State University Center for Urban Studies. (P,
          A)

Miller, George A.
   1968   "Some psychological perspectives on the year
          2000." Pp. 251-264 in Daniel Bell (ed.), Toward
          the Year 2000. Boston: Houghton Mifflin
          Company.

Miller, S. M. and H. J. Bryce
* 1970   "The promotion of social mobility." Pp. 333-344
          in Transactions of the Sixth World Congress of
          Sociology, Sepember 1966. Volume IV. Interna-
          tional Sociological Association. (C, P)

Miller, S. M., Martin Rein, Pamela Roby, and Bertram M.
Gross
* 1967   "Poverty, inequality, and conflict." The Annals
          of the American Academy of Political and Social
          Science 373 (September):16-52. (Reprinted in

Bertram M. Gross (ed.), 1969 Social Intelligence
for America's Future. Boston: Allyn and
Bacon). (CS, P)

Mindlin, Albert
* 1970 "A social indicator system for city and
neighborhood--Some issues." A memorandum from
the Chief, Statistical Systems Group, Office of
Budget and Executive Management, Executive
Office of the Mayor-Commissioner, Government of
the District of Columbia, Washington, D.C. (C,
M)

Mitchell, Arnold
* 1967 Alternative Futures: An Exploration of a
Humanistic Approach to Social Forecasting. Research Note-EPRC 6747-2. Menlo Park,
California: Stanford Research Institute, Educational Policy Research Center. (M)

Mitchell, Joyce M. and William C. Mitchell
* 1968 "The changing politics of American life." Pp.
247-294 in Eleanor B. Sheldon and Wilbert Moore
(eds.), Indicators of Social Change: Concepts
and Measurements. New York: Russell Sage Foundation. (A, P)

Mittlebach, Frank G. and Joan W. Moore
1968 "Ethnic endogamy--the case of Mexican Americans." American Journal of Sociology 74:50-62.

Mohring, Herbert
1965 "Urban highway investments." In Robert Dorfman
(ed.), Measuring Benefits of Government
Investment. Washington, D.C.: Brookings Institution.

Moles, Abraham
* 1970 "The future oriented society: Axioms and
methodology." Futures 2 (December):312-326.
(C)

Mondale, Walter F.
* 1967a "New tools for social progress." The
Progressive 31 (September):28-31. (C, CS)

* 1967b "Some thoughts on stumbling into the future."
American Psychologist 22 (November):972-973.
(P, CS)

1969   "S.5---introduction of bill---full opportunity
act of 1969." Congressional Record, 115, No. 9
(January 15).

* 1970a   Full Opportunity Act, 91st Congress 2nd Session,
Senate (July 1) Hearings before the Special
Subcommittee on Evaluation and Planning of
Social Programs. Report No. 91-998. Washing-
ton, D.C.: U.S. Government Printing Office.
(P, CS)

1970b   "Reporting on the social state of the union."
Pp. 107-117 in Fred R. Harris (ed.), Social Sci-
ence and National Policy. Chicago, Illinois:
Aldine Publishing Company.

* 1970c   "Social advisers, social accounting, and the
presidency." Law and Contemporary Problems
(Summer):496-504. (P)

* 1971a   "Behavioral scientists urge establishment of
council of social advisors." U.S. Senate,
Congressional Record (August):S13107-13113.
(P)

* 1971b   "S.5--Introduction of the full opportunity and
national goals and priorities act." U.S.
Senate, Congressional Record 117 (January
25):S119-S127. (P)

* 1971c   "Social advisers, social accounting, and the
presidency." U.S. Senate, Congressional Record
117 (August 6):S13437-S13439. (P)

Moore, Wilbert E.
    1963   Social Change. Englewood Cliffs, New Jersey:
Prentice-Hall.

    1967   "Forecasting the future: The U.S. in 1980." In
W. E. Moore, Order and Change: Essays in Comparative Sociology. New York: Wiley.

Moore, Wilbert E. and Eleanor Bernert Sheldon
 * 1965   "Monitoring social change: A conceptual and
programmatic statement." Pp. 144-152 in
Proceedings of the Social Statistics Section,
American Statistical Association, Washington,
D.C. (GT)

Morgan, James N. and James D. Smith
* 1969   "Measures of economic well-offness and their
          correlates." The American Economic Review,
          Proceedings and Papers 59 (May):450-462. (R)

Moriyama, Iwao M.
   1964   The Change in Mortality Trend in the United
          States (Public Health Service Publication No.
          1000, Series 3, no. 1). Washington, D.C.:
          National Center for Health Statistics.

* 1968   "Problems in the measurement of health status."
          Pp. 573-599 in Eleanor B. Sheldon and Wilbert
          Moore (eds.), Indicators of Social Change: Con-
          cepts and Measurements. New York: Russell Sage
          Foundation. (A, P)

Morrison, Denton E., Kenneth E. Hornback and W. Keith
Warner
* 1971   "The environmental movement: Some preliminary
          observations." A paper presented at the Annual
          Meeting of the Rural Sociological Society
          (August) Denver, Colorado. (Forthcoming in
          William Burch, Neil Cheek and Lee Taylor (eds.),
          Social Behavior, Natural Resources and the Envi-
          ronment, New York: Harper and Row). (P)

Morrison, Peter A.
   1972   Future Urban Growth and the Nonmetropolitan Pop-
          ulation: Policies for Coping with Local De-
          cline. No. P 4001. Santa Monica, California:
          The Rand Corporation.

Morss, Elliott R.
   1971   "A very partial survey of social indicator work
          and its implications for future research and or-
          ganizational strategies." A paper presented at
          the National Science Foundation Conference on
          Social Indicators (November 5-6) George Washing-
          ton University, Washington, D.C.

Moser, Claus A.
* 1957   The Measurement of Levels of Living with Special
          Reference to Jamaica. Colonial Research Study
          No. 24. London, England: Her Majesty's
          Stationery Office. (A, P)

   1969   An Integrated System of Social and Demographic
          Statistics. Geneva: United Nations Statistical

Commission and ECE, Conference of European
Statisticians, XVII Plenary Session. Conf.Eur.
Stat./273, 29.5.69.

* 1970   "Some general developments in social statis-
          tics." Pp. 7-11 in Muriel Nissel (ed.), Social
          Trends. London: Her Majesty's Central Statis-
          tical Office. (M, A)

  1971a   Federal Support of Applied Research. Washing-
          ton, D.C.: National Academy of Engineering.

  1971b   "Social indicators: Systems, methods and prob-
          lems." Unpublished manuscript. London,
          England: Central Statistical Office.

Moses, Stanley
  1969   "The learning force: An approach to the
          politics of education." A paper presented at
          the 65th Annual Meeting of the American
          Political Science Association (September) New
          York, New York.

Moss, Milton
* 1968a   "Consumption: A report on contemporary issues."
          Pp. 449-523 in Eleanor B. Sheldon and Wilbert
          Moore (eds.), Indicators of Social Change: Con-
          cepts and Measurements. New York: Russell Sage
          Foundation. (A, P)

  1968b   "The relationship of federal to local authori-
          ties." Pp. 169-176 in Daniel Bell (ed.), Toward
          the Year 2000. Boston: Houghton Mifflin
          Company.

  1969a   "New directions in the federal information
          system." The American Statistician 23
          (April):25-29.

  1969b   "The urban environment: General." Pp. 495-520
          in Bertram M. Gross (ed.), Social Intelligence
          for America's Future: Explorations in Societal
          Problems. Boston: Allyn and Bacon.

  1969c   "Toward a national urban policy." The Public
          Interest 17 (Fall):3-20.

Most, Kenneth S.
  1971   "Another look at socio-economic accounting."
          The Accountant (December 30):875-879.

352

Motes, W. C.
* 1971   "Rural development: Economic criteria for as-
          sessment of outcome, and for research inputs."
          A paper presented at the Annual Meeting of the
          Rural Sociological Society (August 27) Denver,
          Colorado. (C)

Moynihan, Daniel P.
* 1967   "Urban conditions: General." The Annals of the
          American Academy of Political and Social Science
          371 (May):159-177. (Reprinted in Bertram M.
          Gross (ed.), 1969 Social Intelligence for
          America's Future. Boston: Allyn and Bacon).
          (CS)

* 1969   "Toward a national urban policy." Appalachia
          (August):1-9.   (CS)

Moynihan, Thomas P.
  1962   "When married couples part: Statistical trends
          and relationships in divorce." American
          Sociological Review 27:625-633.

Mugge, Robert H.
  1966   "Demographic analysis and public assistance." A
          paper presented to the Annual Meeting of the
          Population Association of America (April 30) New
          York, New York.

Munson, Byron E.
* 1971   "Substandard housing and social problems." A
          paper presented at the Annual Meeting of the
          American Sociological Association (August
          30-September 2) Denver, Colorado. (C, M)

Murie, Martin
* 1971   "Evaluation of natural environments." A paper
          presented at the Annual Meeting of the American
          Association for the Advancement of Science (De-
          cember 27) Philadelphia, Pennsylvania. (C, M)

Murphy, Kathryn R.
* 1964   "Contrasts in spending by urban families."
          Monthly Labor Review 87 (November):1249-1253.
          BLS Report No. 238-8.   (A)

* 1965 "Spending and saving in urban and rural areas."
Monthly Labor Review 88 (October):1169-1176.
BLS Report No. 238-14. (A)

Myers, John G. and Francesco M. Nicosia
1970 "Time-path types: From static to dynamic
typologies." Management Science 16 (June):
B584-B596.

Nam, Charles B.
1967 "Discussion of social indicators articles." Pp.
184-186 in Proceedings of the Social Statistics
Section of the American Statistical Association,
Washington, D.C.

National Academy of Engineering, Committee on Public
Engineering Policy
1971a Federal Support of Applied Research. Washington, D.C.: National Academy of Engineering.

* 1971b Priorities in Applied Research: An Initial
Appraisal. Washington, D.C.: National Academy
of Engineering. (CS, C)

National Academy of Engineering, Committee on
Telecommunications
1970 "The application of social and economic values
to spectrum management." Final Report to the
Director of Telecommunications Management under
Contract OEP-SE-69-101. Washington, D.C.:
National Academy of Engineering.

National Academy of Sciences
1964 Toward Better Utilization of Scientific and
Engineering Talent: A Program for Action.
Washington, D.C.: National Academy of Sciences.

National Academy of Sciences and the Social Science Research Council
1969 Behavioral and Social Sciences: Outlook and
Needs. Englewood Cliffs, New Jersey: Prentice-
Hall, Inc.

National Bureau of Economic Research, Inc.
1968 Toward Improved Social and Economic Measurement.

48th Annual Report (June) New York: National
Bureau of Economic Research, Inc.

National Commission on the Causes and Prevention of
Violence
    1970   Crime in America.   AFL-CIO American
            Federationist 77:6-13.

National Commission on Technology, Automation, and Economic Progress
    1966   Technology and the American Economy.   Washing-
            ton, D.C.:   U.S. Government Printing Office.

National Goals Research Staff
 * 1970   Toward Balanced Growth: Quantity with Quality
            (July 4) Washington, D.C.:   U.S. Government
            Printing Office.   (P)

National Planning Association
    1970   Looking Ahead.   Vol. 18 (August).

National Research Council, Advisory Committee on Government Programs in the Behavioral Sciences
    1968   The Behavioral Sciences and the Federal Govern-
            ment.   Publication Number 1680.   Washington,
            D.C.:   National Academy of Sciences.

National Science Board and National Science Foundation
    1969   Knowledge into Action: Increasing the Nation's
            Use of the Social Sciences.   Report of the Spe-
            cial Commission on the Social Sciences (the Brim
            Report).   NSB 69-3.

National Science Foundation
    1969   Knowledge into Action: Improving the Nation's
            Use of the Social Sciences.   Washington, D.C.:
            U.S. Government Printing Office.

National University Extension Association
    1970   Our Urbanizing Society: A Search for
            Perspective.   A position paper of the Division
            of Community Development, National University
            Extension Association.

National Wildlife Federation
 * 1971   1971 EQ Index. Reprinted from October-November,
           1971 National Wildlife magazine. Washington,
           D.C.: National Wildlife Federation. (C)

New York State, Office of Planning Coordination
     1970   New York State's Central Social Environment
             Study. (January) Albany, N.Y.: OPC.

Nicosia, Francesco M.
     1972   "Marketing management scientists and social
             indicators: Opportunities and challenges." A
             paper to be presented to the Institute of
             Management Science (April). (in preparation)

Nisbet, Robert A.
 * 1968   "The year 2000 and all that." Commentary 45
           (June):60-66. (CS)

Nixon, Richard M.
 * 1969   "Statement by President Nixon on creating a
           National Goals Research Staff." Futures 1
           (September):458-459. (CS)

 * 1971a   The First Annual Report on Financial Assistance
           to Rural Areas, Pursuant to Title 9 of the
           Agricultural Act of 1970. 92nd Congress, 1st
           Session, House Document No. 92-147. July 26.
           Washington, D.C.: U.S. Government Printing
           Office. (P)

 * 1971b   The First Annual Report on Government Services
           to Rural America, Pursuant to the Agricultural
           Act of 1970. 92nd Congress, 1st Session, House
           Document No. 92-55. March 1. Washington, D.C.:
           U.S. Government Printing Office. (P)

 * 1972   "Problems of population growth." Pp. 249-255 in
           Rex R. Campbell and Jerry L. Wade (eds.),
           Society and Environment: The Coming Collision.
           Boston, Massachusetts: Allyn and Bacon, Inc.
           (P, CS)

Ochavkov, Jivko
     1970   "La sociologie et le pronostic social." A paper
             presented at the Seventh World Congress of Soci-
             ology (September 14-19) Varna, Bulgaria.

O'Connell, Harold J.
  * 1972 Toward a Social Policy Model: Methodology and
          Design. Unpublished M.S. Thesis. Ames, Iowa:
          Iowa State University. (P, A, M, GT)

Office of Development Programs, Bureau for Latin America
     1971 Summary Economic and Social Indicators 18 Latin
           American Countries: 1960-1970. Washington,
           D.C.: Agency for International Development.

Office of Management and Budget
     1970 "Outline for a social statistics publication."
           (May 18, Draft 4) Washington, D.C.: Office of
           Statistical Policy and Management, Information
           Systems Division.

Official Summary of HEW Toward a Social Report
  * 1969 "A social report in practice." The Public
          Interest 15:98-105. (CS)

Ogburn, William F.
    1946a "On predicting the future." Pp. 32-57 in The
           Social Effects of Aviation. New York: Houghton
           Mifflin Company.

  * 1946b The Social Effects of Aviation. Cambridge,
           Massachusetts: Houghton Mifflin (Riverside
           Press). (M, CS)

Okun, Arthur M.
     1971 "Should GNP measure social welfare?" The
           Brookings Bulletin VIII:4-7.

Olson, Mancur, Jr.
     1967 Social Indicators and Social Accounts. A paper
           presented at the Symposium on Operations Analy-
           sis of Education. Washington, D.C.

    1968a An Agenda for the Development of Measures of the
           Progress of a Racial or Ethnic Group. Washing-
           ton, D.C.: U.S. Dept. of Health, Education, and
           Welfare.

  * 1968b "Economics, sociology, and the best of all pos-
           sible worlds." The Public Interest 12
           (Summer):96-118. (GT)

* 1969a   "Social indicators and social accounts." Socio-
          Economic Planning Science 2:335-346. (CS)

* 1969b   "The plan and purpose of the social report."
          The Public Interest 15 (Spring):85-99. (CS)

  1969c   "Toward a social report: Its plan and purpose."
          The Public Interest (Spring):1-17.

* 1970a   "An analytic framework for social reporting and
          policy analysis." The Annals of the American
          Academy of Political and Social Science 388
          (March):112-126. (M, P, CS)

  1970b   "Recent progress in social accounts." A paper
          presented at the Annual Meeting of the American
          Statistical Association (December 27-30)
          Detroit, Michigan.

  1970c   "The national income and the level of welfare."
          Unpublished manuscript. Baltimore, Maryland:
          University of Maryland.

  1971a   "Indicators of development." Draft written for
          TA/PM/M, May 18. Pp. 1-8. Washington, D.C.:
          Agency for International Development.

* 1971b   "Social indicators for less developed
          countries." Draft, August 5. TA/PM/M. Wash-
          ington, D.C.: Agency for International Develop-
          ment. (C, P)

Ontell, Robert
* 1971   "What is a social indicator?" Unpublished
         manuscript. San Diego, California: Urban
         Observatory. (D, C)

OECD (Organization for Economic Cooperation and Development)
* 1970   "Demographic accounts: A step towards social
         accounting." OECD Observer 49 (December):35-37.
         (CS, M)

Orlans, Harold
  1967   The Use of Social Research in Federal Domestic
         Programs. Staff Study for the Committee on Gov-
         ernment Operations, 90th U.S. Congress, 1st Ses-
         sion (April).

  1968   "Educational and scientific institutions." Pp.
         191-200 in Daniel Bell (ed.), Toward the Year
         2000. Boston: Houghton Mifflin Company.

* 1971a   "Social science research policies in the United
          States." Minerva 9 (January):7-31. (P)

  1971b   "The political uses of social research." The
          Annals of the American Academy of Political and
          Social Science 394 (March):28-35.

Orshansky, Mollie
  1965a   "Counting the poor: Another look at the poverty
          profile." Social Security Bulletin 28
          (January):3-29.

  1965b   "Who's among the poor." Social Security
          Bulletin 28 (July):3-32.

Osman, John
* 1969   "Alternative futures for the American city."
         Public Management 51 (September):2-3. (CS)

Ostrom, Elinor
* 1971a   "Institutional arrangements and the measurement
          of policy consequences in urban areas." Urban
          Affairs Quarterly 6 (June):447-475. (M, P)

* 1971b   "On the meaning and measurement of output and
          efficiency in the production of urban policy
          services." Unpublished manuscript.
          Bloomington, Indiana: Indiana University, De-
          partment of Political Science. (C, M, D)

Ozbekhan, Hasan
* 1969   "Planning theory." Ekistics 28 (October):
         296-299. (GT, P)

Palley, Marian L. and Howard A. Palley
  1969   "Social welfare indicators as predictors of
         racial disorders in black ghettos." A paper
         presented at the 65th Annual Meeting of the
         American Political Science Association (Septem-
         ber) New York, New York.

* 1971   "Social policy analysis--the use of social
         indicators." Welfare in Review 9 (March-April):
         8-14. (CS, P)

Pardee, Frederick S., Nake M. Kamrany, Joseph L. Midler
and Charles T. Phillips

* 1971   "Developing tools for regional environmental as-
          sessment: A study design." A report prepared
          for Special Assistant to the Secretary for
          Regional Economic Development, U.S. Department
          of Commerce, Washington, D.C. Los Angeles,
          California: The Institute for Analysis. (P, M)

Patrick, Donald and J. W. Bush
* 1971   "Toward an operational definition of health." A
          paper presented before the statistics section of
          the Annual Meeting of the American Public Health
          Association (October 14) Minneapolis, Minnesota.
          (D, C, M)

Patrick, Ruth
* 1971   "Aquatic communities as indices of pollution."
          A paper presented at AAAS Symposium "Indicators
          of Environmental Quality" (December)
          Philadelphia, Pennsylvania. (M, CS)

Pelz, Donald C. and Ray E. Faith
* 1970   "Some effects of causal connections in simulated
          time-series data." A paper presented at the
          American Sociological Association Symposium on
          Methodological Problems in Longitudinal Studies
          (December 27) Ann Arbor, Michigan. (M)

Perle, Eugene D.
* 1970a   "Editor's introduction." Urban Affairs
          Quarterly 6 (December):135-144. (CS)

* 1970b   "Notes on urban information systems and urban
          indicators." A paper presented at the Annual
          Meeting of the Association for Computing Machin-
          ery (September 1) New York City. (CS)

  1970c   Social Reporting in Michigan: Problems and
          Issues. Detroit, Michigan: Wayne State Univer-
          sity Center for Urban Studies.

  1970d   Toward Regular Public Reporting on the Quality
          of Life. Detroit, Michigan: Wayne State Uni-
          versity Center for Urban Studies.

  1970e   "Urban indicators: Editor's introduction."
          Urban Affairs Quarterly 6 (December):135-143.

  1970f   "Urban indicators: The state of the art."
          Urban Affairs Quarterly 6 (December). (Special
          issue).

* 1971   "Local societal indicators: A progress report."
          Pp. 114-120 in Proceedings of the Social Sta-
          tistics Section, American Statistical Associa-
          tion, Washington, D.C.   (CS)

Perloff, Harvey S.
   1968   "Modernizing urban development." Pp. 157-168 in
          Daniel Bell (ed.), Toward the Year 2000.
          Boston: Houghton Mifflin Company.

* 1969a "A framework for dealing with the urban environ-
          ment: Introductory statement." Baltimore,
          Maryland: The Johns Hopkins Press. (C)

* 1969b The Quality of the Urban Environment.
          Baltimore, Maryland: The Johns Hopkins Press.
          (C, C3)

Pett, Saul
   1972   "The quality of life." Pp. 13-22 in Rex R.
          Campbell and Jerry L. Wade (eds.), Society and
          Environment: The Coming Collision. Boston,
          Massachusetts: Allyn and Bacon, Inc. (C, CS)

Pfaff, Anita B.
* 1971   "An index of consumer satisfaction." A paper
          presented at the Annual Meeting of The American
          Economic Association jointly with the Associa-
          tion for the Study of the Grants Economy (Decem-
          ber 27) New Orleans, Louisiana. (A)

Pfaff, Martin
   1971   "Summary information on (1) index of consumer
          satisfaction and (2) index of citizen satisfac-
          tion." November 5. Detroit, Michigan: Depart-
          ment of Economics, Wayne State University.

Phillips, Derek L.
   1967   "Social participation and happiness." American
          Journal of Sociology 72 (March):479-488.

* 1971   "Sociologists and their knowledge." American
          Behavioral Scientist 14 (March-April):563-582.
          (P, CS)

Pierce, John R.
   1968   "Communication." Pp. 297-309 in Daniel Bell
          (ed.), Toward the Year 2000. Boston: Houghton
          Mifflin Company.

Pikul, Robert, Charles Bisselle and Martha Lilienthal
 * 1971   "Development of environmental indices: Outdoor
           recreational resources and land use shift." A
           paper presented to the American Association for
           the Advancement of Science (December 26) McLean,
           Virginia: The MITRE Corporation. (M, C)

Porter, David O.
    1969   "The who and what of future forecasting in
           politics." A paper presented at the 65th annual
           meeting of the American Political Science
           Association (September) New York, New York.

    1970   "Questions for discussion: Workshop on social
           indicators." Held at the Annual Meeting of the
           American Political Science Association, (Septem-
           ber 8) Los Angeles, California.

Powers, Ronald C.
    1967   "What is quality life--conflicts in values."
           Remarks prepared for the 46th annual conference
           of the American Country Life Association (July
           11-12) Ames, Iowa, Iowa State University.

    1971   "Sociological strategies in a multi-county de-
           velopment program: A case in sociologing." In
           George M. Beal, Ronald C. Powers and E. Walter
           Coward, Jr. (eds.), Perspectives on Domestic De-
           velopment. Ames, Iowa: Iowa State University.

President's Commission on Federal Statistics
    1971   Federal Statistics: A Report of the President's
           Commission. Volumes I and II. Washington,
           D.C.: U.S. Government Printing Office.

President's Commission on National Goals
 * 1960   "The commission report." Pp. 1-23 in Goals for
           Americans. New York: Prentice-Hall. (P)

President's Research Committee on Social Trends
    1933   Recent Social Trends. New York: McGraw-Hill.

Prest, A. R. and R. Turvey
    1966   "Cost-benefit analysis: A survey." Pp. 155-207
           in Surveys of Economic Theory: Resource Analy-
           sis. New York: St. Martins Press.

Price, Daniel O.
    1968   "Needed statistics for minority groups in
            metropolitan areas." _Pp. 118-131 in David M.
            Heer (ed.), Social Statistics and the City.
            Cambridge, Massachusetts: MIT - Massachusetts
            Institute of Technology, Harvard Joint Center
            for Urban Studies.

Price, Daniel O. and Melanie M. Sikes
  * 1971   "Rural-urban migration and poverty: A synthesis
            of research findings, with a look at the litera-
            ture." A paper presented at the Annual Meeting
            of the American Sociological Association (August
            30-September 2) Denver, Colorado. (A)

Pritzker, Leon and N. D. Rothwell
    1968   "Procedural difficulties in taking past censuses
            in predominately Negro, Puerto Rican, and
            Mexican areas." Pp. 55-79 in David M. Heer
            (ed.), Social Statistics and the City.
            Cambridge, Massachusetts: MIT - Harvard Joint
            Center for Urban Studies.

Quarton, Gardner C.
    1968   "Deliberate efforts to control human behavior
            and modify personality." Pp. 205-221 in Daniel
            Bell (ed.), Toward the Year 2000. Boston:
            Houghton Mifflin Company.

Rappaport, Carl
  * 1971   "A framework for evaluating the impact of the
            model cities program." A paper presented at the
            National Meeting of the Operations Research
            Society of America, (October 28-30) Detroit,
            Michigan. (M, P, A)

Ratajczak, Rosalinda
  * 1969   "Problems in the evaluation of poverty pro-
            grams." Working paper. Santa Monica,
            California: System Development Corporation.
            (P, D, A)

Ray, Paul H.
  * 1968   "Human ecology, technology, and the need for
            social planning." The American Behavioral Sci-
            entist 11 (July-August):16-19. (C, M)

Raymond, Robert S. and Elizabeth Richards
* 1971   "Social indicators and business decisions."
         Michigan State University Business Topics
         (Autumn):42-46.   (CS, P)

Redick, Richard
* 1971   1970 Census Data Used to Indicate Areas with
         Different Potentials for Mental Health and Re-
         lated Problems.   No. 3 of Series C, "Mental
         Health Statistics," National Institute of Mental
         Health Series.   Public Health Service Publica-
         tion No. 2171.   Stock number 1724-0131, 1971
         0-426-439.   Washington, D.C.:   U.S. Government
         Printing Office.   (C, M)

Reed, John Shelton
   1971   "To live--and die--in Dixie: A contribution to
          the Study of Southern violence."   Political Sci-
          ence Quarterly 86 (September):429-443.

Reeder, William W. and Nelson L. LeRay
* 1971   "Some implications of social theory for public
         policy."   A paper presented at the Annual
         Meeting of the Rural Sociological Society
         (August) Denver, Colorado.   (C)

Reiquam, Howard
   1971   "Establishing priority ranking among environmen-
          tal stresses."   A paper presented at the Ameri-
          can Association for the Advancement of Science
          Symposium, Indications of Environmental Quality
          (December 27) Philadelphia,

Report of the Advisory Council on Public Welfare
   1966   Having the Power, We Have the Duty.   Report to
          the Secretary of Health, Education, and Welfare,
          U.S. Department of Health, Education, and
          Welfare, Welfare Administration, Washington,
          D.C., (June 29).

The Report of the President's Task Force on Science Policy
   1970   Science and Technology: Tools for Progress.
          (April) Washington, D.C.:   The U.S. Government
          Printing Office.

Review Symposium
    1970   The Behavioral and Social Sciences: Outlook and
            Needs and Sociology. Reviews by Philip M.
            Hauser, Charles P. Loomis, Alvin W. Gouldner,
            and Kenneth Lutterman. American Sociological
            Review 35:329- 341.

Rice, Stuart A.
 * 1967   "Social accounting and statistics for the great
            society." Public Administration Review 27
            (June):169-174. (C, D)

Richard, Robert
 * 1969   Subjective Social Indicators. Chicago,
            Illinois: National Opinion Research Center,
            University of Chicago. (M, CS)

Richta, Radovan and Oto Sulc
 * 1969   "Forecasting and the scientific and
            technological revolution." International Social
            Science Journal 21:563-573. (GT)

Ridley, Clarence E. and Herbert A. Simon
 * 1938   Measuring Municipal Activities: A Survey of
            Suggested Criteria and Reporting Forms for
            Appraising Administration. Chicago, Illinois:
            The International City Managers' Association.
            (A, M)

Riecken, Henry W.
 * 1969   "Social sciences and social problems." Social
            Science Information 8 (February-June):101-129.
            (CS)

    1971   "The federal government and social science
            policy." The Annals of the American Academy of
            Political and Social Science 394
            (March):100-113.

Riesman, David
    1968   "Notes on meritocracy." Pp. 265-276 in Daniel
            Bell (ed.), Toward the Year 2000. Boston:
            Houghton Mifflin Company.

Robinson, John P.
    1969   "Social change as measured by time budgets."
            Journal of Leisure Research 1 (Winter):75-77.

Robinson, John P., Jerrold G. Rusk and Kendra B. Head
    1968   Measures of Political Attitudes. Ann Arbor,
            Michigan: Survey Research Center.

Robinson, John P. and Phillip R. Shaver
    1969   Measures of Social Psychological Attitudes. Ann
            Arbor, Michigan: Survey Research Center.

Robinson, John P., Robert Athanasiou and Kendra B. Head
    1969   Measures of Occupational Attitudes and
            Occupational Characteristics. Ann Arbor,
            Michigan: Survey Research Center. .

Rochberg, Richard, Theodore J. Gordon and Olaf Helmer
    * 1970   The Use of Cross-Impact Matrices for Forecasting
            and Planning. (April) Middletown, Connecticut:
            Institute for the Future, Riverview Center. (M)

Rogers, Carl R.
    * 1968   "Interpersonal relationships: U.S.A. 2000."
            Journal of Applied and Behavioral Science 4
            (July-September):265-279.   (C)

Rogers, Everett M.
    1969   Modernization Among Peasants: The Impact of
            Communication. New York: Holt, Rinehart and
            Winston, Inc.

Rohrlich, George
    1970   Social Economics for the 1970's. Cambridge,
            Massachusetts: Harvard University Press.

Rokeach, Milton and Seymour Parker
    * 1970   "Values as social indicators of poverty and race
            relations in America." The Annals of the Ameri-
            can Academy of Political and Social Science 388
            (March):97-111.   (A, C, D)

Rose, Richard
    1972   "The market for policy indicators." In Andrew

Shonfield and Stella Shaw (eds.), Social
Indicators and Social Policy. London, England:
Heinemann Educational Books Limited. (In press)

Rosenthal, Robert A. and Robert S. Weiss
* 1969   "Problems of organizational feedback processes."
         Pp. 302-340 in Raymond A. Bauer (ed.), Social
         Indicators. Cambridge, Massachusetts:
         Massachusetts Institute of Technology Press.
         (P)

Ross, M. R.
    1971   "Life style of the coal miner: America's origi-
           nal hard hat." Appalachia Medicine (March):3-9.

Rossi, Peter H.
    1970   Community Social Indicators. Report No. 85.
           Baltimore, Maryland: The Johns Hopkins Univer-
           sity Center for the Study of Social Organization
           of Schools.

Rostow, Eugene V.
    1968   "Thinking about the future of international
           society." Pp. 310-314 in Daniel Bell (ed.),
           Toward the Year 2000. Boston: Houghton Mifflin
           Company.

Roterus, Victor
* 1946   "Effects of population growth and non-growth on
         the well-being of cities." American
         Sociological Review 11 (February):90-97. (A)

Rothenberg, Jerome
    1965   "Urban renewal programs." In Robert Dorfman
           (ed.), Measuring Benefits of Government
           Investments. Washington, D.C.: Brookings
           Institution.

Roumyantzev, A. M.
    1970   "Social prediction and planning in the USSR." A
           paper presented at the Seventh World Congress of
           Sociology (September 14-19) Varna, Bulgaria.

Rummel, Rudolph J.
    1963   "Dimensions of conflict behavior within and be-

tween nations." Yearbook of the Society for
General Systems Research 8:25-26.

1965   "A field theory of social action with applica-
        tion to conflict within nations." Yearbook of
        the Society for General Systems Research
        10:189-195.

* 1969 "Indicators of cross-national and international
        patterns." American Political Science Review 63
        (March):127-147.   (M, C, A)

Runciman, W. G.
    1966   Relative Deprivation and Social Justice: A
            Study of Attitudes to Social Inequality in
            Twentieth-Century England. Berkeley,
            California: University of California Press.

Russett, Bruce M.
* 1970 "Indicators for America's linkages with the
        changing world." The Annals of the American
        Academy of Political and Social Science 388
        (March):82-96.   (M, CS)

Russett, Bruce M. and Robert Bunselmeyer
* 1964 World Handbook of Political and Social
        Indicators. New Haven: Yale University Press.
        (A, M)

Sametz, A. W.
* 1968 "Production of goods and services: The measure-
        ment of economic growth." Pp. 77-96 in Eleanor
        B. Sheldon and Wilbert E. Moore (eds.),
        Indicators of Social Change: Concepts and Meas-
        urements. New York: Russell Sage Foundation.
        (A, P)

Samuelson, Robert J.
* 1967 "Council of social advisers: New approach to
        welfare priorities?" Science 157 (July-August):
        49-50.   (P, C)

Sanders, Barkev S.
* 1964 "Measuring community health levels." American
        Journal of Public Health 54 (July):1063-1070.
        (A, C)

Sanders, Irwin T.
* 1958 "Theories of community development." Rural So-
        ciology 23 (March):1-12.   (GT)

Saunders, Lyle
    1954   Cultural Difference and Medical Care.   New York:
            Russell Sage Foundation.

Sawchuk, R. and A. George Gitter
  * 1971   Eight Subjective Indicators of Quality of Life.
            Communication Research Center.   Report No. 51.
            Boston: Boston University.   (C, M)

Sayre, Nora
    1966   "Predicting delinquency."   New Statesman 72
            (July 22):125.

Scammon, Richard M.
  * 1967   "Electoral participation."   The Annals of the
            American Academy of Political and Social Science
            371 (May):59-71.   (Also Pp. 81-97 in Bertram M.
            Gross (ed.), Social Intelligence for America's
            Future: Explorations in Societal Problems.
            Boston: Allyn and Bacon.)   (A, P)

Schatz, Gerald S.
  * 1970   "Spectrum management: The problems of defining
            the public interest."   National Academy of Sci-
            ences News Report 20 (October):1, 4-5.   (CS)

Scherer, Frederic
    1965   "Government research and development programs."
            In Robert Dorfman (ed.), Measuring Benefits of
            Government Investments.   Washington, D.C.:
            Brookings Institution.

Schick, Allan
    1971   "From analysis to evaluation."   The Annals of
            the American Academy of Political and Social
            Science 394 (March):57-71.

Schmandt, H. J. and R. G. Stephens
    1963   Local Government Expenditure Patterns in the
            United States.   Land Economics 39:397-406.

Schmid, A. Allan
  * 1969   "Developing community spending priorities."   A

paper presented at Central Michigan Leadership
Program (December 4) Mount Pleasant, Michigan.
(P)

Schneier, Edward
  * 1970   "The intelligence of congress: Information and
            public policy patterns." The Annals of the
            American Academy of Political and Social Science
            388 (March):14-29.   (CS)

Schnore, Leo F.
  * 1961   "The myth of human ecology." Sociological
            Inquiry 31 (Spring):128-139.   (GT, C)

Schon, Donald A.
    1968   "Forecasting and technological forecasting."
            Pp. 127-138 in Daniel Bell (ed.), Toward the
            Year 2000. Boston: Houghton Mifflin Company.

Schussheim, Morton J.
    1969   Toward a New Housing Policy; The Legacy of the
            Sixties. CED Supplementary paper No. 29. New
            York: (New York) Committee for Economic Devel-
            opment.

    1970   "Housing in perspective." The Public Interest
            19 (Spring):18-30.

    1971   "National goals and local practices: Joining
            ends and means in housing." Pp. 141-158 in U.S.
            92nd Congress, 1st Session. House of Represent-
            atives. Committee on Banking and Currency.
            Papers submitted to Subcommittee on Housing
            Panels on Housing Production, Housing Demand,
            and Developing a Suitable Living Environment,
            Part 1. (June) Washington, D.C.: U.S. Govern-
            ment Printing Office.

Schwartz, Arthur
  * 1970   "PPBS and evaluation and research: Problems and
            promises." Pp. 35-41 in Edward E. Schwartz
            (ed.), Planning-Programming-Budgeting Systems
            and Social Welfare. Chicago, Illinois: The
            University of Chicago, The School of Social
            Service Administration. (P, A, C)

Schwartz, Edward E. (ed.)
  * 1970   Planning-Programming-Budgeting Systems and

Social Welfare. Chicago, Illinois: The University of Chicago, The School of Social Service Administration. (P, M, C)

Schwartz, Mildred A.
* 1967 Trends in White Attitudes toward Negroes. Chicago, Illinois: National Opinion Research Center, The University of Chicago. (A, M)

Scott, Stanley and Edward L. Feder
1957 Factors Associated with Variations in Municipal Expenditure Levels. Berkeley, California: University of California Press.

Sewell, William H., Leonard A. Marscuilo and Harold W. Pfautz
1967 "Review symposium." American Sociological Review 32 (June):475-483.

Shanks, J. Merrill
1971 "Toward the development of model social indicators." Berkeley, California: Survey Research Center.

Shariff, Zahid
* 1971 "Social information and government-sponsored development: A case study from West Pakistan." The Annals of the American Academy of Political and Social Science 393 (January):92-108. (CS, A)

Sheldon, Eleanor Bernert
1967 "Social indicators." Pp. 171-188 in Proceeding of the Social Statistics Section, American Statistical Association, Washington, D.C.

* 1971 "Social reporting for the 1970's." Pp. 403-435 in Volume II, Federal Statistics: A Report of the President's Commission. Washington, D.C.: U.S. Government Printing Office. (P, CS)

Sheldon, Eleanor Bernert and Howard E. Freeman
* 1970 "Notes on social indicators: Promises and potential." Policy Sciences 1 (April):97-111. (CS)

Sheldon, Eleanor B. and Wilbert E. Moore
  1966   "Toward the measurement of social change: Im-
          plications for progress." Pp. 185-217 in
          Leonard Goodman (ed.), Economic Progress and
          Social Welfare. New York: Columbia University
          Press.

  * 1968a Indicators of Social Change: Concepts and Meas-
          urements. New York: Russell Sage Foundation.
          (C, P)

  * 1968b "Monitoring social change in American society."
          Pp. 3-26 in Eleanor B. Sheldon and Wilbert Moore
          (eds.), Indicators of Social Change: Concepts
          and Measurements. New York: Russell Sage Foun-
          dation. (A, P)

Shinn, Allen M., Jr.
  * 1971a "Magnitude estimation: Some applications to
          social indicators." A paper presented at the
          Annual Meeting of the American Political Science
          Association (September) Chicago, Illinois. (M)

  * 1971b "Measuring the utility of housing:
          Demonstrating a methodological approach."
          Social Science Quarterly (June):88-102. (M)

Shiskin, Julius
  1970   "Strengthening federal statistics." The Ameri-
          can Statistician 24 (February):15-20.

Shonfield, Andrew
  * 1969   "Thinking about the future." Encounter 32
          (February):15-26. (CS)

Shonfield, Andrew and Stella Shaw (eds.)
  1972   Social Indicators and Social Policy. London,
          England: Heinemann Educational Books Limited.
          In press.

Shubik, Martin
  1968   "Information, rationality, and free choice in a
          future democratic society." Pp. 139-146 in
          Daniel Bell (ed.), Toward the Year 2000.
          Boston: Houghton Mifflin Company.

Shults, Wilbur D. and J. Beauchamp
  1971   "Statistically based air quality indices." A

paper presented at the Annual Meeting of the
American Association for the Advancement of Science (December 27) Philadelphia, Pennsylvania.
(tm, A, D)

Shultz, James and Marge Shultz
 * 1970   "An annotated review of the literature on
          volunteering." (October) Washington, D.C.:
          Center for a Voluntary Society, NTL Institute
          for Applied Behavioral Science. (R)

Siegel, Jacob S.
   1968   "Completeness of coverage of the nonwhite popu-
          lation in the 1960 census and current estimates,
          and some implications." Pp. 13-54 in David M.
          Heer (ed.), Social Statistics and the City.
          Cambridge, Massachusetts: M.I.T - Harvard Joint
          Center for Urban Studies.

Siegel, Jacob S. and Melvin Feinik
   1968   "An evaluation of coverage in the 1960 census of
          population by techniques of demographic analysis
          and by composite methods." Pp. 132-173 in David
          M. Heer (ed.), Social Statistics and the City.
          Cambridge, Massachusetts: Massachusetts
          Institute of Technology - Harvard Joint Center
          for Urban Studies.

Sill, Maurice L., O. Norman Simpkins and Richard O.
Comfort
   1972   "Measurement in neighborhood development: An
          effort at exploring 'scale' as a frame of refer-
          ence for local level development with implica-
          tions for extension evaluation and an invitation
          for further discussion." A paper presented at
          the Rural Sociology Section of the Association
          of Southern Agricultural Workers Meeting (Febru-
          ary 13-16) Richmond, Virginia.

Sills, David Lawrence
 * 1971   "Unanticipated consequences of population
          policies." A paper presented at the Annual
          Meeting of the Population Association of America
          (April 24) Washington, D.C. (CS)

Simmons, James
   1970   "Interaction patterns." Urban Affairs Quarterly
          6 (December):213-232.

Simon, Rita James
* 1971   "Public attitudes toward population and
           pollution." The Public Opinion Quarterly 35
           (Spring):93-99. (A)

Singer, Fred S.
* 1971   "Can we develop an index for quality of life?"
           Science 173 (September 24):1253-1254. (CS)

Singh, R. N. and Kenneth P. Wilkinson
  1971   "A behavioral measure of levels of involvement."
           A paper presented at the Annual Meeting of the
           American Sociological Association (August
           30-September 2) Denver, Colorado.

Sloan, Helen W.
* 1970   Social Change, Quality of Life, and Urban
           Affairs: A Selective Bibliography of Current
           Popular Literature. (April) Nashville,
           Tennessee: Center for Community Studies. (B)

Smith, Courtland L. and Thomas C. Hogg
* 1971a   "Benefits and beneficiaries: Contrasting eco-
           nomic and cultural distinctions." Water Re-
           sources Research 7 (April):254-263. (CS)

* 1971b   "Cultural aspects of water resource development
           past, present, and future." Water Resources
           Bulletin 7 (August):652-660. (P)

Smith, David Horton and Alex Inkeles
* 1966   "The OM scale: A comparative socio-
           psychological measure of individual modernity."
           Sociometry 29 (December):353-377. (A, M)

  1970   "Individual modernizing experience and overall
           modernity scores: Validation of the OM scales."
           Unpublished manuscript. Cambridge,
           Massachusetts: Harvard University.

Snelling, W. Rodman, Robert F. Boruch and Nancy B. Boruch
* 1971   "Science graduates of private and selective
           liberal arts colleges." College and University
           46 (Spring):231-244. (R, A)

Soderlind, Sterling E.
* 1970   "The outlook: Appraisal of current trends in
          business and finance." Wall Street Journal 51
          (Monday, November 2) Number 14:1. (CS)

Somit, Albert
    1971 Political Science and the Study of the Future.
          New York: Holt, Rinehart, and Winston.

Special Commission on the Social Sciences of the National
Science Board
    1969 Knowledge into Action: Improving the Nation's
          Use of the Social Sciences. Washington, D.C.:
          U.S. Government Printing Office.

Springer, Michael
    1970a "Foreward." The Annals of the American Academy
          of Political and Social Science 388 (March):9.

  * 1970b Political Intelligence for America's Future.
          The Annals of the American Academy of Political
          and Social Science 388 (March). (CS)

  * 1970c "Social indicators, reports, and accounts:
          Toward the management of society." The Annals
          of the American Academy of Political and Social
          Science 388 (March):1-13. (P, CS)

Staats, Elmer B.
    1972 "Governmental auditing in a period of rising
          social concerns." Address by the Comptroller
          General of the United States before the Eastern
          Area Conference of the Financial Executives
          Institute (May 12) Nassau, Bahamas.

Stagner, Ross
  * 1970 "Perceptions, aspirations, frustrations, and
          satisfactions: An approach to urban
          indicators." Ekistics 30 (September):197-199.
          (Also in Bertram Gross and Michael Springer
          (eds.), The Annals: Political Intelligence for
          America's Future 388 (March):59-68). (P, M, CS)

Stanford Research Institute
  * 1969 "Toward master social indicators." Educational
          Policy Research Center. SRI Project 6747, Re-

search Memorandum EPRC-6747-2. Supported by
Bureau of Research, U.S. Office of Education.
(February) Menlo Park, California: Stanford Re-
search Institute. (GT, C)

State of Iowa Office for Planning and Programming
  * 1971   The Quality of Life in Iowa: An Economic and
            Social Report to the Governor for 1970. Des
            Moines, Iowa: State Capitol. (A)

Stein, Maurice A.
    1960   The Eclipse of Community. Princeton, New
            Jersey: Princeton University Press.

Stendahl, Krister
    1968   "Religion, mysticism, and the institutional
            church." Pp. 222-227 in Daniel Bell (ed.),
            Toward the Year 2000. Boston: Houghton Mifflin
            Company.

Stenner, Alfred J.
    1964   "On predicting our future." The Journal of Phi-
            losophy 61:415-428.

Stockdale, Jerry D.
  * 1969   "Social implications of technological change in
            agriculture." A paper presented at the Annual
            Meeting of the Rural Sociological Society
            (August 29) San Francisco, California. (CS)

Stockdale, Jerry D. and Steven Aronson
  * 1970   Technology and Societal Change: Selected
            Sources with Emphasis on Resource Allocation.
            Ithaca, New York: Cornell University. (R)

Stokes, Donald E.
    1962   "Popular evaluations of government: An empiri-
            cal assessment." Pp. 61-72 in Harlan Cleveland
            and Harold D. Lasswell (eds.), Ethics and
            Bigness: Scientific, Academic, Religious,
            Political and Military. New York, New York:
            Harper and Row, Publishers.

Stone, Richard
    1969   Educational Statistics in Relation to Systems of
            Socio-Demographic Accounts and Economic Ac-
            counts. Geneva: United Nations Statistical

376

Commission and ECE, Working Group on Statistics
and Education (jointly with UNESCO and ILO).
Conf.Eur.Stat. /WG23/11, UNESCO/STE/EUR/WG4,
12.6.69.

1972   "Social indicators." Unpublished manuscript.
        Cambridge, England: University of Cambridge.

Stouffer, Samuel, Louis Guttman, Edward A. Suchman, Paul
F. Lazarsfeld, Shirley A. Star, and John A. Clausen
    1950   Measurement and Prediction. Princeton, New
            Jersey: Princeton University Press.

Stringham, Luther W.
  * 1959   "Health, education and welfare indicators and
            trends." Pp. 216-221 in Proceedings of the
            Social Statistics Section, American Statistical
            Association, Washington, D.C. (CS)

Strumpel, Burkhard
    1970   "Indicators of changes in people's goals,
            opportunities and economic well-being." Re-
            search proposal submitted to the National Sci-
            ence Foundation, including an interview sched-
            ule.

Studer, Raymond G.
  * 1970   "Human systems design and the management of
            change." A paper presented at the Second Inter-
            national Conference on the Problems of
            Modernization in Asia and the Pacific, EAST-WEST
            Center (August 9-15) Honolulu, Hawaii. (GT)

Sulc, Oto
  * 1969   "Interactions between technological and social
            changes." Futures 1 (September):402-407. (A)

Sullivan, Daniel F.
  * 1966   Conceptual Problems in Developing an Index of
            Health. Publication No. 1000-Series 2-No. 17.
            Washington. D.C.: National Center for Health
            Statistics, Public Health Service. (C, GT, M)

Sundquist, James L.
  * 1970   "Where shall they live?" The Public Interest 18
            (Winter):88-100. (P)

Suter, Larry E.
* 1971   "A 1966 replication of the 1962 occupational
          change in a generation analysis of older men:
          Path models as indicators of social change."   A
          paper presented at the Annual Meeting of the
          Population Association of America (April 24)
          Washington, D.C.   (GT, A)

Sutton, Willis A., Jr. and Jiri Kolaja
* 1960   "The concept of community."   Rural Sociology 25
          (June): 197-203.   (C, M)

Taeuber, Conrad
    1968a "Needed innovations in 1970 census data
          collection procedures: A census view."   Pp.
          80-90 in David M. Heer (ed.), Social Statistics
          and the City.   Cambridge, Massachusetts: MIT -
          Harvard Joint Center for Urban Studies.

* 1968b   "Population: Trends and characteristics."   Pp.
          27-76 in Eleanor B. Sheldon and Wilbert E. Moore
          (eds.), Indicators of Social Change: Concepts
          and Measurements.   New York: Russell Sage Foun-
          dation.   (A, P)

    1971 "The federal government as a source of data."
          The Annals of the American Academy of Political
          and Social Science 394 (March): 114-124.

Taeuber, Karl E.
* 1970   "Toward a social report: A review article."
          The Journal of Human Resources 5
          (Summer): 354-360.   (CS)

Tait, John L. and Arthur H. Johnson
* 1971   Iowa Population Trends.   Ames, Iowa: Iowa State
          University of Science and Technology,
          Cooperative Extension Service.   (R)

Taylor, Jeremy B.
    1971 "Annotated bibliography and selected references
          on social indicators."   Compiled for use of the
          Task Force on Social Indicators, TA/PM/M.   Wash-
          ington, D.C.:   Agency for International Develop-
          ment.

Tenbruck, Friedrich H.

378

* 1970   "Limits of planning."   A paper presented at the Seventh World Congress of Sociology (September 14-19) Varna, Bulgaria.   (P, CS)

Terleckyj, Nestor
* 1970a   "Data systems for measuring social change."   A paper presented at the Annual Meeting of the American Statistical Association (December 27) Detroit, Michigan.   (CS, P)

* 1970b   "Measuring possibilities of social change." Looking Ahead (Publication of the National Planning Association) 18 (August):1-11.   (M, P)

* 1970c   "Measuring progress towards social goals: Some possibilities at national and local levels." Management Science 16 (August):B765-B778.   (CS)

* 1970d   "The role of efficiency in achieving national goals."   A paper presented at the Annual Meeting of the American Association for the Advancement of Science (December 29) Chicago, Illinois. (GT, M)

  1971   "Goals accounting project: Description of status."   November 3.   Washington, D.C.: National Planning Association.

Thomas, William A.
* 1971   "Indicators of environmental quality."   Science 174 (October 22):437-438.   (CS, C)

Thompson, Jean
* 1970   "The growth of population to the end of the century."   Pp. 21-32 in Muriel Nissel (ed.), Social Trends.   London: Her Majesty's Central Statistical Office.   (M, A)

Thorndike, E. L.
  1940   144 Smaller Cities.   New York: Harcourt, Brace and World.

Tilly, Charles and James Rule
  1965   Measuring Political Upheaval.   Princeton, New Jersey: Center of International Studies, Princeton University.

Todd, Seldon P.
* 1970   "Data sources for computing a system of social

379

indicators for the aged." A paper prepared for the Administration on Aging by the Operations Research and Policy Systems Division. Minneapolis, Minnesota: American Rehabilitation Foundation. (M, C)

Todd, Seldon and Jacqueline Anderson
* 1970   "A system of social indicators for the aged." A paper prepared for the Administration on Aging by the Operations Research and Policy Systems Division. Minneapolis, Minnesota: American Rehabilitaticn Foundation. (M, C)

Toffler, Alvin
* 1967   "The art of measuring the arts." The Annals of the American Academy of Political and Social Science 373 (September):141-155. (Reprinted in Bertram M. Gross (ed.), 1969 Social Intelligence for America's Future. Boston: Allyn and Bacon). (CS, P, M)

Tugac, Ahmet
* 1971   "Social indicators and social prediction in planning process: A review of literature and bibliography." State Planning Organization Pub. No. DPT:1124--SPD:243. Ankara, Turkey: Devlet Planlama Teskilati, Bakanliklar. (B, CS)

Tunstall, Daniel B.
* 1970a   "Developing a social statistics publication." U.S. Office of Statistical Policy. A paper presented at the Annual Meeting of the American Statistical Association (December 27-30) Detroit, Michigan. (C, P)

   1970b   "Outline for a social statistics publication." U.S. Office of Statistical Policy. A paper presented at the Annual Meeting of the American Statistical Association (December 27-30) Detroit, Michigan.

Tussing, A. Dale and John A. Henning
* 1970   "Long-run growth of non-defense government expenditures in the United States." (August, Working draft) Syracuse, New York: Educational Policy Research Center, Syracuse University Research Corporation. (GT, A, P)

Tweeten, Luther G.
* 1969   "Causes of rural poverty."   Ekistics 28
          (December):395-398.   (CS)

Udall, Stewart L.
* 1968   "Population, parenthood, and the quality of
          life."   Pp. 122-137 in Stuart Udall, 1976:
          Agenda for Tomorrow.   New York: Harcourt, Brace
          and World.   (C, P)

Ulrich, Gary
* 1969   "Indicators of equal opportunity for social
          mobility in the occupational structure."   Unpub-
          lished manuscript.   Ann Arbor, Michigan: School
          of Social Work, University of Michigan.   (A, C)

United Nations
* 1961   International Definition and Measurement of
          Levels of Living: An Interim Guide.   New York:
          United Nations.   (D, CS, M)

* 1963   Compendium of Social Statistics: 1963.   New
          York: United Nations.   (M, C)

  1966   "Purposes for which current housing statistics
          are required and the broad types of statistics
          needed for these purposes."   Conference of
          European Statisticians, Statistical Standards
          and Studies No. 7.

* 1968   Compendium of Social Statistics: 1967.   New
          York: United Nations.   (A)

  1971a   Report of the Board of the United Nations
          Institute for Social Development.   December 1,
          1969 to December 1, 1970.   New York: United
          Nations.

  1971b   Social Indicators Development Programme.   Note
          by the Secretariat.   OECD, Social Affairs Divi-
          sion.   August 9.   New York: United Nations.

United Nations, Department of Economic and Social Affairs
* 1964   Handbook of Household Surveys.   New York:
          United Nations.   (M, A)

United Nations, Department of Social Affairs
  1963   1963 Report on the World Social Situation.   New
          York: United Nations Publications.

* 1966 "European programme of current housing statistics." Pp. 1-5 in Conference of European
Statisticians: Statistical Standards and Studies - No. 7 ST/ECE/HOU/29 ST/CES/7. Sales No.
66. II. Mim. 42. New York: United Nations.
(D, C, M, A)

* 1967a "Statistics needed for educational planning."
Pp. 118-150. Conference of European
Statisticians: Statistical Standards and Stud-
ies No. 11. ST/CES/11, Vol. 2. New York:
United Nations. (M, A, D, P)

1967b "Statistics of the educational system." Pp.
59-96. Conference of European Statisticians:
Statistics of the Educational System. ST/CE
S/10. Sales No. 67. II. E/MiM 60. New York:
United Nations.

1967c "Statistical requirements for the promotion of
health." Pp. 151-158. Conference of European
Statisticians: Statistical Standards and Studies No. 11. ST/CES/11, Vol. 2. New York:
United Nations.

United Nations Economic and Social Council
1970 An Integrated System of Demographic, Manpower
and Social Statistics and Its Links with the
System of National Economic Accounts. E/CN
.3/394, May 28. New York: United Nations.

United Nations, Report of the Secretary General
1965 Methods of Determining Social Allocations. The
Report of the Sixteenth Session of the Social
Commission, Economic and Social Council. March
31. New York: United Nations.

* 1970 "Problems of the human environment." Ekistics
29 (April):225-230. (CS)

United Nations Research Institute for Social Development
* 1970a Contents and Measurement of Socio-Economic Development: An Empirical Enquiry. Report No.
70.10. Geneva, Switzerland: United Nations Research Institute for Social Development. (A, M)

* 1970b "The concept of development and its measurement." International Social Development Review
(No. 2):1-6. (C, M)

* 1971 "Proposal for a research project on the measure-

ment of real progress at the local level." Unpublished manuscript. New York: United
Nations. UNRISD/72/C.10. (M, P)

United Nations Social Development Division
* 1969   "Social policy and the distribution of income in
          the nation." Ekistics 28 (December):399-405.
          (P)

United Nations Statistical Office
   1971   "A system of demographic, manpower and social
          statistics series, classifications and social
          indicators. Document No. ST/Stat. 49. New
          York: United Nations.

U.S. Bureau of the Census
   1969   Statistical Abstract of the United States.
          Washington, D.C.: U.S. Government Printing
          Office. (published annually).

United States Congress
   1967a   "Testimony before the Senate Subcommittee on
          Government Research of the Committee on govern-
          ment operations: A bill to create a national
          foundation for the social sciences." American
          Psychologist 22 (November):915-969.

   1967b   "Testimony before the Senate Subcommittee on
          Government Research of the Committee on govern-
          ment operations: Full opportunity and social
          accounting act." American Psychologist 22
          (November):977- 1035.

U.S. Congress, Joint Economic Committee
   1969   The Analysis and Evaluation of Public
          Expenditures: The PPB System. Vols. 1, 2, and
          3. Washington, D.C.: U.S. Government Printing
          Office.

U.S. Council of Economic Advisers
   1970   Economic Indicators. Washington, D.C.: U.S.
          Government Printing Office. (published
          monthly).

U.S. Department of Agriculture
* 1969a   "Rural development program." (November 7) Wash-
          ington, D.C.: Office of the Secretary, U.S. De-
          partment of Agriculture. (P)

* 1969b   Some Notes on Quality of Rural Living. Seminar
          during the meeting of the Northeast Rural Soci-
          ology Committee (April 3) Federal Extension
          Service, United States Department of
          Agriculture, Washington, D.C. ER&E-52 (6/69).
          (C, CS)

  1971   Rural Development: Information and Technical
          Assistance Delivered by the Department of
          Agriculture in Fiscal Year 1971. A report to
          the congress as requested by Title IX, Section
          901(d) of the Agricultural Act of 1970.

U.S. Department of Agriculture, Economic Development Division
* 1971   Rural Development Chartbook. March. Washing-
          ton, D.C.: United States Department of
          Agriculture, Economic Development Division, Eco-
          nomic Research Service. (A)

U.S. Department of Commerce
  1960   Historical Statistics of the United States,
          Colonial Times to 1957. Washington, D.C.: U.S.
          Government Printing Office.

  1962   Statistical Abstract of the United States, 1962.
          Washington, D.C.: U.S. Government Printing
          Office.

U.S. Department of Commerce, Bureau of the Census
* 1968   Report on National Needs for Criminal Justice
          Statistics. (August) Washington, D.C.: U.S.
          Department of Commerce. (A, C)

* 1971a   Environmental Quality Control: Expenditure for
          Selected Large Governmental Units: Fiscal Year
          1968-69. State and Local Government Special
          Studies No. 57. Washington, D.C.: U.S. Govern-
          ment Printing Office. (A)

* 1971b   National Data Needs: Fire Service Statistics.
          Washington, D.C.: U.S. Department of Commerce.
          (A)

U.S. Department of Health, Education, and Welfare
* 1963   New Directions in Health, Education, and
          Welfare. Washington, D.C.: U.S. Government
          Printing Office. (R)

1964   Medical Care, Health Status, and Family Income. Series 10, No. 9. Washington, D.C.: U.S. National Center for Health Statistics.

1965a   An Index of Health: Mathematical Models. National Center for Health Statistics, Series 2, Number 5. Washington, D.C.: U.S. Government Printing Office.

1965b   "The health, education and welfare of the nation in retrospect and prospect." U.S. Department of Health, Education and Welfare. Health, Education and Welfare Trends, Part 1: National Trends. Washington, D.C.: U.S. Government Printing Office. 1964-65:S-1-S-120.

1966a   Conceptual Problems in Developing an Index of Health. National Center for Health Statistics, Series 2, Number 17. Washington, D.C.: U.S. Government Printing Office.

1966b   Program Analysis: Disease Control Programs, 1966. Washington, D.C.: Department of Health, Education, and Welfare. Nos. 1-5.

1967   Health, Education and Welfare Indicators. Washington, D.C.: U.S. Government Printing Office. (published monthly between September 1960 through February 1967).

1968   Fifty City Profile (1968). Washington, D.C.: Department of Health, Education, and Welfare.

1969   Toward a Social Report. Washington, D.C.: U.S. Government Printing Office.

* 1970   Social Indicators for the Aged. (October) Minneapolis, Minnesota: Quantitative Social Planning Division, Institute for Interdisciplinary Studies, American Rehabilitation Foundation. (A)

U.S. Department of Health, Education and Welfare, National Committee on Vital and Health Statistics of the Public Health Service
    1970   Report of the Twentieth Anniversary Conference. National Center for Health Statistics, Series 4, #13 (September).

U.S. Department of Housing and Urban Development
    1968   Urban and Regional Information Systems: Support
            for Planning in Metropolitan Areas. Washington,
            D.C.: U.S. Government Printing Office. (R)

U.S. Department of Labor
    1965   "The Negro family: The case for national
            action." Washington, D.C.: U.S. Department of
            Labor, Office of Policy Planning and Research.

U.S. Department of Labor, Bureau of Labor Statistics
  * 1970   Three Budgets for a Retired Couple in Urban
            Areas of the United States 1967-68. Bulletin
            1570-6. Washington, D.C.: U.S. Government
            Printing Office. (Supplement included) (A)

U.S. Department of Labor/Workplace Standards Administration
  * 1970   State Economic and Social Indicators. Workplace
            Standards Administration, Bureau of Labor Stan-
            dards, Bulletin 328. Washington, D.C.: U.S.
            Government Printing Office. (A)

U.S. President, Research Commission on National Goals
  * 1960   Goals for Americans: Programs for Action in the
            Sixties. Englewood Cliffs, New Jersey:
            Prentice-Hall. (P, C)

U.S. President, Research Committee on Social Trends
    1933   Recent Social Trends in the United States. New
            York: McGraw-Hill.

    1962   Manpower Report of the President. Washington,
            D.C.: U.S. Government Printing Office.

    1969   Statement by the President on the Establishment
            of a National Goals Research Staff - July 13,
            1969.

United States Senate
  * 1967a   Hearings before the 90th Congress - 1st Session.
            Congressional Record 113 (February 6, June 19).
            (CS)

    1967b   "S. 836: National foundation for the social
            sciences act of 1966." American Psychologist 22
            (November):911-914.

386

1967c   "S. 843: Full opportunity and social accounting act." American Psychologist 22 (November): 974-976.

1968   Hearings before the 90th Congress - 2nd Session. Congressional Record 114 (May 8, June 3). (CS)

1969a   "Full opportunity act." House of Representatives Bill #9483. 91st Congress - 1st Session (March).

 * 1969b   "Full opportunity and social accounting act." House of Representatives Bill #10116, 91st Congress - 1st Session (April). (P)

 * 1969c   Hearings before the 91st Congress - 1st Session. Congressional Record 115 (January 15, January 22, January 23, February 4, February 7, February 25, March 4, March 24, March 25, March 26, March 27, October 27, December 16). (CS)

U.S. Senate Bill #S.843
   1967   "The full opportunity and social accounting act of 1967." American Psychologist 22 (November):974- 983.

United States Senate, Committee on Labor and Public Welfare
 * 1971   Full Opportunity and National Goals and Priorities Act. Hearings before the Special Subcommittee on Evaluation and Planning of Social Programs, on S.5, 92nd Congress, 1st Session. (CS, P, B)

United States Senate Committee on Public Welfare
 * 1970   Full Opportunity Act. Hearings before the special subcommittee on Evaluation and Planning of Social Problems, on S.5, 91st Congress, 1st and 2nd Session. (P, CS, B)

United States Senate, Subcommittee on Government Research of the Committee on Government Operations
 * 1967   Full Opportunity and Social Accounting Act - Seminar. Hearings before the Subcommittee on Government Research of the Committee on Government Operations, 90th Congress, 1st Session on S.843. Washington, D.C.: U.S. Government Printing Office. (CS, P, GT)

The Urban Institute
* 1971   "Developing urban indicators: Some first
         steps." Search/A Report from the Urban
         Institute (May-June):3-6.   (CS)

Utah State Planning Coordinator
    1970   Utah Multi-County Districts for Planning and De-
           velopment. Salt Lake City, Utah: Office of the
           Governor.

Vandermark, Elzo
* 1970   "Measuring the quality of urban environment."
         Australian Journal of Social Issues 5:179-200.
         (CS)

    1972   "G.N.P. - The modern golden calf." Australian
           Journal of Social Issues 7 (February).

Van Til, Sally Bould and Jon Van Til
* 1971   "The lower class and the future of inequality."
         A paper presented at the Annual Meeting of the
         American Sociological Association (August)
         Denver, Colorado.   (GT, CS, P)

Van Valey, Thomas L.
* 1971   "Industrialization and urbanization: An empiri-
         cal assessment of two models." A paper present-
         ed at the Annual Meeting of the Rural
         Sociological Society (August) Denver, Colorado.
         (C, A)

Vayda, Andrew P.
    1969   Environment and Cultural Behavior: Ecological
           Studies in Cultural Anthropology. Garden City,
           New York: The Natural History Press.

Verba, Sidney
* 1967   "Democratic participation." The Annals of the
         American Academy of Political and Social Science
         373 (September):53-78. (Reprinted in Bertram M.
         Gross (ed.), 1969 Social Intelligence for
         America's Future. Boston: Allyn and Bacon).
         (P, C)

Ver Eecke, Wilfried
* 1970   "Law, morality, and society: Reflections on
         violence." Ethics 80 (January):140-145.   (C)

Vestermark, S. D., Jr.
    1968a   Indicators of Social Vulnerability. McLean,
             Virginia: Human Science Research, Inc.

 * 1968b   "Social indicators of social effects and the
           social inventory after attack." Pp. 327-363 in
           Proceedings of the Symposium on Postattack Re-
           covery from Nuclear War, held at Fort Monroe,
           Virginia, November 6-9, 1967, under auspices of
           Advisory Committee on Civil Defense, Advisory
           Committee on Emergency Planning, Office of Civil
           Defense, and Office of Emergency Planning.
           Washington, D.C.: National Academy of Sciences.
           (C, M)

Vlachos, Evan and Bert Ellenbogen
 * 1971   "Organizational aspects of irrigation systems."
           A paper presented at the Annual Meeting of the
           Rural Sociological Society (August) Denver,
           Colorado. (C)

Voight, Robert B.
 * 1970   "Costs, response rates, and other aspects of
           data collection in the 1970 census." A paper
           presented at the Annual Meeting of the American
           Statistical Association (December 28) Detroit,
           Michigan. (M)

Wallis, George W.
    1971   "Dynamic assessments and social change." A
            paper presented at the Annual Meeting of the
            American Sociological Association (August)
            Denver, Colorado.

Warner, W. Keith
    1971   "The structural matrix of development." In
            George M. Beal, Ronald C. Powers, and E. Walter
            Coward, Jr. (eds.), Perspectives on Domestic De-
            velopment. Ames, Iowa: Iowa State University
            Press.

Warren, Roland L.
 * 1965   "Types of purposive social change at the
           community level." No. 11 Brandeis University
           Papers in Social Welfare. Waltham,
           Massachusetts: The Florence Heller Graduate
           School for Advanced Studies in Social Welfare.
           (C, D)

* 1970a   "The good community--What would it be?"   Journal
          of Community Development Society 1
          (Spring):14-24.   (C)

  1970b   "Toward a non-utopian normative model of the
          community." American Sociological Review 35
          (April):219-228.

Wasserman, Paul and Fred S. Silander
  1964   Decision-Making: An Annotated Bibliography,
          Supplement 1958-1963. Ithaca, New York: Gradu-
          ate School of Business and Public Administra-
          tion, Cornell University.

Wasson, K. William and Harold J. O'Connell
  * 1971   "Social indicators: The bibliographic review as
          a first step toward scientific inquiry." Unpub-
          lished paper. Department of Sociology. Ames,
          Iowa: Iowa State University. (CS)

Waterston, Albert
  * 1965   "What do we know about planning?" International
          Development Review 7 (December):2-10.   (P, GT)

Watt, Kenneth
  * 1970   "A model of society." Simulation 14 (April):
          153-164.   (GT, C)

Wayman, Morris
  * 1971a   "Socio-ecologic analysis in industrial
          enterprise development planning." A paper pre-
          sented at the Conference on Environmental
          Studies-The Role of the University (May 19-21)
          Toronto, Canada. (A, P)

  1971b   "Towards a technology of social responsibility -
          I. Problems in the identification of acceptable
          net benefit-risk ratios." Socio-Economic
          Planning Sciences 5 (October):483-489.

Webber, Melvin M.
  * 1965   "The roles of intelligence systems in urban-
          systems planning." Journal of the American
          Institute of Planners 31 (November):289-296.
          (C, P)

Weisbrod, Burton
    1965   "Preventing high school dropouts." In Robert
            Dorfman (ed.), Measuring Benefits of Government
            Investment. Washington, D.C.: Brookings Insti-
            tution.

Weiss, S. F., T. G. Donnelly and E. S. Kaiser
    1966   "Land value and land development influence
            factors: An analytical approach for examining
            policy alternatives." Land Economics
            42:230-233.

Welch, F.
    1970   "The NBER approach to human resource problems."
            A paper presented at the American Economic Asso-
            ciation Meetings (December) Detroit, Michigan.

Wells, Alan
  * 1971   "Nation-building models and the Nigerian
            dilemma." A paper presented at the Annual
            Meeting of the American Sociological Association
            (August 30-September 2) Denver, Colorado. (C,
            A, P)

Werlin, Robert J.
    1970   "Political power and the great society: A re-
            sponse to Etzioni." Sociological Inquiry
            40:126-129.

Westat Research, Inc., Data Services Division
    1971   "Social indicators report: Revealing statisti-
            cal measures computed from 1970 census data."
            Rockville, Maryland: Westat Research, Inc.,
            Data Services Division. (a brochure)

Wheeler, David N.
  * 1971   "The measurement of job relatedness for
            vocational program evaluation." Minneapolis,
            Minnesota: University of Minnesota, Minnesota
            Research Coordinating Unit for Vocational Educa-
            tion. (M, CS)

Wheeler, Stanton
    1967   "Criminal statistics: A reformulation of the
            problem." The Journal of Criminal Law,

Criminology and Police Science 58
(1967):327-334.

Wheelock, Gerald
* 1969   "National agricultural structure and its rela-
           tion to agricultural productivity: A Cross
           National Study." Unpublished manuscript.
           Ithaca, New York: Cornell University, Depart-
           ment of Rural Sociology. (M, C)

Whitehead, F. E.
* 1971   "Trends in certificated sickness absence."
           Social Trends No. 2:13-23. (M)

Widdison, Harold A. and James K. Skipper, Jr.
* 1971   "The use of an interval scale technique with
           occupational prestige rankings." A paper pre-
           sented at the Annual Meeting of the American
           Sociological Association (August 30-September 2)
           Denver, Colorado. (M)

Wilbur, George L.
* 1971   "Determinants of poverty." A paper prepared for
           the joint session of American Sociological Asso-
           ciation and the Rural Sociological Society
           (August 30) Denver, Colorado. (M)

Wilcox, Leslie D.
  1972   "Social indicator models in rural community de-
           velopment." In preparation for publication in
           the Russell Sage Foundation monograph, Social
           Indicator models.

Wilcox, Leslie D. and Gerald E. Klonglan
  1972   "Measure of social change: Social indicators."
           A paper presented at the seminar on Rural
           Community Development: Focus on Iowa. Iowa
           State University: Center for Agricultural and
           Rural Development.

Wilcox, Leslie D. and Ralph M. Brooks
* 1971a   "Social indicators: An alternative approach for
           future research." A paper presented at the
           Annual Meeting of the Rural Sociological Society
           (august 27-30) Denver, Colorado. (M, C, D)

* 1971b   "Toward the development of social indicators for
           policy planning." A paper presented at the Ohio
           Valley Sociological Society (April) Cleveland,
           Ohio. (P, CS, D)

Wilcox, Leslie D., Ralph M. Brooks, George M. Beal and
Gerald E. Klonglan
    1972a   "Social and economic indicators of rural devel-
            opment from a sociological viewpoint: A sug-
            gested empirical approach." A paper presented
            at the Association of Southern Agricultural
            Workers Conference (February) Richmond,
            Virginia.

    1972b   Social Indicators and Societal Monitoring: An
            Annotated Bibliography. Amsterdam: Elsevier
            Publishing Company.

*   1972c   "Social indicators: Recent trends and select
            bibliography." Sociological Inquiry 42
            (Winter):37-50. (B, CS)

Wilensky, Harold L.
* 1967   Organizational Intelligence: Knowledge and
           Policy in Government and Industry. New York:
           Basic Books. (P, A)

* 1970   "Intelligence in industry: The uses and abuses
           of experts." The Annals of the American Academy
           of Political and Social Science 388
           (March):46-58. (P, C)

Wiles, Peter
* 1971   "Crisis prediction." The Annals of the American
           Academy of Political and Social Science 393
           (January):32-39. (CS)

Willhelm, Sidney M.
* 1964   "The concept of the 'ecological complex': A
           critique." The American Journal of Economics
           and Sociology 23 (July):241-249. (C, GT, M)

Williams, Anne S.
    1971   "Adequacy of community services: A measurement
            problem." In Working Papers on Rural Community
            Services compiled by S. M. Leadley, Department
            of Agricultural Economics and Rural Sociology,
            The Pennsylvania State University for the
            National Workshop on Problems of Research on De-

livery of Community Services in Rural Areas (December 13-16) Lincoln, Nebraska.

Williams, Anne S. and William R. Lassey
* 1971   "Pluralistic leadership and area development."
          A paper presented at the Annual Meeting of the
          Rural Sociological Society (August 27-29)
          Denver, Colorado. (C, A)

Williams, Faith M.
* 1956   "Standards and levels of living of city-worker
          families." Monthly Labor Review 79
          (September):1-9. Bureau of Labor Statistics.
          Reprint No. 2204. (A)

Williams, Robin M.
  1960   American Society. New York: Alfred A. Knopf.

* 1967   "Individual and group values." The Annals of
          the American Academy of Political and Social
          Science 371 (March):20-37. (Also Pp. 163-185 in
          Bertram M. Gross (ed.), Social Intelligence for
          America's Future: Explorations in Societal
          Problems. Boston: Allyn and Bacon.) (P, CS,
          D)

* 1968   "A model of society--the American case." Pp.
          32-57 in Bertram M. Gross (ed.), A Great
          Society? New York: Basic Books, Inc. (CS)

Wilson, Albert and Donna Wilson
* 1971   "Futures-orientation: Toward the
          institutionalization of change." Pp. 85-113 in
          Magoroh Maruyama and James A. Dator (eds.),
          Human Futuristics. Honolulu, Hawaii: Social
          Science Research Institute, University of
          Hawaii. (C, P)

Wilson, Ian H.
* 1971   "Futures planning: A new dimension of the
          corporate planner." Remarks made at the International Conference on Corporate Planning (December 8) Montreal. (C, P)

Wilson, James Q.
  1968   "Violence." Pp. 277-296 in Daniel Bell (ed.),
          Toward the Year 2000. Boston: Houghton Mifflin
          Company.

Wilson, John O.
    1968a   Inequality of Racial Opportunity--An Excursion
             into the New Frontier of Socioeconomic
             Indicators. New Haven: Yale University Depart-
             ment of Economics.

    1968b   "Regional differences in social welfare." A
             paper presented at the Inter-University
             Consortium for Political Research. Ann Arbor,
             Michigan.

  * 1969   Quality of Life in the United States: An
             Excursion into the New Frontier of Socio-
             Economic Indicators. Kansas City: Midwest
             Research Institute. (A, CS)

Winchester, Edward E. and Peter W. Finkel
    1970   "The role of analysis in establishing program
             priorities." Proceedings of the Association for
             Public Program Analysis.

Winthrop, Henry
  * 1968   "The sociologist and the study of the future."
             The American Sociologist 3 (May):136-145. (CS)

  * 1969   "Social costs and studies of the future."
             Futures 1 (December):488-499. (P, CS)

Wirtz, W. Willard et al.
    1970   "The case for a national social science founda-
             tion." Pp. 119-152 in Fred R. Harris (ed.),
             Social Science and National Policy. Chicago,
             Illinois: Aldine Publishing Company.

World Future Society
    1967   Futurist 1 (February).

World Health Organization
    1957   "Measurements of levels of health." In Report
             of a Study Group: World Health Organization
             Technical Report Ser. 137. New York: United
             Nations.

Wright, Arthur F. and John Whitney Hall
    1967   "Chinese and Japanese historiography: Some

Trends, 1961-1966." The Annals of the American
Academy of Political and Social Science 371
(May):178-193.

Wright, Christopher
* 1969   "Some requirements for viable social goals."
          Pp. 194-197 in R. Jungk and J. Galtung (eds.),
          Mankind-2000. London, England: Allen and
          Unwin. (P)

Yates, Aubrey J.
   1962   Frustration and Conflict. New York: Wiley.

Yoesting, Dean R., Richard D. Warren and Dan L. Burkhead
* 1971   "Leisure orientation scale--replication and
          measurement analysis." A paper presented at the
          Annual Meeting of the Rural Sociological Society
          (August) Denver, Colorado. (M)

Young, Ruth C.
* 1968   "A structural approach to development." The
          Journal of Developing Areas 2 (April):363-372.
          (C, A)

Zapf, Wolfgang
   1971a   "Social indicators: Prospects for social ac-
           counting systems?" A paper presented to the In-
           ternational Social Science Council Symposium on
           Comparative Analysis of Highly Industrialized
           Societies (August) Bellagio, Italy.

   1971b   "Some problems of time-series analysis in re-
           search on modernization." Social Science Infor-
           mation 10 (3):53-102.

   1972a   "Measuring the quality of life." A paper pre-
           sented at the Social Science Research Council
           Committee on Comparative Politics Conference (
           January) Princeton, New Jersey.

   1972b   "Work on social indicators in the German Federal
           Republic." A report on a conference (January)
           Frankfurt, Germany.

Zucker, Charles
* 1971   "Environmental measurement." New York: City
          College of the City University of New York,

School of Architecture and Environmental Studies, Urban Research Group. (GT, M)

Zweers, W.
    1971   "Research on Dutch theatre audiences."
            Sociologia Neerlandica 7:42-49.

Administration

Administration, delivery of services
Anderson, James G.	1971	(M)
Bevan, William	1971	(R)
Gordon, Andrew C. et al.	1970	(M)

Administration, municipal
Alford, Robert B.	1970	(CS)
Howard, William A.	1969	(CS)
Ridley, Clarence E. et al.	1938	(A)

Aged
Anderson, Jacqueline et al.	1969	(A)
Hawes, Mary H.	1969	(A)
Todd, Seldon P.	1970	(M)
Todd, S. and J. Anderson	1970	(M)
U.S. Dept. HEW	1970	(A)
U.S. Dept. Labor/WSA	1970	(A)

Agriculture
Stockdale, Jerry D.	1969	(CS)
Wheelock, Gerald	1969	(M)

Air (See Environment, physical, air)

Argentina (See Geographic Areas)

Art (See Indicators)

Bibliographies
Agocs, Carol	1970	(B)
Andrzejewski, Norm	1970	(B)
Beal, George M. et al.	1971	(B)
Bonjean, Charles M. et al.	1967	(B)
Brady, Henry	1970	(B)
Gebert, Gordon A.	1972a	(B)
Gebert, Gordon A.	1972b	(B)
Harland, Douglas G.	1971a	(B)
Harland, Douglas G.	1971b	(B)
Inst Nat Stat Etudes Econ	1971	(B)
Knezo, Genevieve J.	1971a	(B)

```
Knezo, Genevieve J.          1971b      (B)
Marien, Michael D.           1971       (B)
Schultz, James et al.        1970       (R)
Sloan, Helen W.              1970       (B)
Tugac, Ahmet                 1971       (B)
Wilcox, Leslie D. et al.     1972       (B)
```

Budget(s) (See Family)

Bureau of Labor Statistics (See United States, agencies)

Business (See Corporate)

Canada (See Geographic Areas)

Case study (See Research Design)

Census (See Population)

Ceylon (See Geographic Areas)

Change Agent (See Social Change)

Change, Planned (See Social Change)

Chile (See Geographic Areas)

Cities (See Metropolitan)

Civil strife (See Conflict)

Classification (See Typology)

Community
```
     Becker, Harold S. et al.     1971a      (A)
     Becker, Harold S. et al.     1971b      (A)
     Cebotarev, E. A. et al.      1971       (A)
     Cummings, Gordon J.          1970       (CS)
     Elazar, Daniel J.            1966b      (A)
     Elazar, Daniel J.            1966c      (A)
```

```
         Eldridge, Eber                    1970        (GT)
         Heady, Earl O.                    1972        (GT)
         Jackson, Edward Neill             1970        (A)
         Jones, Kenneth J. et al.          1970        (M)
         Manley, Vaughn Porter             1967        (P)
         Perle, Eugene D.                  1971        (CS)
         Sanders, Barkev S.                1964        (A)
         Sanders, Irwin T.                 1958        (GT)
         Sutton, W. A., Jr. et al.         1960        (C)
         Warren, Roland L.                 1965        (C)
         Warren, Roland L.                 1970        (C)

Community, action(See Planning)


Computer(See Research Design)


Conflict
         Kriesberg, Louis                  1970        (D)
         Miller, S. M. et al.              1967        (CS)

Conflict, civil strife
         Gurr, Ted and C. Ruttenburg       1968        (M)

Conflict, violence
         Biderman, Albert D.               1969        (CS)
         Blumenthal, Monic  D. et al.      1970a       (A)
         Blumenthal, Monic  D. et al.      1971        (A)
         Gerbner, G.                       1970        (CS)
         Kahn, Robert L.                   1971        (C)
         Ver Ecke, Wilfried                1970        (C)


Consequences, secondary(See Indicators)


Consumer(See Indicators)


Consumption(See Indicators)


Corporate
         Wilson, Ian H.                    1971        (C)

Corporate, business
         Raymond, Robert S. et al.         1971        (CS)
         Soderlind, Sterling E.            1970        (CS)

Corporate, social responsibility
         General Electric                  1970        (M)
         Holden, Constance                 1971        (A)
```

Crime
    AFL-CIO Amer. Fed.   1970   (A)
    Bryce, Herrington J.   1971   (A)
    Gitter, A. and S. Lewis   1971   (C)
    Glaser, Daniel   1967   (P)
    U.S. Dept. of Commerce   1968   (A)

Crime, delinquency
    Lowe, Jay   1966   (A)

Cross National
    Wheelock, Gerald   1969   (M)

Cross National, international
    Finsterbusch, Kurt   1971   (A)
    Rummel, Rudolph J.   1969   (M)

Cultural(See Indicators)

Data
    Boruch, Robert F.   1971b   (M)

Data, data needs
    Bauer, Raymond A.   1963   (CS)
    Clavel, Pierre et al.   1971   (CS)
    Gross, Bertram M. et al.   1967a   (CS)

Data, multivariate
    Boruch, R. and L. Wolins   1970   (M)
    Boruch, Robert F. et al.   1970   (M)
    Gitter, A. George   1970   (M)
    Terleckyj, Nestor E.   1970a   (CS)

Decision(s)(See Planning)

Decision-mak(ers)(ing)(See Planning)

Delinquency(See Crime)

Delivery of services(See Administration)

Delphi Technique(See Methodology, measurement)

Demographic(See Population)

Development
    Adelman, Irma and C. Morris   1967   (GT)
    Andrade, Preston   1970   (P)
    Area Analysis Branch   1970   (P)
    Becker, Harold S. et al.   1970   (P)
    Canada Dep. Reg. Econ. Exp.   1970   (P)
    Edwards, Clark et al.   1972   (M)
    Eisenstadt, Samuel   1971   (GT)
    Finsterbusch, Kurt   1971   (A)
    Fox, Karl A.   1969b   (GT)
    Heady, Earl O.   1972   (GT)
    Horowitz, Irving Louis   1969   (GT)
    Jackson, Edward Neill   1970   (A)
    Johnson, Helen W.   1971   (P)
    Manley, Vaughn Porter   1967   (P)
    McGranahan, Donald   1972   (CS)
    Motes, W. C.   1971   (C)
    Sanders, Irwin T.   1958   (GT)
    U.S. Dept. of Agriculture   1969   (P)
    U.S. Dept. of Agriculture   1971   (A)
    Wells, Alan   1971   (C)
    Young, Ruth C.   1968   (C)

Development, human resource
    Eldridge, Eber   1970   (GT)
    Lamson, Robert W.   1971b   (P)

Development, leadership
    Gross, Bertram M.   1968   (P)
    Williams, Anne S. et al.   1971   (C)

Development, resource
    Carnegie Endowment St. Group   1960   (CS)
    Cebotarev, E. A. et al.   1971   (A)
    Cummings, Gordon J.   1970   (CS)

Development, social development
    Day, L. H. and A. T. Day   1971   (M)
    Drewnowski, Jan   1966   (CS)
    Drewnowski, Jan et al.   1970   (A)
    Drewnowski, Jan et al.   1970   (C)
    Edwards, Clark et al.   1972   (M)
    Fox, Karl A.   1971   (CS)
    Freeman, David M.   1971   (C)
    Lochhead, A. V. S.   1969   (C)
    McGranahan, Donald V.   1971   (A)
    Olson, Mancur   1971   (C)
    United Nations   1970   (A)
    United Nations   1971   (M)
    United Nations Res. Inst.   1970   (C)

Divorce (See Family)

Economic(See Indicators)

Economic 'well-offness'(See Indicators)

Ecosystem(See Environment)

Education
Boruch, Robert F.	1971b	(M)
Brolin, K. G.	1967	(CS)
Byrnes, James C.	1970	(P)
Cohen, Wilbur J.	1967	(CS)
Duncan, Beverly	1968	(A)
Ferriss, Abbott L.	1969	(A)
Flax, Michael J.	1970	(M)
Gitter, A. George et al.	1970	(A)
Hanushek, Eric A.	1970	(C)
Hogg, Thomas C. et al.	1969	(R)
Inst Nat Stat Etudes Econ	1971	(C)
Levin, Lowell S.	1969	(CS)
Sewell, William H. et al.	1967	(A)
Snelling, W. Rodman et al.	1971	(R)
Stringham, Luther W.	1959	(CS)
United Nations	1967	(M)
U.S. Dept. of HEW	1963	(R)
Wheeler, David N.	1971	(M)

Education, university
Bayer, Alan E. et al.	1969	(A)
Jantsch, Erich	1969	(P)

Elderly(See Aged)

Employment(See Labor)

Environment
Biderman, Albert D.	1971	(GT)
Campbell, Rex R. et al.	1972b	(CS)
Cassidy, Michael W. A.	1970	(C)
Centr Natl-Rech Scient	1971	(C)
Citizens Comm. E v. Quality	1971	(A)
Gebert, Gordon A.	1972a	(B)
Gebert, Gordon A.	1972b	(B)
Klausner, Samuel Z.	1971	(GT)
Lamson, Robert W.	1970b	(P)
Morrison, Denton E. et al.	1971	(P)
Pardee, Frederick S. et al.	1971	(P)
Perloff, Harvey	1969b	(C)

Pett, Saul	1972	(C)
Thomas, William A.	1971	(CS)
U.S. Dept. of Commerce	1971a	(A)
Zucker, Charles	1971	(GT)

Environment, ecology
Schnore, Leo F.	1961	(GT)

Environment, ecosystem
Duncan, Otis Dudley	1961	(CS)
Kormondy, Edward J.	1972	(GT)

Environment, physical
Broady, Maurice	1970	(C)
Fisher, Joseph L.	1967	(CS)
Kimball, Thomas L.	1971	(M)
Lipscomb, David M.	1971	(A)
MacDonald, Gordon J.	1971	(P)
Murie, Martin	1971	(C)
National Wildlife Federation	1971	(C)
Perloff, Harvey	1969a	(C)

Environment, physical, air
Babcock, L. R., Jr. et al.	1971	(M)
Engen, Trygg	1971	(M)
Shults, Wilbur D. et al.	1971	(M)

Environment, physical, water resource
Becker, Catherine et al.	1971	(A)
Brown, Robert M. et al.	1971	(M)
Hogg, Thomas C.	1966	(GT)
Patrick, Ruth	1971	(M)
Smith, Courtland L. et al.	1971	(CS)
Smith, Courtland L. et al.	1971	(P)
Vlachos, Evan et al.	1971	(C)

Environment, physical, weather
Haas, J. Eugene et al.	1971	(P)

Environment, pollution
Alexander, Robert M.	1971	(C)
Campbell, Rex R. et al	1972a	(CS)
Patrick, Ruth	1971	(M)

Evaluation
Alberts, David S.	1971	(P)
Anderson, Claire M. et al.	1970	(P)
Blaisdell, Thomas C., Jr.	1954	(P)
Bush, J. W. and S. Fanshel	1970	(A)
Cabello, Octavio	1959	(CS)
Campbell, Donald T.	1969	(P)
Chaiklin, Harris	1970	(P)
Davidson, Frank P.	1968	(P)

Gordon, Andrew C. et al.	1970	(M)
Linowes, David	1971	(CS)
Meyer, John R.	1969	(CS)
Rappaport, Carl	1970	(M)
Ratajczak, Rosalinda	1969	(P)
Ridley, Clarence E. et al.	1938	(A)
Schwartz, Arthur	1970	(P)

Expenditure, public(See Planning)

Factor analysis(See Methodology)

Family
Day, Lincoln H. et al.	1969	(CS)
Goode, William J.	1968	(A)
Williams, Faith M.	1956	(A)

Family, budget
Murphy, Kathryn R.	1964	(A)

Family, divorce
Land, Kenneth C.	1971	(A)

Family, living costs
Hawes, Mary H.	1969	(A)

Feedback(See Information)

Financing(See Planning)

Forecast(s)(ing)
Abt, Clark C.	1970	(CS)
De Brigard, Raul et al.	1970	(P)
Dror, Yehezkel	1969	(C)
Fontela, E.	1969	(M)
Gordon, Theodore J. et al.	1969	(P)
Hage, Jerald et al.	1971	(R)
Holmans, A. E.	1970	(M)
Horowitz, Irving Louis	1969	(GT)
Hunt, H.	1969	(A)
Ikle, Fred Charles	1971	(CS)
Johnston, Denis F.	1970	(CS)
Johnston, Denis F.	1971	(CS)
Marien, Michael D.	1971	(B)
Michael, Donald N.	1967	(CS)
Mitchell, Arnold	1967	(M)
Richta, Radovan et al.	1969	(GT)
Rochberg, Richard et al.	1970	(M)

```
          Thompson, Jean                    1970        (M)

Forecast, prediction
     De Jouvenel, Bertrand               1966        (M)
     Wiles, Peter                        1971        (CS)


France(See Geographic Areas)


Full Opportunity and National Goals and Priorities Act(See
     United States, congress)


Full Opportunity and Social Accounting Act(See United
     States, congress)


Future(s)
     Abrams, Mark                        1968        (C)
     Bestuzhev-Lada, Igor                1969        (D)
     Boucher, Wayne I.                   1971        (M)
     Boulding, Kenneth E.                1967        (GT)
     Calder, Nigel                       1967        (C)
     Cerha, Jarko                        1969        (C)
     David, Henry                        1970        (C)
     Day, Virgil B.                      1971        (C)
     Dyck, Harold J. et al.              1970        (M)
     Emery, R. E.                        1967        (GT)
     Fontela, E.                         1969        (M)
     Gordon, Theodore J.                 1971        (P)
     Gross, Bertram                      1967a       (CS)
     Johnson, Paul                       1969        (C)
     Jungk, Robert                       1968        (CS)
     Kopkind, Andrew                     1967        (CS)
     Kriesberg, Louis                    1970        (C)
     Lamson, Robert W.                   1969        (P)
     Lamson, Robert W.                   1971a       (P)
     Lompe, Klaus                        1968        (CS)
     Markley, O. W.                      1970        (P)
     McHale, John                        1969        (GT)
     Mitchell, Arnold                    1967        (M)
     Moles, Abraham                      1970        (C)
     Osman, John                         1969        (CS)
     Shonfield, Andrew                   1969        (CS)
     Springer, Michael (ed.)             1970        (CS)
     Wilson, Albert and D. Wilson        1971        (C)
     Wilson, Ian H.                      1971        (C)
     Winthrop, Henry                     1968        (CS)
     Winthrop, Henry                     1969        (P)

Future, 1970's
     Carey, Charles B. et al.            1966        (CS)
     Sheldon, Eleanor Bernert            1971        (P)
```

```
        Udall, Stuart                        1968        (C)
        Wilcox, Leslie D. et al.             1971        (M)

Future, 1970-2000
        Bell, Daniel                         1970        (C)
        De Brigard, Raul et al.              1970        (P)
        Iowa Development Commission          1970        (P)
        Iowa State Dept. of Health           1970        (A)
        Nisbet, Robert A.                    1968        (CS)
        Rogers, Carl R.                      1968        (C)

Future, post-industrial society
        Bell, Daniel                         1970        (CS)


General systems(See Methodology)


Geographic Areas

Geographic Area, Albuquerque
        Albuquerque Urban Observatory        1971        (M)

Geographic Area, Argentina
        Smith, David Horton et al.           1966        (A)

Geographic Area, Canada
        Canada Dep. Reg. Econ. Exp.          1970        (P)
        Dyck, Harold J. et al.               1970        (M)
        Economic Council of Canada           1971        (P)
        Haas, J. Eugene et al.               1971        (P)
        Harland, Douglas G.                  1971a       (B)
        Harland, Douglas G.                  1971b       (B)
        Harland, Douglas G.                  1971        (P)
        O'Connell, Harold J.                 1972        (P)
        Wayman, Morris                       1971        (A)

Geographic Area, Chile
        Smith, David Horton et al.           1966        (A)

Geographic Area, France
        Hage, Jerald                         1971        (M)
        Inst de Rech Econ et de Plan         1971        (CS)
        Inst Nat Stat Etudes Econ            1971        (B)
        Inst Nat Stat Etudes Econ            1971        (CS)
        Inst Nat Stat Etudes Econ            1971        (P)
        Johnston, Denis F.                   1971        (CS)

Geographic Area, Germany
        Hage, Jerald                         1971        (M)

Geographic Area, Great Britain
        Central Statistical Office           1971        (P)
        Hage, Jerald                         1971        (M)
```

```
            Holmans, A. E.                      1970        (M)
            Thompson, Jean                      1970        (M)

Geographic Area, India
            Andrade, Preston                    1970        (P)
            Smith, David Horton et al.          1966        (A)

Geographic Area, Iowa
            Area Analysis Branch                1970        (P)
            Iowa Development Commission         1970        (P)
            Manley, Vaughn Porter               1967        (P)
            State of Iowa -  1. and Pr.         1971        (A)
            Tait, John L. et al.                1971        (R)

Geographic Area, Israel
            Smith, David Horton et al.          1966        (A)

Geographic Area, Italy
            Hage, Jerald                        1971        (M)

Geographic Area, Jamaica
            Moser, Claus A.                     1957        (A)

Geographic Area, Kansas
            Jackson, Edward Neill               1970        (A)

Geographic Area, Michigan
            Michigan Off. of Plan. Coor.        1970        (P)
            Schmid, A. Allan                    1969        (P)

Geographic Area, Midwest
            Elazar, Daniel J.                   1970        (R)

Geographic Area, Missouri
            Bryan, C. Hobson et al.             1970        (P)

Geographic Area, New York
            Gordon, David M.                    1969        (A)
            Gottehrer, Barry                    1967        (A)
            McDevitt, Matthew et al.            1970        (M)

Geographic Area, Nigeria
            Smith, David Horton et al.          1966        (A)
            Wells, Alan                         1971        (C)

Geographic Area, Pakistan
            Shariff, Zahid                      1971        (CS)
            Smith, David Horton et al.          1966        (A)

Geographic Area, Puget Sound
            Barnard, R. C. (ed.) et al.         1970        (P)

Geographic Area, Regional
            Bryce, Herrington J.                1972        (A)
```

```
Christakis, Alexander N.            1970        (P)
Clague, Ewan                        1963        (P)
Fitzgerald, Sherman                 1970        (A)
Harland, Douglas G.                 1971        (P)
Pardee, Frederick S. et al.         1971        (P)
U.S. Dept. of HUD                   1968        (R)

Geographic Area, Turkey
    Tugac, Ahmet                    1971        (B)

Geographic Area, United States
    Wilson, John C.                 1969        (A)

Geographic Area, Washington, D. C.
    Jones, Martin V. et al.         1970        (A)


Germany(See Geographic Areas


Goals(See Planning)


Goals, national(See Planning)


Great Britain(See Geographic Areas)


Growth (rate)(centers)(See Planning)


Health
    Anderson, James G.              1970        (GT)
    Anderson, James G.              1970        (M)
    Anderson, Claire M. et al.      1970        (P)
    Austin, Charles J.              1971        (GT)
    Bevan, William                  1971        (R)
    Bush, J. W. et al.              1971        (A)
    Bush, J. W. and M. M. Chen      1972        (GT)
    Bush, J. W. and  s. Fanshel     1970        (A)
    Central Statistical Office      1971        (P)
    Chen, M. M. and J. W. Bush      1971        (GT)
    Chiang, C. L.                   1965        (GT)
    Culyer, A. J. et al.            1971        (C)
    Iowa State Dept. of Health      1970        (A)
    Kaplan, H. Roy et al.           1971        (A)
    Krohn, Edward                   1967        (CS)
    Lee, Philip R.                  1967        (C)
    Levin, Lowell S.                1969        (CS)
    Malenbaum, Wilfred              1971        (CS)
    Moriyama, Iwao M.               1968        (A)
    Patrick, Donald a d J. Bush     1971        (D)
    Redick, Richard                 1971        (C)
```

```
        Sanders, Barkev S.                    1964        (A)
        Stringham, Luther W.                  1959        (CS)
        Sullivan, Daniel F.                   1966        (C)
        U.S. Dept. of HEW                     1963        (R)

Health, sickness
        Whitehead, F. E.                      1971        (M)


History of 'movement'(See Indicators)


Housing
        Aiken, Michael et al.                 1970        (A)
        Andrews, Frank M. et al.              1970        (A)
        Dluhy, Milan                          1969        (C)
        Fedkiw, John                          1969        (P)
        Holmans, A. E.                        1970        (M)
        Huttman, E. D.                        1971        (A)
        Josowitz, Aaron                       1970        (A)
        Marcuse, Peter                        1970        (GT)
        Munson, Byron E.                      1971        (C)
        Shinn, Allen M., Jr.                  1971b       (M)
        United Nations                        1966        (D)


Human Resource(See Development, human resource)


India(See Geographic Areas)


Indicators
        Bauer Raymond A. et al.               1960        (GT)
        Dillman, Don A. et al.                1971        (GT)
        Finsterbusch, Kurt                    1971a       (GT)
        Garn, Harvey A. et al.                1971        (A)
        Martin, Margaret E.                   1971        (C)
        McGranahan, Donald                    1972        (CS)
        Merriam, Ida C.                       1967        (C)
        Mindlin, Albert                       1970        (C)
        National Wildlife Federation          1971        (C)
        Ostrom, Elinor                        1971        (C)
        Perle, Eugene D.                      1971        (CS)
        Sawchuk, R. and A. Gitter             1971        (C)
        Sheldon, Eleanor B. et al.            1968        (C)

Indicators, art
        Toffler, Alvin                        1967        (CS)

Indicators, attitude(s)
        Blumenthal, Monic D. et al.           1970a       (A)
        Blumenthal, Monica D.                 1971        (A)
        Blumenthal, Monic D. et al.           1971        (A)
```

```
Boruch, Robert F. et al.            1972       (A)
Demerath, N. J. III                 1968       (A)
Fontaine, Andre                     1967       (P)
Lingoes, James C. et al.            1971       (M)
Schultz, James et al.               1970       (R)
Schwartz, Mildred A.                1967       (A)
Simon, Rita James                   1971       (A)
Stagner, Ross                       1970       (P)

Indicators, civil liberties
     Konvitz, Milton R.             1967       (CS)

Indicators, consequences, secondary
     Anderson, James G.             1971       (A)
     Maimon, Zvi                    1971       (P)

Indicators, consumer
     Pfaff, Anita B.                1971       (A)

Indicators, consumption
     Moss, Milton                   1968       (A)
     Murphy, Kathryn R.             1964       (A)

Indicators, cultural
     Gerbner, G.                    1970       (CS)

Indicators, economic
     Bratt, Elmer C.                1971       (R)
     Drewnowski, Jan                1966       (CS)
     Lamale, Helen H.               1958       (C)
     Motes, W. C.                   1971       (C)
     Sametz, A. W.                  1968       (A)
     United Nations                 1969       (P)
     U.S. Dept. Labor/WSA           1970       (A)

Indicators, economic 'well-offness'
     Morgan, James N. et al.        1969       (R)

Indicators, history of the 'movement'
     Carter, Genevieve W.           1971       (CS)

Indicators, participation, citizen
     Johnson, Norman J. et al.      1970       (M)
     Verba, Sidney                  1967       (P)

Indicators, participation, electoral
     Scammon, Richard M.            1967       (A)

Indicators, political
     Long, Norton E.                1970       (C)
     Mitchell, Joyce M. et al.      1968       (A)
     Russett, Bruce M.              1970       (M)
     Russett, Bruce M. et al.       1964       (A)
```

Indicators, savings
    Murphy, Kathryn R.   1965   (A)

Indicators, social effects
    Ogburn, William Fielding   1946   (M)

Indicators, social impact
    Bauer, Raymond A.   1969   (CS)

Indicators, social indicators

Author	Year	Code
Andrzejewski, Norm	1970	(B)
Bauer, Raymond A.	1966	(CS)
Bauer, Raymond A. (ed.)	1966	(GT)
Bauer, Raymond A.	1968	(CS)
Beal, George M. et al.	1971	(B)
Beal, George M. et al.	1971	(CS)
Biderman, Albert D.	1966	(P)
Biderman, Albert D.	1971	(M)
Brady, Henry	1970	(B)
Brooks, Ralph M. et al.	1971	(GT)
Cohen, Wilbur J.	1968	(CS)
D'agostino, Ralph B.	1971	(M)
De Neufville, Judith I.	1972	(P)
Dial, O. E.	1970	(CS)
Drewnowski, Jan	1966	(CS)
Etzioni, Amitai	1970b	(C)
Flax, Michael J.	1971	(CS)
Gastil, Raymond D.	1970	(CS)
Harland, Douglas G.	1971	(P)
Hauser, Philip M.	1971	(P)
Henriot, Peter J.	1970a	(CS)
Henriot, Peter J.	1970b	(CS)
Horowitz, Irving Louis	1968	(CS)
Inst Nat Stat Etudes Econ	1971	(B)
Inst Nat Stat Etudes Econ	1971	(CS)
Inst Nat Stat Etudes Econ	1971	(P)
Johnston, Denis F.	1971	(CS)
Kamrany, Nake M.	1968	(D)
Krendel, Ezra S.	1969	(GT)
Krendel, Ezra S.	1971b	(GT)
Krieger, Martin H.	1971a	(C)
Land, Kenneth C.	1970	(GT)
Land, Kenneth C.	1971	(D)
Lehman, Edward W.	1971	(CS)
Marcuse, Peter	1970	(GT)
McDevitt, Matthew et al.	1970	(M)
McHale, John	1967	(GT)
McIntosh, William Alex	1971	(A)
Olson, Mancur, Jr.	1969a	(D)
Olson, Mancur	1971	(C)
Ontell, Robert	1971	(D)
Palley, Howard A. et al.	1971	(CS)
Raymond, Robert S. et al.	1971	(CS)
Richard, Robert	1969	(M)

```
Russett, Bruce M. et al.            1964        (A)
Sheldon, Eleanor B. et al.          1970        (CS)
Soderlind, Sterling E.              1970        (CS)
Springer, Michael                   1970        (P)
Stanford Research Institute         1969        (GT)
Suter, Larry E.                     1971        (GT)
Tugac, Ahmet                        1971        (B)
U.S. Dept. Labor/WSA                1970        (A)
Vestermark, S. D., Jr.              1968        (C)
Wasson, K. William et al.           1971        (CS)
Wilber, George L.                   1971        (M)
Wilcox, Leslie D. et al.            1971        (P)
Wilcox, Leslie D. et al.            1972        (B)

Indicators, social mobility
Bryan, C. Hobson et al.             1970        (P)
Miller, S. M. et al.                1970        (C)
Ulrich, Gary                        1969        (A)

Indicators, social statistics
Moser, C. A.                        1970        (M)
United Nations                      1963        (M)
United Nations                      1968        (A)

Indicators, technology
Bell, Daniel                        1968        (A)
Boucher, Wayne, I.                  1971        (P)
Lamson, Robert W.                   1969        (A)
Stockdale, Jerry D. et al.          1970        (R)

Indicators, values
Blumenthal, Monic  D. et al.        1970b       (A)
Clark, Terry N.                     1971        (M)
Gordon, Theodore J.                 1971        (P)
Konvitz, Milton R.                  1967        (CS)
Rokeach, Milton et al.              1970        (A)
Williams, Robin M., Jr.             1967        (P)

Indicators, women
Ferriss, Abbott L.                  1971        (A)


Inference (See Methodology)


Information
Dubin, Robert                       1971        (GT)
Liu, William T. et al.              1971        (GT)

Information, feedback
Bauer, Raymond A.                   1967        (P)
Biderman, Albert D.                 1969        (CS)
Krendel, Ezra S.                    1971b       (GT)
Rosenthal, Robert A. et al.         1969        (P)
```

Information, information systems
    Bauer, Raymond A.   1967   (P)
    Hoos, Ida R.   1971   (CS)
    Judge, Anthony J. N.   1971   (CS)
    Perle, Eugene D.   1970b   (CS)
    U.S. Dept. of HUD   1968   (R)

Information, information utilization
    Bauman, Zygmunt   1971   (CS)
    Brady, Edward L. et al.   1972   (P)
    Johnson, Norman J. et al.   1970   (M)

Information, intelligence
    Etzioni, Amitai et al.   1967   (M)
    Schneier, Edward   1970   (CS)
    Springer, Michael (ed.)   1970   (CS)
    Webber, Melvin M.   1965   (C)
    Wilensky, Harold L.   1967   (P)
    Wilensky, Harold L.   1970   (P)

Information, knowledge
    Bell, Daniel   1968   (A)

Information, social information
    Galnoor, Itzhak   1971   (P)
    Gross, Bertram   1967b   (CS)
    Shariff, Zahid   1971   (CS)

Information, utilization(See Information)

Intelligence(See Information)

International(See Cross National)

Inter-organization(s)(al)(See Research Design)

Interval Scale(See Methodology, measurement)

Iowa(See Geographic Areas)

Israel(See Geographic Areas)

Italy(See Geographic Areas)

Jamaica(See Geographic Areas)

414

```
Justice
     Law Enforcement  ssis. Adm.      1970       (A)
     Law Enforcement  ssis. Adm.      1971       (A)
     Law Enforcement  ssis. Adm.      1971       (R)
     U.S. Dept. of Commerce           1968       (A)


Kansas(See Geographic Areas)


Knowledge(See Information)


Labor
     Lebergott, Stanley               1967       (M)
     Marie, Michel et al.             1971       (C)

Labor, employment
     De Neufville, Judith I.          1972       (P)
     Keyserling, Leon H.              1967       (P)
     Lebergott, Stanley               1968       (A)

Labor, occupation
     Form, William H. et al.          1971       (GT)
     Lionberger, Herbert F. et al.    1969       (M)
     Suter, Larry E.                  1971       (GT)
     Ulrich, Gary                     1969       (A)
     Widdison, Harold A. et al.       1971       (M)

Labor, working conditions
     Herrick, Neal Q. et al.          1971       (M)


Leadership(See Development, leadership)


Leisure
     Burkhead, Danny L.               1971       (C)
     Ennis, Philip                    1968       (C)
     Kaplan, Max                      1968       (P)
     Yoesting, Dean R. et al.         1971       (M)

Leisure, outdoor recreation
     Pikul, Robert et al.             1971       (M)


Levels of Living
     Baster, Nancy et al.             1969       (A)
     Brackett, Jean C.                1969       (A)
     Cowhig, James C. et al.          1965       (C)
     Drewnowski, Jan                  1970       (M)
     Lamale, Helen H.                 1965       (A)
     Moser, Claus A.                  1957       (A)
```

United Nations	1961	(D)
United Nations	1964	(M)
U.S. Dept. of Agriculture	1969	(C)

Levels of Living, living standards

Bennett, M. K.	1937	(M)
Lamale, Helen H.	1968	(A)
Williams, Faith M.	1956	(A)

Levels of Living, quality of life

Barnard, R. C. (ed.) et al.	1970	(P)
Center for Comm. Studies	1970	(CS)
Clausen, A. W.	1971	(CS)
Corning, Peter	1971	(C)
Discussion at Delos	1969	(P)
Gastil, Raymond D.	1970	(CS)
Gitter, A. and S. Franklin	1971	(C)
Gitter, A. George et al.	1971	(M)
Harland, Douglas G.	1971a	(B)
Harland, Douglas G.	1971b	(B)
Jones, Martin V. et al.	1970	(A)
Jones, Martin V. et al.	1970	(M)
King-Hele, Desmond	1970	(CS)
Krieger, Martin H.	1969	(CS)
Little, Dennis et al.	1970	(A)
Pett, Saul	1972	(C)
Sawchuk, R. and A. Gitter	1971	(C)
Singer, Fred S.	1971	(CS)
Sloan, Helen W.	1970	(B)
Soderlind, Sterling E.	1970	(CS)
State of Iowa - 1. and Pr.	1971	(A)
Udall, Stuart	1968	(C)
Wilson, John C.	1969	(A)

Living costs(See Family)

Living standards(See Levels of Living)

Longitudinal analysis(See Research Design)

Longitudinal studies(See Research Design)

Macro(See Indicators)

Macrosociology(See Sociology, macrosociology)

Management(See Corporate)

Measurement (See Methodology)

Methodology
    Boruch, Robert F. et al.   1970   (M)
    Moles, Abraham   1970   (C)
    Willhelm, Sidney M.   1964   (C)

Methodology, factor analysis
    Gitter, A. George   1970   (M)
    Gitter, A. George et al.   1971   (M)
    Jackson, Edward Neill   1970   (A)
    Rummel, Rudolph J.   1969   (M)

Methodology, general systems
    Gross, Bertram M. et al.   1967b   (CS)

Methodology, inference
    Martin, Thomas et al.   1971   (M)

Methodology, measurement
    Alberts, David S.   1970   (M)
    Bennett, M. K.   1937   (M)
    Bonjean, Charles M. et al.   1967   (B)
    Drewnowski, Jan   1970   (M)
    Dubin, Robert   1971   (GT)
    Etzioni, Amitai et al.   1967   (M)
    Ford, Joseph B.   1971   (GT)
    United Nations Res. Inst.   1970   (C)
    Zucker, Charles   1971   (GT)

Methodology, measurement, Delphi technique
    Sulc, Oto   1969   (A)

Methodology, measurement, interval scale
    Widdison, Harold A. et al.   1971   (M)

Methodology, measurement, modernity scale
    Smith, David Horton et al.   1966   (A)

Methodology, measurement, scaling
    Shinn, Allen M., Jr.   1971a   (M)

Methodology, measurement, trend analysis
    Duncan, Otis Dudley   1968   (C)

Metropolitan
    Alford, Robert B.   1970   (CS)
    Bixhorn, Herbert   1971   (M)
    Bryce, Herrington J.   1971   (M)
    Elazar, Daniel J.   1970   (R)
    Flax, Michael J.   1970   (M)

Flax, Michael J.	1971	(CS)
Friedly, Philip H.	1969	(M)
Garn, Harvey A. et al.	1971	(A)
Goldstein, Sidney et al.	1964	(M)
Gottehrer, Barry	1967	(A)
Hawes, Mary H.	1969	(A)
Howard, William A.	1969	(CS)
Jones, Kenneth J. et al.	1970	(M)
Josowitz, Aaron	1970	(A)
Krendel, Ezra S.	1971b	(GT)
Lamale, Helen H. et al.	1959	(M)
Liu, William T. et al.	1971	(GT)
Mead, Margaret	1970	(P)
Mindlin, Albert	1970	(C)
Moynihan, Daniel P.	1967	(CS)
Murphy, Kathryn R.	1964	(A)
Osman, John	1969	(CS)
Ostrom, Elinor	1971	(C)
Perle, Eugene D.	1970a	(CS)
Perle, Eugene D.	1970b	(CS)
Perloff, Harvey	1969a	(C)
Perloff, Harvey	1969b	(C)
Rappaport, Carl	1970	(M)
Stagner, Ross	1970	(P)
U.S. Dept. of HUD	1968	(R)
Urban Institute, The	1971	(CS)
Vandermark, E. H.	1970	(CS)
Webber, Melvin M.	1965	(C)
Williams, Faith M.	1956	(A)

Model(s)(ing)

Anderson, James G.	1970	(M)
Anderson, James G.	1971	(M)
Chen, M. M. and 8j. W. Bush	1971	(GT)
Chiang, C. L.	1965	(GT)
Coleman, James S.	1971	(C)
Cornblit, Oscar et al.	1968	(M)
Corning, Peter A.	1970	(GT)
Dodd, Stuart C.	1971	(R)
Featherman, David	1971	(C)
Finsterbusch, Kurt	1971a	(GT)
Finsterbusch, Kurt	1971b	(GT)
Flora, Cornelia Butler et al.	1971	(M)
Fontela, E.	1969	(M)
Forrester, Jay W.	1971	(M)
Fox, Karl A.	1969	(C)
Fox, Karl A.	1969b	(GT)
Gross, Bertram M. et al.	1967b	(CS)
Gurr, Ted and C. Ruttenburg	1968	(M)
Hogg, Thomas C.	1966	(GT)
Inst de Rech Econ et de Plan	1971	(CS)
Klausner, Samuel Z.	1971	(GT)
Krendel, Ezra S.	1971a	(GT)

```
Kriesberg, Louis                        1970      (C)
Kunkel, John H.                         1971      (GT)
Land, Kenneth C.                        1970      (M)
Land, Kenneth C.                        1971      (A)
Lowe, Jay                               1966      (A)
Markley, O. W.                          1970      (P)
McGranahan, Donald V.                   1971      (A)
McGranahan, Donald                      1972      (CS)
McHale, John                            1967      (GT)
O'Connell, Harold J.                    1972      (P)
Perloff, Harvey                         1969a     (C)
Suter, Larry E.                         1971      (GT)
Van Til, Sally  ould et al.             1971      (GT)
Van Valey, Thomas L.                    1971      (C)
Warren, Roland L.                       1970      (C)
Watt, Kenneth                           1970      (GT)
Wells, Alan                             1971      (C)
Williams, Robin M.                      1968      (CS)
Wilson, Albert and D. Wilson            1971      (C)
Young, Ruth C.                          1968      (C)
```

Michigan(See Geographic Areas)

Midwest(See Geographic Areas)

Missouri(See Geographic Areas)

Modernity Scale(See Methodology, measurement)

Multivariate(See Data)

Municipal(See Administration)

Natality(See Population)

National Goals Research Staff,Office of the President,(See
    United States, agencies)

National Science Foundation(See United States, agencies)

Needs(See Planning)

New York(See Geographic Areas)

Nigeria (See Geographic Areas)

Non-metropolitan
Andrade, Preston	1970	(P)
Area Analysis Branch	1970	(P)
Beal, G. and G. Klonglan	1970	(CS)
Bender, Lloyd D. et al.	1971	(A)
Edwards, Clark et al.	1972	(M)
Heady, Earl O.	1972	(GT)
Kaplan, H. Roy et al.	1971	(A)
Madden, J. Patrick	1970	(CS)
Mather, William G.	1971	(R)
Nixon, Richard M.	1971a	(P)
Nixon, Richard M.	1971b	(P)
Tweeten, Luther G.	1969	(CS)
U.S. Dept. of Agriculture	1969	(C)
U. S. Dept. of Agriculture	1971	(A)

Occupation (See Labor)

Operations Research (See Research Design)

Organizational analysis (See Research Design)

Outdoor recreation (See Leisure)

Pakistan (See Geographic Areas)

Panel study (See Research Design)

Participation, citizen (See Indicators)

Participation, electoral (See Indicators)

Planned Change (See Social Change)

Planning
Burke, Edmund M.	1965	(P)
Fromm, Erich	1970	(GT)
Gross, Bertram M.	1965	(P)
Gross, Bertram	1967a	(CS)
Ozbekhan, Hasan	1969	(GT)

```
Rochberg, Richard et al.          1970        (M)
Tenbruck, Friedrich H.            1970        (P)
U.S. Dept. of Agriculture         1969        (P)
Waterston, Albert                 1965        (P)
Wayman, Morris                    1971        (A)

Planning, community action
    Becker, Harold S. et al.      1970        (P)
    Becker, Harold S. et al.      1971a       (A)
    Becker, Harold S. et al.      1971b       (A)

Planning, decision(s), decision-makers(ing)
    Economic Council of Canada    1971        (P)
    Smith, Courtland L. et al.    1971        (CS)

Planning, financing
    Abel-Smith, Brian             1970        (M)
    Elazar, Daniel J.             1966a       (A)
    Henning, John et al.          1970        (C)
    Tussing, A. Dale et al.       1970        (GT)

Planning, goals(national)
    Bettman, James R.             1971        (M)
    Biderman, Albert D.           1963        (P)
    Colm, Gerhard                 1966        (P)
    Hauser, Philip M.             1967        (P)
    National Goals Res. Staff     1970        (P)
    President's Comm. Nat. Goals  1960        (P)
    Terleckyj, Nestor             1970        (GT)
    Terleckyj, Nestor E.          1970b       (CS)
    Tunstall, Daniel B.           1970        (C)
    U.S. President                1960        (P)
    Wright, Christopher           1969        (P)

Planning, growth (rate), (centers)
    Andrade, Preston              1970        (P)

Planning, needs
    Carnegie Endowment St. Group  1960        (CS)
    Ellickson, Katherine Pollak   1959        (CS)

Planning, policy
    Holleb, Doris                 1968        (D)
    Horowitz, Irving Louis        1968        (CS)
    Krendel, Ezra S.              1969        (GT)
    Lamson, Robert W.             1971a       (P)
    Moynihan, Daniel P.           1969        (CS)
    Ostrom, Elinor                1971        (M)
    Palley, Howard A. et al.      1971        (CS)
    United Nations                1969        (P)
    Wilcox, Leslie D. et al.      1971        (P)

Planning, priorit(y)(ies)
    Asso. for Pub. Prog. Anal.    1970        (CS)
```

Bettman, James R.	1971	(M)
Boucher, Wayne I.	1971	(M)
Krieger, Martin H.	1970	(P)
Lewis, Wilfred, Jr.	1971	(CS)
Natl. Acad. of Engineering	1971	(CS)
Schmid, A. Allan	1969	(P)

Planning, program(s)

Alberts, David S.	1970	(M)
Asso. for Pub. Prog. Anal.	1970	(CS)
Meyer, John R.	1969	(CS)

Planning, public policy

Beal, George M. et al.	1971	(CS)
Clavel, Pierre et al.	1971	(CS)
Cohen, Wilbur J.	1968	(CS)
Gross, Bertram	1967b	(CS)
Hoos, Ida R.	1971	(CS)
Katzman, Martin T.	1968	(D)
Lewis, Wilfred, Jr.	1971	(CS)
Linowes, David	1971	(CS)
Madden, J. Patrick	1970	(CS)
Mather, William G.	1971	(R)
Orlans, Harold	1971	(P)
Reeder, William W. et al.	1971	(C)
Schatz, Gerald S.	1970	(CS)
Schneier, Edward	1970	(CS)

Planning, role of planner

Duhl, Leonard J.	1968	(P)
Kopkind, Andrew	1967	(CS)

Planning, science policy

Lamson, Robert W.	1969	(A)
Lamson, Robert W.	1971a	(A)
Lamson, Robert W.	1971b	(A)

Policy(See Planning)

Pollution(See Environment)

Population

Duncan, Otis Dudley	1969	(C)
Lamson, Robert W.	1970a	(P)
Lamson, Robert W.	1971b	(P)
Martin, Margaret E.	1971	(C)
Nixon, Richard M.	1972	(P)
Sills, David Lawrence	1971	(CS)
United Nations	1970	(CS)

Population, census

```
Voight, Robert B.                    1970        (M)

Population, demographic
     Applied Urbanetics, Inc.        1968        (M)
     Farley, Reynolds                1971        (A)
     Fox, Karl A.                    1970        (CS)
     Goldstein, Sidney et al.        1964        (M)
     Mayer, Lawrence A.              1972        (CS)
     Org. for Econ. C op./Devel.     1970        (CS)
     Price, Daniel O. et al.         1971        (A)
     Roterus, Victor                 1946        (A)
     Sundquist, James L.             1970        (P)
     Taeuber, Conrad                 1968        (A)
     Tait, John L. et al.            1971        (R)
     Thompson, Jean                  1970        (M)

Population, natality
     Day, Lincoln H. et al.          1970        (CS)
     Day, L. H. and A. T. Day        1971        (M)


Post-industrial society(See Future(s))


Poverty
     Bender, Lloyd D. et al.         1971        (A)
     Bryce, Herrington J.            1972        (A)
     Lamale, Helen H.                1965        (A)
     Lamale, Helen H.                1965        (D)
     Madden, J. Patrick              1971        (CS)
     Miller, S. M. et al.            1967        (CS)
     Price, Daniel O. et al.         1971        (A)
     Ratajczak, Rosalinda            1969        (P)
     Rokeach, Milton et al.          1970        (A)
     Tweeten, Luther G.              1969        (CS)
     Wilber, George L.               1971        (M)


PPBS(See United States, agencies)


Prediction(See Forecast(s)(ing)


Priorit(y)(ies)(See Planning)


Program(s)(See Planning)


Public policy(See Planning)


Public Welfare(See Welfare, public welfare)
```

Puget Sound (See Geographic Areas)

Quality of Life,Living,(See Levels of Living)

Race
Bayer, Alan E. et al.	1969	(A)
Bryce, Herrington J.	1972	(A)
Cowhig, James C. et al.	1965	(C)
Duncan, Otis Dudley	1967	(P)
Flax, Michael J.	1970	(A)
Rokeach, Milton et al.	1970	(A)
Schwartz, Mildred A.	1967	(A)

Regional (See Geographical Areas)

Research
Heberlein, Thomas A.	1971	(GT)
Hunt, H.	1969	(A)
Natl. Acad. of Engineering	1971	(CS)

Research, social research
Beal, G. and G. Klonglan	1970	(CS)
Bennis, Warren G.	1970	(P)
Biderman, Albert D.	1966	(CS)
Boruch, Robert F.	1971a	(M)
Ellickson, Katherine Pollak	1959	(CS)
Lippett, Ronald	1965	(C)

Research Design
Bixhorn, Herbert	1971	(M)
Boruch, Robert F. et al.	1970	(M)
Boruch, R. and L. Wolins	1970	(M)
Bryce, Herrington J.	1971	(A)
Ford, Joseph B.	1971	(GT)
Krendel, Ezra S.	1969	(GT)

Research Design, case study
Krendel, Ezra S.	1970	(M)

Research Design, computer
Forrester, Jay W.	1971	(M)

Research Design, inter-organization (s) (al)
Elazar, Daniel J.	1966b	(A)
Elazar, Daniel J.	1966c	(A)
Judge, Anthony J. N.	1971	(CS)

Research Design, longitudinal analysis

```
        Hage, Jerald                        1971        (M)

Research Design, longitudinal studies
        Pelz, Donald C. et al.              1970        (M)

Research Design, operations research
        Alberts, David S.                   1971        (P)
        Fox, Karl A.                        1969a       (GT)
        Rappaport, Carl                     1970        (M)

Research Design, organizational analysis
        Burke, Edmund M.                    1965        (P)
        Fitzgerald, Sherman                 1970        (A)
        Rosenthal, Robert A. et al.         1969        (P)

Research Design, panel study
        Lionberger, Herbert F. et al.       1969        (M)

Research Design, sample surveys
        Bauer, Raymond A.                   1966        (CS)

Research Design, simulation
        Little, Dennis et al.               1970        (A)

Research Design, social trends
        Central Statistical Office          1970        (M)
        Central Statistical Office          1971        (P)
        Lebergott, Stanley                  1968        (A)
        Nixon, Richard M.                   1971a       (P)
        Nixon, Richard M.                   1971b       (P)
        Schwartz, Mildred A.                1967        (A)
        Taeuber, Conrad                     1968        (A)
        Whitehead, F. E.                    1971        (M)

Research Design, system analysis
        General Electric                    1970        (M)
        Kunkel, John H.                     1971        (GT)
        Olson, Mancur, Jr.                  1970        (M)

Research Design, time-series data
        Pelz, Donald C. et al.              1970        (M)


Resource(See Development)


Retired(See Aged)


Role of planner(See Planning)


Role, sociologist(See Sociology, sociologist's role)
```

Rural(See Non-metropolitan)

Sample surveys(See Research Design)

Saving(s)(See Indicators)

Scaling(See Methodology, measurement)

Science

Science policy(See Planning)

Science, social science

American Psycholo ical Asso.	1967	(CS)
Boulding, Kenneth E.	1967	(CS)
Caldwell, Catherine	1970	(C)
Deutsch, Karl W. et al.	1971	(A)
Hackes, Peter M. et al.	1971	(CS)
Hauser, Philip M.	1946	(CS)
Hauser, Philip M.	1949	(P)
Knezo, Genevieve J.	1971a	(B)
Knezo, Genevieve J.	1971b	(B)
Orlans, Harold	1971	(P)
Riecken, Henry W.	1969	(CS)

Sickness(See Health)

Simulation(See Research Design)

Social Accounting(s)

Bell, Daniel	1968	(C)
Bowman, R. T. et al.	1960	(CS)
Eisner, Robert	1970	(C)
Flora, Cornelia Butler et al.	1971	(M)
Gross, Bertram M.	1966	(GT)
Hauser, Philip M.	1967	(CS)
Horowitz, Irving L. et al.	1967	(P)
Mondale, Walter F.	1967	(C)
Org. for Econ. C op./Devel.	1970	(CS)
Rice, Stuart A.	1967	(C)

Social Accounting(s), social costs

Winthrop, Henry	1969	(P)

Social Change

Abt, Clark C.	1970	(CS)
Bell, Daniel	1968	(A)

```
Biderman, Albert D.                          1963      (P)
Blumenthal, Monica D.                        1971      (A)
Bryan, C. Hobson et al.                      1970      (P)
Brzezinski, Zbigniew                         1968      (C)
Center for Comm. Studies                     1970      (CS)
Coleman, James S.                            1971      (GT)
Cornblit, Oscar et al.                       1968      (M)
Demerath, N. J. III                          1968      (A)
Hauser, Philip M.                            1969      (C)
Inst de Rech Econ et de Plan                 1971      (CS)
Madden, J. Patrick                           1970      (CS)
McHale, John                                 1968      (C)
Mitchell, Joyce M. et al.                    1968      (A)
Moore, Wilbert E. et al.                     1965      (GT)
Sheldon, Eleanor B. et al.                   1968      (A)
Sheldon, Eleanor B. et al.                   1968      (C)
Sloan, Helen W.                              1970      (B)
Stockdale, Jerry D. et al.                   1970      (R)
Terleckyj, Nestor E.                         1970a     (CS)
Terleckyj, Nestor                            1970      (M)

Social Change, change agent
    McIntosh, William Alex                   1971      (A)

Social Change, planned change(change, planned)
    Alpbach European Forum                   1969      (P)
    Cohn, Edwin J.                           1971      (C)
    Iowa Development Commission              1970      (P)
    Jantsch, Erich                           1969      (C)
    Long, Norton E.                          1968      (CS)
    Mauro, John T.                           1968      (CS)
    Ray, Paul H.                             1968      (C)
    Studer, Raymond G.                       1970      (GT)
    Warren, Roland L.                        1965      (C)


Social Cost(s)  (See Social Accounting(s))


Social development(See Development)


Social Disorganization
    Goldman, Nathan                          1967      (CS)


Social effects(See Indicators)


Social impact(See Indicators)


Social indicators(See Indicators,
```

Social information(See Information)

Social mobility(See Indicators)

Social Monitoring
    Campbell, Angus et al.   1970   (C)
    Moore, Wilbert E. et al.   1965   (GT)

Social Problems
    Applied Urbanetics, Inc.   1968   (M)
    Duncan, Otis Dudley   1967   (P)
    Guttman, Louis   1971   (M)
    Huttman, E. D.   1971   (A)
    Krieger, Martin H.   1970   (P)
    Lehman, Edward W.   1971   (CS)
    Munson, Byron E.   1971   (C)
    Riecken, Henry W.   1969   (CS)
    Van Til, Sally ould et al.   1971   (GT)

Social Report(s)(ing)
    Albuquerque Urban Observatory 1971   (M)
    Bell, Daniel   1969   (P)
    Etzioni, Amitai   1970a   (C)
    Gross, Bertram   1966a   (CS)
    Gross, Bertram   1966b   (CS)
    Krieger, Martin H.   1971b   (C)
    Michigan Off. of Plan. Coor.   1970   (P)
    Official Summary of HEW   1969   (CS)
    Olson, Mancur, Jr.   1969b   (D)
    Sheldon, Eleanor Bernert   1971   (P)
    Taeuber, Karl E.   1970   (CS)
    Tunstall, Daniel B.   1970   (C)
    U.S. Dept. of Agriculture   1971   (A)
    U. S. President   1960   (P)
    Voight, Robert B.   1970   (M)
    Williams, Robin M.   1968   (CS)

Social research(See Research}

Social responsibility(See Corporate)

Social Science(See Science, social science)

Social Service Systems(See Welfare, social service
    systems)

Social statistics(See Indicators)

Social trends(See Research Design)

Social Welfare(See Welfare, social welfare)

Society
Bauer, Raymond A.	1967	(P)
Campbell, Donald T.	1971	(M)
Watt, Kenneth	1970	(GT)

Sociology
Coleman, James S.	1969	(CS)
Hahn, Erich	1970	(GT)
Olson, Mancur, Jr.	1968	(GT)

Sociology, macrosociology
Dodd, Stuart C.	1971	(R)

Sociology, sociologist's role
Boulding, Kenneth E.	1967	(CS)
Hackes, Peter M. et al.	1971	(CS)
Phillips, Derek L.	1971	(P)
Winthrop, Henry	1968	(CS)

System(s) analysis(See Research Design)

Taxonomy(See Typology)

Technology(See Indicators)

Time-series data(See Research Design)

Turkey(See Geographic Areas)

Typology
Alford, Robert R.	1972	(A)
Jones, Martin et al.	1970	(M)
Wasson, K. William et al.	1971	(CS)

United Nations
Drewnowski, Jan	1970	(M)
Krohn, Edward	1967	(CS)
United Nations	1963	(M)

```
            United Nations                    1964        (M)
            United Nations                    1967        (M)
            United Nations                    1968        (A)
            United Nations                    1969        (P)
            United Nations                    1970        (A)
            United Nations                    1971        (M)


United States
            Carey, Charles B. et al.         1966        (CS)
            De Brigard, Raul et al.          1970        (P)
            Mayer, Lawrence A.               1972        (CS)
            Nisbet, Robert A.                1968        (CS)
            Orlans, Harold                   1971        (P)
            Osman, John                      1969        (CS)
            Russett, Bruce M.                1970        (M)
            Sheldon, Eleanor Bernert         1971        (P)
            Springer, Michael (ed.)          1970        (CS)
            U.S. Dept. of Agriculture        1971        (A)
            U.S. President                   1960        (P)
            Voight, Robert B.                1970        (M)
            Williams, Robin M.               1968        (CS)

United States(See Geographic Areas)

United States, agencies

United States, agencies, Bureau of Labor Statistics
            Brackett, Jean C.                1969        (A)
            Lamale, Helen H.                 1968        (A)
            U. S. Dept. Labor/WSA            1970        (A)

United States, agencies, National Goals Research Staff
            Nixon, Richard M.                1969        (CS)

United States, agencies, National Science Foundation

United States, agencies, PPBS
            Anderson, Claire M. et al.       1970        (P)
            Chaiklin, Harris                 1970        (P)
            Engquist, Carlton L.             1970        (P)
            Grosse, Robert H.                1970        (P)
            Harris, Fred R.                  1970        (CS)
            Schwartz, Arthur                 1970        (P)
            Schwartz, Edward E. (ed.)        1970        (P)

United States, congress
            American Psycholo ical Asso.     1967        (CS)
            Harris, Fred R.                  1967        (P)
            Mondale, Walter F.               1971a       (P)
            Mondale, Walter F.               1971c       (P)

United States, congress, Full Opportunity and National
            Goals and Priorities Act
```

```
        Ink, Dwight A.                          1971        (P)
        Mondale, Walter F.                      1971b       (P)
        United States Senate                    1971        (CS)

United States, congress, Full Opportunity and Social Ac-
        counting Act
        Hauser, Philip M.                       1967        (CS)
        Mondale, Walter F.                      1967        (P)
        Mondale, Walter F.                      1970a       (P)
        Mondale, Walter F.                      1970b       (P)
        Samuelson, Robert J.                    1967        (P)
        U.S. Senate                             1967        (CS)
        U.S. Senate                             1968        (CS)
        U.S. Senate                             1969        (CS)
        U.S. Senate                             1969        (P)
        U.S. Sen. Comm. Pub. Wel.               1970        (P)
        U.S. Sen./Subc. Gov. Res.               1967        (CS)

University(See Education)

Urban(See Metropolitan)


Values(See Indicators)


Violence(See Conflict)


Washington, D.C.(See Geographical Areas)


Water Resource(See Environment, physical, water resource)


Weather(See Environment, physical, weather)


Welfare
        Bryce, Herrington J.                    1971        (M)
        Gordon, David M.                        1969        (A)
        Lamale, Helen H.                        1959        (D)
        Lingoes, James C. et al.                1971        (M)
        Merriam, Ida C.                         1967        (C)
        Merriam, Ida C.                         1968        (C)
        Schwartz, Edward E. (ed.)               1970        (P)
        Stringham, Luther W.                    1959        (CS)
        U.S. Dept. of HEW                       1963        (R)

Welfare, fire(safety)
        U.S. Dept. of Commerce                  1971b       (A)

Welfare, public welfare
        Clague, Ewan                            1963        (P)
```

```
              Friedly, Philip H.                  1969        (M)

Welfare, social service systems
      Anderson, Claire M. et al.        1970        (P)

Welfare, social welfare
      Chaiklin, Harris                  1970        (P)
      Engquist, Carlton L.             1970        (P)
      Madden, J. Patrick                1971        (CS)


Working conditions(See Labor)
```

Aborn, Murray. National Science Foundation, Washington,
   D.C.   20550

Adelson, Marvin. Institute of Urban Planning, University
   of California, Los Angeles, 405 Hilgard Avenue, Los
   Angeles, California   90024

Administration on Aging. Social and Rehabilitation Service, U.S. Department of Health, Education, and Welfare,
   Washington, D.C.   20201

Agency for International Development. Washington, D.C.
   20523

Aigner, Stephen M. 2263 Parkwood, Ann Arbor, Michigan
   48104

Akman, Dogan D. Department of Social Work, Memorial University of Newfoundland, St. John's Newfoundland,
   Canada

Albers, Walter T., Jr. Head, Societal Analysis Activity,
   General Motors Research Laboratory, General Motors
   Technical Center, Warren, Michigan   48090

Alers-Montalvo, Manuel. Department of Sociology, Colorado
   State University, Fort Collins, Colorado   80521

Alfeld, Louis E. Massachusetts Institute of Technology, E
   40-214, Cambridge, Massachusetts   02139

Alford, Robert. Department of Sociology, University of
   Wisconsin, Madison, Wisconsin   53706

Allen, David. Social Science Research Council, State
   House, High Holborn, London, England, WC1

American Institute of Certified Public Accountants.   666
   Fifth Avenue, New York, New York   10019

American Marketing Association. Public Policy and Issues
   Division, 230 North Michigan Avenue, Chicago, Illinois
   60601

American Telephone and Telegraph Company. Atten: Phillip
   E. Davis, 123 William Street, 20th Floor, New York, New
   York   10007

Anderson, W. David. Assistant Director of Public Relations, Interdisciplinary Roundtable on Social Measure-

ment, American Institute of Certified Public
Accountants, 666 Fifth Avenue, New York, New York
10019

Anderson, Jacqueline. Director, Quantitative Social
Planning Division, Institute for Interdisciplinary
Studies, 123 East Grant Street, Minneapolis, Minnesota
55403

Anderson, James G. Department of Sociology, Purdue University, Lafayette, Indiana   47907

Anderson, Keith. Bureau of the Census, General Federal
Office Buildings 3 & 4, Suitland, Maryland   20023

Anderson, Kenneth E. Acting Chief, Governments Division,
Bureau of the Census, U.S. Department of Commerce,
Washington, D.C.   20233

Anderson, Marvin A. Dean and Director, University
Extension Service, 110S Curtiss, Iowa State University,
Ames, Iowa   50010

Andrade, Preston. The Ford Foundation, 55 Lodi Estate,
New Delhi 3, India

Andrews, Frank. Institute for Social Research, University
of Michigan, Ann Arbor, Michigan   48104

Andrews, Wade H. Department of Sociology, Utah State University, Logan, Utah   84321

Andrzejewski, Norman S. Assistant Director for Area Development, Project ALPHA (Areawide and Local Planning
for Health Action), 1100 Hills Building, 217 Montgomery
Street, Syracuse, New York   13702

Averch, Harvey. Director, Division of Social Systems and
Human Resources, National Science Foundation, Washington, D.C.   20550

Bailey, Laurence A. Urban Observatory Director, c/o City
Planning Department, 222 East Saratoga Street,
Baltimore, Maryland   21202

Baker, Martin K. Department of Sociology, University of
Montana, Missoula, Montana   59801

Baker, Michael. Project Computer Data Banks, National
Academy of Sciences, 2101 Constitution Avenue, Washington, D.C.   20418

Balloch, Susan. Consultant, Education Division, 1211
Geneve 10, Geneva, Switzerland

Balyeat, Ralph R. Director, The Urban Observatory of
    Metropolitan Nashville-University Centers, 205 Howard
    School, 700 Second Avenue South, Nashville, Tennessee
    37210

Bancroft, T. A. Director and Head, Statistical Laborato-
    ry, 102A Snedecor Hall, Iowa State University, Ames,
    Iowa   50010

Baranowski, Tom. Research and Evaluation, Kansas Regional
    Medical Program, 3909 Eaton, Kansas City, Kansas
    66103

Barrows, Richard. The University of Wisconsin, College of
    Agricultural & Life Sciences, Agricultural Hall, 1450
    Linden Drive, Madison, Wisconsin   53706

Bartholomai, R. Head of Division, Federal Ministry of
    Labour and Social Order, 5300 Bonn 12, Germany

Bateson, Bernice M. Cooperative Extension Service, B4
    Curtiss Hall, Iowa State University, Ames, Iowa   50010

Baty, Carl F. Institute for Community Studies, 2 West
    40th Street, Kansas City, Missouri   64111

Baudot, M. Jacques. Social Affairs Division, UNRISD, 1211
    Geneve 10, Geneva, Switzerland

Bauer, Raymond A. Graduate School of Business Administra-
    tion, Harvard University, Soldiers Field, Boston,
    Massachusetts   02163

Beal, George M. Head, Department of Sociology and
    Anthropology, Iowa State University, Ames, Iowa   50010

Beale, Calvin L. Leader, Population Group, Human Re-
    sources Branch, Economic Research Service, U.S. Depart-
    ment of Agriculture, Washington, D.C.

Beauregard, Robert A. Department of City and Regional
    Planning, West Sibley Hall, Cornell University, Ithaca,
    New York   14850

Becker, Hal. The Futures Group, 124 Hebron Avenue,
    Glastonbury, Connecticut   06033

Bell, Daniel. Department of Sociology, William James Hall
    370, Harvard University, Cambridge, Massachusetts
    02138

Bell, Norman W. Clarke Institute of Psychiatry, 250 Col-
    lege Street, Toronto 2B, Canada

435

Bender, Lloyd D. Associate Professor of Agricultural Economics, University of Missouri, Columbia, Missouri 65201

Bertrand, Rene. National Accounts and Growth Studies, Head of Division, 1211 Geneve 10, Geneva, Switzerland

Biderman, Albert D. Bureau of Social Science Research, Inc., 1200 Seventeenth Street N.W., Washington, D.C. 20036

Bixhorn, Herbert J. Mathematical Statistician, Government of the District of Columbia, Executive Office, Washington, D.C. 20004

Bloomberg, L. Bureau of the Budget, Washington, D.C. 20201

Blumenthal, Monica D. Survey Research Center, University of Michigan, Ann Arbor, Michigan 48104

Bonnen, James T. Department of Agricultural Economics, Michigan State University, East Lansing, Michigan 48823

Boruch, Robert. Department of Psychology, Northwestern University, Evanston, Illinois 60201

Boucher, Wayne I. The Futures Group, 124 Hebron Avenue, Glastonbury, Connecticut 06033

Boulding, Kenneth E. Department of Economics, University of Colorado, Boulder, Colorado 80302

Bova, Patrick. Library, National Opinion Research Center, 6030 South Ellis Avenue, Chicago, Illinois 60637

Bricker, George B. KOBA Associates Inc., 1710 N Street, N.W., Washington, D.C. 20036

Brictson, Bob. Director of Research Programs, University of Pittsburgh, Pittsburgh, Pennsylvania 15213

Bridgeman, J. M. Assistant Secretary, H.M. Treasury, Great George Street, London, S.W.1. England

Brogan, Donna R. Department of Statistics and Biometry, Emory University, Atlanta, Georgia 30322

Brooks, Ralph M. Department of Agricultural Economics, Krannert Building, Purdue University, Lafayette, Indiana 47906

Brown, Lois S. Extension Nutrition, 105 Ricks Hall, North

Carolina State University, Raleigh, North Carolina
27607

Brown, Robert M. President, National Sanitation Foundation, P.O. Box 1468, 2355 West Stadium Boulevard, Ann
Arbor, Michigan   48106

Bryce, Herrington J. Senior Research Staff, The Urban
Institute, 2100 M Street, N.W., Washington, D.C.
20037

Bureau of Social Science Research. 1200 Seventeeth
Street, N.W., Washington, D.C.   20036

Burns, Virginia. The Center for the Study of Welfare
Policy, The University of Chicago, The School of Social
Service Administration, 969 East Sixtieth Street,
Chicago, Illinois   60637

Bush, J. W., M.D., M.P.H. Assistant Professor of
Community Medicine, School of Medicine, University of
California, San Diego, La Jolla, California   92037

Butcher, Bernard. Administration Officer, Bank of
America, Box 37000, San Francisco, California   94137

Butz, Earl L. Secretary, Department of Agriculture,
U.S.D.A., Washington, D.C.   20250

Campbell, Angus. Institute of Social Research, University
of Michigan, Ann Arbor, Michigan   48106

Carlson, William A. Director, Planning, Evaluation and
Programming Staff, Office of the Secretary, South
Building, U.S.D.A., Washington, D.C.   20250

Carr-Hill, Roy. Consultant, Education Division, 1211
Geneve 10, Geneva, Switzerland

Carter, Genevieve W. Director, Regional Research
Institute in Social Welfare, School of Social Work,
University of Southern California, Los Angeles,
California   90007

Cauley, Jon T. Economics Department, University of
Colorado, Boulder, Colorado   80302

Cebotarev, E. A. Assistant Professor, Department of Sociology and Anthropology, University of Guelph, Guelph,
Ontario, Canada

Center for Community Studies. Box 60 - George Peabody
College, Nashville, Tennessee   37203

Chapin, June R.   1190 Bellair Way, Menlo Park, California
94025

Chesney, Alan P.   Director, Cleveland Urban Observatory,
501 City Hall, Cleveland, Ohio   44114

Christakis, A.   Consultant, Office of Regional Economic
Development, U.S. Department of Commerce, 14th and Constitution Avenue, N.W. - Room 5225, Washington, D.C.
20230

Christian, David E.   Chief, Division of Social Affairs,
OECD, No. 2 Rue Andre-Pascal, Paris XVI, France

Christiansen, John R.   Sociology Department, 1216 Smith
Family Living Center, Brigham Young University, Provo,
Utah   84601

Churchill, Neil C.   Graduate School of Business Administration, Harvard University, Soldiers Field, Boston,
Massachusetts   02163

Clark, Stephen C.   Social Rehabilitation Services - HEW,
Room 5431 South, Washington, D.C.   20201

Clark, Terry N.   University of Chicago, Department of Sociology, 1126 E. 59th Street, Chicago, Illinois   60637

Clayton, M. G. (Miss).   Library, Foreign and Commonwealth
Office, Overseas Development Administration, Eland
House Stag Place, London SW1 England

Coffey, Joseph D.   Assistant to the Deputy Under Secretary
for Rural Development, Office of the Secretary, South
Building, U.S.D.A., Washington, D.C.   20250

Coleman, James S.   Department of Social Relations, Johns
Hopkins University, Baltimore, Maryland   21218

Colombo, Bernardo.   Dean, Facolta Di Scienze Statistiche,
Demografiche Ed Atturiali, Universita Degli Studi Di
Padova, Padova, Italy

Colonial Research Studies.   Colonial Office, Church Ho,
Great Smith Street SW1, London, England

Comprehensive Mental Health Center of Tacoma-Pierce
County.   Building #2 Tacoma Medical Center, 1206 South
11th Street, Tacoma, Washington   98405

Converse, James W.   Assistant Professor, Department of
Rural Sociology, Warren Hall, Cornell University,
Ithaca, New York   14850

Converse, Philip E. Institute for Social Research, University of Michigan, Ann Arbor, Michigan   48106

Copp, James H. Chief, Human Resources Branch, Room 4937 South Building, EDD-ERS, U.S.D.A., Washington, D.C. 20250

Corning, Peter A. Institute for Behavioral Genetics, University of Colorado, Boulder, Colorado   80302

Corteel, Paul-Louis M. Charge de mission, Commissariat General du Plan, 18, rue de Martignac, Paris, 7eme France

Coughenour, Milton C. Department of Sociology, University of Kentucky, Lexington, Kentucky   40506

Council of Planning Librarians. Exchange Bibliographies, P.O. Box 229, Monticello, Illinois   61856

Cowhig, James. RANN, National Science Foundation, Washington, D.C.   20550

Cummings, Gordon. 436 Warren Hall, Department of Rural Sociology, Cornell University, Ithaca, New York   14850

Daft, Lynn. Assistant Deputy Administrator, Office of the Secretary, South Building, U.S.D.A., Washington, D.C. 20250

D'Agostino, Ralph. Department of Mathematics, Boston University, 725 Commonwealth Avenue, Boston, Massachusetts 02215

Davidson, H. Justin. Dean, Graduate School of Business and Public Administration, Cornell University, Ithaca, New York   14850

Davis, James W. Political Service Department, Washington University, St. Louis, Missouri

Dawson, Richard. Department of Political Science, Washington University, St. Louis, Missouri   63130

Day, Alice T. 115 Blake Road, Hamden, Connecticut   06517

Day, Lincoln H. Chief, Demographic and Social Statistics Branch, Statistical Office, United Nations, New York, New York

De Jong, Gordon F. Professor of Sociology, 107 Burrowes Building, The Pennsylvania State University, University Park, Pennsylvania   16802

Demerath, Nicholas J. Department of Sociology, Box 1113,
    Washington University, St. Louis, Missouri 63130

DeNeufville, Judith I. 10 Acacia Street, Cambridge,
    Massachusetts 02138

Department of Political Science. The Ohio State Universi-
    ty, 216 North Oval Drive, Columbus, Ohio 43210

Dial, O. Eugene. 9 Possum Hollow Lane, Natick,
    Massachusetts 01760

Dillman, Don A. Director Public Opinion Laboratory, De-
    partment of Rural Sociology, Washington State Universi-
    ty, Pullman, Washington 99163

Director. Office of Program Analysis, Department of
    Health, Education and Welfare, Washington, D.C. 20201

Donhowe, Charles E. Assistant Dean, University Extension
    Service, 108 Curtiss Hall, Iowa State University, Ames,
    Iowa 50010

Drewnowski, Jan. Institute of Social Studies, 27
    Molenstraat, The Hague, Holland

Duncan, Otis Dudley. Population Studies Center, Depart-
    ment of Sociology, University of Michigan, Ann Arbor,
    Michigan 48104

Dunkelberger, J. E. Rural Sociology, Auburn University,
    Auburn, Alabama 36830

Dunn, Diana. Director of Research, National Recreation &
    Park Association, 1700 Pennsylvania Avenue N.W., Wash-
    ington, D.C. 20006

Eberts, Paul R. Department of Rural Sociology, Cornell
    University, Ithaca, New York 14850

Eckhardt, Kenneth W. Social Systems, Battelle Memorial
    Institute, 505 King Avenue, Columbus, Ohio 43210

Edwards, G. Franklin. Department of Sociology, Howard
    University, Washington, D.C. 20010

Effrat, Andrew. Editor, Sociological Inquiry, 252 Bloor
    Street West, Toronto 5, Ontario, Canada

Eichman, Charles J. Box 983, Tallahassee, Florida 32302

Eisner, Robert. Department of Economics, Northwestern
    University, Evanston, Illinois 60201

Eldin, Gerard. Deputy Secretary General, O.E.C.D.,
Geneva, Switzerland

Emslie, Graham. Commissioner of Development, Development
Department, City Hall, Toronto 100, Ontario, Canada

Engen, Trygg. Professor of Psychology, Brown University,
Providence, Rhode Island   02912

Etzioni, Amitai. Center for Policy Research, Inc., 475
Riverside Drive, Suite 7221, New York, New York   10027

Evans, James F. University of Illinois, Agricultural Communications, Urbana, Illinois   61801

Evans, Lynn A. Project Director, Institute for Interdisciplinary Studies, 123 East Grant Street, Minneapolis,
Minnesota   55403

Ewing, Solon Alex. Assistant Director, Agricultural Research Administration, 104 Curtiss Hall, Ames, Iowa
50010

Falkner, Bruce. 1257 Logan, #302, Denver, Colorado
80203

Farlee, Coralie. Health Care Systems Research, Rutgers
University, 26 Mine Street, New Brunswick, New Jersey
08901

Fegan, I. (Mrs.). United Kingdom Scientific Mission,
British Embassy, 3100 Massachusetts Avenue N.W., Washington, D.C.   20008

Feldmesser, Robert A. Research Sociologist, Educational
Testing Service, Division of Educational Studies,
Princeton, New Jersey   08540

Fine, Ruth. Librarian, Executive Office of the President,
Office of Management and Budget Library, Washington,
D.C.   20503

Fink, Elizabeth M. Assistant Director, IRSS--Manning
Hall, The University of North Carolina, Chapel Hill,
North Carolina   27514

Finsterbusch, Kurt. Executive Associate, American
Sociological Association, 1001 Connecticut Avenue,
N.W., Washington, D.C.   20036

Firebaugh, Francille M. Department of Home Economics,
1787 Neil Avenue, The Ohio State University, Columbus,
Ohio   43210

441

Flax, Michael J. Senior Research Staff, The Urban
    Institute, 2100 M Street N.W., Washington, D.C.   20037

Flora, Jan. Department of Sociology, Kansas State Univer-
    sity, Manhattan, Kansas

Fournier, M. Jacques. Chef du Service des Affaires
    Sociales, Commissariat General du Plan, 18, rue de
    Martignac, Paris, 7eme France

Fox, Karl. Chairman, Department of Economics, 266B East
    Hall, Iowa State University, Ames, Iowa   50010

Foy, S. R. U.S. Delegation to OECD, Paris, France

Freeman, David M. Department of Sociology and
    Anthropology, Colorado State University, Fort Collins,
    Colorado   80521

Freeman, Howard E. Florence Heller Graduate School,
    Brandeis University, Waltham, Massachusetts   02154

Fry, R. E. Chief Statistician, Central Statistical
    Office, 71 Whitehall, London, S.W.1. England

Fuguitt, Glenn V. Professor of Rural Sociology, Universi-
    ty of Wisconsin, Madison, Wisconsin

Fujimoto, Isao. Department of Applied Behavioral Scienc-
    es, University of California, Davis, California   95616

Fuller, Wayne A. Department of Statistics, 221 Snedecor
    Hall, Iowa State University, Ames, Iowa   50010

Gaard, Thomas J. Assistant Secretary, The Bankers Life,
    Des Moines, Iowa

Garn, Harvey. The Urban Institute, Washington, D.C.
    20037

Garnick, Daniel H. 816 Hyde Court, Silver Springs,
    Maryland   20902

Gastil, Raymond D. Battelle Memorial Institute, Battelle,
    Seattle Research Center, 4000 N.E. 41st Street,
    Seattle, Washington   98105

Gebert, Gordon. Senior Research Architect, School of
    Architecture, The City College of the University of New
    York, New York, New York   10031

Geis, Sally. Assistant Professor of Sociology, Temple
    Buell College, 1800 Pontiac Street, Denver, Colorado
    80220

442

Gibbons, Jean D. Department of Business Statistics, School of Commerce and Business Administration, University of Alabama, University, Alabama 35486

Gibson, Duane L. Institute for Community Development and Services, Kellogg Center, Michigan State University, East Lansing, Michigan 48823

Gitter, A. George. Chairman, Communication Research Center, School of Public Communication, Boston University, 640 Commonwealth Avenue, Boston, Massachusetts 02215

Glaser, Daniel. Department of Sociology, University of Southern California, Los Angeles, California 90007

Glover, Charles. Head of Urban Section, International Cooperation in Science Division, 1211 Geneve 10, Geneva, Switzerland

Goldstein, Gerald. Leader, Analytical Biochemistry Group, Oak Ridge National Laboratory, Oak Ridge, Tennessee 37830

Gordon, Theodore. The Futures Group, 124 Hebron Avenue, Glastonbury, Connecticut 06033

Greeley, Andrew M. National Opinion Research Center, University of Chicago, 6030 South Ellis Avenue, Chicago, Illinois 60637

Green, James W. Chief TA Methodology Division, Room 2937 NS, AID, Washington, D.C. 20523

Gregg, Christina F. State of Nebraska, Department of Health, Section of Hospitals and Medical Facilities, State House Station, Box 4757, Lincoln, Nebraska 68509

Grigsby, Eugene. School of Architecture and Urban Planning, University of California, 405 Hilgard Avenue, Los Angeles, California 90024

Gross, Bertram. Department of Political Science, Wayne State University, Detroit, Michigan 48202

Gutmann, P. Principal Administrator, National Accounts and Growth Studies, Social Affairs Division, 1211 Geneve 10, Geneva, Switzerland

Hackes, Peter. Correspondent, NBC News, 4001 Nebraska Avenue, N.W., Washington, D.C. 20016

Hage, Jerald. Department of Sociology, University of

Wisconsin, Madison, Wisconsin   53706

Hahn, Erich.   Prenzlauer Promenade 165a, 110 Berlin, DDR

Hair, Feather D.   Department of Health, Education, and
    Welfare, Public Health Service, Health Services and
    Mental Health Administration, Rockville, Maryland
    20852

Hamburg, Morris.   Editor, The American Statistician, E-242
    Dietrich Hall, University of Pennsylvania,
    Philadelphia, Pennsylvania   19104

Hanson, James.   Manager, Cultural Change Surveillance
    System, General Mills, Inc., 9200 Wayzata Boulevard,
    Minneapolis, Minnesota   55440

Harland, Douglas G.   Social Statistician, Social and Human
    Analysis Branch, Canada Department of Regional Economic
    Expansion, 161 Laurier Avenue West, Ottawa, Canada K1A
    OM4

Harman, Willis W.   Director, Educational Policy Research
    Center, Stanford Research Institute, Menlo Park,
    California   94025

Harris, Senator Fred.   Senate Office Building, Washington,
    D.C.   20201

Hauser, Philip M.   Director, Population Research Center,
    University of Chicago, 1413 East 60th Street, Chicago,
    Illinois   60637

Heberlein, Thomas A.   Department of Sociology, University
    of Wisconsin, Madison, Wisconsin   53706

Hedges, Jim.   1350 20th - Apartment E-15, Boulder,
    Colorado   80302

Heller, Clemens.   Directeur de la Bibliotheque, Services
    des Dons et des Echanges, Bibliotheque, Maison des Sci-
    ences de l'Homme, 54, boulevard Raspail, 75 - Paris 6e,
    France

Helm, Stanley T.   Mendocino State Hospital, Box X,
    Talmage, California   95481

Henderson, David.   Economic Council of Canada, P.O. Box
    527, Ottawa, Ontario, Canada, Post Code Postal K1P 5V6

Henriot, Peter J.   Staff Associate, Center of Concern,
    3700 13th Street, N.E., Washington, D.C.   20017

Her Majesty's Stationery Office.   Government Statistical

Service, P. O. Box No. 569, London, S.E. 1 England

Hernandez, Pedro. Louisiana State University, Baton
    Rouge, Louisiana

Hetman, F. Administrator, Science Policy Division, 1211
    Geneve 10, Geneva, Switzerland

Hilton, Helen. Dean, Home Economics Administration, 122A
    MacKay Hall, Ames, Iowa   50010

Hines, Howard. Division Director, Social Sciences,
    National Science Foundation, Washington, D.C.   20550

Hirsch, Abraham. Office of Program and Methodology,
    Bureau for Technical Assistance, AID - Washington, D.C.
    20523

Hirsch, Ralph B. Chief, Division of General Research,
    13th Floor City Planning Commission, Philadelphia,
    Pennsylvania   19107

Hjort, Shirley. Center for the Study of Local Government,
    St. John's University, Collegeville, Minnesota   56321

Hodge, Robert W. Center for Advanced Study in the Behav-
    ioral Sciences, 202 Junipero Serra Boulevard, Stanford,
    California   94305

Hoffmann, Alain. Institut National de la Statistique et
    des Etudes Economiques, 29, quai Branly, Paris, 7
    France

Hofstetter, Richard. The Ohio State University, Depart-
    ment of Political Science, 216 North Oval Drive,
    Columbus, Ohio   43210

Hogg, Thomas C. Associate Professor, Department of
    Anthropology, Oregon State University, Corvallis,
    Oregon   97331

Hollingworth, J. E., Jr. Emerson College, Boston,
    Massachusetts   02163

Holmfeld, John D. Science Policy Consultant, Committee on
    Science and Astronautics, House of Representatives,
    Suite 2321 Rayburn House Office Building, Washington,
    D.C.   20515

Horowitz, Irving Louis. Department of Sociology, Rutgers
    University, New Brunswick, New Jersey   08903

Hoyer, Hans. Inter-American Social Development Institute,
    1515 Wilson Boulevard, Rosslyn, Virginia   22209

Hughes, Senator Harold. Senate Office Building, Washington, D.C. 20201

Human Relations Resources Research Council of Alberta. 11507 74th Avenue, Edmonton 62, Alberta, Canada

Human Sciences Research, Inc. Westgate Research Park, 7710 Old Springhouse Road, McLean, Virginia 22101

Ink, Dwight A. Assistant Director, Office of Management and Budget, Executive Office of the President, Washington, D.C. 20503

Institute for Interdisciplinary Studies. American Rehabilitation Foundation, 123 East Grant Street, Minneapolis, Minnesota 55403

Institute for the Future. Middletown, Connecticut

Institute for Social Research. The University of Michigan, Ann Arbor, Michigan 48106

Institute of Behavioral Science Library. University of Colorado, Boulder, Colorado 80302

Inter America Social Development Foundation. William Dial, Jr., 1515 Wilson Boulevard, Rosslyn, Virginia 22209

Irwin, Linda F. 314 Social Science Tower, School of Public Affairs, University of Minnesota, Minneapolis, Minnesota 55455

Jackson, C. Wesley, Jr. Associate Professor, Frances Payne Bolton School of Nursing, Case Western Reserve University, Cleveland, Ohio 44106

Jasper, Herb. Legislative Assistant, Senator Walter F. Mondale, United States Senate, Washington, D.C. 20510

Jaumin, Anne M. Stratford Hours, Apartment 209, 433 West Gilman Street, Madison, Wisconsin 53703

Jehlik, Paul J. Director, Social Sciences, Cooperative State Research Service, U.S. Department of Agriculture, Washington, D.C. 20250

John, M. E. Department of Agricultural Economics and Rural Sociology, Pennsylvania State University, University Park, Pennsylvania 18602

Johnson, Helen W. Economic Development Division, Economic Research Service, U.S.D.A., Washington, D.C. 20250

Johnston, Denis F. Senior Demographic Statistician, Office of Manpower Structure and Trends, Bureau of Labor Statistics, U.S. Department of Labor, Washington, D.C. 20212

Jones, Martin V. The MITRE Corporation, Westgate Research Park, McLean, Virginia 22101

Julius, Marvin B. 568D East Hall, Department of Economics, Iowa State University, Ames, Iowa 50010

Kacser, Pamela Haody. Adviser on Socio-Economic Research, U.S. Department of Labor, Bureau of Labor Statistics, Washington, D.C. 20212

Kahn, Robert L. Institute for Social Research, Box 1248, Ann Arbor, Michigan 48106

Kaiser, J. L. University of Illinois, Purchasing Division - Business Office, 223 Administration Building, Urbana, Illinois 61801

Kamrany, Nake M. Department of Economics, University of Southern California, University Park, Los Angeles, California 90007

Kaplan, Max. Center for Studies of Leisure, University of South Florida, Tampa, Florida 33620

Karpinos, B. Office of the Surgeon General, Health, Education, and Welfare, 400 Maryland Avenue S.W., Washington, D.C. 20014

Kaufman, Harold F. Department of Sociology, Mississippi State University, State College, Mississippi 39762

Kimball, William J. Community Resource Development, 323 Natural Resources Building, Michigan State University, East Lansing, Michigan 48823

Kimball, Thomas L. Executive Director, National Wildlife Federation, 1412 16th St., N.W., Washington, D.C. 20036

Klassen, David H. Coordinator, Mid-America Urban Observatory, 27th Floor, City Hall, 414 East 12th Street, Kansas City, Missouri 64416

Klessig, Lowell L. Organizational Analyst, Environmental Resources Unit, University Extension, The University of Wisconsin, 215 North Brooks Street, Madison, Wisconsin 53706

Klonglan, Gerald E. Department of Sociology and

Anthropology, Iowa State University, Ames, Iowa   50010

Knezo, Genevieve J.   Analyst, Science and Technology, Science Policy Research Division, Congressional Research Service, Library of Congress, Washington, D.C.   20540

Kolmer, Lee.   Assistant Dean, University Extension Service, 109 Curtiss Hall, Ames, Iowa   50010

Krendel, Ezra S.   Professor of Statistics and Operations Research, Wharton School of Finance and Commerce, University of Pennsylvania, Philadelphia, Pennsylvania   19104

Krieger, Martin.   University of California Center for Planning and Development Research, University of California, Berkeley, Berkeley, California   94720

Kriesberg, Louis.   Educational Policy Research Center, Syracuse University Research Corporation, 1206 Harrison Street, Syracuse, New York   13210

Kunkel, John H.   Department of Sociology, Arizona State University, Tempe, Arizona   85281

Lackner, Irene (Miss).   Economic Council of Canada, P.O. Box 527, Ottawa, Canada

Lamale, Helen H.   Division of Living Conditions Studies, Bureau of Labor Statistics, U.S. Department of Labor, Washington, D.C.   20212

Lambert, Richard D.   The Annals, 3937 Chestnut Street, Philadelphia, Pennsylvania   19104

Lamson, Robert W.   Science Policy Research Section, National Science Foundation, Washington, D.C.   20550

Land, Kenneth C.   Mathematical Sociologist, Russell Sage Foundation, 230 Park Avenue, New York, New York   10017

Lanham, Orville E.   Assistant Professor, Rural Sociology Department, Agricultural Hall 246, Brookings, South Dakota   57006

Larson, Olaf F.   Department of Rural Sociology, Cornell University, Ithaca, New York   14850

Lassey, William R.   Director Center for Planning and Development, Montana State University, Bozeman, Montana   59715

Latane, Bibb.   Ohio State University, Columbus, Ohio   43210

Laurmann, John A. Executive Secretary, Advisory Committee
    to HUD, 2101 Constitution Avenue, Washington, D.C.
    20418

Lazarsfeld, Paul. Columbia University, New York, New York
    10027

Lecoultre, D. (Miss). Principal Administrator, Social
    Affairs Division, 1211 Geneve 10, Geneva, Switzerland

Lehman, Edward W. Department of Sociology, New York Uni-
    versity, New York, New York

Levine, Jonathan, Instructor of History, Department of
    History, University of Pittsburgh, Pittsburgh,
    Pennsylvania   15213

Levy, M. Emile. Professeur a la Faculte de Droit, et des
    Sciences Economiques, Universite de Paris-Ouest, 92
    Nanterre, France

Lieberson, Stanley. Professor of Sociology, The Universi-
    ty of Chicago, Population Research Center, 1413 East
    60th Street, Chicago, Illinois   60637

Lind, Marvin. Director of Research, Iowa Development
    Commission, 250 Jewett Building, Des Moines, Iowa
    50309

Lind, Roger. School of Social Work, 1065 Frieze Building,
    University of Michigan, Ann Arbor, Michigan   48104

Lionberger, Herbert F. Department of Rural Sociology,
    University of Missouri, Columbia, Missouri   65201

Linowes, David F., CPA. Laventhol, Krekstein, Horwath and
    Horwath, 919 Third Avenue, New York, New York   10022

Lipscomb, David M. Associate Professor of Audiology &
    Speech Pathology, Director, Noise Study Laboratory,
    University of Tennessee, Knoxville, Tennessee   37916

Loomis, Charles. Department of Sociology, Michigan State
    University, East Lansing, Michigan   48823

Loomis, Ralph A. Economic Development Division, Depart-
    ment of Agricultural Economics, Washington State Uni-
    versity, Pullman, Washington   99163

Lowry, Roye L. American Statistical Association, Suite
    640, 806 - 15th Street, N.W., Washington, D.C.   20005

Lueptow, Lloyd B. Department of Sociology, The University
    of Akron, Akron, Ohio   44304

Lyell, Edward H. 1350 - 20th Street, Apt. D-11, Boulder,
    Colorado   80302

MacDonald, Gordon J. F. Council on Environmental Quality,
    Executive Office cf the President, Washington, D.C.

Madden, J. Patrick. Associate Professor, Department of
    Agricultural Economics and Rural Sociology, Weaver
    Building, The Pennsylvania State University, University
    Park, Pennsylvania   16802

Magnus, Jennifer V. (Mrs.) Library of Congress, Order Di-
    vision, Receiving Unit (0723R), Washington, D.C.
    20540

Magnussen, Olav. Administrator, Education Division, 1211
    Geneve 10, Geneva, Switzerland

Mahlstede, John P. Associate Director, Agricultural Re-
    search Administration, 104 Curtiss Hall, Iowa State
    University, Ames, Iowa   50010

Maimon, Zvi. Research Associate, Center for Urban Stud-
    ies, Wayne State University, Detroit, Michigan   48202

Malone, David W. Grissom Hall - Purdue University,
    Lafayette, Indiana   49707

Manges, Binnie L. Director, Community Health Education
    Livision, Saint Louis County Health Department, 801
    South Brentwood Boulevard, Clayton, Missouri   63105

Marien, Michael. Educational Policy Research Center,
    Syracuse University Research Corporation, 1206 Harrison
    Street, Syracuse, New York   13210

Markley, O. W. Educational Policy Research Center,
    Stanford Research Institute, Menlo Park, California
    94025

Marlin, Alice Tepper. Council on Economic Priorities, 456
    Greenwich Street, New York, New York   10013

Marple, Gary A. Arthur D. Little, Inc., Acorn Park,
    Cambridge, Massachusetts   02140

Marshall, Colonel Donald. Office of the Secretary of De-
    fense, Viet Nam Task Force, Washington, D.C.

Mason, Karen Oppenheim. Research Triangle Institute, P.O.
    Office Box 12194, Research Triangle Park, North
    Carolina   27709

Mast, Robert H. The Institute of Race Relations, 36

Jermyn Street, London, S.W.1., England

Masters, Kenneth W.   Professor of Social Science,
    Pennsylvania State University, Middletown, Pennsylvania
    17057

Mayhew, James.   Area Community Development Specialist,
    Warrenton, Missouri   63383

Mazery, J. P.   Consultant, International Cooperation in
    Science Division, 1211 Geneve 10, Geneva, Switzerland

McComb, James B.   Director, Environmental Development,
    Dayton Hudson Corporation, 777 Nicollet Mall,
    Minneapolis, Minnesota   55402

McCullough, Paul.   Western Interstate Commission for
    Higher Education, P.O. Drawer P, Boulder, Colorado
    80302

McElyea, Stewart D.   Deputy Director, Field Operations Di-
    vision, U.S. General Accounting Office, Washington,
    D.C.   20548

McGranahan, Donald V.   United Nations Research Institute
    for Social Development, Geneva, Switzerland

McLaughlin, Jim.   Delaware Valley Regional Planning
    Commission, 1317 Filbert Street, Philadelphia,
    Pennsylvania   19107

Medalia, Nahum.   Chairman, Oakland University, Department
    of Sociology and Anthropology, Rochester, Michigan
    48063

Messick, Samuel.   Educational Testing Services, Princeton,
    New Jersey   08540

Metzen, E. J.   Department of Home Economics, Stanley Hall
    Room 238, University of Missouri, Columbia, Missouri
    65201

Michigan Office of Planning Coordination.   Bureau of
    Policies and Programs, Lansing, Michigan

Midwest Research Institute.   425 Volker, Kansas City,
    Missouri   64110

Miller, Warren E.   Director, Center for Political Studies,
    Institute for Social Research, Ann Arbor, Michigan
    48106

Mindlin, Albert.   Chief Statistician, Office of Planning
    and Management, Room 113 - District Building, Washing-

ton, D.C.   20024

Miyasaki, Isamu.   Counsellor, Coordination Buro, Economic
    Planning Agency, 3-1-1 Kasumijasiki, Chiyoda-ku, Tokyo,
    Japan

Moe, Ed.   Division of Community and Urban Development,
    P.O. Box 200, University of Utah, Salt Lake City, Utah
    84112

Mondale, Senator Walter F.   Senate Office Building, Wash-
    ington, D.C.   20201

Montgomery, Ann (Miss).   Administrative Assistant,
    Institute for Behavioral Research, York University,
    4700 Keele Street, Downsview 463, Ontario, Canada

Moore, Wilbert E.   College of Law, University of Denver,
    200 West 14th Avenue, Denver, Colorado   80204

Morrison, Peter A.   The Rand Corporation, 1700 Main
    Street, Santa Monica, California   90406

Morss, Elliott R.   Department of Economics, George Wash-
    ington University, Washington, D.C.   20006

Mortvedt, Marjorie.   Home Economics Extension, Ohio State
    University, Columbus, Ohio   43210

Motes, William C.   Director, Economic Development Divi-
    sion, Economic Research Service, U.S. Department of
    Agriculture, Washington, D.C.

Moynihan, Daniel P.   Harvard University, Cambridge,
    Massachusetts   02138

Murie, Martin.   Professor of Biology, Environmental Stud-
    ies Center, Antioch College, Yellow Springs, Ohio
    45387

Murray, Alex L.   Associate Professor, York University,
    4700 Keele Street, Downsview 463, Ontario, Canada

Naftalin, Arthur.   School of Public Affairs, University of
    Minnesota, 314 Social Sciences Building, Minneapolis,
    Minnesota   55455

Nakatani, Shigeru.   Japanese Delegation to the OECD, 7,
    Avenue Hoche, Paris, 8eme France

Nanus, Burt.   Senior Research Associate, Public Systems
    Research Institute, 3551 University Avenue, University
    of Southern California, Los Angeles, California   90007

National Academy of Sciences and Engineering. Office of
General Services, 2101 Constitution Avenue, N.W., Washington, D.C.   20418

National Bureau of Economic Research. 261 Madison Avenue,
New York, New York   10016

National Center for Health Statistics. Public Health
Service, Washington, D.C.

National Opinion Research Center. University of Chicago,
6030 South Ellis Avenue, Chicago, Illinois   60637

National Technical Information Service. U.S. Department
of Commerce, 5285 Port Royal Road, Springfield,
Virginia   22151

Nelson, Glenn L. Policy Research Division, Office of Economic Opportunity, Executive Office of the President,
Washington, D.C.   20506

Nelson, Jean W. (Miss). Program Manager, Long Range
Planning Service, Stanford Research Institute, Menlo
Park, California   94025

Nelson, K. P. Oak Ridge National Laboratory, P.O. Box X,
Oak Ridge, Tennessee   37830

Newbrough, J. Robert. Coordinator, Center for Community
Studies, President, Nashville Urban Observatory, De-
partment of Psychology, Peabody College, Box 60,
Nashville, Tennessee   37203

Newman, D. National Urban League, 425 13th N.W., Washington, D.C.

Nicoll, David. 5152 Earl Drive, La Canada, California
91011

Nicosia, Francesco M. Professor and Director, Consumer
Research Program, University of California, Berkeley,
California   94720

Nissel, Muriel (Mrs.). Cabinet Office, Central Statistical Office, Great George Street, London S.W.1., England

Noack, Horst R. 7911 Oberelchingen, Eichenweg 7, West
Germany

Oborn, Parker T. 2475 S. Vine St. - Apt. 104, Denver,
Colorado   80210

Ochavkov, J. Institute of Sociology at the Bulgarian
Academy of Sciences, 6, Patriarch Evtimii Str., Sofia,

Bulgaria

Ohio State University, Department of Political Science.
216 North Oval Drive, Columbus, Ohio   43210

Oliphant, Walter J.   President, American Institute of
Certified Public Accountants, 666 Fifth Avenue, New
York, New York   10019

Olson, Mancur.   Department of Economics, University of
Maryland, College Park, Maryland   20742

Ontell, Robert.   Social Indicators Project Director, Urban
Observatory, San Diego State College, San Diego,
California   92115

Orshansky, M.   Social Security Administration, 400
Maryland Ave. S.W., Washington, D.C.   20014

Osman J.   Brookings Institution, 1775 Massachusetts Avenue
N.W., Washington, D.C.   20036

Ossorio, Elizabeth D.   Statistics Consultant, Department
of Health, Education and Welfare, Federal Building, 601
East 12th Street, Kansas City, Missouri   64106

Ostrom, Elinor.   Department of Political Science, Woodburn
Hall 320, Indiana University, Bloomington, Indiana
47401

Ouellet, Hector.   29, Sheraton Drive, Ithaca, New York
14850

Palley, Marian L.   Department of Political Science, University of Delaware, Newark, Delaware   19711

Palmer, Boyd Z.   Governmental Studies & Systems, 3401
Market St. - Suite 3000, Philadelphia, Pennsylvania
19104

Pardee, Fred.   The Institute for Analysis, 12218 Paisley
Lane, Los Angeles, California   90049

Patrick, Donald L.   Research Sociologist, School of
Medicine, University of California, San Diego, La
Jolla, California   92037

Patrick, Ruth.   Chairman, Department of Limnology, The
Academy of Natural Sciences, Philadelphia, Pennsylvania

Pearl, Robert B.   Office of Statistical Policy and
Management, Information Systems Division, Executive
Office of the President, Office of Management and
Budget, Washington, D.C.   20503

Percy, Myrtle (Mrs.). Buyer, Washington State University, Division of Purchasing, Pullman, Washington 99163

Perle, Eugene D. Associate Director, Center for Urban Studies, Wayne State University, Detroit, Michigan 48202

Perloff, Harvey S. (Dean). School of Architecture and Urban Planning, University of California, Los Angeles, California 90024

Petersen, LeRoy. Office of Program and Planning, State Capitol, Des Moines, Iowa 50319

Pfaff, Martin. Department of Economics, Wayne State University, Detroit, Michigan 48202

Pikul, Robert P. Head, Environmental Quality Sub-Department, MITRE Corporation, McLean, Virginia 22101

Pinney, Neil J. Urban Systems Laboratory, Massachusetts Institute of Technology, Cambridge, Massachusetts 02139

Poleck, D. National Safety Council, 1735 De Sales NW, Washington, D.C. 20036

Porter, David O. Assistant Professor, Graduate School of Administration, University of California, Riverside, California 92502

Pounds, Russell G. 560A East Hall, Department of Economics, Iowa State University, Ames, Iowa 50010

Powell, M. National Planning Association, Washington, D.C.

Powers, Ronald C. Head, Family Environment, 52A MacKay Hall, Iowa State University, Ames, Iowa 50010

Price, Daniel O. University of Texas, Department of Sociology, Austin, Texas 78712

Public Policy Program. c/o Marion Ezell, Littauer Center, JFK School of Government, Harvard University, Cambridge, Massachusetts 02138

Puget Sound Governmental Conference. Research, Division, Seattle Ferry Terminal, Seattle, Washington 98104

Puryear, Paul L. Russell Sage Foundation, 230 Park Avenue, New York, New York 10017

Ralston, N. P. (Pat). Associate Director, Science and Ed-

ucation, Office of the Secretary, South Building,
U.S.D.A., Washington, D.C.   20250

Rapkin, Chester. Professor of Urban Planning, Director,
Institute of Urban Environment, Columbia University,
New York, New York   10025

Rappaport, Carl. Program Coordinator, Office of the
Assistant Secretary for Environment and Urban Systems,
U.S. Department of Transportation, Washington, D.C.
20590

Ratcliffe, Allen W. Committee on Public Engineering
Policy, National Academy of Engineering, Washington,
D.C.

Rathbun, Daniel. President's Commission on Federal Statistics, Room 400, 1016 Sixteenth Street, N.W., Washington, D.C.   20036

Ray, Michael L. Associate Professor of Marketing, Graduate School of Business, Stanford University, Stanford,
California   94305

Redick, Richard. Biometry Branch, National Institute of
Mental Health, Department of HEW Public Health Service,
5600 Fisher Lane, Rockville, Maryland   20852

Reiquam, Howard. Senior Meteorologist, Battelle Memorial
Institute, 505 King Avenue, Columbus, Ohio   43201

Renter, Lois (Mrs.). Corporate Headquarters, The American
College Testing Program, P.O. Box 168, Iowa City, Iowa
52240

Research Foundation for Mental Hygiene, Inc. New York
Psychiatric Division, 722 West 168th St., New York, New
York   10032

Richardson, Fred. Research Assistant, Public Systems Research Institute, 3717 S. Grand Street, Room 347, Los
Angeles, California   90007

Riecken, Henry W. President, Social Science Research
Council, 230 Park Avenue, New York, New York   10017

de Rita, Giuseppe. CENSIS, Corso Vittorio Emanuele 251,
Rome, Italy

Rivlin, Alice M. Department of Health, Education and
Welfare, Washington, D.C.   20201

Rodgers, Willard. Study Director, Survey Research Center,
Institute for Social Research, The University of

Michigan, Ann Arbor, Michigan   48106

Ross, Douglas. National Urban Coalition, 111 West 57th
    Street, New York, New York   10019

Rossi, Ino. St. John's University, Department of Sociolo-
    gy, Jamaica, New York

Rossi, Peter H. Johns Hopkins University, Department of
    Social Relations, Baltimore, Maryland   21218

Roy, Prodipto. Research Director, Council for Social De-
    velopment, Indian Information Center, 44 Lodi Estate,
    New Delhi 3, India

Sapolsky, Harvey M. University of Michigan, Ann Arbor,
    Michigan   48106

Sargent, Charles. Agricultural and Applied Economics De-
    partment, 312 Coffey Hall, University of Minnesota, St.
    Paul, Minnesota   55101

Savoie, Leonard M., CPA. Executive Vice President, Ameri-
    can Institute of Certified Public Accountants, 666
    Fifth Avenue, New York, New York   10019

Scanlon, J. National Institute of Mental Health, 5454
    Wisconsin Ave., Washington, D.C.   20015

Scarlott, C. L. Public Affairs Department, Standard Oil
    Company of New Jersey, 30 Rockefeller Plaza, New York,
    New York   10020

Schackne, Stewart. American Institute of Certified Public
    Accountants, 666 Fifth Avenue, New York, New York
    10019

Schmid, A. Allan. Department of Agricultural Economics,
    Agriculture Hall, Michigan State University, East
    Lansing, Michigan   48823

Schreiner, Robert N. President, Foreign and International
    Book Company, P.O. Box 126, Flushing, New York   11364

Schulze, Paul. Statistician, Office of Technical Serv-
    ices, Division of Dental Health, Department of Health,
    Education, and Welfare, Bethesda, Maryland   20014

Schussheim, Martin J. University of Pennsylvania,
    Philadelphia, Pennsylvania   19104

Schweitzer, H. J. 2320 Phinney Drive, Champaign, Illinois
    61820

Scott, Wolf. United Nations Research Institute for Social
Development, Geneva, Switzerland

Seaton, Richard W. Environmental Psychologist, Office of
Academic Planning, The University of British Columbia,
Vancouver 8, Canada

Shanks, J. Merrill. Director, Survey Research Center,
University of California, Berkeley, California   94720.

Sharp, Emmit. Department of Sociology, Colorado State
University, Fort Collins, Colorado   80521

Shaw, Hiram. Assistant Director, Albuquerque Urban
Observatory, 1805 Roma, N.E., Albuquerque, New Mexico
87106

Shaw, Stella (Miss). Secretary, Sociology and Social Administration Committee, Social Science Research
Council, State House High Holborn, London WC1, England

Shearer, John C. Department of Economics, Oklahoma State
University, Stillwater, Oklahoma   74074

Sheldon, Eleanor B. Sociologist and Executive Associate,
Russell Sage Foundation, 230 Park Avenue, New York, New
York   10017

Shinn, Allen. Division of Social Science, National Science Foundation, Washington, D.C.

Shiskin, Julius. Assistant Director for Statistical Standards, Office of Management and Budget, Bureau of
Budget, Washington, D.C.   20201

Shoup, Donald S. Social Science Research Council, 230
Park Avenue, New York, New York   10017

Shults, Wilbur D. Environmental Index Group, Oak Ridge
National Laboratory, Oak Ridge, Tennessee   37830

Siedl, John. HEW, Washington, D.C.

Sills, David. The Population Council, 245 Park Avenue,
New York, New York   10017

Simons, Nat. Battelle Memorial Institute, 505 King
Avenue, Columbus, Ohio   43201

Singer, S. Fred. University of Virginia, Charlottesville,
Virginia   22903

Singh, K.K. Indian Institute of Technology, P.O. IIT,
Kanpur, U.P., India

458

Sizer, Leonard M. Associate Professor of Sociology, 316
    Spring Road, Morgantown, West Virginia   26506

Slipy, Dave. Center for the Study of Local Government,
    St. John's University, Collegeville, Minnesota   56321
    ¢+1
Smelser, Neil J. Associate Director, Institute of Inter-
    national Studies, University of California, Berkeley,
    California   94720

Smith, Courtland L. Department of Anthropology, Oregon
    State University, Corvallis, Oregon   97331

Smith, George L., Jr. Consultant, Economic Research Divi-
    sion, State of Ohio, Department of Development, 65
    South Front Street, Columbus, Ohio   43215

Smock, Robert. Department of Sociology, University of
    Michigan, Dearborn, Michigan   48128

Social Science Panel of the Advisory Committee to HUD.
    National Academy of Sciences, JH-713, 2101 Constitution
    Avenue, Washington, D.C.   20418

Social Welfare Research Institute. 303 Bradley Hall, Uni-
    versity of Kentucky, Lexington, Kentucky   40506

Soderlind, Sterling E. Wall Street Journal, 30 Broadway,
    New York, New York   10004

Solomon, Henry. Chairman, Department of Economics, George
    Washington University, Washington, D.C.   20006

Space Sciences Laboratory. University of California,
    Berkeley, California   94720

Springer, Michael. Department of Political Science, Wayne
    State University, Detroit, Michigan   48202

Stagner, Ross. Psychology Department, Wayne State Univer-
    sity, Detroit, Michigan   48202

Stanback, Howard. School of Social Work, Atlanta Univer-
    sity, 223 Chestnut, S.W., Atlanta, Georgia   30314

Steelman, Lucille (Mrs.). Order Librarian, Library,
    G-021, Stanford Research Institute, Menlo Park,
    California   94025

Stendenbach, Franz. Administrator, Social Affairs Divi-
    sion, 1211 Geneve 10, Geneva, Switzerland

Stiff, Ronald. Department of Sociology, Stuart Building,
    Illinois Institute of Technology, Chicago, Illinois

60616

Stith, Robert J.   Research Director, City of Charlotte,
    307 Executive Building, 623 East Trade Street,
    Charlotte, North Carolina   28202

Strumpel, Burkhard.   Institute for Social Research, Ann
    Arbor, Michigan   48104

Studer, Raymond G.   Man-Environment Relations, S-126 Human
    Development Building, The Pennsylvania State Universi-
    ty, University Park, Pennsylvania   16802

Suranyi-Unger, Theodore Jr.   Economics Department, George
    Washington University, Washington, D.C.   20006

Suter, Larry.   Bureau of Census, Population Division, U.S.
    Department of Commerce, Washington, D.C.   20233

Sutton, Bruce.   P.O. Box 2237, Boulder, Colorado   80302

Swedner, Harald.   Mantalskroken 3, S-222 47 Lundl, Sweden

System Development Corporation.   Santa Monica, California

Tait, John L.   Extension Sociologist, Department of Soci-
    ology, Iowa State University, Ames, Iowa   50010

Talbot, Ross B.   Chairman, Department of Political Sci-
    ence, 321B Beardshear, Iowa State University, Ames,
    Iowa   50010

Tannenbaum, Percy H.   Graduate School of Public Policy,
    University of California, Berkeley, California   94720

Taylor, Jeremy B.   AID, Technical Assistance Bureau,
    Methodology Division, Room 2941 N.S., Washington, D.C.
    20523

Tenbruck, F. H.   University of Tubingen, Tubingen, Federal
    Republic of Germany

Terleckyj, Nestor.   National Planning Association, 1606
    New Hampshire Avenue, N.W., Washington, D.C.   20009

Texas Agricultural Extension Service.   Jack W. Rose,
    Systems Building, College Station, Texas   77843

The Citizens' Advisory Committee on Environmental Quality.
    1700 Pennsylvania Avenue, N.W., Washington, D.C.
    20006

The Institute for Analysis.   12218 Paisley Avenue, Los
    Angeles, California   90049

The Library of Congress, Nathan R. Einhorn, Chief, Exchange and Gift Division, Washington, D.C.   20540

The Ohio State University. Business Office, 190 N. Oval
Drive, Columbus, Ohio   43210

Thomas, William A. Group Leader, Environmental Indices,
ORNL-NSF Environmental Program, Oak Ridge National Laboratory, P.O. Box X, Oak Ridge, Tennessee   37830

Tiryakian, Edward A. Department of Sociology, Duke University, Durham, North Carolina   27706

Toan, Arthur B., Jr., CPA. Price Waterhouse and Company,
60 Broad Street, New York, New York   10004

Tugac, Ahmet. State Planning Organization, Bakanliklar,
Ankara, Turkey

Tumin, Melvin M. Consultant, Educational Testing Service,
Division of Educational Studies, Room PO64, Princeton,
New Jersey   08540

Tunstall, Daniel. Statistical Policy Division, Federal
Office of Management and Budget, 17th and Pennsylvania
Avenue, N.W., Washington, D.C.   20503

Tweeten, Luther. Department of Agricultural Economics,
Oklahoma State University, Stillwater, Oklahoma   74074

Tyler, Ralph W. Acting President, Social Science Research
Council, 230 Park Avenue, New York, New York   10017

University of California. Survey Research Center, Los
Angeles, California   90024

University of Nebraska, 105 Home Economics, East Campus,
Lincoln, Nebraska   68503

University of Nevada. College of Agriculture, Fiscal
Office, Reno, Nevada   89507

Updegraff, G. E. Department of Agricultural Economics,
Michigan State University, College of Agriculture, East
Lansing, Michigan   48823

USDA National Agricultural Library. Current Serial
Record, Beltsville, Maryland   20705

U.S. Department of Labor, Bureau of Labor Statistics, GAO
Building, Washington, D.C.   20212

Vallance, Ted. 104 Human Development Building,
Pennsylvania State University, University Park,

Pennsylvania   16802

van den Ban, A. W.   Agricultural University, Department of
    Extension Education, Herenstraat 25, Wageningen
    (Netherlands)

Vandermark, Elzo.   Urban Research Unit, Research School of
    Social Sciences, Australian National University,
    Canberra, Australia

Vatter, Ethel L.   Department of Consumer Economics &
    Public Policy, College of Human Ecology, Cornell Uni-
    versity, Ithaca, New York   14850

Vestermark, Seymour D.   Human Sciences Research, Inc.,
    Westgate Research Park, 7710 Old Springhouse Road,
    McLean, Virginia   22101

Viswanathan, N., D.S.W.   University of Illinois, Chicago
    Division at Chicago Circle Campus, P.O. Box 4348,
    Chicago, Illinois   60680

Vlachos, Evan.   Department of Sociology, Colorado State
    University, Fort Collins, Colorado   80521

Waingrow, Selwyn M.   NCSH; RMPS; HSMHA, 5600 Fishers Lane,
    Rockville, Maryland   20852

Walker, Jack.   Department of Political Science, University
    of Michigan, Ann Arbor, Michigan   48104

Walker, Marella.   Assistant University Librarian, Robert
    W. Woodruff Library, Emory University, Atlanta, Georgia
    30322

Walters, Dorothy (Miss).   The Economic Council of Canada,
    P.O. Box 527, Ottawa, Canada

Warner, W. Keith.   Sociology Department, 183 Faculty
    Office Building, Brigham Young University, Provo, Utah
    84601

Warren, Roland L.   Florence Heller Graduate School,
    Brandeis University, Waltham, Massachusetts   02154

Wasson, K. William.   Department of Sociology, Iowa State
    University, Ames, Iowa   50010

Wayman, Morris.   Department of Chemical Engineering and
    Applied Chemistry, University of Toronto, Toronto 5,
    Canada

Webber, Melvin.   University of California, Berkeley,
    California   94720

Weber, H. United Community Funds, Councils of America, 1701 18th N.W., Washington, D.C.

Weber, Jeanne (Miss). Chief, Reference Unit, Information Services Section, U.S. Department of Commerce, National Technical Information Service, 5285 Port Royal Road, Springfield, Virginia   22151

Weiner, Alan J. Community Analysis Bureau, 316 West Second Street, Los Angeles, California   90012

Wells, Alan. Department of Sociology, Tulane University, New Orleans, Louisiana

Weston, Frank T., CPA. Arthur Young and Company, 277 Park Avenue, New York, New York   10017

Wheelock, Gerald. Research Associate, Department of Rural Sociology, Cornell University, Ithaca, New York   14850

Whiting, Gordon. 1 Agriculture Hall, University of Wisconsin, Madison, Wisconsin   53706

Wicklund, Lee A. Northwest Regional Educational Laboratory, 313 South 129th, Tacoma, Washington   98444

Widdison, Harold A. Assistant Professor, Department of Sociology and Anthropology, Eastern Illinois University, Charleston, Illinois   61920

Wiebe, Richard A. Director, State Office of Planning Services, 488 Broadway, Albany, New York   12207

Wilcox, Leslie D. Department of Sociology and Anthropology, Iowa State University, Ames, Iowa   50010

Wilkening, E. A. University of Wisconsin, College of Agricultural and Life Sciences, Department of Rural Sociology, 240 Agriculture Hall, Madison, Wisconsin 53706

Williams, Anne S. Center for Planning and Development, Montana State University, Bozeman, Montana   59715

Williams, C. A. Deputy Administrator, United States Department of Agriculture, Federal Extension Service – South Building, Washington, D.C.   20230

Williams, Charles. Staff Director, National Goals Research Staff, The White House, Washington, D.C.   20006

Williams, Robin. Department of Sociology, Cornell University, Ithaca, New York   14850

Wilson, Albert. Director, Eomega Grove, Box 113, Topanga, California   90290

Wilson, Ian H. Consultant, Business Environment Studies, General Electric Company, 570 Lexington Avenue, New York, New York   10022

Wilson, John O. Director, Office of Planning, Research and Evaluation, Office of Economic Opportunity, 1200 19th St., Room 717, Washington, D.C.   20506

Wolfgang, Marvin E. Department of Sociology, University of Pennsylvania, Philadelphia, Pennsylvania   19104

Wright, Deil S. Professor, Department of Political Science, The University of North Carolina, Chapel Hill, North Carolina   27514

Young, Frank W. Warren Hall, Department of Rural Sociology, Cornell University, Ithaca, New York   14850

Zapf, Wolfgang. Johann Wolfgang Goethe-Universitat, Seminar fur Gesellschaftslehre, 6 Frankfurt, Germany

Zuiches, James J. Research Assistant, Department of Rural Sociology, University of Wisconsin, Madison, Wisconsin 53706

Zweben, I. P. (Mrs.). 2800 Anchor Avenue, Los Angeles, California